Gendered Poverty and Well-being

Gendered Poverty and Well-being

Shahra Razavi

Copyright © Institute of Social Studies 2000

ISBN: 0-631-21793-2

Blackwell Publishers Ltd
108 Cowley Road
Oxford OX4 1JF, UK

Blackwell Publishers Inc
350 Main Street
Malden, Massachusetts 02148, USA

British Library Cataloguing in Publication Data has been applied for

Library of Congress Cataloguing in Publication Data has been applied for

Typeset by Polestar

This book is printed on acid-free paper

This text was originally published as special issue 30(3) of *Development and Change*, published by Blackwell Publishers on behalf of the Institute of Social Studies, The Hague.

Contents

1

Gendered Poverty and Well-being: Introduction

Shahra Razavi

After more than a decade of preoccupation with 'stabilization' and growth, by the early 1990s mainstream policy institutions pronounced a renewed interest in attending to the problems of global poverty. These concerns were given greater voice and urgency through the series of global summits that inscribed the early part of the decade and signalled, at the very least, a discursive shift in development policy. One outcome has been the 'New Poverty Agenda'[1] of multilateral development agencies which identifies 'labour-intensive growth' as its central tenet. Another is the extension of the social exclusion approach from French and European social policy debates into development thinking as a way of reconceptualizing and understanding social disadvantage.

Recently there has been some apprehension about the way women and their needs are being addressed in anti-poverty analyses and policies, and concern that gender subordination — an equity issue — is being collapsed into an agenda about increasing welfare (Jackson, 1996).[2] Notwithstanding the relatively wide-ranging bodies of literature on gender and on poverty, it is argued that the interlinkages between the two have escaped careful analytical scrutiny.

At one level, the relationship between gender disadvantage and poverty appears to be quite straightforward, as in the tendency to equate women or female-headed households with the vulnerable or the poor. In fact, one frequently-made link between gender and poverty is the equation of women-headed households with the poor (Jazairy et al., 1992). A second approach,

Most of the chapters in this volume were first presented at a workshop that was co-organized by United Nations Research Institute for Social Development (UNRISD) and the Centre for Development Studies (CDS), 24–27 November 1997, Trivandrum, India. The workshop and the research project on which it was based have been generously funded by the United Nations Development Programme (UNDP) and the Swedish International Development Co-operation Agency (SIDA). The author would like to thank Yusuf Bangura, Solon Barraclough, Barbara Harriss-White, Carol Miller, Ruhi Saith and S. Sudha for their useful comments on an earlier draft of this chapter. Special thanks go to Uzma Hashmi for support in library searches, checking references and proof-reading under severe time constraints. Responsibility for the content of the chapter, however, lies with the author.

1. The 'New Poverty Agenda' (Lipton and Maxwell, 1992) refers to the poverty-oriented policy agenda articulated in *World Development Report 1990* (World Bank, 1990).
2. A similar concern was voiced by Buvinic (1983) in relation to the poverty focus of development agencies in the 1970s.

more instrumental in tone, is the 'win-win' scenario whereby 'investing in
women', their education in particular, is seen as an effective means for
increasing welfare or reducing fertility (World Bank, 1994). The links between
gender and poverty have also been captured through the gender-disaggregation of well-being *outcomes*, which has served to highlight significant female
disadvantage (UNDP, 1995).

While all of these arguments provide some insight into the relationship
between gender and poverty and have some empirical validity, although to
varying degrees in different contexts, they tend to be invoked in a highly
generalized manner. Thus generalizations have tended to replace contextualized social analyses of how poverty is created and reproduced. The gender
analysis of poverty also needs to unravel *how* gender differentiates the social
processes leading to poverty. This is an important consideration which has
received relatively little attention in recent policy debates.

The question that arises with some urgency is: Why does gender appear in
policy discussions of poverty in such generalized and problematic forms? One
of the arguments of this volume is that there are both methodological and
political reasons for this which need to be clearly understood because of their
implications for future poverty measurement and analysis, as well as for
policy formulation aimed at gender-sensitive poverty reduction. At the same
time some new ways of understanding the relationship between gender and
poverty need to be elaborated which can illuminate the ways in which both
the trajectories leading to poverty, and the escape from destitution, are
gendered. A gendered understanding of poverty also raises some difficult
questions about whether it can be assumed, as is often done, that the kinds of
asset interventions that can strengthen the position of poor men are going to
have much the same impact on poor women.

To take this project forward, the present volume makes contributions at
two inter-related levels. First, it provides a critical and selective assessment of
the attempts to measure gender disadvantage through a wide range of
indicators. It considers how reliable these indicators are in identifying gender
bias. It also asks questions about what these indicators mean in different
social contexts, what kinds of contextual information would be needed to
facilitate their interpretation, and how well they are able to reveal the social
processes creating poverty. An enquiry into these causal mechanisms in turn
leads to a second set of questions about how women and men, in particular
social contexts, relate differently to important assets such as land and labour,
given the ways in which their livelihood strategies are distinct. To explore
these issues, the social institutions within which production and distribution
take place, and their 'unruly'[3] practices are scrutinized.

One of the main themes emerging from this volume is that gender analysis
can illuminate the diverse processes leading to poverty, and thereby enrich its

3. The term 'unruly practice' is taken from Fraser (1989).

analysis. But at the same time, without a contextualized understanding of how poverty is created and reproduced, it is difficult to capture the ways in which gender shapes, and differentiates, those causal processes.

MAKING GENDER VISIBLE: SOME METHODOLOGICAL TRAPS

At the conceptual level, poverty is increasingly seen as a multi-dimensional phenomenon, which includes market-based consumption (or income), as well as the public provision of goods and services, access to common property resources and the intangible dimensions of a good life such as clean air, dignity, autonomy, and low levels of disease and crime. The proponents of the conventional approach argue that the income/consumption measure is still the best single proxy for poverty since it can incorporate non-market goods and services and a wide range of other utilities (clean air, democracy) and disutilities (noise, pollution), through 'shadow prices', into a monetary equivalent that is easy to compare over time and across contexts. Their critics argue that common property resources and state-provided commodities have usually been ignored in practice, and the consumption of non-traded goods has been under-estimated (Baulch, 1996). It is also questionable whether 'shadow prices' can meaningfully translate the different kinds of values that are embodied in non-market goods and services into monetary equivalents that are comparable.

A telling illustration of the methodological bias appears from Whitehead and Lockwood's analysis in this volume of some of the Poverty Assessments (PAs) for sub-Saharan Africa carried out by the World Bank.[4] The relevance of their argument, however, extends to the technocratic circles of other donor agencies as well as recipient states engaged in the measurement and analysis of poverty.

While most PAs begin by asserting the multi-dimensionality of poverty, ultimately it seems, all give priority to an income and/or consumption definition, a poverty line measure and a quantitative estimate of the percentage of people in poverty. At the same time, many of the potential insights about the nature of impoverishment, or poverty processes, which emerge from the qualitative and 'participatory' research are either marginalized or dropped from the analysis. Whitehead and Lockwood see this as a fundamental methodological choice, since it locks the PAs into reliance on expenditure data from household surveys, which in addition to being narrow, also tend to be unreliable and non-comparable.

---

4. These Poverty Assessments (PAs) are country studies about poverty carried out by the World Bank as part of the New Poverty Agenda. By 1996 almost fifty PAs had been carried out; for some countries there is more than one Assessment.

In most African and Latin American countries, household budget surveys are one-off (non-repetitive) exercises, which makes them unsuited as a device for monitoring poverty.[5] There is also little consistency in how the poverty line is established, even for the same country: some of the PAs define the poverty line in absolute terms and others in relative terms; some deflate household expenditure by average household size while others use expenditure per adult equivalent. Such methodological inconsistency effectively defeats the purpose of collecting quantitative data, since one of the rationales for using quantitative data is precisely that they are comparable over time and across context.

Kandiyoti (this volume) points to some of the specific problems that plague standard household surveys in transitional economies such as Uzbekistan. In this context, with the collapse of public sector employment and the precipitous drops in wages, what used to be 'subsidiary' activities and incomes have now become the mainstay of household budgets. However, for the purposes of surveys — an official activity *par excellence* — many respondents still report the place where their workbook is registered, and the 'official' salary that goes with it. This makes the calculation of income quite problematic. The issue of whether salaries are actually received or not, at what intervals, and the calculation of money equivalents of in-kind payments are all pertinent but difficult to capture within the formal context of the household survey.

More significantly, though, the reliance on poverty lines and household expenditure data has profound implications for how gender issues are analysed. Measuring poverty on the basis of household expenditure data effectively ignores the long-standing feminist concerns about intra-household distribution. It is very rare to find standard surveys, such as those carried out in the context of the PAs, embarking on a quantitative exploration of intra-household poverty. Per capita and adult equivalent measures make assumptions about *equal* intra-household distribution of resources. Hart's (1995) interrogation of the claims made by those using collective models of the household to be able to recover intra-household distributional patterns from household surveys using sophisticated econometric techniques also reveals that they are for the most part exaggerated. In other words, if household surveys are to become useful tools for capturing and monitoring gender differentials in poverty, then intra-household distribution issues need to be addressed at the very early stage and specifically built into questionnaire design.

The reliance on household expenditure data also means that one of the easier ways to make gender visible is by dividing the households into male-headed and female-headed ones, given that the characteristics of household heads (their gender, age, etc.) are invariably collected through these surveys and form a ready basis for sorting the data.

---

5. See for example, Appleton (1996) on Uganda, and Lustig (1993) for Latin America.

The tendency to equate female headship with poverty has, however, been queried on both empirical and methodological grounds. The trajectories leading to female headship are clearly divergent, and the category of households labelled 'female-headed' is a highly heterogeneous one. It includes lone female units, households of single women wage earners with young dependants, households in which women earners receive significant remittances from absent males, and so on. Some of these conditions may constitute what can be reasonably thought of as poverty risk factors, such as households with young children maintained by women alone (Folbre, 1990). But by aggregating these distinct categories of households generated through different social processes (e.g. migration, widowhood, divorce), and constructing a simple dualism between male-headed and female-headed households, it becomes impossible to interpret the evidence in a meaningful way.

At the same time, the identification of certain types of female-headed households as poorer, such as lone widows, begs the question of why some widows end up living alone while others do not. As Whitehead and Lockwood (this volume) put it, the characteristics of the poor say very little about the reasons why they have become impoverished, and it is methodologically incorrect to treat these characteristics as independent variables. In this particular case, they argue, the chain of causation may run the other way: it may very well be that it is poor widows whose children leave the household (through labour migration, for example) and that when more economically secure women are widowed they do not end up living alone. In practice, causes and effects always interact and do so differently in diverse contexts of time and place. In the case of Uzbekistan described by Kandiyoti (this volume) a likely poverty risk factor may be the gender composition of a widow's offspring. Widowed women are less likely to be taken into a married daughter's household, and often end up living alone sometimes in a state of destitution, whereas widowed mothers of sons are routinely to be found living with their sons and also in control of household finances.

In short, the contributions to this volume document persisting reticence on the part of administrative and governmental structures responsible for data collection exercises to probe the intra-household arena. This is surprising in view of the significant body of evidence and argument that has been brought to bear on this issue over the past two decades. This has effectively shaken the micro foundations of the conventional economic approach, and yet few national level surveys attempt to collect data at a more disaggregated level.

Social Indicators, Functionings and Capabilities

One of the more positive responses to the conceptual shortcomings of the 'money-metric' approach has been to look more directly at what people can do or be — indicators of the physical quality of life (Morris, 1979) or functionings (Sen, 1985a). Ironically, the work on social indicators seems to meet the requirements of neo-classical micro-economic analysis, individualism, far more easily than the poverty line measures. Given that these beings and doings are directly measurable on the individual, gender inequalities can be made more readily visible. The framework has inspired a large body of feminist research on well-being outcomes, documenting significant and sometimes alarming incidence of female disadvantage. The contributions to this volume explore this issue from a number of different perspectives and at different levels of aggregation. As might be expected from the large body of literature on 'missing females' in South and East Asia, life and death questions take up considerable space in this volume too.

Das Gupta and Li's broadbrush historical account (this volume) traces the patterns of female disadvantage in child survival during the twentieth century for three countries which show the highest levels of 'missing girls' in the world: India, China and South Korea. One of the hypotheses they explore is the extent to which levels of discrimination against daughters, in these particular cultural contexts, may intensify when people experience a tightening of circumstances relative to *their own* previous position.[6] These stresses could be experienced when people are caught up in a war, a famine, or during periods of fertility decline when the number of opportunities to have a son is effectively reduced.

The impact of major national crises, in particular the Japanese invasion of China in the 1930s, the Korean War (1950–3) and the large-scale Chinese famine (1959–61), on girls is evident in the juvenile sex ratios (i.e. number of males to females in the 0–4 year age group) which reflect the *excess* mortality of girls, over and above the fact that children of both sexes undoubtedly suffered during these crises. Fertility decline, which has taken place in all three countries in recent decades, has also been accompanied by rising female disadvantage in survival (and more masculine sex ratios for children) as parents manipulate the gender composition of their desired family size. The main rise in sex ratios in all three countries, however, has taken place after 1980 and seems to suggest that the impact of fertility decline on sex ratios is substantially raised by the spread of pre-natal sex-selection techniques.

This last point is the subject of Sudha and Irudaya Rajan's contribution to this volume, which presents both demographic and qualitative evidence on the incidence of prenatal sex selection and female infanticide in India. Their analysis of sex ratios *at birth* for the period 1981–91 suggests that in some parts of the country parents may be adding pre-natal sex selection techniques to traditional post-natal ones to create a 'double jeopardy' for their daughters. The excess masculinity of sex ratios at birth is concentrated especially in the north and north-west of the sub-continent, and in the urban

---

6. As the authors note, the hypothesis that the poor discriminate against their daughters more than the non-poor in these countries does not seem to find empirical support; a similar conclusion emerges from Saith and Harriss-White's contribution to this volume.

areas of some central states, while the southern states appear to have on the whole normal sex ratios at birth — a regional contrast with some historical precedence that has been the subject of intense debate and theorizing.

While sex ratios at birth show the most masculinity in the north and north-west, and this increasing masculinity is not a nationwide phenomenon, Sudha and Irudaya Rajan also show that sex ratios of child mortality definitely indicate increasing female disadvantage *over all of India*. Only one or two very small areas of the country show less female disadvantage in 1991 than they did in 1981, while areas in the south that had normal mortality ratios in 1981 show female disadvantage in 1991. This pattern is consistent with recent micro-level studies documenting excess female child mortality in parts of south India where such extreme forms of discrimination have been hitherto unknown, and where it has appeared in a class-specific form among landed households (Harriss-White, forthcoming; Miller, 1997).

The evidence on female disadvantage in early age survivorship does not, however, imply a consistent pattern of anti-female bias in food intake and nutritional status as is often assumed. Even in north and north-western India, where the evidence on discrimination against young girls in terms of survivorship is most compelling, findings from nutritional surveys not infrequently show that adult women fare better than their male counterparts (Harriss, 1990). Confirming the problematic nature of these generalized assumptions of female disadvantage, Saith and Harriss-White's comprehensive review (this volume) of the micro-level literature for South Asia reaches the conclusion that the evidence on gender differentials in nutritional status is inconclusive, showing no *consistent* indication of gender bias.

An interesting instance of the inconsistency is captured in a village-level study of nutritional status in the north-western Indian state of Uttar Pradesh (Kynch and McGuire, 1994). Here age and gender interact in complex ways over the life cycles of men and women. Starting with female nutritional disadvantage during childhood, the pattern is reversed among child-bearing couples where adult men seem to be the ones at greater risk of illness or low working ability, because of thinness. Male disadvantage in this particular context is explained by the compulsions on husbands to 'provision' their families, which among the agricultural households means undertaking effort-intensive farm work (ploughing and digging).

This analysis, in particular, echoes the point made by Jackson and Palmer-Jones (this volume) that while time use studies have been of great value in making women's work visible, it is important to recognize how male gender roles in divisions of labour can also involve vulnerabilities for specific groups of men. They argue that an explicit concern with the *physical arduousness* of work may better illuminate how work and well-being are connected for women and men. In poor South Asian households effort-intensive work (high energy expenditure) can, more often than inequitable food intake, be the cause of differences in adult anthropometry. In these cases, after adjusting for energy expenditures, energy intakes are often equitable. In some cases, however, the greater calorie consumption of men might not even compensate for their greater average daily energy expenditure.

The contributions to this volume also raise some thorny methodological questions about gender-disaggregation, and the difficulties of making meaningful comparisons between male and female well-being when men's and women's bodies are different in form and function. One problematic area, highlighted by Saith and Harriss-White (this volume), is that of morbidity, where a significant proportion of the conditions that cause morbidity are sex-specific and defy simple male/female comparisons — reproductive health problems being the most glaring example. Other diseases may be sex-specific due to genetic predispositions. Somewhat similar questions can be raised about life expectancy data. While it is misleading to conclude from the overall increase in female life expectancy that there has been an improvement in female health in younger, especially reproductive, ages (Saith and Harriss-White, this volume), it may be equally misleading to attribute male disadvantage to biological factors alone (Jackson and Palmer-Jones, this volume). The life expectancy disadvantage of men may suggest that in addition to 'natural' biological disadvantage there are also *social processes* which disadvantage men in health and longevity terms.

Another controversial area is nutrition monitoring where meaningful comparisons between men's and women's nutritional status can only be made once 'norms' and 'cut-off points' have been adjusted for gender difference — a process that is fraught with difficulty (Saith and Harriss-White, this volume). As Harriss-White (1997) recently showed, the conclusions of studies carried out using even the *same data set* can differ depending on the assumptions made about norms and cut-off points as well as the use of gendered or ungendered standards.

The point of raising these issues here is to highlight the methodological controversies (and arbitrariness) involved in making well-being comparisons between men and women — issues that tend to be overlooked when global comparisons are made. In the broader scheme of things these technical problems are merely the tip of the iceberg. As those familiar with this field have repeatedly argued, data problems to do with reliability and comparability are as debilitating in the area of social indicators as they are in the case of economic data.

Very few developing countries, for example, have comprehensive and reliable vital registration systems from which demographic data can be obtained — India being perhaps an exception. And even for those with complete vital registration systems the estimates of mortality and life expectancy produced by international agencies may not be accurate because of the overuse of model life tables (Murray, 1991). UNICEF (1993: 8) admits that many of the statistics used for estimating under-five mortality are based on mathematical models rather than recent measurements. Even for an apparently straightforward indicator like literacy there are few up-to-date estimates; for 19 of the 145 (including developed) countries there are no data on adult literacy since 1970, and for 41 more the data relate to a year in the decade 1970–9 (Srinivasan, 1994).

Moreover, social indicators while useful in revealing gender differences in well-being *outcomes*, are limited in the kind of *causal* analysis they can generate. This is a very important qualification, and is discussed at some length later. Data users thus need to be realistic about the extent to which findings and policy recommendations that rely on correlations and regressions, without enough complementary contextual information, can be trusted (see below on 'triangulation'). A pertinent example is the human capital argument for investing in education — especially female education.

According to Whitehead and Lockwood (this volume) the World Bank's analyses of gender gaps in primary education in sub-Saharan Africa provide an extremely partial and misleading picture of the causal dynamics behind low levels of female education. The analysis of female education in the PAs is based exclusively on efficiency arguments — about how female education will increase child and household welfare. It does not shed any light on the reproduction of structural gender inequalities, or say anything substantive about how gender inequalities underlie educational outcomes. It is also stated widely in the PAs that education is intimately related to agricultural productivity and thus to the escape from poverty. According to Whitehead and Lockwood, besides the weak evidence documented in the PAs to support this hypothesis, there are also serious problems in how the weak association between education and income is being interpreted. The relationship between the two variables, they argue, may be being read spuriously as causal when both income and education may be affected by underlying patterns of wealth organized through families.

Ironically, such over-reliance on simple econometric techniques also marks some of the emerging micro-level feminist research, which uses interview techniques to capture different aspects of female autonomy such as intra-household decision making, mobility in the public sphere and domestic violence. As Kabeer (this volume) usefully illustrates, here too the results can be uncontextualized, single-stranded and difficult to interpret, with a heavy reliance on simple correlations and regressions using a few variables.

Power, Freedom and Agency

From a gender perspective, broader concepts of poverty are more useful than a focus purely on household income levels because they allow a better grasp of the multi-dimensional aspects of gender disadvantage, such as lack of power to control important decisions that affect one's life (Sen, this volume). Along somewhat similar lines, it can also be argued that confining the analysis of gender inequality to basic well-being outcomes alone serves to convey the impression that female disadvantage is largely a matter of poverty (Kabeer, this volume). This is misleading for two reasons. On the one hand, prosperity within a society may help to reduce gender inequalities in basic well-being outcomes, but intensify social restrictions on women's autonomy. On the other hand, a focus on basic needs failures such as child mortality misses out on other dimensions of gender disadvantage among the poor which do not take such extreme forms, such as women's heavier workloads.

In recent years, issues of empowerment and autonomy have entered poverty debates through a number of different channels. The capability framework, in particular, embraces both basic functionings, such as longevity, as well as more complex capabilities such as freedom to which intrinsic value is attached (Sen, 1985b). In practice, however, the proponents of this approach have tended to concentrate on the first set of functionings, which lend themselves to measurement.[7] At the same time certain strands of policy discourse have identified female empowerment as an effective means for reducing poverty. Its value here tends to be instrumental and the aim has been to establish the nature of the association between the 'degrees of autonomy' permitted to women in different contexts and certain demographic, economic or social outcomes deemed desirable — hence the search for easily quantifiable indicators of empowerment.

The methodological problems and the difficulties of interpretation which were noted above in relation to well-being outcomes become particularly daunting when we move from basic achievements, such as longevity and education, onto the difficult terrain of power, agency and choice. As Kabeer (this volume) rightly notes, indicators not only compress a great deal of information into a single statistic, but also embody assumptions about what this information means. In the case of complex and culturally embedded notions like autonomy, it is impossible to have any faith in whether or not the indicator means what it is intended to mean without contextual evidence to support the assumptions that are being made.

These issues are explored by Kabeer (this volume). She sees empowerment as being inescapably bound up with disempowerment and about the *process* by which those who have been denied the ability to make choices acquire such an ability. She argues that it is only through grounded analyses that issues of power and disempowerment can be meaningfully assessed, because it is only at that level that the *context, content and consequences* of choice can be understood and interpreted. Statistical perspectives on intra-household

---

7. In his earlier writings, Sen (1985a) makes a distinction between the realms to which functionings and capabilities belong. A functioning is an achievement of a person, what he or she can be or do. In other words, functionings are constitutive of well-being, whereas a capability set is a freedom-type notion meant to assess the 'real opportunities faced by the person' (1985a: 51). But Sen is not satisfied with this separation and in his later works suggests different ways of bridging the gap, in particular by recourse to the notion of 'capability to function' whereby actual achievements (e.g. being healthy) are seen as proxies for the capabilities to function (Sen, 1987). Thus both well-being and positive freedom are inferred from the achievement.

decision-making are clearly limited. They may provide a brief glimpse of the processes of decision-making, but they say very little about the subtle negotiations that go on between men and women in their private lives.

Besides the methodological problems confronting analyses of power there are further questions to do with the interpretation of results. A case in point is the kind of behaviour on the part of women which seems to suggest that they have internalized their social status as persons of lesser value, such as women's secondary claims on household resources (their 'altruism'), or their willingness to bear children to the detriment of their own health and survival in order to satisfy their own or their husband's preferences for sons — the problem of 'physical condition neglect' as Sen (1985a) calls it. The acceptance of gender biased norms can also lead women to discriminate against other women, their daughters for example (Das Gupta and Li; Sudha and Irudaya Rajan, this volume). How can a feminist analysis of agency and power come to terms with these forms of behaviour?

One of the key points emerging from Kabeer's analysis of empowerment is the need to *cross-check* evidence on women's agency against the outcomes or consequences of the choices they make (while Sen prefers to *infer* agency from outcomes, see footnote 7). Thus according to Kabeer power relations are expressed not only through the exercise of agency and choice, but also through the *kinds* of choices people make. Her contribution also reminds us of the strong rationale that women are likely to have in certain contexts for making choices which are essentially disempowering and also detrimental to their own, or their daughters', health and well-being. Deeply entrenched rules, norms and practices help influence behaviour, define values and shape choices. Kabeer's understanding of agency is therefore qualified in two important ways: first, by being anchored within an institutional understanding of the conditions of choice (i.e. structures of constraint); second, by including the consequences of choice within her account of agency, which effectively overcomes the problem of 'physical condition neglect'.

The connections between agency and bodily well-being are also central to the argument put forward by Jackson and Palmer-Jones (this volume). They criticize both structuralist and bargaining analyses of gender divisions of work and well-being for their failure to show the 'structuring actions of women and men', i.e. agency. They argue that intra-household social processes of contestation and negotiation about work, which are significantly influenced by the *personal experiences of the pleasures and pains of work*, mediate the gendered connections between work and well-being. Bargaining models with their emphasis on structures of constraint and opportunity (generalized 'fall back positions'), they argue, have not been particularly useful for describing the actual or implicit discourses between individual members of a particular domestic group, and have thus tended to underplay women's agency.

This critique reverberates the point made by Kabeer (this volume) that the critical aspects of women's agency are often embedded in the subtle negotiations that go on between men and women, and are thus difficult to capture. But in contrast to Kabeer's stress on how structures of constraint limit the choices that women make (as in cultures where daughter disfavour becomes a 'rational' response to social norms), Jackson and Palmer-Jones emphasize how women seek to subvert and reformulate those social norms. The ways in which a woman faced with onerous and well-being threatening work may ensure her bodily well-being (by hiring labour, or persuading a husband, child or daughter-in-law to do it) is taken as evidence of such agency.[8] They thus ask whether the alleged high levels of work ('time famine') by poor rural women are actually reflected in well-being outcomes? And how, if one does not see patriarchy as all-determining, do women as active agents come to be the victims of such an inequitable order?

Similarly, the micro-level studies of women workers in Third World manufacturing discussed in Razavi's contribution (this volume) highlight the possibilities and the spaces for agency that entry into these labour markets has opened up for some groups of women. In some contexts, it has allowed them to re-negotiate the terms of their domestic relationships, and in some cases to walk out of, or not enter into, unsatisfactory relationships. This is not to deny the fact that the increased field of manoeuvring at home may be matched by different patriarchal controls in the factory setting which help keep the women workers poorly paid and vastly unprotected in jobs that are sometimes dangerous.

This also raises difficult methodological questions, such as the tension between objective criteria (skills, wages, health issues and bodily well-being more generally) and subjective criteria (perceptions of work and its value), for assessing the implications of this form of work for both poverty eradication and wider issues of discrimination and subordination. While reference to some objective criteria of well-being is clearly needed in order to get us away from the utilitarian insistence in taking subjective preferences as the only criteria for making judgements about values and welfare (Sen, this volume), there is also a need for women's own perceptions and values to find some space in these discussions if only because they allow us to better understand the choices that women make.

Three tentative conclusions may be taken from this section. *First*, an obvious methodological observation would be that issues of agency and informal power are difficult to capture through interview techniques (Kabeer) and problematic to represent through generalized fallback positions (Jackson and Palmer-Jones). *Second*, the question as to whether social structures of constraint limit women's choices, or alternatively whether women are able to subvert gender-biased social norms finds different answers

---

8. Ironically the ability of senior women to shift their onerous domestic tasks onto daughters and daughters-in-law is cited as evidence of power asymmetries (rather than agency) in Kandiyoti's contribution (this volume).

depending on the issue and context at hand. Where there are multiple discourses with contradictory elements, such as around work and value (Jackson and Palmer-Jones, Razavi), there may be greater possibility for agency than in the case of daughter disfavour in some parts of India (Kabeer), where devaluing discourses overlap and reinforce each other (in dowry obligations, and in religious asymmetries between daughters and sons for ritual purposes). And *third*, there is a degree of consensus among these different contributors on the need to *include* issues of bodily well-being within gender analyses of choice and agency.

Participatory Methods

In contrast to the formality of the conventional approach to poverty measurement, what have become known as participatory approaches determine both the constituents and the sources of well-being through an iterative process involving the PRA (participatory rural appraisal) facilitator and participants. Their proponents claim that participatory methods of research and policy analysis enable the local people — including the poor, illiterate, women and the marginalized — themselves to appraise, analyse, plan and act.

A puzzling observation that emerges from Whitehead and Lockwood's contribution to this volume is how standard qualitative research methods used in both sociology and anthropology, such as unstructured interviews, are labelled 'participatory' in the context of the World Bank Poverty Assessments. They suggest that arguments over what constitutes a 'participatory' method and its relation to qualitative methods is not simply a turf war. Rather it seems to be related to the long-standing epistemological competition between quantitative and qualitative methods in the social sciences in general, and the difficulties of the latter in gaining legitimacy in the World Bank, in particular. For these authors the use of the new participatory methods by the World Bank 'represents a foothold for non-quantitative methods'. It also 'begs the question of whether there should not be a greater role for conventional qualitative research' in the form of the existing published local level case studies which have appropriate data for the analysis of socio-economic processes, but which are hardly used in the PAs.

There has been a long-running debate about the claims made by the proponents of PRA that their methods in effect 'hand over the stick' to the local people themselves. Critics point out that PRAs involve highly formal and public social events, which collect information in ways that are strongly influenced by existing social relationships and hierarchies (Mosse, 1994). Questions have also been raised over any expectations that poor village people willingly divulge truthful and accurate information in one-off 'participatory' research exercises (Jackson, 1997a).

Quite apart from how participatory data are collected, Whitehead and Lockwood (this volume) draw attention to the importance of how the data are then selected, interpreted/analysed and presented. The strong moral emphasis on accessing the voices of the poor, and the subsequent focus on methods and tools for data collection in participatory approaches, they note, side-step fundamental questions about the validity and reliability of the data, and about the role of data collectors themselves. The fieldworker, they note, 'is a crucial figure in selecting and transmitting the voices of the poor, but is largely invisible in the PPAs [participatory poverty assessments], or assumed to be somehow transparent'.

There are also some fundamental questions as to whether subjective perceptions of ill- and well-being can, on their own, reveal all that there is to know about individual welfare. More broadly though, what do not emerge from the perceptions of the poor themselves are those factors and relationships that they do not perceive directly, either because of ideology or scale (Whitehead and Lockwood, 1999). The PPAs produce no analyses of the macro-economic causes of poverty, or of how people in poor households may be locked into cycles of food insecurity and labour shortage. To access these from the participatory research exercises, they argue, the evidence must be 'read'. The interpretation of the evidence emerging from participatory exercises is crucial as far as gender analysis is concerned since the statements made by poor men and women can divulge critical gender differences in how poverty is created and experienced. Participatory methodologies tend to underplay the importance of interpreting the data, and hence the meanings emerging from the raw data may not be taken up. The job of interpreting the data is in fact always done, but in the PRA tradition it is not extensively discussed, thereby creating the potential for all sorts of errors.

Triangulation

Several contributors to this volume highlight the need for cross-checking and 'triangulation' if the estimates and analyses that are arrived at are to inspire any confidence — this is not a new insight (see Scott, 1981), but bears reaffirming in view of its significance to poverty analyses. This is presumably one of the reasons why participatory research techniques have been included in the World Bank's Poverty Assessments. But this raises many difficult and unresolved questions about what the relations between different methodologies should be, and how conflicting results should be handled or reconciled (Baulch, 1996).

Some of these questions are taken up by the contributors to this volume, whose chapters provide insights into this difficult methodological area, as well as some useful suggestions for future research. Jackson and Palmer-Jones highlight the importance of triangulating well-being outcomes (longevity, nutritional status) with analytical accounts of processes and mechanisms (implicit and explicit negotiations between men and women over the division and valuation of work, for example). Kabeer's empowerment framework also entails checking of different kinds of evidence across three different dimensions of power: 'resources' (not only access, but also future claims, to both material and human and social resources); 'agency' (including processes of decision making, as well as less measurable manifestations of agency such as negotiation, deception and manipulation); and 'achievements' (well-being outcomes). These three dimensions, she argues, are indivisible in determining the meaning of an indicator and hence its validity as a measure of empowerment.

Kandiyoti, and Whitehead and Lockwood argue that qualitative data and existing case studies need to feed into definitions and analyses of poverty in particular country settings and not be used simply to illustrate points derived from survey data. In her fascinating discussion of the shifting boundaries of domestic units in Uzbekistan, Kandiyoti reminds us that the choice of appropriate unit of analysis may depend on the nature of the research question posed. To be able to grapple with the complex and fluid boundaries of domestic units she highlights the advantages of a more 'flexible and exploratory approach ... one that is more open to trial and error'. These suggestions basically turn current practice on its head.

The need for contextual analyses, which is reiterated by these authors, hints at some of the inherent and fundamental limitations of indicators, and highlights the need to supplement data from indicators with other kinds of information. But in some contexts relevant and up-to-date information from case studies may not even be available. Kandiyoti's contribution raises some sensitive issues about the politics of poverty research. In the case of Uzbekistan and other Central Asian Republics, she argues, there is a serious scarcity of local level case studies that may assist the analysis of socio-economic processes that are generative of new forms of vulnerability. The relatively modest body of ethnographic research from the Soviet period is becoming quickly outdated. The drying up of local research funds since the breakup of the Union has meant that social science research, which was relatively weak in this region, is now grinding to a halt. The priorities of major donors have been to fill this gap with large-scale surveys which may not be the most appropriate research tools in an environment where a host of new socio-economic processes are changing the landscape of social provision, redistribution and livelihoods. While this problem may be more acute in Central Asia, Kandiyoti's arguments no doubt have wider relevance given the on-going crisis that engulfs research institutions in many developing countries, affecting their budgets, incentive structures, priorities and agendas.

FROM OUTCOME TO PROCESS: INSTITUTIONS AND ENTITLEMENTS

One of the arguments thus far has been that an exclusive focus on poverty outcomes very often means that the processes leading to poverty are either overlooked or otherwise analysed through regressions and correlations of a few variables abstracted from a far more complex scenario wherein a wide range of institutions interact. It also, inevitably, means that gender will be dealt with through a process of disaggregation — either of households (using the gender of the head as the stratifier) or of social indicators (differentiating males and females). The question that has not been explicitly addressed, but which is clearly central to our discussion, is: How can the focus of poverty analyses be sharpened and shifted so that the social, economic, cultural and political processes and institutions that are implicated in the creation and perpetuation of poverty, become more lucid and central to the enquiry?

An important contribution to poverty analyses has come from the literature on hunger and famines, namely the 'entitlements' framework (Sen, 1981; Drèze and Sen, 1989). Entitlement analysis has been useful in directing attention to the processes through which individuals gain access to commodities and other resources (or fail to do so), which is said to depend on their socio-economic position and on the rules which render claims over commodities 'legitimate'. Inasmuch as these rules and norms entitle people differently and unequally, they draw attention to the likelihood that deprivation will be diversely constituted across a population along the lines of gender, caste, class, etc. (Kabeer, 1997).

Taking on board the important qualifications and criticisms made of this framework, especially of its excessively marketized and 'legalistic' view of the rules of entitlement, entitlements can now be seen more broadly to encompass not only state-enforced legal rules, but also socially-enforced moral rules which constrain and enable command over commodities.

The household is a central terrain where the gendered rules of entitlement (to work, rest and food) are negotiated and enforced. One of the important contributions of Gore's (1993) critique of entitlement analysis, however, was to highlight the fact that these moral rules are by no means limited to domestic institutions (family, household), as Sen's original formulation of 'extended entitlements' would have it. 'Sen's entitlement analysis', he argues, 'marginalises non-governmental sites of rule-making and rule-enforcing which affect entitlement by either downplaying the role of socially enforced moral rules, or compartmentalising them to the domestic sphere' (Gore, 1993: 444). And conversely, the boundaries of the domestic sphere, the position of the household head and his degree of control over the lives of other household members are all significantly influenced by state-sanctioned legal rules which authorize particular gendered subjects and deny personhood to others. Consequently, a person's entitlements are determined precisely through this *interplay* between state-enforced legal rules and social norms.

Gender-Based Entitlements: Kinship Structures and Social Norms

The evidence on daughter disfavour in some parts of India and East Asia, accentuated in the context of rapid fertility decline, provides one of the more extreme manifestations of anti-female discrimination at the hands of mothers and fathers under great social pressure. Yet the causal explanations are all contested.

In this volume, Sudha and Irudaya Rajan and Das Gupta and Li provide somewhat different interpretations of the causal mechanisms underlying discriminatory practices. Both chapters contend that the rigid patrilineal and patrilocal kinship systems characteristic of East Asia and north-west India lead to a daughter's marginality to her family of birth. This also affects the way in which the question of marriage and its costs are perceived. Both chapters also note (although explanations are not offered) that in the face of social and economic change these patrilineal kinship systems have been remarkably robust, while the more egalitarian marriage systems have been much less resilient. However, the forces and mechanisms which are implicated in order to explain how women and girls come to be victims in this scheme of things are quite distinct.

Das Gupta and Li's chapter, pitched at the aggregate country level, explores the *demographically* determined reasons behind changes in marriage payments (dowry, brideprice). Using data from national population censuses, they show how changing fertility and mortality patterns over the past century, together with discriminatory forces affecting sex ratios (intensified during famines, wars, and periods of fertility decline), modified the potential supply of males and females in the marriage market ('spousal availability') and also transformed marriage payments. They also consider how these demographic changes influence the extent and manifestation of violence against women.

The chapter by Sudha and Irudaya Rajan has little discussion of how changing numbers of females versus males in successive birth cohorts might alter marriage payments and accentuate or dampen the adverse treatment of women. They argue that socio-economic developments in India, strongly influenced by state policies, have institutionalized women's alienation from the most critical productive resource, land, and marginalized them in labour markets. This has accentuated culturally sanctioned social norms, rules and practices which shape parental perceptions and treatment of daughters. At the same time 'welfarist' state responses addressing women's societal devaluation have either not been implemented, or have had very little impact, and state legislation such as the recent ban on the abortion of healthy female foetuses, has only addressed the symptoms of women's social devaluation rather than its root causes. The efforts by NGOs and social movements to tackle infanticide and women's devaluation through consciousness-raising have hardly made a dent on demographic behaviour when the material pressures pulling in the opposite direction have been overwhelming.

The contrasting approaches of these two chapters are also reflected in some of the conclusions they draw. Das Gupta and Li suggest that, in India, one kind of discrimination — against girls through selective abortion of females and excess female child mortality — might dampen another kind of discrimination — against women through dowry related violence and deaths — by lowering the supply of women in the marriage market. Sudha and Irudaya Rajan conclude that since social and economic developments in

India continue to favour males, discrimination against females of whatever age is unlikely to ameliorate in the near future. Neither contribution predicts an amelioration in the treatment of daughters — even if dowry payments taper off and dowry related harassment and deaths are abated (Das Gupta and Li). The latter chapter considers fertility decline in the context of unchanging social norms as a far more powerful explanation for daughter disfavour than dowry.

A number of tentative conclusions emerge. The first is that in cultural contexts marked by patrilineal kinship systems the implications of rapid fertility decline for the treatment of daughters can be quite adverse as the gender composition of a household becomes the more important. This is particularly the case in the absence of state-provided old age pensions and where sons are still crucial for old age.

The second point that emerges from this analysis is that while there is some evidence of women's collective activism and resistance against discriminatory social practices (Sudha and Irudaya Rajan), the constraints on women at the local level remain very severe and their status is tied up with conforming to the social norms that deny them (and their daughters) agency. As Kabeer (this volume) explains, in these circumstances it is not just difficult, but also dangerous, for individual women, isolated within their families, often cut off from the communities in which they grew up, to challenge the social norms that define them (and their daughters) as lesser beings. Collective action in the public arena makes the project of social transformation an act of solidarity and is therefore likely to be effective in the long run. But the pathways between collective action and transformations at the individual level are complex, diffuse and unpredictable.

Women and Land Tenure Arrangements

The other relevant point emerging from some of the micro-level studies on Indian sex ratios relates to the evolving connections between kinship and land, whereby excess girl child mortality seems to be most severe among propertied households. This is indeed an extreme illustration of how 'household' assets in the hands of men may fail to enhance the well-being of women. A less extreme situation is described by Kandiyoti (this volume) for Uzbekistan, where changes in land tenure and in the composition of rural livelihoods are shifting the balance of gendered divisions of labour within households and creating new burdens for women. The increasing reliance of *kolkhoz* (collective farm) employees, who no longer receive wages, on personal subsidiary plots has meant an intensification of women's labour inputs into subsistence farming, as well as women constituting the majority of workers in the work brigades. At the other end of the social scale, among the thin layer of private peasant farmers, wives are also experiencing a major change in their work conditions — from being *kolkhoz* workers or public sector employees with attendant social benefits, they have become unpaid family labourers. This also raises questions about approaches to poverty advocating the transfer of assets to poor households (through land reforms, settlement schemes, or social forestry projects).

Gender equity calls attention to the question of land rights. For some women discriminatory inheritance laws and poor land access are significant constraints. At one level therefore the current emphasis on land rights in policy documents is an encouraging sign of the success of equal rights lobbyists in getting the issue on the agenda. But, at the same time, the issue of land rights and its relation to women's poverty in developing countries, as elsewhere, is a very complex one, intimately bound up with at least three sets of issues: first, the politics of how women's interests are represented in both the state and civil society, *and* struggled for at the local level; second, the nature of rural livelihoods and women's place as distinct actors within the agrarian structures; third, the specificities of gender and conjugal relations. This includes most importantly kinship and marriage institutions that impinge on how claims, rights, needs and obligations are defined and negotiated. These issues are not always adequately addressed in policy documents. In some of the PAs, for example, the extended discussions of 'women and agriculture' centre on land rights. But the references to land rights remain somewhat detached from the specificities of rural livelihoods, gender relations and poverty processes (Whitehead and Lockwood, this volume). Some of the emerging literature on social exclusion takes it as axiomatic that women need better legal entitlements, while at the same time they persuasively show, at least for sub-Saharan Africa, that in situations where the law and official procedures do not discriminate against women, women still often end up without direct rights to land (see discussion and references in Gore, 1994).

The connections between customary rights, *de jure* (legal) rights and *de facto* control are quite complex and varied across different contexts of time and place. Kabeer's discussion (this volume) of land rights in Muslim and Hindu communities of India (and Bangladesh and Iran) raises a number of additional points about the significance of these different rights, bearing in mind the important qualification that gender divisions of labour in this part of the world bear little resemblance to those in sub-Saharan Africa where women's provisioning roles as well as their engagement in production for the market are socially recognized.

In the Indian literature the critical measure of women's access to land has tended to be *de facto* rather than *de jure* entitlement; on this basis the difference between Hindu and Muslim communities is considered to be inconsequential since in both contexts women are effectively propertyless. However, as Kabeer goes on to argue, there are problems in assuming that *de facto* ownership can reveal all that there is to know about women's entitlements. Evidence from a number of different Muslim communities shows that even though Muslim women do waive their land rights to their brothers, they see it as constituting a possible future claim (should their marriages break down), and in some contexts they do in fact press for their property rights. These are potentials which are not easily available to women in communities where such rights have not been recognized by customary law and tradition, even if they have subsequently been brought into existence by legislative action. This raises an important question which has yet to be satisfactorily answered: how do attempts to change deeply entrenched structures, in this case, pitting the law against rules legitimized by custom and religion, translate into individual agency and choice?

The recent attempt in South Africa to deliver land to women provides some useful insights into this difficult policy area. The South African Constitution and the intricate policy framework for land reform that has been put in place are testimony to the explicit commitment made by the government to gender equality. However, there seem to be serious gaps between policy directives and on-the-ground results, and significant obstacles in implementing gender-sensitive, redistributive policies (Walker, 1998). The role of the judiciary (the Land Claims Court), the institution of chieftaincy, and community-level dynamics, all present varying constraints on the process of implementation. It is also feared that the pursuit of tenure security could *in practice* end up entrenching existing inequalities in access to land by formalizing what are today informal rights and registering such rights in the name of the household heads only, 'thereby fixing women's marginality in a legal trap ... This is not policy, but the pressures propelling harried officials in this direction are strong' (Walker, 1998: 12).

This is a useful observation and hints at two interrelated sets of issues. First is the argument that in social contexts marked by huge differences in educational levels and by differential access to state administration, there is much reason to fear that the adjudication/registration process will be manipulated by the élite in its favour, and thereby result in new sources of tenure insecurity for less influential rightholders; both colonial and modern attempts to reform customary tenurial practices in sub-Saharan Africa, it is argued, have fallen into such traps (Platteau, 1995).

What this also suggests is that where women have some customary usufruct rights, as is the case in many sub-Saharan African countries, there may be fewer arguments for formalizing those rights even if tenure security is defined in very broad terms (as it is in the South African case) and even if women are explicitly targeted as beneficiaries. Second, it is also questionable whether inadequate access to land plays an important part in the creation and perpetuation of women's impoverishment in sub-Saharan Africa. For some women in sub-Saharan Africa, Whitehead and Lockwood (this volume) point out, discriminatory inheritance laws and poor land access are significant constraints, but only in a minority of cases is inadequate access to land, because of an inability to secure usufruct rights, by itself a cause of poverty. 'That land rights rarely emerged as a voiced concern of rural women in the PPAs we take as some support for this view'.

The limited conclusion that may be drawn from this brief discussion of women's land rights is that customary rights affect women's attempts to secure a livelihood for themselves and their dependants in ways that are quite distinct across different contexts. One generalization that can be made is that whatever the nature of the economic system in terms of its productive and exchange relations, women's ability to function as fully acting subjects in relation to property is always less than that of men, and mediated through their relationships with men (Whitehead, 1984). While it is desirable to make women's rights to resources more formal and less conditional on relations with men (or local patriarchal institutions), it also needs to be recognized that ambiguity may have strategic advantages for women: it may arouse less resistance and yet deliver subtle forms of influence and control (Jackson, 1997b). State-enforced legal reforms with an explicit commitment to gender equality can, under some circumstances, strengthen women's position. But whether this potential is realized in practice largely depends on the local and community-level dynamics and institutions through which policy intentions work themselves out, and in particular, on the extent to which poorer women can be effectively organized to engage with and make use of the formal structures and legal opportunities that are being put in place.

'The Poor's Most Abundant Asset: Labour'?

The 'New Poverty Agenda' first articulated in the *1990 World Development Report (WDR)*, which identified 'labour-intensive growth' as its central tenet, is discussed at some length in some of the contributions to this volume.

Whitehead and Lockwood's contribution reveals the deep influence of *1990 WDR* on the analysis and, in particular, the policy prescriptions emerging from the PAs, namely market-led (particularly export-led) agricultural growth; the role of education; and 'safety nets'. One of the main characteristics of the *1990 WDR* analysis of poverty, they argue, is that it is fundamentally about the actions of individuals or individual households in markets, while social and economic relations are largely absent. Not surprisingly, one of the main shortcomings of the PAs is the limited poverty analysis which they contain, in particular the lack of analysis of relational processes of impoverishment or accumulation. It is further argued that this strong Bank orthodoxy on how to reduce poverty (i.e. the three-pronged approach) interferes with any detailed interpretation of the evidence and findings from the specific countries. In other words, the PAs as World Bank documents, are the product of a particular policy climate, 'which effectively imposes assumptions about what can or cannot be done, and what should or should not be done, in the realm of policy'.

The other conclusion they reach is that the three-pronged strategy carries significant implications for how gender issues are analysed, or made visible, in the PAs. Gendered policy appears to be relatively visible in the area of vulnerability and safety nets, where ad hoc groups of women are taken to be vulnerable as a whole, such as widows. The 'gender jewel in the policy crown' is female education — the only high profile gendered policy prescription in most of the PAs. It is rare, however, to find a gendered analysis of agricultural growth strategies. Where there is any gender analysis of this issue, the gender division of labour appears as a 'rigidity' and a potential barrier to the expansion of agricultural growth (e.g. in the PA on Zambia). This approach reflects one of the main ways in which micro-economists (both inside and outside the World Bank) have taken up gender issues in the 1990s.

Using elements of neo-classical micro-economics, this approach combines the disaggregation of agents by gender with a sectoral disaggregation of activities to show that gender can act as a serious constraint on the mobility of resources (especially labour) between different sectors, thereby frustrating the aims of structural adjustment (Collier, 1989). It makes the policy exhortation that women's 'reproductive burden' be reduced *in order to* enable them to respond more easily to price incentives, switching their labour from the production of non-tradables and protected tradables, to tradables (the sector that is set to expand under adjustment). Although it would be difficult to dispute the need for social investments to reduce women's reproductive burden, these particular arguments present some serious analytical and policy blindspots which need to be approached with caution. Two problems in particular are relevant to our discussion.

First, according to this model there are no justifications for reducing women's work burdens, through labour-saving domestic or agricultural technologies, if they use their free time for other purposes, such as rest or even leisure. This style of thinking is not new. The need for domestic water provision, for example, has very often been justified in terms which suggest that women who spend less time on water collection will spend more time on farming. However, as Jackson and Palmer-Jones (this volume) forcefully argue, this kind of policy obsession with extracting work from the poor, which is being validated through the New Poverty Agenda, needs to be viewed with concern since it may not provide much of an escape from poverty; in some contexts and for some groups it may in fact generate what they refer to as 'energy traps', undermining their bodily well-being.

The other problem with the model is that it fails to problematize the wider policy framework, which is assumed to be inherently benign. It would be quite short-sighted, for example, if this kind of analysis were taken as a suggestion that women's labour bottlenecks should be removed so that women could switch their resources to the production of tradables, without asking further questions about what kinds of market opportunities would be opened up to them, or how this intensified market integration would impact on household food security. There is little mention of the food security risks (at the household and national levels) that may be involved in relying on export crop production, nor is there any recognition of the long-term price risks involved if agricultural export strategies are pursued in many countries simultaneously — the fatal 'fallacy of composition' that characterized agricultural policy prescriptions under traditional SAPs and continues to do so under the New Poverty Agenda.

The other question that needs to be raised, which takes us beyond the issue of labour constraints in agriculture *per se*, concerns the strategic importance of farming as a poverty-alleviating mechanism. There are serious doubts about whether agriculture can generate the route out of poverty and destitution in the absence of substantial and sustained developmental support from the government, which in the current policy climate seems difficult to achieve.

Whitehead and Lockwood's (1999) reading of the survey evidence produced in the Poverty Assessments on Tanzania, Zambia, Uganda and Ghana is that off-farm activities, such as trading, transporting and state employment, have important poverty-alleviating repercussions. But these are not explored in the policy discussions of the PAs, which simply emphasize raising agricultural productivity through better technology, research and extension ('modernization' of agriculture), and the need for diversification into non-traditional export crops. The preoccupation with agriculture as the sector that can produce labour-intensive growth in sub-Saharan Africa, they suggest, produces a lack of analysis and policy interest in how off-farm activities might become a more important source of income for the poor, or what policies might help an increase in such activities.

This is not meant to endorse the global policy prescriptions for the agricultural sector, which condemn in advance any attempt by the public sector to intervene in agricultural markets through protective tariffs, quotas and subsidies, as well as transfers of wealth. Nor is it meant to suggest that the off-farm sector can be the panacea for poor women.

The linkages between poverty and the labour process in the off-farm sector, which have been the source of long-standing tensions between neo-classical and institutionalist approaches, are explored at some length by Razavi (this volume). As far as labour market issues are concerned, the 'New Poverty Agenda' offers very little that is 'new'. Both trade liberalization and labour market deregulation, which are its hallmarks, have featured prominently as policy conditionalities, and their gender implications remain deeply contested. The fact that the agenda remains wedded to an abstract theory of labour markets means that it cannot explain the dynamics of female employment (i.e. its causes and implications). Nor can it explain how labour market arrangements themselves can perpetuate poverty and discrimination.

On the other hand, while power hierarchies (between labour and capital) are central to institutional approaches, the failure to analyse adequately the *interplay* between class (labour/capital) and gender (male/female) hierarchies *across* different institutional arenas (labour market, conjugal/familial sphere) means that the distinctiveness of women's experiences of work is sometimes missed. To address these blindspots feminist analysts have drawn attention to the gendered nature of the labour contract, the significance of looking beyond the boss/worker dyad (i.e. at the familial and conjugal sphere) and

24 — S. Razavi

the importance of listening to women workers' subjective assessments of their work and its meanings.

Finally, the fact that feminist analyses of factory work constantly move beyond poverty issues into the wider domain of power and subordination is testimony to the fact that gender analyses of poverty cannot be 'collapsed' into a welfare agenda, and also a reminder of the fact that for women workers the process of becoming a worker and earning a monetary wage can be an empowering one in itself by triggering off a sense of independence and self-worth, as well as facilitating new forms of solidarity (with co-workers) that are independent of kinship and residence.

REFERENCES

Appleton, S. (1996) 'Problems of Measuring Poverty Over Time: The Case of Uganda', *IDS Bulletin* 27(1): 43–55.

Baulch, B. (1996) 'Neglected Trade-offs in Poverty Measurement', *IDS Bulletin* 27(1): 36–42.

Buvinic, M. (1983) 'Women's Issues in Third World Poverty: A Policy Analysis', in M. Buvinic, M. A. Lycette and W. P. McGreevy *Women and Poverty in the Third World*, pp. 14–31. Baltimore, MD: The Johns Hopkins University Press.

Collier, P. (1989) *Women and Structural Adjustment*. Oxford: Oxford University, Centre for the Study of African Economies.

Drèze, J. and A. Sen (1989) *Hunger and Public Action*. Oxford: Clarendon Press.

Folbre, N. (1990) *Mothers on their Own: Policy Issues for Developing Countries*. New York: Population Council and International Centre for Research on Women.

Fraser, N. (1989) *Unruly Practices: Power, Discourse and Gender in Contemporary Social Theory*. Cambridge: Polity Press.

Gore, C. (1993) 'Entitlement Relations and "Unruly" Social Practices: A Comment on the Work of Amartya Sen', *The Journal of Development Studies* 29(3): 427–60.

Gore, C. (1994) 'Social Exclusion and Africa South of the Sahara: A Review of the Literature'. IILS Discussion Paper Series No. 62. Geneva: IILS.

Harriss, B. (1990) 'The Intra-family Distribution of Hunger in South Asia', in J. Drèze and A. Sen (eds) *The Political Economy of Hunger: Volume I. Entitlement and Well-being*, pp. 351–424. Oxford: Clarendon Press.

Harriss-White, B. (1997) 'Gender Bias in Intrahousehold Nutrition in South India: Unpacking Households and the Policy Process', in L. Haddad, J. Hoddinot, and H. Alderman (eds) *Intrahousehold Resource Allocation in Developing Countries: Models, Methods and Policy*, pp. 194–212. Baltimore, MD and London: The Johns Hopkins University Press for the International Food Policy Research Institute.

Harriss-White, B. (forthcoming) 'Gender Cleansing: The Paradox of Development and Deteriorating Life Chances in Tamil Nadu', in R. Sundar Rajan and U. Butalia (eds) *Gender and Modernity in Post-Independence India*. New Delhi: Kali for Women.

Hart, G. (1995) 'Gender and Household Dynamics: Recent Theories and their Implications', in M. Quibria (ed.) *Understanding Economic Process*, pp. 39–74. Lanham, MD: University Press of America.

Jackson, C. (1996) 'Rescuing Gender from the Poverty Trap', *World Development* 24(3): 489–504.

Jackson, C. (1997a) 'Sustainable Development at the Sharp End: Field-worker Agency in a Participatory Project', *Development in Practice* 7(3): 237–47.

Jackson, C. (1997b) 'Gender, Irrigation and Environment: Arguing for Agency', paper prepared for the Workshop on Women and Water, IIMI, Colombo (15–19 September).

Jazairy, I., M. Alamgir and T. Panuccio (1992) *The State of World Rural Poverty: An Inquiry into its Causes and Consequences*. London: IT Publications.

Kabeer, N. (1997) 'Editorial — Tactics and Trade-offs: Revisiting the Links between Gender and Poverty', *IDS Bulletin* 28(3): 1–13.

Kynch, J. in collaboration with M. Maguire (1994) 'Food and Human Growth in Palanpur', The Development Economics Research Programme No. 57. London: London School of Economics, Suntory-Toyota International Centre for Economics and Related Disciplines.

Lipton, M. and S. Maxwell (1992) 'The New Poverty Agenda: An Overview'. Discussion Paper No. 306. Brighton: Institute of Development Studies.

Lustig, N. (1993) 'Measuring Poverty in Latin America: The Emperor Has No Clothes', paper presented at the Symposium on Poverty: New Approaches to Analysis and Policy, International Institute for Labour Studies, Geneva (22–4 November).

Miller, B. (1997) 'Social Class, Gender and Intrahousehold Food Allocations to Children in South Asia', *Social Science and Medicine* 44(11): 1685–95.

Morris, M. D. (1979) *Measuring the Condition of the World's Poor: The Physical Quality of Life Index*. Oxford: Pergamon Press.

Mosse, D. (1994) 'Authority, Gender and Knowledge: Theoretical Reflections on the Practice of Participatory Rural Appraisal', *Development and Change* 25(3): 497–526.

Murray, Christopher (1991) 'Development Data Constraints and the Human Development Index'. Discussion Paper No. 25. Geneva: UNRISD.

Platteau, J. P. (1995) 'Reforming Land Rights in Sub-Saharan Africa: Issues of Efficiency and Equity'. Discussion Paper No. 60. Geneva: UNRISD.

Scott, W. (1981) *Concepts and Measurement of Poverty*. Report No. 81.1. Geneva: UNRISD.

Sen, A. (1981) *Poverty and Famines: An Essay on Entitlement and Deprivation*. Oxford: Clarendon Press.

Sen, A. (1985a) *Commodities and Capabilities*. Amsterdam: Elsevier Science Publishers.

Sen, A. (1985b) 'Well-being, Agency and Freedom', *The Journal of Philosophy* 132(4): 169–221.

Sen, A. (1987) 'Freedom of Choice: Concepts and Content'. WIDER Working Paper No. 25. Helsinki: WIDER.

Srinivasan, T. N. (1994) 'Human Development: A New Paradigm or Reinvention of the Wheel?', *The American Economic Review* 84(2): 238–43.

UNDP (1995) *Human Development Report 1995*. New York: Oxford University Press.

UNICEF (1993) *The State of the World's Children 1993*. New York: UNICEF.

Walker, C. (1998) 'Land Reform and Gender in Post-Apartheid South Africa'. Discussion Paper No. 98. Geneva: UNRISD.

Whitehead, A. (1984) 'Women and Men; Kinship and Property: Some General Issues', in R. Hirschon (ed.) *Women and Property — Women as Property*, pp. 176–92. London: Croom Helm.

Whitehead, A. and M. Lockwood (1999) 'Gender in the World Bank's Poverty Assessments: Six Case Studies from Sub-Saharan Africa'. UNRISD Discussion Paper 99. Geneva: UNRISD.

World Bank (1990) *World Development Report 1990*. New York: Oxford University Press.

World Bank (1994) *Enhancing Women's Participation in Economic Development*. World Bank Policy Paper. Washington, DC: The World Bank.

2

Resources, Agency, Achievements: Reflections on the Measurement of Women's Empowerment

Naila Kabeer

CONCEPTUALIZING EMPOWERMENT

Introduction

Advocacy on behalf of women which builds on claimed synergies between feminist goals and official development priorities has made greater inroads into the mainstream development agenda than advocacy which argues for these goals on intrinsic grounds. There is an understandable logic to this. In a situation of limited resources, where policymakers have to adjudicate between competing claims (Razavi, 1997), advocacy for feminist goals in intrinsic terms takes policy makers out of their familiar conceptual territory of welfare, poverty and efficiency, and into the nebulous territory of power and social injustice. There is also a political logic in that those who stand to gain most from such advocacy carry very little clout with those who set the agendas in major policy-making institutions.

Consequently, as long as women's empowerment was argued for as an end in itself, it tended to be heard as a 'zero-sum' game with politically weak winners and powerful losers. By contrast, instrumentalist forms of advocacy which combine the argument for gender equality/women's empowerment with demonstrations of a broad set of desirable multiplier effects offer policy makers the possibility of achieving familiar and approved goals, albeit by unfamiliar means.

However, the success of instrumentalism has also had costs. It has required the translation of feminist insights into the discourse of policy, a process in which some of the original political edge of feminism has been lost. Quantification is one aspect of this process of translation. Measurement is, of course, a major preoccupation in the policy domain, reflecting a justifiable concern with the cost/benefit calculus of competing claims for scarce resources. And given that the very idea of women's empowerment epitomizes for many policy makers the unwarranted intrusion of metaphysical concepts into the concrete and practical world of development policy, quantifying empowerment appears to put the concept on more solid and objectively

A longer version of this chapter has been published as UNRISD Discussion Paper 108 (May 1999).

verifiable grounds. There has consequently been a proliferation of studies attempting to measure empowerment, some seeking to facilitate comparisons between locations or over time, some to demonstrate the impact of specific interventions on women's empowerment, and others to demonstrate the implications of women's empowerment for desired policy objectives.

However, not everyone accepts that empowerment can be clearly *defined*, let alone *measured*. For many feminists, the value of the concept lies precisely in its 'fuzziness'. As an NGO activist cited in Batliwala (1993: 48) puts it: 'I like the term empowerment because no one has defined it clearly yet; so it gives us a breathing space to work it out in action terms before we have to pin ourselves down to what it means'. A critical analysis of attempts to measure women's empowerment thus provides a useful standpoint from which to assess both the narrower implications of attempting to measure what is not easily measurable as well as the broader implications of replacing intrinsic arguments for feminist goals with instrumentalist ones. However, given the contested nature of the concept, it is important to clarify at the outset how we will be using it in this chapter, since it will be from this standpoint that various measurement attempts will be evaluated. This makes up the rest of this section. In subsequent sections, I will be reviewing various measures of women's empowerment, the extent to which they mean what they are intended to mean, the values they embody and the appropriateness of these values in capturing the idea of empowerment.

Conceptualizing Empowerment: Resources, Agency and Achievements

One way of thinking about power is in terms of the *ability to make choices*: to be disempowered, therefore, implies to be denied choice. My understanding of the notion of empowerment is that it is inescapably bound up with the condition of disempowerment and refers to the processes by which those who have been denied the ability to make choices acquire such an ability. In other words, empowerment entails a *process of change*. People who exercise a great deal of choice in their lives may be very *powerful*, but they are not *empowered* in the sense in which I am using the word, because they were never disempowered in the first place.

However, to be made relevant to the analysis of power, the notion of choice has to be qualified in a number of ways. First of all, *choice necessarily implies the possibility of alternatives*, the ability to have chosen otherwise. There is a logical association between poverty and disempowerment because an insufficiency of the means for meeting one's basic needs often rules out the ability to exercise meaningful choice. However, even when survival imperatives are no longer dominant, there is still the problem that not all choices are equally relevant to the definition of power. Some choices have greater significance than others in terms of their consequences for people's lives. We therefore have to make a distinction between first- and second-order choices, where the former are those strategic life choices which are critical for people to live the lives they want (such as choice of livelihood, whether and who to marry, whether to have children, etc.). These strategic life choices help to frame other, second-order, less consequential choices, which may be important for the quality of one's life but do not constitute its defining parameters. Inasmuch as our notion of empowerment is about change, it refers to the expansion in people's ability to make strategic life choices in a context where this ability was previously denied to them.

The ability to exercise choice can be thought of in terms of three inter-related dimensions:

resources	agency	achievements
(pre-conditions)	(process)	(outcomes)

Resources include not only material resources in the more conventional economic sense, but also the various human and social resources which serve to enhance the ability to exercise choice. Resources in this broader sense of the word are acquired through a multiplicity of social relationships conducted in the various institutional domains which make up a society (such as family, market, community). Such resources may take the form of actual allocations as well as of future claims and expectations. Access to such resources will reflect the rules and norms which govern distribution and exchange in different institutional arenas. These rules and norms give certain actors authority over others in determining the principles of distribution and exchange so that the distribution of 'allocative' resources tends to be embedded within the distribution of 'authoritative resources' (Giddens, 1979) — the ability to define priorities and enforce claims. Heads of households, chiefs of tribes or élites within a community are all endowed with decision-making authority within particular institutional contexts by virtue of their positioning within those institutions.

The second dimension of power relates to *agency* — the ability to define one's goals and act upon them. Agency is about more than observable action; it also encompasses the meaning, motivation and purpose which individuals bring to their activity, their *sense* of agency, or 'the power within'. While agency tends to be operationalized as 'decision-making' in the social science literature, it can take a number of other forms. It can take the form of bargaining and negotiation, deception and manipulation, subversion and resistance as well as more intangible, cognitive processes of reflection and analysis. It can be exercised by individuals as well as by collectivities.

Agency has both positive and negative meanings in relation to power.[1] In the positive sense of the 'power to', it refers to people's capacity to define their own life-choices and to pursue their own goals, even in the face of opposition from others. Agency can also be exercised in the more negative sense of 'power

---

1. My use of the concepts of positive and negative agency echoes the distinction between positive and negative freedom made by Amartya Sen (1985a: 208).

over', in other words, the capacity of an actor or category of actors to over-ride the agency of others, for instance, through the use of violence, coercion and threat. However, power can also operate in the absence of any explicit agency. The norms and rules governing social behaviour tend to ensure that certain outcomes are reproduced without any apparent exercise of agency. Where these outcomes bear on the strategic life choices noted earlier, they testify to the exercise of power as 'non-decision-making' (Lukes, 1974). The norms of marriage in South Asia, for instance, invest parents with the authority for choosing their children's partners, but are unlikely to be experienced as a form of power, unless such authority is questioned.

Resources and agency together constitute what Sen (1985b) refers to as capabilities: the potential that people have for living the lives they want, of achieving valued ways of 'being and doing'. He uses the idea of 'functionings' to refer to all possible ways of 'being and doing' which are valued by people in a given context and of 'functioning achievements' to refer to the particular ways of being and doing which are realized by different individuals. Clearly, where the failure to achieve valued ways of 'being and doing' can be traced to laziness, incompetence or individual preferences and priorities, then the issue of power is not relevant. It is only when the failure to achieve one's goals reflects some deep-seated constraint on the ability to choose that it can be taken as a manifestation of disempowerment.

Qualifying Choice: Difference versus Inequality

However, a concern with 'achievements' in the measurement of empower-ment draws attention to the need for further qualifications to our understanding of choice. As far as empowerment is concerned, we are interested in possible *inequalities* in people's capacity to make choices rather than in *differences* in the choices they make. An observed lack of uniformity in functioning achievements cannot be automatically interpreted as evidence of inequality because it is highly unlikely that all members of a given society will give equal value to different possible ways of 'being and doing'. Consequently, where gender differentials in functioning achievements exist, we have to disentangle differentials which reflect differences in preferences from those which embody a denial of choice.

One way of getting around the problem for measurement purposes would be to focus on certain universally-valued functionings, those which relate to the basic fundamentals of survival and well-being, regardless of context. For instance, it is generally agreed that proper nourishment, good health and adequate shelter all constitute primary functionings which tend to be univer-sally valued. If there are systematic gender differences in these very basic functioning achievements, they can be taken as evidence of inequalities in underlying capabilities rather than differences in preferences. This, for instance, is the strategy adopted by Sen (1990). However, focusing on basic needs achievements addresses one aspect of the problem but raises others.

Inequalities in basic functionings generally tend to occur in situations of extreme scarcity. Confining the analysis of gender inequality to these achievements alone serves to convey the impression that women's disempowerment is largely a matter of poverty. This is misleading for two reasons.

On the one hand, it misses forms of gender disadvantage which are more likely to characterize better-off sections of society. Prosperity within a society may help to reduce gender inequalities in basic well-being, but intensify other social restrictions on women's ability to make choices (Razavi, 1992). On the other hand, it misses out on those dimensions of gender disadvantage among the poor which do not take the form of basic functioning failures. For instance, marked gender differentials in life-expectancy and children's nutrition — two widely used indicators of gender discrimination in basic well-being — do not appear to be as widespread in sub-Saharan Africa as they are in South Asia. However, this does not rule out the possibility that gender disadvantage can take other forms in these contexts. Shaffer (1998), for instance, found little evidence of income or consumption disadvantage between male- and female-headed households in Guinea. However, both men and women in his study recognized women's far heavier workloads as well as male domination in private and public decision-making as manifestations of gender inequality within their community.

A second way out of the problem might be to go beyond the concern with basic survival-related achievements to certain other functioning achievements which would be considered to be of value in most contexts. This is the strategy adopted in the UNDP's gender-disaggregated Human Development Index as well as its Gender Empowerment (GEM) index (UNDP, 1995). Such measures play a useful role in monitoring differences in achievements across regions and over time and in drawing attention to problematic disparities. However, while there are sound reasons for moving the measurement of achievements beyond very basic functionings, such as life-expectancy, to more complex achievements, such as political representation, we have to keep in mind that such measurements, quite apart from their empirical shortcomings, entail the movement away from the criteria of women's choices, or even the values of the communities in which they live, to a definition of 'achievement' which represents the values of those who are doing the measuring. We will return in a later section to the problems that external values can raise in the analysis of women's empowerment.

Qualifying Choice: 'Choosing not to Choose'

The use of achievements to measure empowerment draws attention to a second problem of interpretation deriving from the central place given to choice in our definition of power. There is an intuitive plausibility to the equation between power and choice as long as what is chosen appears to contribute to the welfare of those making the choice. In situations where we find evidence of striking gender inequalities in basic well-being achievements, the equation between choice and power would suggest quite plausibly that such inequalities signal the operation of power: either as an absence of choice on the part of women as the subordinate group or as active discrimination by men as the dominant group. However, the equation between power and choice finds it far more difficult to accommodate forms of gender inequality when these appear to have been chosen by women themselves. This problem plays out in the literature on gender and well-being in the form of behaviour on the part of women which suggests that they have internalized their social status as persons of lesser value. Such behaviour can have adverse implications for their own well-being as well as for the well-being of other female family members. Women's acceptance of their secondary claims on household resources, their acquiescence to violence at the hands of their husbands, their willingness to bear children to the detriment of their own health and survival to satisfy their own or their husband's preference for sons, are all examples of behaviour by women which undermine their own well-being. It is worth noting, for instance, that in Shaffer's (1998) study from West Africa cited earlier, both women and men recognized the existence of gender inequalities in terms of women's heavier workloads and men's dominance in decision-making, but neither considered these inequalities *unjust*. In addition, women's adherence to social norms and practices associated with son preference, discrimination against daughters, the oppressive exercise of authority by mothers-in-law over their daughters-in-law (a problem often identified in the South Asian context), are examples of behaviour in which women's internalization of their own lesser status in society leads them to discriminate against other females in that society.

While these forms of behaviour could be said to reflect 'choice', they are also choices which stem from, and serve to reinforce, women's subordinate status. They remind us that power relations are expressed not only through the exercise of agency and choice, but also through the *kinds* of choices people make. This notion of power is a controversial one because it allows for the possibility that power and dominance can operate through consent and complicity as well through coercion and conflict. The vocabulary of 'false consciousness' is not a particularly useful one here, implying as it does the need to distinguish between false and authentic consciousness, between illusion and reality. The consciousness we are talking about is not 'false' as such since how people perceive their needs and interests is shaped by their individual histories and everyday realities, by the material and social contexts of their experiences and by the vantage point for reflexivity which this provides. In any situation, some needs and interests are self-evident, emerging out of the routine practices of daily life and differentiated by gender inasmuch as the responsibilities and routines of daily life are gender-differentiated. However, there are other needs and interests which do not have this self-evident nature because they derive from a 'deeper' level of reality, one which is not evident in daily life because it is inscribed in the taken-for-granted rules, norms and customs within which everyday life is conducted.

One way of conceptualizing this deeper reality is to be found in Bourdieu's (1977) idea of 'doxa' — the aspects of tradition and culture which are so taken-for-granted that they have become naturalized. Doxa refers to traditions and beliefs which exist beyond discourse or argumentation. The idea of doxa is helpful here because it shifts our attention away from the dichotomy between false and authentic consciousness to a concern with differing levels of reality and the practical and strategic interests to which they give rise. Bourdieu suggests that as long as the subjective assessments of social actors are largely congruent with the objectively organized possibilities available to them, the world of doxa remains intact. The passage from 'doxa' to discourse, a more critical consciousness, only becomes possible when *competing* ways of 'being and doing' become available as material and cultural possibilities, so that 'common sense' propositions of culture begin to lose their 'naturalized' character, revealing the underlying arbitrariness of the given social order.

The availability of alternatives at the discursive level, of being able to at least imagine the possibility of having chosen differently, is thus crucial to the emergence of a critical consciousness, the process by which people move from a position of unquestioning acceptance of the social order to a critical perspective on it. This has an obvious bearing on our earlier discussion about functioning achievements as an aspect of empowerment. As was pointed out, the possibility that power operates not only through constraints on people's ability to make choices, but also through their preferences and values and hence the choices that they may make, appears to pose a serious challenge to the basic equation made in this chapter between power and choice. However, it is possible to retain the equation by a further qualification to our notion of 'choice', extending the idea of alternatives to encompass discursive alternatives. In other words, in assessing whether or not an achievement embodies meaningful choice, we have to ask ourselves whether other choices were not only materially possible but whether they were *conceived* to be within the realms of possibility.[2]

---

2. The importance of alternatives, material as well as discursive, is common to a number of analyses of power. Lukes (1974) refers to the absence of actual or imagined alternatives as a factor explaining the absence of protest to the injustices of an unequal order. Geuss (1981) suggests that knowledge about social life and the self requires not only freedom from basic want but also the material and cultural possibility of experimentation, of trying out alternatives.

MEASURING EMPOWERMENT: THE PROBLEM OF MEANING

It is not possible to provide an exhaustive survey of various attempts to measure women's empowerment in this chapter. I have confined myself to analysing a selected number of studies from the development studies literature in order to make some general methodological points about the measurement of empowerment. As we will see, there are some important differences in how these various studies deal with the idea of empowerment. They differ in the dimensions of empowerment which they choose to focus on, and in whether they treat power as an attribute of individuals or a property of structures. They also differ in how social change is conceptualized. What is understandably missing from the measurement literature are examples of the more processual model of social change subscribed to by many feminists (Batliwala, 1993, 1994). A processual understanding of social change tends to treat it as open-ended. It is premised on the unpredictability of human agency and on the diversity of circumstances under which such agency is exercised. While it may identify certain key elements of structure and agency as having a catalytic potential, it does not attempt to determine in advance how this catalytic effect will play out in practice. Consequently, it is a form of social change that tends to be least amenable to measurement.

Measuring 'Resources'

The 'resource' dimension of empowerment would appear at first sight to be the easiest to measure. However, a critical reading of attempts at measurement suggest that the task is less simple than it looks, even when resources are defined in narrow material terms as they generally tend to be. There is a widespread tendency in the empowerment literature to talk about 'access to resources' in a generic way, as if indicating some relationship between women and resources automatically specifies the choices it makes possible. In reality, however, resources are at one remove from choice, a measure of *potential* rather than *actualized* choice. How changes in women's resources will translate into changes in the choices they are able to make will depend, in part, on other aspects of the conditions in which they are making their choices. By way of example, let us take women's 'access' to land.

At the systemic level, this is often captured by distinguishing between different categories of land rights with the assumption that women are likely to exercise a greater degree of autonomy in those regions where they enjoy some rights to land (Boserup, 1970; Dyson and Moore, 1983). Yet studies which use measures of women's access to land as an indicator of empowerment seldom reflect on the pathways by which such 'access' translates into agency and achievement, let alone seeking to understand these pathways empirically. It is noteworthy, for instance, that a causal connection is often made between patrilineal principles of descent and inheritance in the northern plains of the Indian sub-continent (compared to the south) and the low levels of female autonomy there. However, land inheritance rules are by no means uniform within this region. Among Hindus, joint family property is a central tenet shaping inheritance practices with some local variation in how this is interpreted. Joint family property is generally held in a coparcenary system by men, usually fathers and sons, to the total exclusion of women (Mukhopadhayay, 1998). Among Muslims, on the other hand, women have always enjoyed the right to inherit property and to inherit as individuals. Muslim women and men consequently enjoy individual, absolute but unequal rights to property: men tend to inherit twice the share of women. Hindu law has been reformed after Indian independence to give men and women equal rights of inheritance; Muslim inheritance principles have been left untouched.

However, despite these differences in the customary and legal positions of women in the two communities, both Muslim and Hindu women tend to be treated as effectively propertyless in the literature. For Hindu women, older norms and customs remain powerful and Agarwal (1994) provides evidence of the difficulties they face when they seek to assert legal over customary practices around land inheritance. Muslim women, on the other hand, generally prefer, or are encouraged to prefer, to waive their rights to parental property in favour of their brothers with the result that they too are treated as effectively propertyless. Thus the critical measure of women's access to land which characterizes the Indian literature is *de facto* rather than *de jure* entitlement and by this measure, there is little difference between the Hindu and Muslim communities.

Yet it is by no means evident that *de facto* ownership tells us all we need to know about the potential domain of choice. It has, for instance, been pointed out that although Muslim women do waive their land rights to their brothers (and may be under considerable pressure to do so), they thereby strengthen their future claim on their brothers, should their marriage break down. While brothers have a duty under Islam to look after their sisters, the waiving of land rights by sisters in favour of brothers gives a material basis to a moral entitlement. The necessity for such an exchange may reflect women's subordinate status within the community but the fact that women's land rights are in principle recognized by their community gives them a resource to bargain with in a situation in which they have few other resources. Moreover, as the situation changes, they may begin to press their claims on such a resource. I found evidence of women beginning to claim their inheritance rights in rural Bangladesh, although sometimes under pressure from their husbands (Kabeer, 1994), while Razavi (1992) also notes evidence from rural Iran of a greater willingness of women to press for their property rights in court, this time to compensate for their diminishing entitlements to common property resources which provided a subsistence base. These are potentials which are not easily available to women in communities where such rights were not recognized by customary law and tradition, even if they have, as in

India, subsequently been brought into existence by legislative action. Indeed, Das Gupta (1987) has pointed out, in the context of her study of the Jat kinship system in Punjab, that there was no question of a woman owning land: 'If she should insist on her right to inherit land equally under civil law, she would stand a good chance of being murdered' (ibid: 92).

The main methodological point to take out of this discussion, therefore, is that if it is to be useful as a measure of empowerment, the 'resource' dimension has to be defined in ways which spell out the potential for human agency and valued achievements more clearly than simple 'access' indicators generally do. One of the limitations of *de facto* measures of land entitlements discussed here is that they ignore the diverse processes by which the *de facto* possession or dispossession occurs and hence fail to appreciate possible differences in women's choices implied by differences in the *de jure* position. In addition, the power of *customary* constructions of *de jure* rights over recently-introduced legal ones noted by these studies also raises a question about processes of social change which has yet to be satisfactorily answered in the empowerment literature: how do attempts to change deeply entrenched structures, in this case, pitting the law against rules legitimized by custom and religion, translate into changes in individual agency and choice?

The recognition by many analysts of the need to go beyond simple 'access' indicators in order to grasp how 'resources' translate into the realization of choice has led to a variety of concepts seeking to bridge the gap between formal and effective entitlement to resources, generally by introducing some aspect of agency into the measure. The most frequently used of these bridging concepts is that of 'control', usually operationalized in terms of having a say in relation to the resource in question. However, while the focus on 'control' is an important step forward in the measurement of empowerment, control is not an easy measure to operationalize. Consequently, what we find in the literature is a tendency to use concepts such as access, ownership, entitlement and control interchangeably so that there is considerable semantic confusion about what 'control' actually means.

Sathar and Kazi (1997), for instance, equate both 'access' *and* 'control' with having a say in decisions related to particular resources within the household. Their measure of 'access to resources' is based on whether women had a say in household expenses, cash to spend on household expenses and freedom to purchase clothes, jewellery and gifts for their relatives, while 'control over resources' is measured by asking who kept household earnings and who had a say in household expenditure. In Jejeebhoy's (1997) analysis concepts of 'access', 'control' and 'decision-making' are all used in relation to resources, with 'control' sometimes referring to ownership and sometimes to decision-making. In Kishor's (1997) analysis, empowerment is defined as women's control over key aspects of their lives: here 'control' indicators vary between control defined in relation to resources, e.g. earnings and expenditures; control defined in terms of self reliance (can women support themselves without their husband's support); control as decision-making (who has the final say in making decisions about a variety of issues); and control as 'choice' (choosing own spouse or being consulted in the choice of marriage partner). In methodological terms, the point to make is that while 'control' is often used as a means of operationalizing empowerment for measurement purposes, it is as elusive to define and to measure as power, except in the purely formal and legalistic sense.

Measuring 'Agency'

Indicators which focus explicitly on the measurement of agency include measures of both positive as well as negative agency: women's mobility in the public domain, their participation in public action, the incidence of male violence and so on. However, the form of agency which appears most frequently in measurement efforts, and hence the one we will be focusing on here, relates to *decision-making agency*. This is not surprising since decision-making in some form is at the heart of some of the best known attempts to conceptualize power (Lukes, 1974; McElroy, 1992). Measures of decision-making are usually based on responses to questions asking women about their roles in relation to specific decisions, with answers sometimes combined into a single index and sometimes presented separately. Below I have summarized some examples of decisions which typically appear in measurement efforts and the geographical context covered:

Typical Decisions in Decision-making Indicators

Egypt: Household budget, food cooked, visits, children's education, children's health, use of family planning methods (Kishor, 1997).
India: Purchase of food; purchase of major household goods; purchase of small items of jewellery; course of action if child falls ill; disciplining the child; decisions about children's education and type of school (Jejeebhoy, 1997).
Nigeria: Household purchases; whether wife works; how to spend husband's income; number of children to have; whether to buy and sell land; whether to use family planning; whether to send children to school, how much education; when sons and when daughters marry; whether to take sick children to doctor and how to rear children (Kritz, Makinwa and Gurak, 1997).
Zimbabwe: Wife working outside; making a major purchase; the number of children (Becker, 1997).
Nepal: What food to buy; the decision by women to work outside; major market transactions; and the number of children to have (Morgan and Niraula, 1995).
Iran: Food purchase; inputs, labour and sale in agricultural production and other income-earning activities; sale and purchase of assets; children's education; seeking health care for children (Razavi, 1992).
Pakistan: Purchase of food; number of children; schooling of children; children's marriage; major household purchases; women's work outside the home; sale and purchase of livestock; household expenses; purchase of clothes, jewellery and gifts for wife's relatives (Sathar and Kazi, 1997).
Bangladesh: Ability to make small and large consumer purchases; house repair; taking in livestock for raising; leasing in of land; purchase of major assets (Hashemi et al., 1996).

Bangladesh: Children's education; visits to friends and relatives; household purchases; health care matters (Cleland et al., 1994).

Even a preliminary reading of these different decisions suggests that they are not all equally persuasive as indicators of women's empowerment because not all have the same consequential significance for women's lives. Few cultures operate with starkly dichotomous distributions of power with men making all the decisions and women making none. More commonly we find a hierarchy of decision-making responsibilities recognized by the family and community, which reserves certain key areas of decision-making for men in their capacity as household heads while assigning others to women in their capacity as mothers, wives, daughters and so on. Broadly speaking, the evidence from studies on South Asia suggests that, within the family, the purchase of food and other items of household consumption and decisions related to children's health appear to fall within women's arena of decision-making while decisions related to the education and marriage of children, and market transactions in major assets tend to be more clearly male.

This is illustrated by Sathar and Kazi (1997). They found on the basis of data from Pakistan that the only area of decision-making in which women reported not only participating but playing a major decision-making role was in relation to the purchase of food. They participated, but did not have a major role, in decisions relating to numbers of children and their schooling and even less of a role when it came to children's marriage and major economic decisions.

In methodological terms, such distinctions suggest the need for greater care in selecting and quantifying the decisions which are to serve as indicators of empowerment, with attention given to consequential significance of areas of decision-making or of different stages in the decision-making process. Evidence that women played a role in making decisions which were of little consequence or which were assigned to women anyway by the pre-existing gender division of roles and responsibilities, tell us far less about their power to choose than evidence on decisions which relate to strategic life choices or to choices which had been denied to them in the past.

We could also distinguish between various critical 'control points' within the decision-making process itself where such control is defined in terms of the consequential significance of influencing outcomes at these different points (Beneria and Roldan, 1987). Pahl (1989), for instance, distinguishes between the 'control' or policy-making function in making decisions about resource allocation and the 'management' function, decisions which pertain to implementation. This distinction might explain the finding by the Egyptian Male Survey in 1992 (cited in Ali, 1996) that men were dominant in the decision to adopt contraceptives — the policy decision — but tended to leave the choice of contraception largely to women (although Ali's qualitative study found men's continuing involvement in women's choice of contraceptives as well).

'Statistical' perspectives on decision-making, however, should be remembered for what they are: simple windows on complex realities. They may provide a brief glimpse of processes of decision-making, but they tell us very little about the subtle negotiations that go on between women and men in their private lives. Consequently, they may underestimate the informal decision-making agency which women often exercise. This can be illustrated by comparing Silberschmidt's (1992) account of formal and informal decision-making among the Kisii in Kenya. The formal account of decision-making given by women ascribed most of the power to men: the husbands were said to be 'heads' of households and their 'owners'; as an afterthought the wives might add, 'they can buy us just like cattle'. Their accounts of 'actual' decision-making, however, gave a very different picture:

> (Women) admitted that men should be consulted on all sorts of issues ... In reality, however, many women took such decisions themselves. Their most common practice was to avoid open confrontation while still getting their own way ... There is no doubt that many women do often manipulate their menfolk and make decisions independently. For example, since the land belongs to the man, he is expected to decide where the various crops are to be planted. If his wife disagrees, she would seldom say so, but simply plant in what she feels is a better way. If he finds out that she has not followed his instructions, she will apologise but explain that because the seeds did not germinate they had to be replanted in a different manner/spot. (ibid: 248).

The inability of a purely statistical approach to capture this informal aspect is not simply a measurement failure. It has conceptual implications. There is an important body of research from the South Asian context which suggests that the renegotiation of power relations, particularly within the family, is often precisely about changes in informal decision-making, with women opting for private forms of empowerment, which retain intact the public image, and honour, of the traditional decision-maker but which nevertheless increases women's 'backstage' influence in decision-making processes (Basu, 1996; Chen, 1983; Kabeer, 1997). Such strategies reflect a certain degree of caution on the part of women — a strategic virtue in situations where they may have as much to lose from the disruption of social relationships as they have to gain.

Measuring Achievement

As with the other dimensions of empowerment, the critical methodological point to be made in relation to achievement indicators relates once again to the need for analytical clarity in the selection of what is to be measured. I have already pointed out the need to make a distinction between achievement differentials which signal *differences* in choice and those which draw attention to *inequalities* in the ability to make choice. An examination of some of the studies which have included indicators of achievement in their analysis of women's empowerment will help to throw up other criteria for the selection of such indicators.

Kishor (1997) has used national Egyptian data to explore the effects of direct, as well as indirect, measures of women's empowerment on two valued functioning achievements: infant survival rates and infant immunization. These achievements were selected on the basis of her conceptualization of women's empowerment in terms of 'control' which she defined as their ability to 'access information, take decisions, and act in their own interests, or the interests of those who depend on them' (ibid: 1). Since women bore primary responsibility for children's health, Kishor hypothesized that their empower-ment would be associated with positive achievements in terms of the health and survival of their children. Her analysis relied on three categories of composite indicators to measure empowerment: 'direct evidence of empower-ment', 'sources of empowerment' and 'the setting for empowerment'. I have summarized these below, together with the variables which had greatest weight in each indicator:

(1) Direct evidence of empowerment
Devaluation of women: *reports of domestic violence; dowry paid at marriage.*
Women's emancipation: *belief in daughters' education; freedom of move-ment.*
Reported sharing of roles and decision-making: *egalitarian gender roles; egalitarian decision-making.*
Equality in marriage: *fewer grounds reported for justified divorce by husbands; equality of grounds reported for divorce by husband or wife.*
Financial autonomy: *currently controls her earnings; her earnings as share of household income.*

(2) Sources of empowerment
Participation in the modern sector: *index of assets owned; female education.*
Lifetime exposure to employment: *worked before marriage; controlled earnings before marriage.*

(3) Setting indicators
Family structure amenable to empowerment: *does not now or previously live with in-laws.*
Marital advantage: *small age difference between spouses; chose husband.*
Traditional marriage: *large educational difference with husband; did not choose husband.*

The results of a multivariate analysis found that the indirect source/ setting indicators of women's empowerment had far more influence in determining infant survival and immunization. There are two possible and mutually compatible explanations for this finding. One is that Kishor's direct indicators of empowerment did not in fact succeed in capturing empowerment particularly well. This is quite plausible given that many entailed highly value-laden information about attitudes and relationships within marriage (such as, the grounds on which women believed that a husband was justified in divorcing his wife; whether women should speak up if they disagreed with their husbands). However, other more factual direct indicators ('financial autonomy' and 'freedom of movement', for instance) also proved insignificant.

The other possible explanation was that the achievements in question did not in fact depend on whether or not women were directly 'empowered' but on other factors which were better captured by the 'source' and 'setting' variables. A further 'deconstruction' of Kishor's findings suggests that child mortality was higher in households where women were currently, or had previously been, in residence with their parents-in-law as well as in households where there was a large difference in the age and education levels of husband and wife. Child mortality was lower if the mother had been in employment prior to her marriage. As far as immunization was concerned, children were more likely to have been immunized in households where their mothers had extended experience of employment, where they reported exposure to the media, where they were educated and where they were not under the authority of in-laws as a result of joint residence. In addition, where the age difference between husband and wife was small and where women expressed a belief in equality in marriage, children's survival chances were likely to be higher. Thus the only direct measure of empowerment which proved significant in the analysis was her 'equality of marriage' indicator and it proved significant only in relation to child immunization.

Returning to a point made earlier, if, as is likely, the care of infants came within women's pre-assigned sphere of jurisdiction, then improvements in this sphere should be seen as increased efficacy in pre-assigned roles rather than as evidence of empowerment. In other words, what mattered for achievements in relation to children's well-being was women's agency as *mothers* rather than as *wives*. This is why the direct measures of empowerment, which dealt largely with equality in conjugal relationships, proved insignificant in explaining the achievement variables. Instead, it was variables which captured women's ability to take effective action in relation to the welfare of their children which played the significant explanatory role. For instance, women who lived, or had lived, with their in-laws , were more likely to have been subordinate to the authority of a senior female, with less likelihood of exercising effective agency at a time when such agency was critical to children's health outcomes. Women who were less educated than their husbands or much younger were also likely to have been less confident, competent or authoritative in taking the necessary actions to ensure their children's health. Female education and employment both had a role in explaining child welfare outcomes but with slight variations. Lifetime experience of employment by women had a *direct* positive effect on their children's chances of survival as well as the likelihood of child immunization.

Female education influenced children's survival chances indirectly through its association with improved standards of household water and sanitation but had a direct influence on the likelihood of child immunization. The differences in the determinants of the two achievement variables are worth noting. The fact that women's education and employment as well as 'equality in marriage' all had a direct influence on the likelihood of child immunization but only women's employment affected their children's survival chances, suggests that the former activity may have required a more active agency on the part of mothers than did the more routine forms of health-seeking behaviour through which child survival is generally assured.

The case for analytical clarity in the selection of 'empowerment-related' measures of achievement can also be illustrated with reference to a study by Becker (1997) which used data from Zimbabwe to explore the implications of women's empowerment on a different set of functioning achievements: the use of contraception and the take-up of pre-natal health care. Regression analysis was carried out in two stages. First of all, Becker explored the effects of some likely determinants of these outcomes. He found that contraceptive use appeared to be positively related to household wealth, as measured by a possessions index, the number of surviving children, the wife's employment and husband's education. Older women, women who lived in rural areas and who had polygamous husbands were less likely to use contraception. The likelihood that women received pre-natal care was positively related to household possessions, rural residence, women's age, education and employment and husband's education. In the second stage, Becker added a measure of women's empowerment to his equations to see what difference it made. Empowerment was measured by an index of women's role in decision-making in three key areas: the purchase of household items, the decision to work outside and number of children to have. Adding the empowerment indicator did little to improve the fit of the equation in relation to contraceptive use, but significantly improved the fit as far as take up of pre-natal care was concerned.

Speculating on the meaning of these findings, Becker pointed out that, given the commitment of the Zimbabwean government to family planning, contraceptive services were widely available through community-based distribution systems and contraceptive prevalence was correspondingly high. Over 50 per cent of the women in his sample used it. In a context where contraception was both easily available, and had also become a relatively routine form of behaviour, women's employment status increased the likelihood of use, but otherwise, it did not appear to require any great assertiveness on the part of women to access the necessary services. By contrast, women's take-up of pre-natal care was more closely related to their role in intra-household decision-making as well as to both their education levels and their employment status, suggesting that this may have required far greater assertiveness on the part of women than contraceptive use. In other words, women who were assertive in other areas of household decision-making, who were educated and employed, were also more likely to be assertive when it came to active and non-routine health-seeking behaviour on their own behalf.

In both studies discussed here, direct measures of women's agency were far more significant in determining outcomes when women were required to step out of routine forms of behaviour — getting their children immunized, in one case, and seeking pre-natal health care in the other — than outcomes which allowed them to conform to prevailing practice. However, apart from the extent to which outcomes require women to go against the grain of established custom, achievements also have to be assessed for their transformatory implications in relation to the gender inequalities frequently embedded in these customs.

While both child survival and immunization are highly valued achievements from a variety of perspectives — of policy makers, of the family and, above all, of women themselves — and while both were the product of women's greater effectiveness as agents, neither achievement by itself necessarily implied a shift in underlying power relations. In this sense, women's ability to access pre-natal health care is more indicative of the kind of transformative agency we are talking about.

A similar distinction between achievements which testify to women's greater efficacy as agents within prescribed gender roles and those which are indicative of women as agents of transformation would apply to the determinants of under-five child mortality and gender differentials in child mortality in India reported by Dreze and Sen (1995). They found that female literacy reduced under-five child mortality while both female labour force participation and female literacy reduced excess female mortality in the under-five age group. They interpreted these effects as evidence that women's access to education and employment enhanced their ability to exercise agency. While accepting this interpretation, I would nevertheless argue that the meanings conveyed by these two indicators carried rather different implications in terms of women's empowerment. The reduction in under-five mortality can be taken as evidence of more *effective* agency on the part of women but does not, by itself, testify to a *transformatory* agency on their part. On the other hand, the reductions in excess female mortality does suggest something more than greater efficacy of agency. Given that the reduction in excess female mortality represented an increase in the survival chances of the girl child, rather than a decrease in the survival chances of boys, it suggests that women who have some education and are economically active are more likely than others to give equal value to sons and daughters and to exercise equal effort on their behalf.

Triangulation and Meaning: The Indivisibility of Resources, Agency and Achievements

This review of the 'fit' between the dimensions of empowerment and the indicators used to measure them has essentially been a review of the 'fit' between the meanings attributed to a measure and the meanings empirically revealed by it. What the discussion has thrown up very clearly is that it is not possible to establish the meaning of an indicator, whatever dimension of empowerment it is intended to measure, without reference to the other dimensions of empowerment. *In other words, the three dimensions are indivisible in determining the meaning of an indicator and hence its validity as a measure of empowerment.* Specifying 'access' to a resource tells us about potential rather than actual choice and the validity of a 'resource' measure as an indicator of empowerment largely rests on the validity of the assumptions made about the potential agency or entitlement embodied in that resource. It is similarly difficult to judge the validity of an 'achievement' measure unless we have evidence, or can make a reasonable guess, as to whose agency was involved and the extent to which the achievement in question transformed prevailing inequalities in resources and agency rather than reinforcing them or leaving them unchallenged. Similar considerations apply to evidence on 'agency': we have to know about its consequential significance in terms of women's strategic life choices and the extent to which it had transformatory potential.

In methodological terms, the point to emphasize is the critical need to triangulate or cross-check the evidence provided by an indicator in order to establish that it means what it is believed to mean. Indicators not only compress a great deal of information into a single statistic but make assumptions, often implicit, about what this information means. The more evidence there is to support these assumptions, the more faith we are likely to have in the validity of the indicator in question. The importance of triangulation can be demonstrated by examining the very conflicting conclusions arrived at by a number of evaluations exploring the impact on women of a very similar set of credit programmes in rural Bangladesh. As I have sought to argue in greater detail elsewhere, these conflicts lay less in their empirical findings and more in the very different understandings of power on which they were based (Kabeer, 1998).

In one study by Pitt and Khandker (1995), the attempt was made to infer gender differences in bargaining power within the household from the extent to which decision-making outcomes varied according to the gender of the loanee. In terms of the terminology used in this chapter, they were seeking to make assumptions about agency on the basis of evidence on the relationship between resources and achievements. However, the value of their analysis was undermined by the fact that there did not appear to be any clear-cut rationale for the selection of the particular achievement indicators in the study, and the bearing that these achievements might have on the question of empowerment was by no means clear. It is difficult, for instance, to know what to make of their finding that loans to men were likely to have a far greater fertility-reducing effect than loans to women, a finding that goes against received demographic wisdom and for which they do not offer any explanation themselves. Other findings generally lend themselves to alternative and equally plausible interpretations.

For instance, the authors themselves interpreted their finding that women loanees spent *more* time on market-related work than did women in male loanee households as evidence of women's empowerment, but explained as an 'income effect' the finding that men in households that had received credit spent *less* time on market-related work, and probably more time on leisure, regardless of whether the loan in question had been made to a man or a woman. However, the increase in women's market-related work as a result of their access to credit has been given a much more negative interpretation by others who have suggested that increases in women's loan-generated labour may simply add to their increased work burdens, overwork, fatigue and malnutrition (Ackerly, 1995; Goetz and Sen Gupta, 1996). Similarly, men's greater leisure as a result of loans to their household, regardless of who actually received the loan, could quite plausibly be interpreted as evidence of male privilege and power rather than (or as well as) an 'income effect'. Further information on what their findings actually meant would have helped to distinguish between these alternative hypotheses.

A similar absence of information on the agency involved in the achievement of particular decision-making outcomes also characterizes a study by Rahman (1986). However, her selection of 'functioning achievements' at least had a plausible bearing on women's empowerment since she focused on gender differentials in basic welfare outcomes in a context where women have suffered considerable gender discrimination in these areas. She found that women who had received loans enjoyed higher levels of welfare (food, clothing and medical expenditure) compared to women in households where men had received the loans or in economically equivalent households which had not received any loans at all. Her findings would lead us to conclude that women's access to credit reduced, but did not fully eliminate, gender differentials in intra-household welfare. As evidence on women's empowerment, they would have been strengthened by information on whose agency was involved in translating loans into impact. Did increased expenditures on women's well-being represent the more active and direct exercise of purchasing power by women? Did it represent their greater role in decision-making about the distribution of household resources? Or did it represent the greater weight given by the household head to women's well-being in recognition of women's role in bringing in economic resources? Clearly each of these possibilities throws a different light on the issue of power and agency within the household, and women's empowerment.

If there are problems with inferring agency on the basis of inadequate information about achievements, attempts to infer achievement possibilities on the basis of restricted understandings of agency are equally problematic. This is evident in a study by Goetz and Sen Gupta (1996) in which they used an index of 'managerial control' as their indicator of women's empowerment. This index classified women who had no knowledge of how their loans had been utilized or else had played no part in the enterprise funded by their loans as having 'little or no control' over their loans, at one end of the spectrum, while at the other end of the spectrum were those who were described as exercising 'full control' over their loans, having participated in all stages of the enterprise, including marketing of their products. The large numbers of women found to be exercising 'little or no control' over their loans according to these criteria led the authors to extremely pessimistic conclusions about the empowerment potential of credit programmes for women.

However, if we return to our earlier point about the hierarchy of decisions, a major problem with their index of 'managerial control' was that it conflated quite distinct moments in the decision-making processes by which access to loans translates into impact on women's lives. In particular, it conflated 'control' and 'management', making no distinction between the *policy* decision as to how loans were to be utilized and repaid, and the *management* decisions by which decisions regarding loan use were implemented. If this distinction had been taken into account, then apart from the 22 per cent of women in their 'no control' category who reported that they did not even know how their loans were used, the remaining 78 per cent of women in their sample could, *in principle*, have exercised much greater control over their loans than was allowed for by the authors. Putting this point to one side, if, as Goetz and Sen Gupta appear to be hypothesizing, control over the loan-funded activity is in fact a critical 'control' point in the process by which access to loans translates into a range of valued achievements, then certainly 'managerial control' can serve as an *indicator* of empowerment.

However, this hypothesis is directly contradicted by yet another evaluation of a similar set of credit programmes in rural Bangladesh. Hashemi et al. (1996) classified all the women loanees in their sample according to the categories of 'managerial control' spelt out by Goetz and Sen Gupta. While the results varied considerably according to both the length of women's membership of credit organization as well as by credit organization, they confirmed that a large percentage of women in certain villages did indeed 'lose' control over their loans by Goetz and Sen Gupta's criteria. By then going on to examine the relationship between women's access to loans and a range of empowerment indicators, Hashemi et al. (1996) were essentially asking whether women's access to credit could have any transformatory significance for their lives, *regardless* of who exercised 'managerial control'. The indicators they used were: mobility in a number of public locations; the ability to make small purchases as well as larger purchases, including purchases for women themselves; involvement in major areas of economic decision-making; land-related decisions or purchase of major assets; whether women had suffered appropriation of their money or any other asset; been prevented from visiting their natal homes or from working outside; the magnitude of women's economic contribution to the family; participation in public protests and campaigns; political and legal awareness; economic security, viz. assets and savings in their own names.

The results of their analysis suggested that women's access to credit contributed significantly to the magnitude of the economic contributions reported by women, to the likelihood of an increase in asset holdings in their own names, to an increase in their exercise of purchasing power, and in their political and legal awareness as well as in the composite empowerment index. Furthermore, access to credit was also associated with higher levels of mobility, political participation and involvement in 'major decision-making' for particular credit organizations.

This comparison of different approaches to the quantification of empowerment in the context of the same set of credit programmes demonstrates the need for the triangulation of evidence in order to ensure that indicators mean what they are intended to mean. The absence of such supportive evidence carries the danger that analysts will load meanings onto their indicators which reflect their own disciplinary, methodological or political leanings rather than the realities they are seeking to portray. Triangulation requires that multiple sources of information are brought to bear on the interpretation of an indicator, thereby guarding against the interpretative bias of the analyst.

MEASURING EMPOWERMENT: THE PROBLEM OF VALUES

Status, Autonomy and the Relevance of Context

I have so far focused on the problem of *meaning* in the selection of indicators of empowerment — the need to be sure that indicators mean what they are intended to mean. I want to turn now to the question of values and how they complicate attempts to conceptualize and measure women's empowerment. Let me start with the question of 'emic' or insider values before going on to consider the complications introduced by outsider values. The main way in which 'insider values' have been captured in studies dealing with women's empowerment has been through variables measuring 'cultural context'. Such studies tend to be comparative in nature and explore how differences in cultural context influence resources, agency and achievements. For instance, we have already noted the findings reported by Dreze and Sen (1995) that women's literacy and employment status helped to explain variations in overall child mortality and in excess female mortality among children across India. However, the single most important variable in their study explaining excess female mortality was a 'dummy' variable standing for geographical location: gender differentials in mortality rates were far less striking in the southern states of India than in the northern and western states.

These regional 'dummy' variables can be seen as compressing information about a whole range of inter-related norms and practices relating to marriage, mobility and inheritance which make up gender relations in different parts of India. If we accept that investments in the survival and well-being of a family member tell us something important about the value attached to that member, then the analysis by Dreze and Sen tells us that the structural variables which make up gender relations in different parts of India were far more important in determining the extent to which the girl child is valued within the family than the individual characteristics of her parents.

Jejeebhoy's (1997) study, which compares Tamil Nadu, one of the southern states of India, with Uttar Pradesh (UP), one of its northern states, offers some lower-level insights into the relationship between cultural context and individual preference. Her study explores the effects of a range of variables on women's autonomy. Measures of women's autonomy included their role in decision-making; mobility; incidence of domestic violence; access to, and control over, economic resources. Predictably, women in Tamil Nadu fared better on most indicators of autonomy than women in UP. However, she also found that the determinants of women's 'autonomy' varied in the two regions.

In general, the traditional factors conferring status on women — the number of sons they bore, the size of their dowry and nuclear family residence — were more closely linked with the autonomy indicators in the restrictive context of UP than they were in the more egalitarian context of Tamil Nadu. In UP, women who had brought large dowries to their marriages, who lived in nuclear families and who produced sons were far more likely to report a greater role in household decision-making and greater freedom from domestic violence than others. While female employment also had significant and positive implications for most of the autonomy indicators in UP, education had a far weaker and less significant impact. In Tamil Nadu, however, the effects of these more traditional 'status'-related variables were far weaker, while female employment and, even more strongly, female education were both more consistently related to women's autonomy.

Jejeebhoy's study points to the strong rationale that women are likely to have in certain contexts for making choices which are essentially dis-empowering. The contextual variables in her study, as in Dreze and Sen's, are a shorthand for the deeply-entrenched rules, norms and practices which shape social relations in different parts of India and which help to influence behaviour, define values and *shape choice*. Since women are likely to be given greater respect within their communities for conforming to its norms, and to be penalized if they do not, their own values and behaviour are likely to reflect those of the wider community and to reproduce its injustices. There is evidence, for instance, that women in the northern states like UP are far more likely to express strong son preference than those in southern states like Tamil Nadu (Dyson and Moore, 1983). The apparently 'voluntary' nature of such choices should not detract our attention from their consequences. If empowerment is simply equated with a role in decision-making and 'control' over household resources, then having sons and bringing in a large dowry would be considered conducive to women's empowerment. Yet dowry is a practice which simultaneously expresses and reinforces son preference and transforms daughters into financial liabilities for their parents. Both dowry and son preference are central to the values and practices through which women are socially defined as a subordinate category in a state which is associated with some of the starkest indicators of gender discrimination on the Indian subcontinent.

A number of points can be made on the basis of this discussion. First of all, there is a point about strategies of empowerment. The studies here suggest a role for individual agency in challenging gender inequality but they also point to the importance of larger structural change. In a context where cultural values constrain women's ability to make strategic life choices, structural inequalities cannot be addressed by individuals alone. We have cited evidence that individual women can, and do, act against the norm, but their impact on the situation of women in general is likely to remain limited and they may have to pay a high price for their autonomy. The project of women's empowerment is dependent on collective solidarity in the public arena as well as individual assertiveness in the private. Women's organizations and social movements in particular have an important role to play in creating the conditions for change and in reducing the costs for the individual.

In methodological terms, the discussion in this section reminds us why empowerment cannot be conceptualized simply in terms of choice, but must incorporate an assessment of the values embedded in agency and choice, values which reflect the wider context. It points, in other words, to the need to make a distinction between 'status' and 'autonomy' as criteria in evaluating agency and choice. 'Status' considerations relate to the values of the community, whether these communities are hierarchical or egalitarian, and they draw attention to the influence of the larger collectivity in ascribing greater value to certain kinds of individual choices over others and hence in giving greater value to those who abide by these choices.

When such considerations set up a trade-off for women between their ability to make independent choices in critical arenas of their lives — such as marriage, reproduction, friendship and so on — and their ability to enjoy status within the family and community, status becomes antithetical to autonomy. As Gita Sen (1993: 198) comments in relation to reproductive choice: 'The point is especially apparent in gender hierarchies where, for example, a woman's status may be linked to her fertility. Bearing the approved number of children will grant a woman the rights and privileges accorded to a fertile woman, but do not necessarily give her greater autonomy in decision-making'.

More strongly, in such contexts, status is also likely to be antithetical to empowerment. The need to bear the approved number of children in order to secure social status and family approval takes its toll on women's bodies and on their lives as they bear children beyond their capacity. Furthermore, status considerations in cultures of son-preference require women to give birth to a certain number of sons, to favour their sons over their daughters, thereby acting as agents in the transmission of gender discrimination over generations. Status considerations also lead to the more hidden costs of dependency, difficult to measure but testified so eloquently by women all over the world (Kabeer, 1997; Rowlands, 1997; Silberschmidt, 1992). Finally, in the extreme, status considerations can lead to cultures where female infanticide and foeticide, female circumcision, and widow immolation all become 'rational' responses to social norms (see Das Gupta and Li, and Sudha and Irudaya Rajan, this volume).

Outsider Values and Women's Empowerment: Between Altruism and Autonomy

The discussion in the preceding section spells out in greater detail the rationale for the highly qualified notion of choice which informs the understanding of empowerment in this chapter by pointing to the significance of social values in justifying the subordinate status of women and to the internalization of these values by women themselves. However, these qualifications require us to bring in an external normative standpoint, a set of values other than women's own, as the basis for assessing the meaning of their choices. The problem that this raises is not one of a normative standpoint per se — the whole idea of development is, after all, based on some kind of normative standpoint — but in determining the extent to which this normative standpoint expresses values which are relevant to the reality it seeks to evaluate.

The tendency to re-present 'the self' in representing 'the other' has been noted by Mohanty (1991) who describes the way in which Third World women from a variety of contexts tend to get reduced and universalized, particularly in texts coming out of the field of women and development. Although this portrayal of the 'average' disempowered Third World woman was intended to evoke sympathy and action on their behalf, its reductionism reflected the fact that the social distances of location, class, nationality and language which often separate researcher and 'researched' in the social sciences tend to be particularly large in the development field.

The same distances help to explain why attempts to define and measure women's empowerment have given rise to similarly averaging tendencies in the portrayal of the *empowered* woman. I want to point to two distinct examples of these 'averaging' tendencies, coming out of quite different strands of scholarship and advocacy, addressing different dimensions of 'cooperative-conflict' within the household, both containing some elements of truth, but large elements of simplification.

One model promotes what could be called the 'virtuous model' of the empowered woman and is associated with the instrumentalist forms of gender advocacy that we noted earlier. It draws on various examples of gender scholarship which document the greater social connectedness of women in order to endow them with various traits which form the basis of policy advocacy on their behalf: altruism and dedication to the collective family welfare; thrift and risk-aversion; industriousness; a sense of civic responsibility, manifested in their willingness to take on unpaid community work and so on.

While the instrumentalist notions of empowerment tend to emphasize women's greater altruism and 'connectedness', an alternative model of empowerment is also evident which focuses far more on the conflictual element of gender relations and hence favours a more separative model of the empowered woman. What is valued as evidence of altruism in the former model is interpreted in the latter as evidence of women's internalization of their own subordinate status, their tendency to put the needs of others in the family before their own. Fierlbeck (1995), for instance, argues that women would be much more likely to expand their ability to make choices if they were to view themselves as individuals rather than members of a social group, while Jackson (1996: 497) comments: 'It may well be true that women prioritise children's needs, but there is a sense in which one might wish women to be a little less selfless and self-sacrificing'.

It is certainly the case that in contexts where the separation of resources within the family, and indeed, some degree of separation within the family, has cultural sanction, women may view greater autonomy as a desirable goal for themselves. In such contexts it may make sense to ask, as Lloyd (1995: 17) does: 'If income permits, wouldn't a mother-child unit prefer to form a separate household with its own decision-making autonomy rather than join a more complex household under other (most likely male or older female) authority?'.

In the US context, England (1997) suggests that the increasing access to employment by women since the 1950s and the rise of single motherhood, as a result of divorce or non-marital births, is not coincidental: the short version of the story is probably that employment gave women the freedom to leave unhappy marriages. Literature from sub-Saharan Africa points to women setting up on their own households once they have independent economic resources (Roberts, 1989). Hoogenboezem (1997: 85) found that several of the women who had participated in a legal literacy programme run by the Women's Action Group in Zimbabwe stated that once they knew about the procedures to be followed, they sued their husbands for divorce. Moore (1994) cites evidence from Thailand that access to an independent income has given many women the ability to walk out of unsatisfactory marriages. My own research in Bangladesh found that the emergence of new waged opportunities as well as access to loans made it possible for many women to either leave unsatisfactory marriages, or to effect a 'divorce within marriage', remaining with their husbands, but setting up their own parallel economy (Kabeer, 1997, 1998).

However, in contexts where households are organized along more corporate lines, where a powerful ideology of 'togetherness' binds the activities and resources of the family together under the control of the male head, such a question would have very little resonance. In such contexts, even in the situations of rising female employment and wages cited earlier, women do not *actively* seek the opportunity to set up separate units from men because such autonomous units are neither socially acceptable nor individually desired. Instead, they invest considerable time and effort in maintaining their marriages, in strengthening the 'cooperative' dimension of 'cooperative-conflict', seeking separation only in exceptional circumstances.

Indicators of women's empowerment, therefore, have to be sensitive to the ways in which context will shape processes of empowerment. Access to new resources may open up new possibilities for women, but they are unlikely to seek to realize these possibilities in uniform ways. Instead, they will be influenced by the intersection of social relations and individual histories which form the vantage point from which they view these new possibilities. Unless indicators are sensitive to these contextual possibilities, they are likely to miss the significance of those transformations which *do* occur.

CONCLUSION

The ability to choose is central to the concept of power which informs the analysis in this chapter, but the notion of 'choice' has been qualified in a number of ways. One set of qualifications refers to *the conditions of choice*, the need to distinguish between choices made from the vantage point of alternatives and those reflecting the absence, or the punishingly high cost, of alternatives. A second set of qualifications referred to the *consequences of choice*, the need to distinguish between strategic life choices, and second-order choices. The consequences of choice can be further evaluated in terms of their *transformatory significance*, the extent to which the choices made have the potential for challenging and destabilizing social inequalities and the extent to which they merely express and reproduce those inequalities.

Our conceptualization of empowerment has also highlighted the inter-dependence of individual and structural change in processes of empowerment. Structures shape individual resources, agency and achievements. They also define the parameters within which different categories of actors are able to pursue their interests, promoting the voice and agency of some and inhibiting that of others. And finally, they help to shape individual interests so that how people define their goals and what they value will reflect their social positioning as well as their individual histories, tastes and preferences. The qualifications on the notion of choice adopted in this chapter represent an attempt to incorporate the structural dimensions of individual choice: the criterion of *alternatives* relates to the structural conditions under which choices are made while the criterion of *consequences* relates to the extent to which the choices made have the potential for transforming these structural conditions.

Methodologically, the review of attempts to measure empowerment has been about the 'fit' (or lack thereof) between the meanings attributed to an indicator and those revealed by it empirically. It is not possible to establish the meaning of an indicator, whatever dimension of empowerment it is intended to measure, without reference to the other dimensions of empowerment specified in this chapter. Access to a *resource* tells us about potential rather than actual choice and the validity of a resource measure as an indicator of empowerment largely rests on the validity of the assumptions made about the potential agency or entitlement embodied in that resource. It is similarly difficult to judge the validity of an *achievement* measure unless we have evidence, or can make a reasonable guess, as to whose agency was involved and the extent to which the achievement in question transformed prevailing inequalities in resources and agency rather than reinforcing them or leaving them unchallenged. Similar considerations apply to evidence on *agency*: we have to know about its consequential significance in terms of women's strategic life choices and the extent to which it had transformatory potential. The more evidence there is to support these assumptions, the more faith we are likely to have in the validity of the indicator in question.

By definition, indicators of empowerment cannot provide an accurate measurement of changes in women's ability to make choices, they merely have to indicate the direction and meaning of change. However, we have noted some of the reasons why they are likely to be inaccurate and even misleading. Disembedded from their context, indicators can lend themselves to a variety of different, and contradictory, meanings. Given the value-laden nature of the concept of women's empowerment, there is a danger that analysts opt for those meanings which most favour their own values regarding what constitutes appropriate choices for women. We have also noted the importance of ensuring that the values which inform definitions and measures of empowerment are sensitive to the domain of possibilities in which women are located.

Finally, there are measurement and conceptual problems associated with capturing particular kinds of social change. There is an implicit assumption underlying many attempts to measure empowerment that we can somehow predict the nature and direction that change is going to assume. In actual fact, human agency is indeterminate and hence unpredictable in a way that is antithetical to requirements of measurement. Thus giving women access to credit, creating constitutional provision for political participation or equalizing educational opportunities are unlikely to be automatically empowering in themselves, but they do create the vantage point of alternatives which allows a more transformatory consciousness to come into play. The translation of these resources and opportunities into the kinds of functioning achievements which would signal empowerment is likely to be closely influenced by the possibilities for transformation on the ground, and how they are perceived and assessed. To attempt to predict at the outset of an intervention precisely how it will change women's lives, without some knowledge of ways of 'being and doing' which are realizable and valued by women in that context, runs into the danger of prescribing the process of empowerment and thereby violating its essence, which is to enhance women's capacity for self-determination.

REFERENCES

Ackerly, B. A. (1995) 'Testing the Tools of Development: Credit Programmes, Loan Involvement and Women's Empowerment', *IDS Bulletin* 26(3): 56–68.

Agarwal, B. (1994) *A Field of One's Own: Gender and Land Rights in South Asia*. Cambridge: Cambridge University Press.

Ali, K. A. (1996) 'Notes on Rethinking Masculinities. An Egyptian Case', in S. Zeidenstein and K. Moore (eds) *Learning about Sexuality*, pp. 98–109. New York: Population Council and International Women's Health Coalition.

Basu, A. M. (1996) 'Female Schooling, Autonomy and Fertility Change: What do these Words mean in South Asia', in R. Jeffery and A. M. Basu (eds) *Girls' Schooling, Women's Autonomy and Fertility Change in South Asia*, pp. 48–71. New Delhi: Sage.

Batliwala, S. (1993) *Empowerment of Women in South Asia: Concepts and Practices*. New Delhi: FAO-FFHC/AD.

Batliwala, S. (1994) 'The Meaning of Women's Empowerment: New Concepts from Action', in G. Sen, A. Germain and L. C. Chen (eds) *Population Policies Reconsidered. Health, Empowerment and Rights*, pp. 127–38. Cambridge, MA.: Harvard University Press.

Becker, S. (1997) 'Incorporating Women's Empowerment in Studies of Reproductive Health: An Example from Zimbabwe', paper presented at the Seminar on Female Empowerment and Demographic Processes, Lund (20–24 April).

Beneria, L. and M. Roldan (1987) *Crossroads of Class and Gender*. Chicago, IL: University of Chicago Press.

Boserup, E. (1970) *Women's Role in Economic Development*. New York: St. Martin's Press.

Bourdieu, P. (1977) *Outline of a Theory of Practice*. Cambridge: Cambridge University Press.

Chen, M.A. (1983) *A Quiet Revolution. Women in Transition in Rural Bangladesh*. Cambridge, MA: Schenkman.

Cleland, J., J. F. Phillips, S. Amin and G. M. Kamal (1994) *The Determinants of Reproductive Change in Bangladesh: Success in a Challenging Environment*. World Bank, Regional and Sectoral Studies. Washington, DC: The World Bank.

Das Gupta, M. (1987) 'Selective Discrimination among Female Children in Rural Punjab', *Population and Development Review* 13(2): 77–100.

Dreze, J. and A. Sen (1995) *India, Economic Development and Social Opportunity*. Oxford: Oxford University Press.

Dyson, T. and M. Moore (1983) 'On Kinship Structures, Female Autonomy and Demographic Behaviour in India', *Population and Development Review* 9(1): 35–60.

England, P. (1997) 'Conceptualising Women's Empowerment', paper presented at the Seminar on Female Empowerment and Demographic Processes, Lund (20–24 April).

Fierlbeck, K. (1995) 'Getting Representation Right for Women in Development: Accountability and the Articulation of Women's Interests', *IDS Bulletin* 26(3): 23–30.

Giddens, A. (1979) *Central Problems in Social Theory*. London: Macmillan Press.

Geuss, R. (1981) *The Idea of a Critical Theory. Habermas and the Frankfurt School*. Cambridge: Cambridge University Press.

Goetz, A. M. and R. Sen Gupta (1996) 'Who Takes the Credit? Gender, Power and Control over Loan Use in Rural Credit Programmes in Bangladesh', *World Development* 24(1): 45–63.

Hashemi, S. M., S. R. Schuler and A. P. Riley (1996) 'Rural Credit Programs and Women's Empowerment in Bangladesh', *World Development* 24(4): 635–53.

Hoogenboezem, G. (1997) 'Some Men Really are Useless: The Role of Participation in a Women's Project, Empowerment and Gender in the Context of Two Zimbabwean Women's Organisations'. Occasional paper No. 56. Nijmegen: Katholieke Universiteit Nijmegen.

Jackson, C. (1996), 'Rescuing Gender from the Poverty Trap', *World Development* 24(3): 489–504.

Jejeebhoy, S. (1997), 'Operationalising Women's Empowerment: the Case of Rural India', paper presented at the Seminar on Female Empowerment and Demographic Processes, Lund (20–24 April).

Kabeer, N. (1994) *Reversed Realities: Gender Hierarchies in Development Thought*. London: Verso Publications.

Kabeer, N. (1997) 'Women, Wages and Intra-household Power Relations in Urban Bangladesh', *Development and Change* 28(2): 261–302.

Kabeer, N. (1998) 'Money Can't Buy Me Love? Re-evaluating Gender, Credit and Empowerment in Rural Bangladesh'. IDS Discussion Paper No. 363. Brighton: Institute of Development Studies.

Kishor, S. (1997) 'Empowerment of Women in Egypt and Links to the Survival and Health of their Infants', paper presented at the Seminar on Female Empowerment and Demographic Processes, Lund (20–24 April).

Kritz, M. M., P. Makinwa and D. T. Gurak (1997) 'Wife's Empowerment and Fertility in Nigeria: The Role of Context', paper presented at the Seminar on Female Empowerment and Demographic Processes, Lund (20–24 April).

Lloyd, C. (1995) 'Household Structure and Poverty: What are the Connections?'. Population Council Working Papers No. 74. New York: Population Council.

Lukes, S. (1974) *Power: A Radical View*. London: Macmillan.

McElroy, M. (1992) 'The Policy Implications of Family Bargaining and Marriage Markets', in L. Haddad, J. Hoddinott and H. Alderman (eds) *Intra-household Resource Allocation in Developing Countries: Methods, Models and Policy*, pp. 53–74. Baltimore, MD: Johns Hopkins University Press.

Mohanty, C. T. (1991) 'Under Western Eyes: Feminist Scholarship and Colonial Discourses', in C. T. Mohanty, A. Russo and L. Torres (eds) *Third World Women and the Politics of Feminism*, pp. 51–80. Bloomington and Indianapolis, IN: Indiana University Press.

Moore, H. (1994) 'Is There a Crisis in the Family?', UNRISD Occasional paper No. 3. Geneva: UNRISD.

Morgan, P. and B. Niraula (1995) 'Gender Inequality and Fertility in Two Nepali Villages', *Population and Development Review* 21(3): 541–61.

Mukhopadhayay, M. (1998) *Legally Dispossessed. Gender, Identity and the Process of Law*. Calcutta: Stree Publications.

Pahl, J. (1989) *Money and Marriage*. London: Macmillan.

Pitt, M. and Khandker, S. (1995) 'Household and Intrahousehold Impacts of the Grameen Bank and Similar Targeted Credit Programmes in Bangladesh', paper presented at Workshop on Credit Programmes for the Poor: Household and Intrahousehold Impacts and Program Sustainability, Education and Social Policy Department, Washington and Bangladesh Institute of Development Studies, Dhaka.

Rahman, R. I. (1986) 'Impact of Grameen Bank on the Situation of Poor Rural Women'. BIDS Working Paper No. 1, Grameen Evaluation Project. Dhaka: Bangladesh Institute of Development Studies.

Razavi, S. (1992) 'Agrarian Change and Gender Power: A Comparative Study in South Eastern Iran'. D.Phil. dissertation, St. Antony's College, Oxford University.

Razavi, S. (1997) 'Fitting Gender into Development Institutions', *World Development* 25(7): 1111–25.

Roberts, P. (1989) 'The Sexual Politics of Labour in Western Nigeria and Hausa Niger', in K. Young (ed.) *Serving Two Masters. Third World Women in Development*, pp. 27–47. New Delhi: Allied Publishers.

Rowlands, J. (1997) *Questioning Empowerment*. Oxford: Oxfam Publications.

Sathar, Z. A. and S. Kazi (1997) *Women's Autonomy, Livelihood and Fertility. A Study of Rural Punjab*. Islamabad: Pakistan Institute of Development Studies.

Sen, A. K. (1985a) 'Well-being, Agency and Freedom', *The Journal of Philosophy* 132(4): 169–221.

Sen, A.K. (1985b) *Commodities and Capabilities*. Amsterdam: North Holland.

Sen, A. K. (1990) 'Gender and Co-operative Conflict', in I. Tinker (ed.) *Persistent Inequalities*, pp. 123–49. Oxford: Oxford University Press.

Sen, G. (1993) 'Paths to Fertility Decline: A Cross-country Analysis', in P. Bardhan, M. Dattachaudri and T. N. Krishnan (eds) *Development and Change: Essays in Honour of K. N. Raj*, pp. 197–214. New Delhi: Oxford University Press.

Shaffer, P. (1998) 'Gender, Poverty and Deprivation: Evidence from the Republic of Guinea', *World Development* 26(12): 2119–35.

Silberschmidt, M. (1992) 'Have Men Become the Weaker Sex? Changing Life Situations in Kisii District, Kenya', *The Journal of Modern African Studies* 30(2): 237–53.

UNDP (1995) *The Human Development Report 1995*. Oxford: Oxford University Press.

3

The Gender Sensitivity of Well-being Indicators

Ruhi Saith and Barbara Harriss-White

INTRODUCTION

The Fourth World Conference on Women built upon the anti-poverty momentum of the World Summit for Social Development. High on the United Nations agenda is a fight against poverty based not only on economic growth but also on the achievement of social goals — including gender equity. To translate such commitments into effective policies, indicators capable of reliably identifying gender differences in well-being are necessary tools. William Petty's statement 'To measure is the first step to improve', succinctly expresses their importance (Morris, 1979). Despite the proliferation of indicators, their sensitivity to gender differences has not been comparatively reviewed before. This is the object of this chapter, with particular relevance to developing countries.

The chapter is organized as follows. First, the 'functionings' framework within which well-being will be assessed is outlined. The following four sections then focus on indicators of the basic 'functionings' of being healthy, being nourished, and being educated, and on some composite indices which assess a combination of functionings; these are critically analysed with respect to their sensitivity to gender differences. Finally, we summarize the findings and outline some implications for policy and future research.

ASSESSMENT OF WELL-BEING

We propose to use the 'functionings' framework, pioneered by Sen, and based on the notion that well-being is directly concerned with a person's quality of life.[1] Driven by data availability, well-being is measured for the individual through a range of social indicators (Sen, 1985).[2] It is not the possession of the commodity or the utility it provides that proxies for well-being, but rather what the person actually succeeds in doing with the commodity and its characteristics. This is referred to as the 'functioning'.

---

1. Details are given by Sen (1985). For a brief explanation, see Saith and Harriss-White (1998), and for critical appraisals see Dasgupta (1993) and Granaglia (1996) amongst others.
2. Considerable research on social indicators has been done by the United Nations Research Institute for Social Development; see, e.g. Baster and Scott (1969); Drewnoski (1966); and McGranahan et al. (1972) to name a few of the early studies cited by Ghai et al. (1988).

Reasons for preferring the functionings-based framework for assessing gender differences in well-being, over the utility- and commodity-based frameworks, are elaborated in Saith and Harriss-White (1998).

We examine three subjectively identified 'basic' functionings, namely: being healthy, being nourished and being educated.[3] Our objective is to locate social indicators that can reliably capture gender-differentials in these functionings. A complete assessment of well-being should include functionings like human agency, power, autonomy, and so on (a point cogently argued by Razavi, 1996 and 1997). These are the subject of a complementary study undertaken by Kabeer (this volume).

The translation of gender differences in 'basic' functionings, as assessed by appropriate indicators, to corresponding differences in well-being involves certain assumptions. First is the assumption that the functionings considered are so elementary as to be necessary for well-being; the second is that a differential in any one of these functionings will result in a differential in well-being. For example, if an assessment of indicators of 'being healthy' showed female health to be poorer than male, then female well-being is less than male well-being.

Studies from different levels of aggregation (micro-level to international country comparisons) are drawn upon in the discussion. Indicators already used for international comparisons may, however, have differing significance in different countries in specific social contexts. When interpreting, it is important to be aware that indicators provide limited information. For example in the context of this chapter, indicators may be able to demonstrate reliably that gender differences exist, but on their own they are unable to generate explanations for the causes of the differences. Indicators are thus *necessary* to devise and implement action towards the goal of gender equity but they are *not sufficient*.[4]

---

3. Strictly, within the functionings approach well-being is to be assessed by examining the complete capability set (this is the set of all functionings achievable by the various possible combinations of utilizations of commodities in a person's possession; depending on his/her evaluation, a person would choose functionings related to one particular combination). The extent of the freedom to choose determined by the capability set may itself contribute to some extent to well-being. In practice, we are restricted by the fact that data are only available for the functionings actually achieved. By further restricting our study to the elementary functionings listed, this approach shares much in common with that of 'basic needs' which has a separate intellectual history (International Labour Organization, 1976; Streeten et al., 1981).

4. The issue of causality is beyond the scope of our research (but see Kabeer, this volume who elaborates this theme). Further, general issues not specific to gender sensitivity, such as desirable properties of social indicators (e.g. easily measurable, affordable, reliable), and difficulties that arise in the collection and processing of data, especially in developing countries, are discussed by Ghai et al. (1988) and Westendorff and Ghai (1994) and will not be elaborated here.

BEING HEALTHY

The spectrum of health ranges from good health to morbidity to fatal ill-health, or mortality. A difference in mortality and morbidity between the male and female sex reflects a difference in their health.[5] A conclusion that this is caused by gender bias can however be arrived at only after taking into account underlying genetic differences between the sexes in mortality and disease patterns.[6]

Indicators of mortality and of morbidity are considered below. Figure 1 gives an outline of the indicators discussed in the two groups.

Differential Mortality Indicators

Biological factors ensure higher female survival than male, from the foetal stage onwards, given similar care. This difference is reflected in the ratio of females to males. The ratio is low at birth, with an average of 5 per cent more males born than females (probably to compensate for subsequent higher male mortality). Due to higher male than female mortality in infancy (females have higher resistance to infectious diseases) and adolescence (differences in sex hormones causing increased death rates in men by accidents and other violent causes), the ratio is balanced by the age of 30 (Holden, 1987).[7] Female survival continues to be higher than male in later years up to the menopause due to hormonal protection,[8] causing the ratio to tip in favour of females.[9] Countries in Europe and North America have on an average 105 females for every 100 males; in sub-Saharan Africa the figure is 102 females. There are, however, fewer females than males in a number of Asian, Middle Eastern and North African countries like Egypt and Iran with 97, Turkey with 95, China with 94, India with 93, Pakistan with 92 and Saudi Arabia with 84 females per 100 men (Sen, 1995). Errors of enumeration, migration and the ratio at birth fail to explain such masculine

---

5. Sex refers to the biological differences between men and women. Gender refers to socially-constructed differences.
6. Differences in health care, treatment and nutrition are considered the proximate determinants of discrimination while economic and cultural devaluation are considered the underlying causes.
7. Male hormones, particularly androgens, have been shown to contribute to aggressive behaviour (Wuttke, 1989).
8. In middle age, the incidence of ischaemic heart disease in males is three to four times that in females. After the menopause, however, the gap narrows. The reasons proposed to account for this are the loss of protective hormonal effect in women, loss of harmful effect in men and even the fact that male susceptibles could have already died (Marmot and Mann, 1996).
9. The extent to which female survival advantage is culturally linked is debatable. Biological differences could be reinforced by social influences fostering risky behaviour in males, and until recently, the higher tendency of men than women to smoke (Sen, 1995).

Figure 1. Indicators of 'Being Healthy'

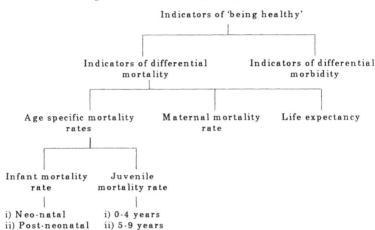

ratios.[10] Increased female mortality (over that of males) seems to be the only reasonable explanation. Since women have a survival advantage right from the intra-uterine period in societies with formally gender-neutral health care systems, an explanation for the increased mortality is sought in social factors.[11] The ratio of females to males can thus be seen as an indicator which gives a summary of gender inequality as it operates over a long time (Sen, 1995). Differentials may in fact be higher in particular age groups which greatly influence the overall masculinization of the ratio. The ratio in these age groups may therefore be a more reliable indicator than the aggregate ratio. Indicators of age-specific death rates are analysed below. Maternal mortality which also contributes to the masculinization of the Female Male Ratio (FMR) in a specific age-group, and life expectancy, which is often used as an indicator of differential mortality, are discussed separately.

Age-specific Death Rates

Age-specific death rates are commonly calculated for groups of five years. The age groups which have a high impact on the FMR are 0–4, 5–9 and 15–34 (largely the impact of maternal deaths).[12]

---

10. Male migrant workers in Saudi Arabia are an exception (Sen, 1995).
11. Economic explanations for the perceived worth of women for India have been theorized by Bardhan (1974) and Miller (1981), and cultural ones by Dasgupta (1987a) and Dyson and Moore (1983) amongst others. Agnihotri (1997) reviews this literature.
12. Internationally the term sex ratio refers to the number of males per thousand female population. In India, however, the same term sex ratio denotes the number of females per thousand males. In order to avoid confusion, the sex ratio *in India* is referred to in this chapter as the Female Male Ratio. The term Juvenile Sex Ratio in the context of India refers to the number of females per thousand male population in the juvenile (under-10) age group.

The under-10 age group (juvenile) is important because, in developing countries with high mortality and high fertility, it constitutes a large proportion of the total population. Differentials in mortality in this age group therefore have a greater impact on the FMR than those among older males and females. Besides, studies in South Asia have demonstrated that under-10 is the age group with the most pronounced female disadvantage and therefore highest mortality differentials (for India, see Chatterjee, 1990).[13] Juvenile mortality rates also have the advantage over overall mortality rates of eliminating the effects of sex-selective migration. Gender disaggregated data on juvenile mortality may, however, not be easily available. A measure which is indirect and therefore less desirable, but capable of capturing largely similar information is the under ten FMR also called the Juvenile Sex Ratio.[14]

Focusing on the under-10 age group for reliably gender-sensitive indicators does not imply the targeting of policy responses specifically in this age group, to the neglect of others. Rather, values obtained for such indicators are considered the outcome of a larger and multi-dimensional process and the findings would have broad policy implications.

Agnihotri (1996) suggests a disaggregation of the Juvenile Sex Ratio. Since there may be large inaccuracies in the reporting of age in developing countries, five-year groupings rather than smaller age groups are conventionally used to reduce the error. Agnihotri therefore took the 0–4 and 5–9 age groups. Although the difference between these two age groups is not as sharp as for the 0–2 (capturing the differential deaths in infancy) and 3–9 groupings, Agnihotri suggests that the FMR04 would reflect both the excess male infant mortality and any excess female mortality by the age of 3 years. The FMR59 would reflect mortality by age group 5 and beyond.

---

13. Within the under-10 age group, the largest proportion of deaths occurs in developing countries in the first year of life. It is therefore usual to distinguish the infant mortality rate (IMR) from overall juvenile mortality rates. The IMR may, however, give a misleading picture because the factors affecting mortality differ between the neo-natal and post-neonatal period. Neo-natal mortality is primarily affected by endogenous factors which affect the foetus intra-uterine and continue to influence its survival for the first four weeks of life. Post-neonatal is mainly determined by exogenous factors relating to the physical environment, for example, infections, respiratory or parasitic diseases (Visaria, 1988). Since females have higher immunity to infections during infancy, a female post-neonatal mortality higher than that of males raises the possibility of social discrimination. Two divergent demographic trends could be concealed in the period labelled 'infancy'. For example, Sample Registration System results for India showed a higher male mortality of 19.5 per 1000 compared to about 17 per 1000 for girls among new-born infants aged 0–29 days (Padmanabha, 1982). Post-neonatal mortality rates were higher for females (about 12 per 1000 compared to about 10 per 1000 for boys). The overall infant mortality rates of about 29 per 1000 for boys as well as girls, however, obscured these differences. In such situations juvenile (under-10) mortality rates are more informative.

14. As mentioned earlier, in the Indian context, we use the term Juvenile Sex Ratio to refer to the number of females per 1000 males in the juvenile (under-10) age group.

Any excess female mortality due to social factors, in childhood, would have 'stabilized' by the age of 5 and would then be reflected by the FMR59 (Miller, 1981; cited by Agnihotri, 1996).[15] Further, since 90 per cent of juvenile deaths occur in childhood, Agnihotri contends that FMR59 is virtually unaffected by deaths in the 5–9 age group. A combination of FMR04 and FMR59 is therefore proposed to identify both the mortality differentials in childhood and the age group at which such differentials set in. Such disaggregation of the juvenile group is also important because differing combinations of FMR04 and FMR59 can give rise to apparently similar Juvenile Sex Ratios. For example, consider a sample that shows a moderate to high FMR04 and a subsequent sharp drop to low FMR59 (indicative of a female child mortality that is higher than the male and which can be confirmed by examining mortality data). The overall Juvenile Sex Ratio in this case could appear balanced, hiding the adverse survival conditions for the older girl child.

In the absence of discrimination, the FMR04 would be expected to be above that at birth (i.e. above 960 for India according to the 1981 census figures) due to higher male infant mortality. If the care of the child were not gendered (and since males do not suffer any additional biological disadvantage in childhood), the FMR59 would be expected to remain the same as the FMR04. Unexpected FMR04 and FMR59 values, deviating from the above pattern, will then point to gender differentials in mortality. Agnihotri's analysis of FMR04 and FMR59 from district level data from the 1981 Indian Census gave the following important results:[16]

• Some regions showed an unusually low FMR04 (below 910) suggesting very strong gender bias with high female mortality even in infancy.[17] Some showed an alarmingly low ratio (below 900), for example, the Salem district, the only district in South India to show a rate below 900. Very recently, Salem has been the object of public concern and action because of the growing incidence of sex selective infanticide (Chunkath and Athreya, 1997; George et al., 1992 cited by Agnihotri, 1996). The FMR04 could also be used to identify regions with lower than normally expected FMRs at birth. Excessively masculine ratios at birth due to

---

15. Children/child/childhood in this context refers to the under-5 age group.
16. In state level averages, districts within the state which have a high FMR are able to compensate for 'rogue' districts with low FMRs (Agnihotri, 1997). Using districts as the unit of analysis prevents such 'masking'. The results presented here are taken from Agnihotri's PhD thesis (Agnihotri, 1997). Agnihotri (1996 and 1997) also present an analysis of FMRs for different social groupings.
17. Agnihotri (1997) assigns four different levels to the FMRs: low (below 910), moderate (910–960), high (960–1000) and very high (above 1000). The cut-off value of 960 was chosen as it was close to the FMR at birth. Other values were chosen by examining the spatial distribution of FMRs which revealed contiguous district clusters with these FMRs as cut-off points.

pre-natal sex identification and selective female abortion have been the subject of recent research on China and South Korea. The FMR04 is particularly apposite for countries like India, where such a practice has been shown to be on the rise and where data on the ratio at birth is not easily available (Sudha and Irudaya Rajan, this volume).

- Some regions showed a drop between FMR04 and FMR59.[18] These, as well as regions with very low FMR59 (below 850), were shown to have high excess girl child mortality.
- Some groups, despite showing a high IMR (and therefore high male infant mortality) were found to have low FMR04 and FMR59.[19] This was also taken to be an indication of strong anti-female discrimination.
- Some regions showed unusually high FMR04 and FMR59 values (typically over 1000). Rather than accepting this as an absence of female discrimination, a further investigation of the tribal population of thirty-six districts in these regions, revealed poorer ante-natal care and immunization coverage than in other parts of the country. Agnihotri suggests that it is possible that this translates into excess foetal wastage and infant mortality. The high IMR with the accompanying high male mortality could result in unusually high FMR04 and FMR59 values. Such values should therefore be investigated for excess male mortality during infancy and childhood. This finding led Agnihiotri to emphasize the distinction between high FMRs and balanced FMRs. A range of 960 to 980 (*for India*) could be considered a balanced figure or 'norm'. Districts with FMRs below this level have to catch up and those with FMRs above this need closer scrutiny (Agnihotri, 1997).[20] Similarly, a very high FMR at birth needs to be investigated for an unsatisfactory health delivery system — as it could be indicative of high male mortality *in utero* due to poor maternal health nutrition and care.

The above results suggest that FMR04 and FMR59 are reliable indicators of a gender differential in the functioning of 'health'. Data are available from certain censuses (such as the Indian ones) and are affordable and relatively easily measurable, compared for example, to indicators of 'being nourished' (see below). The accuracy of census data can be jeopardized

18. Normally the FMR59 would not be expected to be higher than the FMR04, as a pattern of excess female mortality that sets in early is unlikely to be reversed in later years. Agnihotri (1997) suggests that such cases, if stray, could be indicative of data errors. If persistent, he suggests carrying out a detailed micro-level study. It could, however, also be argued that mortality rates for female children could come down in the wake of pre-natal sex selection.
19. With an increase in infant mortality, male infant mortality would be expected to increase more compared to that of females since males are more vulnerable.
20. Agnihotri draws attention to another important distinction, i.e. the decline in FMR through the reduction in IMR and the decline through the increase in female mortality in excess of male, the former being desirable, the latter not.

by under-reporting, age-heaping and other kinds of age distortions which themselves may be gendered (for example the under-reporting of female deaths due to shame at the cause of death). Thus, however robust these findings are for India, it is important to repeat the analysis for other countries. Such an analysis is currently in progress for Nepal (Seddon, 1997).

A Note on Maternal Mortality Rate (MMR)

The differential death rate is high between the ages of 15 and 34 in developing countries, largely due to maternal mortality (Chatterjee, 1990).[21] Lack of care during pregnancy and delivery as well as a long history of neglect with under-nourishment leading to stunting and poor physical growth all contribute to high MMR. An under-investment in pregnancy-related health facilities may reflect the gender bias institutionalized within the public health infrastructure. It could, however, be argued that the prevalence of poverty and poor health care facilities with or without gender inequality itself account for the high MMR. In such sex-specific situations, since cross-sex data is not available for comparisons, it is not possible to reach a definitive conclusion on the question of gender differentials. MMR by itself cannot be used as a sole indicator of gender differences, but as with other sex-specific indicators it may have a corroborating role. Besides, MMR is not capable of assessing differentials in situations where male well-being may be lower than that of the female.

A Note on Life Expectancy

Life expectancy represents the mean length of time an individual is expected to live if prevailing mortality conditions persist throughout the person's life. It can be calculated for individuals at the time of birth or in any subsequent age group. Life expectancy at birth, calculated for males and females, is extensively used as a measure of gender differentials in well-being by national governments as well as international institutions. Often, however, life expectancy evidence is based on model life tables rather than real data. Besides, in the context of gender differentials it can be a misleading indicator. For example the higher mortality of females in India up to the age of 35 is disguised by the estimated female life expectancy at birth which is longer than that of males (Chatterjee, 1990). The higher life expectation is largely the consequence of the greater survival chance of older women which

---

21. Maternal mortality refers to deaths that occur during pregnancy or within 42 days of delivery (or termination), per 100,000 live births.

'more than compensates (mathematically speaking) for the lower survival of younger females' (ibid: 7). While overall life expectancy is useful as a measure of development, the use of male and female life expectancy to capture gender differentials in well-being masks age specific differentials in mortality.

Differential Morbidity Indicators

Conditions that cause morbidity can be classified into two groups. The first is comprised of conditions that are sex specific. This includes genetic pre-dispositions and reproductive disorders (details of which are given in Saith and Harriss-White, 1998). The use of such sex-specific morbidity as a sole indicator of gender differentials, however, suffers from similar constraints expressed with respect to maternal mortality rates above.

The second group is comprised of conditions that affect both sexes, although certain conditions may have a greater preponderance in one sex than in another. This is the case with (a) gendered occupations, such as a high incidence of eye strain amongst young women workers in the *zari* (gold thread) industry in India (Chatterjee, 1990); (b) gendered environments, for instance in rural Karnataka in India, where the male works in the open air while work for the female centres around the 'dark, smoke filled kitchen', in ways which suggest that exposure to infection may be gender-specific (Caldwell and Caldwell, 1987); or (c) differentials in medical care and nutrition, such as gender imbalances in expenditure on health treatment in Punjab (Dasgupta, 1987b; Pettigrew, 1987) and Tamil Nadu (Erb and Harriss-White, 1996). Although morbidity thus reflects differences in underlying nutrition, health care and treatment, as well as gendered occupations and environments, reliable indicators of morbidity have not been developed for use by international agencies or governments. This is because they have a number of limitations which are detailed in Saith and Harriss-White (1998); briefly, these are as follows.

First, 'causes of death' data are quite unreliable as well as difficult to obtain. Furthermore, they can only be employed for inferences about morbidity if it is assumed that sickness follows the same gender and age distribution as death (Harriss, 1993). Second, morbidity data gathered through questionnaires tend to suffer from major biases (Sen, 1995). Women in West Bengal were reported as much more unwilling to perceive or declare their ill-health than were men (Sen, 1985). Boys in Karnataka were believed to be sick more often on account of the perceptions of their relative weakness in childhood (Caldwell and Caldwell, 1987).

Third, although subjectivity may be reduced by using hospital records on the incidence of disease such data would tend to reflect the availability of medical care. The data would also reflect information about those that had been taken to hospital for treatment rather than the true gendered incidence of morbidity. Fourth, even if reliable data on the incidence of disease were available and showed no gender difference, there could well be gender differences in the duration and intensity of treatment. From records related to Punjab in north India, Dasgupta (1987b) and Pettigrew (1987) conclude a marked gender imbalance in health expenditure and treatment (see also McNeill, 1986 for Tamil Nadu, confirming the findings of Chen et al., 1981, and Koenig and D'Souza, 1986, for Bangladesh).

Finally, the bias in morbidity does not invariably operate in a simple and consistent manner and can be misinterpreted. For example, male infants from richer households were found to have a higher incidence of loss of vision than females or males from poor households through pro-male biased use of harmful steroid eye cream (Cohen, 1987).

BEING NOURISHED

Indicators of nutrition are considered here under two headings: indicators of intake, and indicators of outcome.

Indicators of Intake

Consumption of every macro-nutrient (carbohydrates, proteins and fats) and micro-nutrient (vitamins and minerals) can be presented as an indicator. Faced with the interpretation of this cornucopia, most studies of intake concentrate on overall energy adequacy rather than individual nutrients. Energy intake is calculated (usually by noting the consumption of food) and compared to that required for the individual to be in energy balance. Since the quantity of food consumed is measured rather than the outcome, this is a commodity-based approach. Nevertheless, some problems associated with it will be addressed briefly below.

- *Data collection.* In general, an estimation of food intake (and the calculation of calories contained, using standardized conversion tables) is time-consuming, expensive and prone to error. Shortcomings of the different methods used to estimate food consumption are given in brief by Saith and Harriss-White (1998) and in greater detail by Svedberg (1991). A particular methodological disadvantage is that most measurements continue to be based on households and relatively rarely on individuals.
- *Fixing the norm.* Energy intake is compared against the per capita required norm. A calculation of the latter depends on three dimensions (i) energy requirement for the basal metabolic rate per kg of body weight; (ii) body size; and (iii) work activity. The calculation of the

'norm' for each of these dimensions is in dispute.[22] Besides, there is great variability in these dimensions at the individual level. Nutrient requirements based on averages for populations could be abused if applied as cut-off points to individuals. Thus the FAO and WHO suggest that their requirement norms be used for 'prescriptive' purposes and not as cut-off points for estimating under-nutrition at the individual level. When assessing gender differentials in nutrition, an assessment based on absolute amounts of food, rather than relative to the different male/female norms, could result in overestimation of female disadvantage (Harriss, 1995).[23] Underestimating the work load of women, especially those involved in hard agricultural labour and heavy household work, could result in an underestimation of any existing female disadvantage.

These problems are illustrated by several studies of one database, where conclusions differ depending on the assumptions made about intra-household distribution, the norms and the cut-off points, the use of gendered or ungendered standards, the range of nutrients and the age groups (Harriss-White, 1997).[24] Consider also a study by Chen et al. (1981) on data from Bangladesh, which concluded that male intake per caput exceeded that of

---

22. The issues under dispute with respect to each of these are discussed by Svedberg (1991) and are outlined here briefly. 1) Energy requirement for the basal metabolic rate (BMR) per kg of body weight: the BMR could show inter-individual differences among individuals of the same sex, weight and age. Possible explanations are a) genotypic differences affecting the efficiency with which energy is metabolized; b) changes in body composition with increase in weight or even between individuals of same weight, for example, different ratios of fat to lean tissue — the energy expenditure for the maintenance of fat stores being lower than for the sustenance of functions of lean tissue; and c) the controversial notion of adaptation to intake either by increasing energy efficiency or by reducing energy wasted by thermogenesis. Also under dispute is the form of relationship between BMR and body weight; whether BMR increases linearly with an increase in body weight or if the relationship is quadratic (concave). 2) Body size: different body size norms could be used. One possibility is the use of the height and body weight of an average individual in an 'observed' reference population (or a fraction thereof) which has adequate nutrition. The other is the average of an estimated range within which the weight can be changed without impairing health. The weight at the lower end of this range could also be used. 3) Physical activity: with regard to the physical activity of the reference individual, economic return of physical work differs substantially depending on the land, capital, etc., owned. While international organizations base the norm on the 'average' work activity, this actually differs for different people to enable them to survive economically and avoid undernutrition.
23. WHO estimates suggest that an average male expends 36 per cent more energy per day than his female counterpart, due to differences in body weight (and therefore higher maintenance energy) and in the proportion of metabolically active tissue per unit of body weight.
24. Harriss-White (1997) compares five studies (Behrman, 1988; Behrman and Deolalikar, 1989; Behrman and Deolalikar, 1990; Harriss, 1995 and Ryan et al., 1984). All were carried out on the same nutrition database (from the International Crops Research Institute for the Semi-Arid Tropics, ICRISAT), but gave different results with different policy implications.

females in all age groups. Abdullah (1983), however, made adjustments in male and female energy requirements for age groups over five and concluded that in this group there was no female discrimination (beyond that accounted for by male–female differences in body size, activity and physiology).

Indicators of Outcome

Indicators of outcome can be divided into three main groups: biochemical, clinical and anthropometric. Biochemical and clinical indicators are used infrequently and will not be discussed (see Saith and Harriss-White, 1998; Svedberg, 1991). We will focus instead on anthropometric measurements, which are the most commonly used.

Children are normally assessed using height for age, weight for height and weight for age ratios.[25] For adults, the height and the Body Mass Index (weight in kg for height in metres squared — $KGs/(m)^2$) are used. Anthropometric measurements are popular because:

> the anthropometric approach rests on the presumption that people's physical appearance reflects their nutrition (and health) status, i.e. if their body intake and expenditure balance at too low a level, this will show in their body constitution. This means that neither energy intake nor the expenditure has to be measured. The anthropometric approach is therefore more direct and simple and less reliant on data collection than the dietary approach. (Svedberg, 1991: 191)

Despite these advantages, its difficulties are as follows:

- *Fixing the norm.* Most national and international studies use the norms established by the United States Center for Health Statistics. These are obtained from Western populations assuming that the average child is on his or her genetic potential growth path and has a weight assumed to be optimal for health and various mental and physical capabilities (Svedberg, 1991). It is controversial whether these norms should be applied to all populations. The problem is overcome by using norms derived from the local population from amongst a well-fed group. But if gender inequality already exists in such a group use of these norms would result in omission errors (Harriss-White, 1997). Further, when age is wrongly reported such norms give misleading results — for example, where women lie about the age of a daughter saying she is younger (as often is supposed to be the case in South Asia), shortfalls could pass unnoticed.

---

25. Height for age is a measure of stunting and if low, indicates chronic growth retardation; weight for height is a measure of wasting and if low indicates recent or 'acute' growth retardation; weight for age is a measure of overall nutritional status and indicates both long-term and recent growth retardation: if low it is referred to as 'underweight'.

Opinions vary on the choice of the 'cut-off' point (Svedberg, 1991) below which the individual is classified as undernourished. For example with regard to height for age, cut-off points vary from 10 per cent and two standard deviations below the median reference height to below the fifth decile. Setting the cut-off close to the reference median would give high commission and low omission errors and vice versa. Mora (1984) showed that the proportion of children in a sample from Columbia that were classified as wasted or stunted was almost twice as big depending on the cut-off point used (cited in Svedberg, 1991).

- *Adaptation.* The issue of adaptation is still unresolved. Svedberg (1991) questions whether a low anthropometric score is a necessary and/or sufficient condition to label an individual as undernourished. If a child reacts to nutritional stress first by reducing physical activity below a critical level, the child could be undernourished although anthropometric indicators remain normal. On the other hand, if food intake is lowered, the body could adapt in a number of ways (physiologically, behaviourally and metabolically) with costless adjustments to body size. While it is accepted that such adjustments cannot proceed indefinitely, there is no agreement about the crucial cut-off point below which adjustment impairs health (Svedberg, 1991). Rajivan (1996), however, suggests that even if adaptation occurs to an extent up to which it is not harmful, the fact of adaptation (which would be reflected in the anthropometric measurements) can itself be considered as indicating some underlying stress.

- *Failure to capture extreme bias.* Anthropometric measurements are affected by nutrition as well as the 'public health' environment, the prevalence of infections and the availability of health care. Some studies reveal a lack of overlap in gender differentials in anthropometry with those in mortality, such as Ahmad and Morduch (1993), investigating data for Bangladesh, and Basu (1992) for Northern India (both cited in Klasen, 1996a). In both studies, excess female mortality was identified, but this was not reflected in anthropometric indicators. Similarly for Nepal, with a sex ratio favouring males, Martorell et al. (1984) were unable to identify a difference between the sexes in the degree of growth retardation. It is hypothesized that anthropometric surveys could have a selective bias as severely undernourished children could have died and thus would be omitted from survey (Klasen, 1996a).

Given these limitations of anthropometric indicators, studies for populations from the same region give contradictory findings. In Chen's (1982) study in Bangladesh on children under 5, about 14 per cent of the girls showed severe malnourishment (in the weight for age indicator) compared with about 5 per cent of the boys, and 60 per cent of the girls were moderately malnourished compared with about 55 per cent of the boys. By contrast, Abdullah's (1983) longitudinal study, also in Bangladesh but on a smaller sample, gave no clear gender differentials in anthropometric indicators for this age group. In fact, socio-economic factors were found to be more important than gender in determining nutritional status (cited in Watson and Harriss, 1985). Findings in sub-Saharan Africa are similarly controversial. In a study of data on more than fifty populations in the region, Svedberg (1991) concluded that females irrespective of their age, were not at a disadvantage *vis-à-vis* males in anthropometric status. Klasen (1996a), however, questions this evidence and presents data showing an anti-female trend.[26]

Despite their limitations, anthropometric measurements have been used frequently by international agencies as well as national governments. In comparison to intake indicators, they have the advantage of direct measurement on individuals and do not rely on recall or self-reporting. Intrahousehold differences in the nutritional status of individuals, for example, between males and females, can also be assessed. They ascertain joint outcomes of nutrition and health functionings. They can thus easily proxy for morbidity indicators which are numerous, unreliable and difficult to obtain. Once genetic factors are controlled for (by using the appropriate norms) and standardized cut-off points used, these indicators are potentially quite sensitive and reliable (Rajivan, 1996). Outcome measures, however, require more skill to collect than, for example, census enumeration data and mortality statistics, and are thus more costly. A number of countries do nevertheless have data from development programmes directed specifically towards health and nutrition intervention, in which anthropometric measures are collected regularly for young children.

BEING EDUCATED

An extensive literature review has shown us that micro-level research concentrates first on the relevance of formal education to the daily lives of people and second on the causes of low overall literacy as well as causes of gender differentials. Since micro-level studies do not investigate the issue of gender sensitivity of different indicators of education, the discussion here is forced to draw largely on UNESCO's national level investigations. Indicators of education are broadly divided into two groups: indicators of access or participation and indicators of content and purposes (UNESCO, 1995).[27]

26. Controversies on the findings due to problems with norms and interpretations are well-highlighted in the published correspondence between Klasen (1996a and 1996b) and Svedberg (1996).
27. Information provided by *indices* of these indicators of 'being educated' is more transparent, compared to *percentage* values which can be deceptive (Ziarati and Lakin, 1994).

Indicators of Access

These are concerned with access to education from basic literacy up to tertiary education and are of great relevance to developing countries where access is often unequal even at primary levels. Indicators of access are subdivided into stock variables (adult literacy, mean years of schooling) and flow variables (enrolment and drop-out ratios).

Stock Variables

Stock variables give information about the older members of the population. 'Adult literacy' refers to persons (15 years and above) who can, with understanding, read and write a short simple statement on everyday life (illiteracy refers to those in this age group who cannot). Few other indicators are capable of capturing as decisively imbalances in the status of men and women as does this simple measure (UNESCO, 1995). The literacy rate of women is significantly lower than that of men in sixty-six countries (a third of the membership of the United Nations). Literacy rates have, however, attracted criticism on a number of grounds. First, the definition does not spell out either the 'simplicity' of the text or the degree of 'understanding' being sought (Stromquist, 1997). Second, if literacy is defined only with respect to major national languages, it can result in under-estimation (King and Hill, 1993). Third, literacy rates are criticized for conventionally being self-reported rather than proved through testing. Fourth, in rare cases when tests are deployed, they have to be administered individually, making the procedure for assessing literacy time consuming and expensive. Finally, anthropologists and social psychologists question the polarization into literate/illiterate people given the 'wide variation in the way literacy is used, perceived and mastered' (Stromquist, 1997: 5).

The variable 'mean years of schooling' (average number of years of schooling received per person aged twenty-five and over) overcomes some of these problems. Yet, both these stock variables reflect past investment and access to education. Recent progress is better captured by looking at changes over time in gender differentials as revealed by flow variables. This is particularly important in developing countries where younger age cohorts constitute a larger proportion of the population.

Flow Variables

These include gross enrolment, net enrolment and drop-out ratios at the primary, secondary and tertiary levels. The gross enrolment ratio (GER) for any level is the total enrolment in that level, regardless of age, divided by the population of the age-group which officially corresponds to that level. The

Figure 2. Indicators of 'Being Educated'

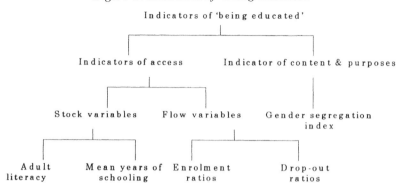

net enrolment ratio only includes enrolment for the age-group corresponding to the official age group for that level. GERs may be misleading compared to net enrolment ratios, especially in developing countries where repetition rates are high. Consider the hypothetical case of a country with a primary GER of 100 per cent and a repetition rate of 12 per cent. The 12 per cent is most likely to also be the percentage of over-age enrolment. A GER of 100 here means that around 12 per cent of children of primary age would not be enrolled in school. GERs can therefore mask the extent of lack of access to education. In practice however, despite this drawback, gross rates are used more commonly than net rates (reasons for this are discussed by Colclough and Lewin, 1993).[28]

The female/male participation ratio, which compares female and male gross enrolment (i.e. the female gross enrolment ratio divided by the male gross enrolment ratio) is often used to assess the gender gap (UNESCO, 1995). It can be calculated at the primary level in countries which have not yet achieved universal primary education. In those that have, participation ratios at the secondary level can be utilized. There is some concern that participation ratios could be misleading. First, in regions where a substantial number of girls are educated at home as in the case of élite women, or at home or in monastery and temple schools for religious reasons, there may be an underestimation of female participation (Bowman and Anderson, 1982). Second, in countries which have compulsory laws with regard to primary school enrolment, enrolments do not invariably imply attendance (Naik, 1982). For example if girls have to miss school more often than boys in order to do household-reproductive work or cannot give as much time as boys to their homework after school for the same reason, this means they have less

---

28. To our knowledge there are no micro-level studies investigating the extent of difference in developing countries between gross and net ratios. In developed countries, the two ratios largely have the same value.

access. Indices of such subtle measures of access which are unaddressed by enrolment ratios can be measured by the proportion that repeat a grade or drop-out (Bowman and Anderson, 1982). The extent of repetition/drop-out can be difficult to quantify if record keeping at schools is poor. In order to assess the relative reliability of indicators (enrolment or drop-out) of the gender gap, UNESCO (1995) conducted a study using two indices, the school life expectancy and the school survival expectancy.[29] It was concluded that the main policy challenge in most of the poorest countries was less one of ensuring the retention of girls once in school than of increasing access by designing ways and means of encouraging parents to send girls to school in the first place. Hyde (1993) provides evidence suggesting that girls have a low mean educational attainment in sub-Saharan Africa due to lower enrolment as well as high wastage (i.e. repetition and drop-out rates). In Bangladesh, drop-out rates for girls were found to be higher than for boys at all levels (Subbarao et al., 1994). Similar evidence across regions has been found in country-specific studies (Herz et al., 1991, cited by Subbarao et al., 1994). The conclusions at the global and national levels need to be further refined by micro-level studies explicitly investigating the reliability of enrolment ratios versus drop-out ratios in capturing gender differentials. Unfortunately most work investigating this question has been conceptual rather than empirical.

Some studies also suggest caution when drawing conclusions about the narrowing of the gender gap based on any of the above indicators of access. Weis (1981) showed that although females in Ghana were proportionally better represented in schools in 1974 than in the 1960s, 57 per cent of the male sample attended high status schools, while less than 14 per cent of females attended schools of a comparable quality. Similar findings were reported for Kenya by Eishwani (1982, cited by Hyde, 1993). These studies, although dated, make an important general point. Since students from high status schools disproportionately occupy higher places in the economy, mere access to education in low quality schools may not increase the social mobility of girls or rectify economic occupational discrimination. A related issue is that of gender differentials in the various subject-fields of education.

Indicators of Content and Purposes

In most countries in South Asia and sub-Saharan Africa, gender gaps in education at the primary and secondary levels which favour males, widen at

---

29. School life expectancy is defined as the total number of years of schooling which the child can expect to receive in the future, assuming that the probability of his or her being enrolled in school at any particular future age is equal to the current enrolment ratio for that age (UNESCO, 1995). The school survival expectancy is basically the school life expectancy for those persons *already in school*.

the tertiary level. In many Latin American/Caribbean countries, however, there are no gaps at any level. In some instances where gaps exist, enrolments favour females at secondary and tertiary levels. While the main reason for this phenomenon in some Southern African countries (Botswana, Lesotho, Namibia and South Africa) is thought to be early school-leaving and the migration of boys to search for work in mines and commercial agriculture, there is no ready explanation for Latin American and Caribbean countries or countries in other regions like Sri Lanka, the Philippines and Gulf countries like Qatar and United Arab Emirates. In most of these countries, however, as elsewhere, women are concentrated in particular subject areas, typically humanities, education and health sciences.

Gender differences in the subjects studied appear at the secondary level and become more pronounced at post-secondary and higher levels (UNESCO, 1995). This phenomenon is common to developing as well as industrial countries.[30] Every country for which data are available to UNESCO, shows a female share of enrolment in the natural sciences, engineering and agriculture that is less than the female share of total enrolment in all fields. The opposite tendency is apparent in the humanities.

To quantify this, UNESCO developed the Gender Segregation Index (statistical notes, UNESCO, 1995). This gives the percentage of persons who would need to change their fields of study for a 'balanced' distribution of the sexes among the fields to be achieved (that is, one where the ratio of females to males is the same in all fields). Low percentages indicate a low degree of segregation or gender-specific specialization. Conversely high percentages indicate a high degree of segregation of the sexes. Calculation of the index for Bangladesh indicated that only 1 per cent of those enrolled in tertiary level education would need to change the field of study, while the corresponding figure for Finland was 23 per cent. This suggests that there is less

---

30. A number of reasons is responsible for the gender segregation in fields of study. In some cases there may be actual restriction of opportunities offered by the education system for access to particular subjects. In others social convention may constrain the supply of female students; possibly a combination of both. Further perceptions of the compatibility of the careers based on different subjects with marriage, household responsibilities and child-rearing are important in girls' attitudes and motivations towards different fields of study. Even in industrial countries women retain the primary responsibility for child care and household management. This affects the kind of employment they are willing to accept and are likely to be offered. Therefore expectations and preferences concerning the nature of future employment are likely to influence the choice of fields girls make at the tertiary level (UNESCO, 1995). Differences in ability (whether females are better suited to particular fields and similarly in case of males), have been raised as a possibility. There are, however, a number of problems with assessment which is widely open to prejudice and misunderstanding (detailed in UNESCO, 1995).

   Given social conventions and certain perceptions, the scope for disagreements when translating a differential in higher education enrolment and segregation in education subjects, into a differential in well-being, could be greater than for differentials in 'being healthy', 'being nourished' or for 'being educated' at the primary or secondary level.

gender segregation in higher education in the former than the latter. But the indicator conceals the fact that there are proportionately fewer females in higher education (16 per cent of total students) in Bangladesh. The proportion of females in the different fields is close to the overall percentage. In Finland, however, females are more proportionally represented in higher education but under-represented in certain fields (for example natural sciences, engineering, and agriculture). To obtain a full picture therefore, differential tertiary enrolment rates must be assessed together with the Gender Segregation Index. To our knowledge, micro-level studies investigating the reliability of this index as an indicator of gender gaps have yet to be undertaken.

COMPOSITE ASSESSMENT

While well-being in each functioning can be assessed by separate indicators as discussed above, efforts have been made to identify a single indicator capable by itself of reflecting overall social development (social development is assumed to map on to well-being). Such an indicator would have great practical value. For example, consider countries where financial and other constraints result in limited data collection. A single reliable indicator which would allow the monitoring of changes in other unobserved sectors would be of great benefit. Yet, using a single indicator of one sector (or functioning) as a proxy for others can be open to misinterpretation (McGranahan et al., 1985a). Sub-Saharan countries show a balanced FMR, but the region still has the highest gender gap in education from primary levels upwards. Further, correlations between indicators which may hold good in one region, may not do so in others. Besides, information from single functionings may be inadequate as a representative of over-all well-being (even measures like income/consumption are considered aggregations; see Lipton and Ravallion, 1995). In the absence of a single universal proxy indicator, efforts have been made to develop a composite index which is an aggregation of indicators of key dimensions of development. The construction of such composite indices, however, first requires the dimensions or functionings represented to be in a large enough number to provide comprehensive information but few enough to allow easy understanding. Value judgements have therefore to be made of the dimensions considered most important. Second, having selected the dimensions, a further act of subjective judgement may be involved in selecting the indicator(s) to represent the dimension. Third, criticisms have been made about the use of average values of the indicator over a group. The use of values which take into account distributional differences has been suggested. Fourth, the question of the weights to be attached to each is highly contentious. Weights need to take into account the 'presumed relative importance of the component represented by the statistical indicator' as well as 'weighting in terms of the technical adequacy of the indicator and the quality of the data available for it' (McGranahan et al., 1985b: 297). Fifth, changes in all dimensions of development will not always move in the same direction as indicated by the composite index. Composite indices have thus been criticized for 'concealing more than they reveal'. Despite these criticisms, such indices are much like averages over a range of variables and play a role in general assessment before exploring particular components. They have been used frequently for preliminary broad brush comparisons in global analyses by the UN and its agencies prior to focusing on particular regions or countries. Further, composite indices constructed for specific purposes (rather than to encapsulate socio-economic development) are valuable tools. For example, the Human Development Index and the Physical Quality of Life Index are primarily intended to draw attention to the fact that comparisons of countries based solely on GNP do not take into account other aspects of human development.

We concentrate on composite indices (composed of conventional indicators) that explore the issue of gender inequality, viz. the Gender-related Development Index (and its precursor the Human Development Index) and the Physical Quality of Life Index (PQLI). The other composite index relevant to this issue is the Gender Empowerment Measure. The conceptualization of empowerment and the scope, indeterminacy and the interpretation of its measurable indicators are discussed elsewhere in this volume by Kabeer.

The Human and Gender-related Development Indices

The Human Development Index (HDI) was designed by the United Nations Development Programme (UNDP) to focus on three essential dimensions of human life: longevity (or 'being healthy'), measured using the indicator life expectancy at birth; knowledge (or 'being educated'), measured by the indicators adult literacy and average primary, secondary and tertiary enrolment; and access to resources to enable a decent living standard, measured using the indicator 'per capita income' adjusted for purchasing power parity (PPP). Normalized values for indicators are obtained and averaged to give the HDI. This is thus considered a reflection of the combined well-being in the dimensions assessed and gives a value on a scale between one (maximum development) and zero (minimum). The Gender-related Development Index (GDI) which is of particular interest to this chapter is a special type of HDI which takes note of inequalities between any two groups. The two groups considered here are male and female (the same index could, however, be used to assess the inequalities between groups of different castes, different ethnicity, etc.). Details on the differences in the calculations to obtain HDI and GDI are given in Saith and Harriss-White (1998).

Deficiencies of data used to construct such indices include, amongst others, the use of projections and estimates rather than real data, extrapolation from household/small surveys to the national level and comparisons of non-comparable national indicators (Barraclough, 1997).[31] Further, the HDI and GDI have been designed for international comparisons between countries.[32] For the purpose of using the GDI specifically for comparisons within and between developing countries, we examine adaptations pertaining to each component of the index below. General criticisms pertaining to the conceptual and methodological aspects of HDI, some of which are relevant to the GDI, have been made by McGillivray (1991), McGillivray and White (1993), and Srinivasan (1994), and are also presented in a separate section in the Human Development Report (UNDP, 1993) to which readers are referred.

- *Longevity*: This component (reflecting the functioning 'being healthy') is presently measured by life expectancy which was selected over other suggestions such as 'infant mortality rate' and 'potential lifetime' (Desai, 1990). This was because the 'IMR' and 'potential lifetime' were unable to distinguish between developed industrial countries. However, for our purpose of assessing well-being within and amongst developing countries, instead of 'life expectancy', an indicator reflecting mortality rates in younger age groups would be more appropriate. Further, 'life expectancy at birth' has little or no value as a measure of gender differentials. As discussed above, 'FMR04' and 'FMR59' may be the more appropriate gender-sensitive indicators of the functioning 'being healthy' that life expectancy proposes to capture.
- *Knowledge*: This component (reflecting the functioning 'being educated') is measured by combining the indicators 'adult literacy' (2/3 weight) and 'mean primary, secondary and tertiary enrolment' (1/3 weight). It evolved from the first Human Development Report in 1990 in which 'adult literacy' (the percentage of literate people aged above 15) was used (UNDP, 1990). Since the adult literacy rate was unable to distinguish between industrial countries, the 'mean years of schooling' (average number of years of schooling received per person aged 25 and over) was added. However, since a majority of the population in developing countries is under 15, these stock variables were unable to capture the *flow* of educational attainment (Smith, 1992 cited by UNDP, 1993). Subsequently 'mean years of schooling' was replaced by 'average primary, secondary and tertiary enrolment'. However, the 1/3 weightage given to the average enrolment measure in the GDI makes it subordinate to the adult literacy measure. It would be worth investigating empirically

31. Murray (1994) in fact suggests that by giving a false impression of the availability of information in important spheres in all countries, the HDI may even devalue efforts towards obtaining 'real and timely' information from developing countries.
32. UNDP, 1993: Technical note 2, Table 2.4 makes some suggestions for using different indicators to measure the three dimensions of the HDI for countries at similar stages (low, medium or high) of human development.

whether a reversal of weights — such that 'adult literacy' accounts for 1/3 and the 'average enrolment' for 2/3 — would be more appropriate for use in developing countries.

• *Income*: For the purposes of the GDI, the shares of earned income for women and men are derived by calculating their wage as a ratio to the average national wage and multiplying this ratio by their shares of the labour force. Any differential in the income indicator therefore relies on two differentials: the ratio of female wages to male wages and the female to male ratio of the labour force. The income indicator does not aim to reflect women's access to income for consumption or other uses, as women who earn money may not have any control over it within the household. In other cases women who do not earn income could, in principle, control what is earned by male members of the household. Rather, the inclusion of the income variable is justified as a reflection of a family member's earning power, which is argued to be an important factor in economic recognition, independence and reward (UNDP, 1995).[33]

Methodologically, the income component has many shortcomings, particularly with regard to the data used. These are admitted by UNDP (1995). For example it is assumed that gender differentials in wages in the agricultural sector are similar to those in the non-agricultural sector. Also, income disparities based on non-labour resources, such as gendered control over land or physical capital have been excluded due to lack of data. Some methodological problems which arise when the GDI is constructed at sub-national levels are discussed by Prabhu et al. (1996). These particularly concern difficulties encountered in measuring female workforce participation rates. Using five different measures of proportional income shares of women, for fifteen Indian states, a variety of rankings of gender-related income attainment of GDI were obtained.

Criticizing the conceptual basis and interpretation of the income component (as reflecting a family member's earning power), Prabhu et al. express doubts about the empowering role of income in third world economies. They suggest that while the work burden is very high for low caste and tribal women, their participation in the work force 'is more an indication of their poor economic status than their empowerment' (Prabhu et al., 1996: WS-74). The income indicator has the potential in theory to play a role in providing inherent information over and above its current intent of reflecting the earning power of women. For example, given equal productivity and holding all other aspects of

---

33. The issue here therefore is of including income from waged work. Suggestions (for example Hirway and Mahadevia, 1996 and Prabhu et al., 1996) pertaining to the inclusion of unpaid work are important. The information captured by such an indicator would, however, be different to that which the 'earnings' are expected to capture.

employment constant, a lower wage rate for women for jobs standardized for skill is a clear indicator of overt discrimination. But the wage ratio part of the income indicator in the GDI is not standardized for skill, making it ambiguous to interpret. An exercise we consider worth pursuing is to supplement an income standardized for skill with a 'drudgery' indicator which captures the differential in the number of hours (paid and unpaid) that males and females work. The inherent information that such 'time allocation' data provides could be seen as important in itself, rather than as is conventionally proposed, to reflect the 'true' economic contributions of males and females. In groups where differentials exist in the number of hours of work (*intensity of work being similar*), a translation into differentials in well-being would be apparent. Taking the work intensity into consideration is essential for correct interpretation, as individuals involved in high energy intensive work may be forced to work for fewer hours and have longer periods of rest to recover than somebody involved in low energy intensive work (Jackson and Palmer-Jones, this volume). Problems with the collection of data could prove to be major impediments, although Jain (1996) conducted a study measuring time allocation at the state as well as village level in Rajasthan and West Bengal in India and suggests that the collection of such data is not impossible. Standardizing for intensity of work would, however, require the duration and nature of work to be incorporated into a single value which would take account of differences in the type of work.

The indicators currently used to construct the GDI thus *reduce* its ability to reflect gender inequality in developing countries. Further, the GDI value gives information about the level of overall development (HDI) discounted for gender inequality. To assess the extent of gender inequality alone, it is misleading to look at the GDI value directly. This Gender Inequality Value can be obtained by the following formula: [(HDI-GDI)/HDI] × 100 (UNDP, 1995). For example take the case of Tanzania which has a GDI value of 0.352, on the zero to one scale (UNDP, 1997). It would be wrong to conclude from this that the country has a large gender differential due to its low GDI value. Its HDI value is 0.357 and Gender Inequality Value calculated following the formula mentioned above is 1.4 per cent. Compare this with Ireland with a 'high' GDI value of 0.851 and a 'high' HDI value of 0.929. Despite higher overall development, Ireland's Gender Inequality Value is 8.4 per cent reflecting a higher gender differential in the combined functionings of 'being healthy' and 'being educated' together with income. Other countries which are high in the scale of human development (high HDI) but show a high gender differential (i.e. low Gender Inequality rank) include, for example, middle Eastern countries like Bahrain, United Arab Emirates and Qatar (see Table 3 in Saith and Harriss-White, 1998). On further examination, however, it is apparent that quite often it is the female income component of the GDI in these countries which is very low and which in turn lowers the GDI value and gives the country a poor gender inequality rank. For example, in both United Arab Emirates and Qatar, female achievements are higher than male in life expectancy as well as in education, but the percentage of female and male contributions to income are about 10 per cent and 90 per cent respectively in both countries. Countries with such high differentials in the income component could thus have ranks indicating high overall inequality. Such findings question the validity of the normative assumptions made in the GDI that differentials in the income (unstandardized for skill) reflect inequality or discrimination. They also indicate the possibility that though gender equality may be achieved in basic functioning vectors, there could be inequality in taking advantage of other opportunities (like economic and political participation, decision making power and control over economic resources). The gender empowerment measure (GEM) has been formulated by the UNDP to assess such inequalities (UNDP, 1995). A discussion of issues related to autonomy and power is presented by Kabeer (this volume).

The Physical Quality of Life Index

The PQLI is a composite of infant mortality rate (to reflect social improvements in the home, especially women's well-being), life expectancy at age one (to reflect improvements in the external environment), and literacy (which crudely assesses the extent to which people can participate in shaping their environment). Although the PQLI was not constructed specifically to assess gender differentials, it lends itself easily to this task as its component indicators can be assessed on individuals. It was designed by Morris in 1979 for use alongside GNP, but as an explicit measure of social performance. The word 'Physical' is used to indicate the narrowness of the target the index aims to measure. Although retrospectively these component indicators of PQLI have been recognized to assess 'basic functionings', they were originally considered simply as reflectors of social performance, and illustrate how the study of functioning is tyrannized by data availability.

Morris proposed using the index to assess gender differentials in India in the 1980s (Morris, 1996).[34] It was suggested that the behaviour of the PQLI (and its components) between 1961 and 1971 would provide evidence of changes in the social condition of women in India, at least as characterized by the index, and allow an assessment of the impact of Indian development policies. Using data from the Registrar General of India, for the period

---

34. Each of the three component indicators of the PQLI — infant mortality rate, life expectancy at age one and literacy — has equal weight and is first indexed on a 0 to 100 scale. 0 represents an internationally defined 'worst' performance and 100 the 'best'. The PQLI is obtained by averaging the normalized value for each indicator.

1961–71, male and female PQLI values were calculated. The study demonstrated that while the absolute PQLI values for both males and females had improved during the decade, the standing of women relative to men had worsened. Unpacking the index revealed this to be mainly due to a superior decline in the male infant mortality rate compared to female. Literacy for the period for females had improved at exactly the same pace and female life expectancy had improved at a somewhat faster rate than for males.

The unreliability of each of the components of the PQLI, viz. IMR, life expectancy and literacy in assessing gender differentials has already been discussed above. Furthermore, the extent to which the information on gender bias obtained by two indicators of the same functioning (being healthy) overlaps, possibly rendering one redundant, would be worth assessing.[35] Notwithstanding the need to alter the component indicators of the PQLI if it is to be used to assess gender differentials, the approach itself is quite simple and potentially useful for preliminary comparative analysis and for allowing a separate assessment of the impact of policies on male and female well-being.

Although composite indices have several limitations, they may have selective uses. Ultimately the purpose of assessment should be used to guide the component indicators to be included in the composite index.

CONCLUSION

We have attempted to evaluate and discuss the ability of a large number of indicators to identify reliably gender differentials in well-being. Well-being was assessed within the functionings approach developed by Sen. We looked at indicators relating to the elementary functionings of 'being healthy', 'being nourished' and 'being educated', together with certain composite indices.

Of the indicators of 'being healthy' reviewed here, the most useful from the perspective of gender disadvantage appears to be the disaggregated juvenile sex ratio, the FMR04 and FMR59. These age-specific FMRs are relatively easily measurable, ought to be made available by census authorities and are reliable. By contrast, the morbidity and nutrition outcome indicators suffer methodological and conceptual problems which render them unreliable. Anthropometric measures are potentially useful, given appropriate norms

---

35. When the PQLI was originally designed for international comparisons, overall IMR was included to reflect social conditions in the home, especially women's well-being and life expectancy at age one to reflect the external environment. In the context of assessing gender differences, however, the male and female IMRs are used as indicators of gender differential mortality as is the life expectancy indicator. A re-evaluation of the extent to which each of these indicators reliably reflects gender differences in mortality in developing countries and an assessment of the extent of overlap of information provided, would be appropriate.

and standardized cut-off points and provided their limitations are borne in mind when interpreting the findings. While the marginal cost of obtaining additional information on FMRs from censuses is low, obtaining representative anthropometric measures is relatively more expensive. Enrolment ratios appear to be useful indicators of 'being educated' in developing countries. Micro-level studies comparing enrolment and drop-out ratios, however, are most urgently required to identify the variables best able to reflect gender gaps in education. The Gender Segregation Index has the capacity to reveal gender differences in the subject-fields of education, in countries with no gender gaps in primary, secondary and tertiary education.

Assessing indicators of a single functioning as with each of the indicator groups above, may give the false impression of equality if there is inequality in other functionings. In sub-Saharan Africa, for example, some countries may show a balanced FMR but large gender gaps in enrolment rates. As it is evident that the set of indicators of disadvantage does not generate a single or even a few reliable proxies, in order to obtain a reliable picture of gender differentials at national and sub-national levels, it may be necessary to have a check list of gender inequality indicators of different functionings, which need analysis one by one.

Currently there is a trend to compress multiple elements of a functioning vector into composite indices. While this approach has the merit of reflecting the multiple dimensions of gender inequalities, it has been criticized for raising more problems than it solves. None the less, composite indicators constructed with specific purposes in mind can be useful and have proven helpful for preliminary comparisons in global analyses. Indicators like the GDI (and the gender inequality rank derived from it) and the PQLI have some merit in drawing comparisons between countries away from comparisons based solely on income towards including other essential aspects of development. They are also useful within countries for preliminary comparisons of regions and assessments of the impact of policy. They could have the additional advantage over individual indicators of drawing attention to the existence of gender inequality on a broad plane, thus promoting policies with multiple prongs to tackle gender inequality, rather than concentrating on single functionings. The PQLI and GDI may, however, need some adaptations if they are to be used for assessing and comparing development taking into account gender gaps, specifically in developing countries in which a larger proportion of the population belongs to younger age groups. Some adaptations with respect to the GDI which we suggest as being worthy of further investigation are: (a) replacement of life expectancy at birth in an appropriate manner by age-specific disaggregated FMRs (for the under-10 age group), to yield information about differentials in 'being healthy'; (b) the reversal of weights currently attached to the adult literacy and average enrolment components of the education indicator, such that the former has a lesser weight than the latter; (c) use of the income indicator to provide inherent information over and above that provided by the functionings, by standardizing for skills; (d) supplementation of the income indicator with a 'drudgery' indicator, i.e. the number of hours of work (paid or unpaid) by men and women ensuring that intensity of work is taken into account.

Implications for Policy and for Research

There is a strong case for investing in the improvement of existing indicators in order to make them both systematic and appropriate to developing countries (rather than investing in the development of new composite indices) given that the marginal cost of adding questions to national decennial censuses and to intermediate, census style surveys would be expected to be low. The analytical returns, should census authorities make gender differentiated juvenile mortality data available in as disaggregated a form as possible (by region, income/property, by caste/ethnic and religious groups) especially for the age groups 0–4 and 5–9, would be very rich. While data for educational enrolment ratios appear satisfactory, systematic data on other flow variables (especially drop-out rates) and gender segregation in educational fields are desirable. Sample time allocation data, if made a regular feature of census data collection, would provide useful information for the design of a 'drudgery' indicator. Further, gender disaggregated data needs to be analysed at different levels — class, region, ethnicity, caste and others, as appropriate. It would then be possible to have a more comprehensive picture of forms and sites of gender disadvantage.

Second, micro-level research in education is presently at the pre-indicator stage. Since existing in-depth case study research is both fragmented and not addressed to the identification or creation of appropriate indicators, new micro-level studies comparing the ability of different flow variables (especially enrolment versus drop-out ratios) to capture reliably gender differentials in access to education need to be undertaken. Appropriate studies to obtain unbiased norms and a consensus on cut-off points would contribute towards rendering results of anthropometric measures, easier to interpret and more reliable.

Lastly, the comparative use of indicators of well-being, while necessary for revealing bias, discloses nothing about their social meanings or about the social processes giving rise to gender differentials. In the absence of information on causality, policies can easily be restricted to specific interventions in the areas revealed by indicators to show gender difference, to the neglect of underlying determinants. Such policies address symptoms rather than causes. Indicators are *necessary* to direct interventions but they are not *sufficient*. If supplemented with information on causality and on the policy process, they may serve as a powerful basis for policy action. It is extremely important therefore to conduct research into the social processes of discrimination and the politics of access, control, agency and empowerment. Little can be assumed about gendered relations of disadvantage. They require empirical specification which in turn requires micro-level research. Yet, while such research is useful *per se* for its contribution to understanding micro-level evidence about gender relations, it is vulnerable to neglect (on grounds of lack of representativity) by policy makers. It is therefore crucial that such research is also supplied to other actors in the policy making process (for example the media, activist lobbies, political parties). At the same time the support and legitimization by international aid agencies and by the United Nations, both for the authority and value of a range of specific indicators and for the detailed insights from analyses of process and access, would best advance the use of indicators out of the ghettos of ranking and comparison and into the arenas of policy.

ACKNOWLEDGEMENTS

A longer version of this chapter has been published as UNRISD Discussion Paper 95 (September 1998). We are grateful to Shahra Razavi, other participants of the CDS/UNRISD/UNDP workshop on 'Gender, Poverty and Well-being: Indicators and Strategies', and the referees of *Development and Change* for their valuable comments. Thanks are due to Ashwin Srinivasan for his help with an understanding of the mathematics of the functionings approach. A literature review related to poverty was carried out under a Department for International Development, Government of UK, project. Ruhi Saith is currently supported by a Wingate scholarship.

REFERENCES

Abdullah, M. (1983) 'Dimensions of Intrahousehold Food and Nutrient Allocation: A Study of a Bangladesh Village', PhD Thesis, London School of Hygiene and Tropical Medicine, London.
Agnihotri, S. (1996) 'Juvenile Sex Ratios in India: A Disaggregated Analysis', *Economic and Political Weekly* 31(52): 3369–82.
Agnihotri, S. (1997) 'Sex Ratio Imbalances in India — A Disaggregated Analysis', PhD Thesis, University of East Anglia, Norwich.
Ahmad, A. and J. Morduch (1993) 'Identifying Sex Bias in the Allocation of Household Resources: Evidence from Linked Household Surveys from Bangladesh'. Boston, MA: Harvard University (mimeo).
Bardhan, K. (1974) 'On Life and Death Questions', *Economic and Political Weekly* Special Number, 9 (32,33,34): 1293–304.
Barraclough, S. (1997) 'Comments on Human Development Report (1995, 1996 and 1997)', Geneva: UNRISD (mimeo).
Baster, N. and W. Scott (1969) *Levels of Living and Economic Growth: A Comparative Study of Six Countries, 1950–1965.* UNRISD: Geneva.
Basu, A. M. (1992) *Culture, the Status of Women, and Demographic Behaviour.* Oxford: Clarendon Press.
Behrman, J. (1988) 'Intrahousehold Allocation of Nutrients in Rural India: Are Boys Favoured? Do Parents Exhibit Inequality Aversion?', *Oxford Economic Papers* 40(1): 32–54.
Behrman, J. and A. Deolalikar (1989) 'Seasonal Demands for Nutrient Intakes and Health Status in Rural South India', in D. Sahn (ed.) *Seasonal Variability in Third World Agriculture: The Consequences for Food Security*, pp. 66–78. Baltimore, MD: Johns Hopkins University Press for the International Food Policy Research Institute.

Behrman, J. and A. Deolalikar (1990) 'The Intrahousehold Demand for Nutrients in Rural South India: Individual Estimates, Fixed Effects, and Permanent Income', *The Journal of Human Resources* 25(4): 665–96.

Bowman, M. J. and C. A. Anderson (1982) 'The Participation of Women in Education in the Third World', in G. P. Kelly and C. M. Elliott (eds) *Women's Education in The Third World: Comparative Perspectives*, pp. 11–30. Albany, NY: State University of New York Press.

Caldwell, P. and J. Caldwell (1987) 'Where there is a Narrower Gap between Female and Male Situations: Lessons from South India and Sri Lanka', chapter prepared for workshop on Differentials in Mortality and Health Care in South Asia, BAMANEH/SSRC Dhaka (June).

Chatterjee, M. (1990) 'Indian Women: Their Health and Economic Productivity', World Bank Discussion Paper No. 109. Washington, DC: World Bank.

Chen, L. C. (1982) 'Where Have the Women Gone?', *Economic and Political Weekly* 17(10): 365–72.

Chen, L., E. Huq, and S. D'Souza (1981) 'Sex Bias in the Family Allocation of Food and Health Care in Rural Bangladesh', *Population and Development Review* 7(1): 55–70.

Chunkath, S. R. and V. Athreya (1997) 'Female Infanticide in Tamil Nadu: Some Evidence', *Economic and Political Weekly*, Review of Women's Studies, 32(17): WS 21–8.

Cohen, N. (1987) 'Sex Differences in Blindness and Mortality in the Indian Subcontinent: Some Paradoxes Explained', paper prepared for the workshop on Differentials in Mortality and Health Care in South Asia, BAMANEH/SSRC Dhaka (June).

Colclough, C. and K. W. Lewin (1993) *Educating all the Children — Strategies for Primary Schooling in the South*. Oxford: Clarendon Press.

Dasgupta, M. (1987a) 'Selective Discrimination against Female Children in Rural Punjab, India', *Population and Development Review* 13(1): 77–100.

Dasgupta, M. (1987b) 'The Second Daughter: Sex Differentials in Child Mortality, Nutrition and Health Care in Rural Punjab', paper prepared for the workshop on Differentials in Mortality and Health Care in South Asia, BAMANEH/SSRC Dhaka (June).

Dasgupta, P. (1993) *An Inquiry Into Well-Being and Destitution*. Oxford: Clarendon Press.

Desai, M. (1990) 'Potential Lifetime (PLT): A Proposal for an Index of Social Welfare', in *Redefining Wealth and Progress: New Ways to Measure Economic, Social and Environmental Change, The Caracas Report on Alternative Development Indicators*, pp. 75–9. Indianapolis: Bootstrap Press (2nd edn).

Drewnowski, J. (1966) *Social and Economic Factors in Development*. Geneva: UNRISD.

Dyson, T. and M. Moore (1983) 'On Kinship Structure, Female Autonomy and Demographic Balance', *Population and Development Review* 9(1): 35–60.

Eishwani, G. S. (1982) 'A Study of Women's Access to Higher Education with a Special Reference to Science and Maths Education', Working Paper 500. Nairobi: Kenyatta University College, Bureau of Educational Research.

Erb, S. and B. Harriss-White (1996) 'Outcast from Social Welfare: Adult Disability in Rural South India'. Report to Overseas Development Administration, London and Queen Elizabeth House, Oxford.

George, S., R. Abel and B. Miller (1992) 'Female Infanticide in Rural South India', *Economic and Political Weekly* 27: 1153–6.

Ghai, D., M. Hopkins and D. McGranahan (1988) 'Some Reflections on Human and Social Indicators for Development', UNRISD Discussion Paper No. 6. Geneva: UNRISD.

Granaglia, E. (1996) 'Two Questions to Amartya Sen', *Notizie di Politeia*, special issue, 12: 43–4.

Harriss, B. (1993) 'Differential Female Mortality and Health Care in South Asia', Famine and Society Series, Monograph I. New Delhi: Centre for the Study of Administration of Relief.

Harriss, B. (1995) 'The Intrafamily Distribution of Hunger in South Asia', in J. Dreze, A. Sen and A. Hossein (eds) *The Political Economy of Hunger. Selected Essays*, pp. 224–97. Oxford: Clarendon Press and Oxford University Press, for WIDER (first published 1990).

Harriss-White, B. (1997) 'Gender Bias in Intrahousehold Nutrition in South India: Unpacking Households and the Policy Process', in L. Haddad, J. Hoddinott and H. Alderman (eds) *Intrahousehold Resource Allocation in Developing Countries: Models, Methods and Policy*, pp. 194–212. Baltimore, MD and London: The Johns Hopkins University Press for the International Food Policy Research Institute.

Herz, B., K. Subbarao, M. Habib and L. Raney (1991) 'Letting Girls Learn: Promising Approaches in Primary and Secondary Education'. World Bank Discussion Paper No. 113. Washington, DC: The World Bank.

Hirway, I. and D. Mahadevia (1996) 'Critique of Gender Development Index: Towards an Alternative', *Economic and Political Weekly*, Review of Women's Studies, 31(43): WS 87–96.

Holden, C. (1987) 'Why do Women Live Longer than Men', *Science* 238(4824): 158–60.

Hyde, K. (1993) 'Sub-Saharan Africa' in E. King and M. Hill (eds) *Women's Education in Developing Countries*, pp. 100–35. Baltimore, MD and London: The Johns Hopkins University Press, for the World Bank.

International Labour Organisation (1976) *Employment, Growth and Basic Needs: A One World Problem*. Geneva: ILO.

Jain, D. (1996) 'Valuing Work: Time as a Measure', *Economic and Political Weekly*, Review of Women's Studies, 31(43): WS 46–57.

King, E. and M. Hill (1993) *Women's Education in Developing Countries*. Baltimore, MD and London: The Johns Hopkins University Press, for the World Bank.

Klasen, S. (1996a) 'Nutrition, Health and Mortality in Sub-Saharan Africa: Is there a Gender Bias?', *Journal of Development Studies* 32(6): 913–32.

Klasen, S. (1996b) 'Rejoinder', *Journal of Development Studies* 32(6): 944–8.

Koenig, M. and S. D'Souza (1986) 'Sex Differences in Childhood: Mortality in Rural Bangladesh', *Social Science and Medicine* 22(1): 15–22.

Lipton, M. and M. Ravallion (1995) 'Poverty and Policy', in J. Behrman and T. N. Srinivasan (eds) *Handbook of Development Economics, Volume 3B*, pp. 2551–657. Amsterdam: Elsevier Science BV.

Marmot, M. and J. Mann (1996) 'Epidemiology and Prevention', in D. J. Weatherall, J. G. Ledingham, and D. A. Warrell (eds) *Oxford Textbook of Medicine, Vol. 2*, Section 15.10.1, pp. 2305–18. New York: Oxford University Press.

Martorell, R., J. Leslie and P. Mock (1984) 'Characteristics and Determinants of Child Nutritional Status in Nepal', *American Journal of Clinical Nutrition* 39: 84–6.

McGillivray, M. (1991) 'The Human Development Index: Yet Another Redundant Composite Development Indicator', *World Development* 19(10): 1461–8.

McGillivray, M and H. White (1993) 'Measuring Development: the UNDP's Human Development Index', *Journal of International Development* 5(2): 183–92.

McGranahan, D., D. V Richard-Proust, N. V. Sovani and M. Subramanian (1972) *Contents and Measurement of Socio-economic Development*. New York: Praeger.

McGranahan, D., E. Pizzaro and C. Richard (1985a) 'Relationships between Development Indicators: Correspondence and Correlations', in D. McGranahan, E. Pizzaro and C. Richard *Measurement and Analysis of Socio-Economic Development*, pp. 237–58. Geneva: UNRISD.

McGranahan, D., E. Pizzaro and C. Richard (1985b) 'Development Profiles, Typology and General Indices', in D. McGranahan, E. Pizzaro and C. Richard *Measurement and Analysis of Socio-Economic Development*, pp. 259–302. Geneva: UNRISD.

McNeill, G. (1986) 'Energy Nutrition of Adults in Rural South India', in the Report of UNICEF, the FORD Foundation and ODA, London School of Hygiene and Tropical Medicine, London.

Miller, D. (1981) *The Endangered Sex*. Ithaca, NY: Cornell University Press.

Mora, J. (1984) 'Anthropometry in Prevalence Studies', in J. Brosek and B. Schurch (eds) *Malnutrition and Behaviour: Critical Assessment of Key Issues*. Lausanne: Nestlé Foundation.

Morris, D. M. (1979) *Measuring the Condition of the World's Poor: The Physical Quality of Life Index*. New York: Pergamon.

Morris, D. M. (1996) 'Measuring the Changing Condition of the World's Poor: The Physical Quality of Life Index, 1960–1990', Working Paper 23/24. Providence: Centre for the Comparative Study of Development, Watson Institute for International Studies, Brown University.

Murray, C. L. (1994) 'Development Data Constraints and the Human Development Index', in D. Westendorff and D. Ghai (eds) *Monitoring Social Progress in the 1990s*, pp. 40–64. Aldershot: Avebury for UNRISD.

Naik, C. (1982) 'An Action-Research Project on Universal Primary Education — The Plan and the Process', in G. P. Kelly and C. M. Elliot (eds) *Women's Education in The Third World: Comparative Perspectives*, pp. 152–72. Albany, NY: State University of New York Press.

Padmanabha, P. (1982) 'Mortality in India, a Note on Trends and Implications', *Economic and Political Weekly* 17(32): 1285–90.

Pettigrew, J. (1987) 'The Household and the Community Context of Diarrhoeal Illness Among the Under Twos in Rural Punjab', paper prepared for workshop on Differentials in Mortality and Health Care in South Asia, BAMANEH/SSRC Dhaka (June).

Prabhu, K., P. Sarker and A. Radha (1996) 'Gender-Related Development Index for Indian States, Methodological Issues', *Economic and Political Weekly*, Review of Women's Studies, 31(43): WS 72–9.

Rajivan, A. (1996) 'Measuring of Gender Differences using Anthropometry', *Economic and Political Weekly*, Review of Women's Studies, 31(43), WS 58–62.

Razavi, S. (1996) 'Excess Female Mortality: an Indicator of Female Subordination? A Note Drawing on Village-Level Evidence from South-eastern Iran', *Notizie di Politeia*, special issue, 12(43–4): 79–95.

Razavi, S. (1997) 'From Rags to Riches: Looking at Poverty from a Gender Perspective', *IDS Bulletin* 28(3): 49–62.

Ryan, J., R. Bidinger, R. Prahlad and P. Pushpamma (1984) 'The Determinants of Individual Diets and Nutritional Status in Six Villages of South India'. ICRISAT Research Bulletin 7. Hyderabad: International Crops Research Institute for the Semi-Arid Tropics.

Saith, R. and B. Harriss-White (1998) 'Gender Sensitivity of Well-Being Indicators', UNRISD Discussion Paper No. 95. Geneva: UNRISD.

Seddon, D. (1997) 'The Sex Ratio and Discrimination Against Females in Nepal', draft, work in progress. Norwich: School of Development Studies, University of East Anglia.

Sen, A. (1985) *Commodities and Capabilities*. Amsterdam: Elsevier Science Publishers.

Sen, A. (1995) 'Mortality as an Indicator of Economic Success and Failure', Innocenti Lectures. Florence: UNICEF International Child Development Centre.

Smith, P. (1992) 'Measuring Human Development', University of Southampton (mimeo).

Srinivasan, T. N. (1994) 'Human Development: A New Paradigm or Reinvention of the Wheel?', *American Economic Review* 84(2): 238–43.

Streeten, P., S. Burki, M. Haq, N. Hicks and F. Stewart (1981) *First Things First, Meeting Basic Human Needs in Developing Countries*. New York: Oxford University Press, for the World Bank.

Stromquist, N. P. (1997) *Literacy for Citizenship: Gender and Grassroots Dynamics in Brazil*. Albany, NY: State University of New York Press.

Subbarao, K., L. Raney, H. Dundar and J. Haworth (1994) 'Women in Higher Education', World Bank Discussion Paper No. 244. Washington, DC: The World Bank.

Svedberg, P. (1991) 'Poverty and Undernutrition in Sub-Saharan Africa: Theory, Evidence and Policy'. Monograph Series No. 19. Stockhom: Institute for International Economic Studies, Stockholm University.

Svedberg, P. (1996) 'Gender Biases in Sub-Saharan Africa: Reply and Further Evidence', *The Journal of Development Studies* 32(6): 933–43.

UNDP (1990) *Human Development Report*. New York: Oxford University Press.

UNDP (1993) *Human Development Report*. New York: Oxford University Press.
UNDP (1995) *Human Development Report*. New York: Oxford University Press.
UNDP (1997) *Human Development Report*. New York: Oxford University Press.
UNESCO (1995) *Third World Education Report*. Paris: UNESCO.
Visaria, L. (1988) 'Level, Trends and Determinants of Infant Mortality in India', in A. Jain and
    P. Visaria (eds) *Infant Mortality in India: Differentials and Determinants*, pp. 67–126. Delhi:
    Sage.
Watson, E. and B. Harriss (1985) 'Health, Nutrition and Work: A Review of Relationships of
    Discrimination Against Women in South Asia', Discussion Paper No. 179. Norwich: School
    of Development Studies, University of East Anglia.
Weis, L. (1981) 'Schooling and Patterns of Access in Ghana', *Canadian Journal of African
    Studies* 15(2): 311–22.
Westendorff, D. and D. Ghai (eds) (1994) *Monitoring Social Progress in the 1990s*. Aldershot:
    Avebury, for UNRISD.
Wuttke, W. (1989) 'Sexual Functionings', in R. F. Schmidt and G. Thews (eds) *Human
    Physiology: Part IX*, pp. 774–84. Berlin, Heidelberg and New York: Springer-Verlag.
Ziarati, S. and M. Lakin (1994) *Education for All: Status and Trends 1994*. Education for All
    Secretariat. Paris: UNESCO.

4

Poverty in Transition: An Ethnographic Critique of Household Surveys in Post-Soviet Central Asia

Deniz Kandiyoti

INTRODUCTION

Transition to the market in the former Soviet Union has occasioned an extensive overhaul of the statistical and planning apparatuses inherited from the Soviet period in all the newly independent states, including the republics of Central Asia. The creation of a new informational infrastructure, prompted by the demands of major international donor and lending agencies, appears to be an intrinsic, if little noticed, adjunct of market reforms. Part of the rationale behind these changes is to bring certain indices and measurements (such as definitions of employment, the measurement of prices, living standards and poverty) into line with internationally agreed standards set by bodies such as the ILO, WHO, OECD and the IMF. The data collection tools inherited from the era of central planning (such as the Soviet Union Family Budget Survey) are being revised and modified while, simultaneously, a range of externally funded sample surveys are being carried out (see Falkingham and Micklewright, 1997, for details). The shift from universal welfare provision under the Soviet system to 'targeted' assistance and poverty monitoring also requires the development of new policy tools. These changes are still in their early stages if we consider, for instance, that the Poverty Assessments (PAs) carried out in many countries by the World Bank (see Whitehead and Lockwood, this volume) and the use of Participatory Poverty Assessments (PPAs) have only just started. The same applies to Living Standard Measurement Surveys (LSMS) which are also new to the region. However, the design and implementation of development projects funded by various donor agencies has created a growing demand for social and economic data and the volume of social research conducted in the private and NGO sectors has increased substantially. This has resulted in a proliferation of sample surveys, mainly based on closed-ended questionnaires and relying on quantitative techniques of data analysis. In particular, household surveys have emerged as a prime tool for generating policy relevant information.

An earlier version of this chapter has been published as UNRISD Discussion Paper 106 (April 1999).

The main contention of this chapter is that transition economies present us with specific methodological and conceptual challenges that need to be adequately reflected in research designs. In the absence of an in-depth understanding of the local meanings attached to the categories that are most routinely employed in questionnaires and interview schedules, survey findings can be of limited utility, and may even be quite misleading. This is not to suggest that the sources of error and bias discussed in the remainder of this text are in any way unique to the post-Soviet context. I am arguing, none the less, that the limitations of survey methodologies may become even more acute in settings where there is a serious scarcity of local level case studies that may assist the analysis of socio-economic processes that are generative of new forms of vulnerability. This is particularly pertinent to achieving an understanding of gender-differentiated outcomes of transition since these are embedded in local cultural practices and expectations. The relatively modest compendium of ethnographic and sociological research produced during the Soviet period is not only outdated but the drying-up of research funds since the break-up of the Union has meant that social science research — which was relatively weak in the Central Asian region in the first place — has come to a standstill. This vacuum is now being filled by surveys, mainly commissioned by external donors, in a context where local sociological and anthropological research has ground to a virtual halt.

In what follows, I will argue that surveys may not be the most appropriate research tools in an environment where a host of new and, thus far, uncharted socio-economic processes are producing fundamental alterations in the landscape of social provision, redistribution and employment. These changes are at the root of new forms of poverty which need to be analysed and interpreted in their regionally and culturally-specific contexts. In particular, I will attempt to show how the combination of Soviet categories of 'official' registration, local cultural understandings and recent changes introduced by agrarian reforms may act to foil the best intentioned attempts to obtain meaningful answers to seemingly straightforward questions.

My illustrations will be drawn from a household survey conducted in four villages from two regions of Uzbekistan, Andijan and Kashkadarya, between October 1997 and August 1998.[1] The survey was preceded by in-depth household case studies and detailed observations in order to avoid errors and biases stemming from the lack of adequate qualitative

---

1. The household survey was part of a broader project supported by a grant of the Department for International Development with participation from UNDP, Tashkent for a project entitled 'Rural Domestic Economy and Female Labour Supply in Uzbekistan'. It was carried out in four villages with contrasting livelihood systems (irrigated farming, dry farming and animal husbandry and farming and rural industry) in the provinces of Andijan and Kashkadarya. Two interview schedules were used; a household interview and a women's interview conducted with all co-resident adult women in the household. My thanks are due to Nadira Azimova who acted as national consultant on this project.

information. The dangers of such oversight were brought home to me by the results of the EUI/Essex Survey carried out in 1995 in three regions of Uzbekistan. This survey attempted, among other things, to estimate the incidence of private transfers among households, whether these take the form of gifts, exchanges or loans in cash or in kind (Couduel et al., 1997). This information was obtained by asking household heads or other persons answering the questionnaire whether they had received help from relatives or friends in the thirty days prior to the interview. Although the survey established that a substantial number of households had been involved in either making or receiving cash or in-kind transfers, it completely missed out on the most pervasive mechanism for private transfers, namely *gaps*. *Gaps* are social get-togethers functioning as rotating savings associations where all the members of a network pay in a fixed sum of money each month which they receive as a lump sum when it is their turn to hold a gathering at their own home.[2] Since these networks are primarily presented — and experienced — as venues for recreation and sociability there is no reason why they should have been reported in answer to the question posed. Yet *gaps* account for the largest volume of cash in circulation based on private transfers. These sums help to alleviate the shortage of ready cash and assist in making more important purchases or defraying non-routine expenses. However, the cultural embeddedness of *gaps* meant that their economic functions could escape detection altogether (Kandiyoti, 1998).

Despite a high level of awareness concerning the possibility of such errors, the household survey referred to throughout this text none the less demonstrated the intrinsic ambiguities of some of the categories employed and the limitations of the survey as a tool in a context where the meanings attached to many concepts are in a state of flux.[3] More specifically, I shall describe these difficulties in relation to five central concepts, namely, those of *household, employment, access to land, income* and *expenditure*. I shall attempt to illustrate how the contents of these categories are not only context-specific but are also shifting in response to changes in the rural environment of Uzbekistan. Since these concepts also constitute the basic building blocks used in conventional measurements of poverty, this critique is of more general relevance to an assessment of changing living standards in transition economies.

---

2. *Gaps* may involve single sex (all male or all female) or mixed sex participation and different levels of payment ranging from symbolic to substantial sums. The payments are inflation linked either by being calculated in dollars or, as in the case of Andijan, being pegged to the price of meat. Although no hard data exists on this question, my observations suggest that substantially higher sums circulate in all-male groups as compared to women's *gaps*.
3. I choose to label these limitations as 'heuristic errors' since an analysis of the reasons behind some apparent inconsistencies and omissions effectively reveals how existing arrangements work and how respondents map out their worlds.

HOUSEHOLDS: ELUSIVE BOUNDARIES

The household (or domestic unit) generally refers to a group of co-resident persons who share most aspects of consumption and draw upon a common pool of resources for their livelihood. However, the sheer diversity of patterns of rural householding documented in ethnographic accounts makes this definition too simplistic and renders the concept itself rather elusive. On the other hand, 'official' definitions of what constitutes a household, deployed for the purposes of enumeration and the delivery of social benefits and entitlements, have an undeniable concreteness. The effects of these definitions may not be overlooked, although they may take different forms in different contexts.

There are significant differences between studies of households carried out in the industrialized West and those based in the less industrialized economies of the South. In the case of the former, the state and the welfare system are acknowledged as important agents informing both livelihood strategies and decisions about employment and the allocation of household tasks and budgetary resources (see for instance, Morris, 1984, 1987; Pahl, 1984, 1988). In the latter, there is generally little reference to the role of suprahousehold or non-kin based agencies, reflecting the weakness or absence of social safety nets, especially in rural areas. Societies that have experienced collectivization occupy a rather distinctive place in this respect since their rural populations have access to a range of benefits and entitlements through membership in collective enterprises and state welfare legislation. However, here as elsewhere, the question of the degree of 'fit' between the actual practices of entities registered as households and the official assumptions made about them constitutes a vexed and complicated issue.[4] Rural households in Uzbekistan present specific problems for researchers using standard sampling techniques based on *selsoviet* (village administration) records, the most commonly used sampling frame for surveys. This is due to the fact that the relationship between official registration as separate units of co-residence and actual separateness as budgeting and production units can be quite tenuous and variable.

Physically, rural domestic units cluster around a courtyard (*auli*) where the garden plot, poultry and animals may be kept and where separate living quarters may be built for married sons. A distinction is made in the Uzbek language between household (*hodjalik*) and family (*oila*), and multiple family households are quite commonplace. Post-marital residence is virilocal and

---

4. The literature on agricultural development projects in sub-Saharan Africa, for instance, is rife with examples of how assumptions about households as income-pooling, corporate units come up against the actual realities of different customary practices. In cases where the automatic control of the male household head over the production and labour time of women cannot be taken for granted, and where projects make the assumption that such control exists, intensified intra-household conflict along gender lines is frequently reported.

although it is typically the youngest son who inherits the parental home and cohabits with elderly or widowed parents, other married sons are, if possible, accommodated around the same *auli*. Some sons may leave the courtyard altogether and set up residentially and financially separate households. This becomes inevitable when there is no spare plot to house them or when circumstances take them elsewhere. Parental expectations of co-habitation with at least one married son are high although, in practice, many households diverge from this pattern. Married couples working for collective enterprises that provide them with purpose built apartment accommodation (*zhil dom*) tend to live in smaller household units. Elderly couples who have no sons or co-resident unmarried children may be found living either on their own or with grandchildren.

Within this framework, village records provide an imperfect guide to the actual number of households since there is a tendency for families, whether they are co-resident in the same *auli* or not, to register as separate units. This entitles them to separate private plots and to child benefit and income support when their income falls below a certain level.[5] Moreover, families sharing the same courtyard may have different budgeting arrangements. In local parlance, they may either 'share the same cooking pot' (*kazan bir*) or keep separate pots (*kazan alahada*) and constitute separate budgeting units. The decision of whether to share daily consumption, or not, involves a wide range of considerations, both monetary and relational, and may undergo modifications depending on changing circumstances.

Mindful of these distinctions, the interview schedule used in the survey referred to above did not simply take the households registered in the *selsoviet* records at face value, but also ascertained whether they had separate cooking pots or not. Such was the case of Omina and Abdulkarim, a newly married couple, who had set up a residentially separate household and reported keeping a separate budget and 'their own' cooking pot. However, they had not been allocated a private plot, apart from the land on which their house was built, and appeared to have no visible means of support since the one was unemployed and the other a *kolkhoz* (collective farm) worker who had not received wages for months. It was only later, in connection with questions on crops harvested and sold, that it became apparent that this couple was still working on the plots of Abdulkarim's paternal household and receiving a portion of their harvest and income. This was a clear-cut case where the separation of residence and daily consumption gave few clues to the actual allocation of agricultural and

---

5. Despite legal entitlement to private plots, the actual probability of being allocated one depends on the availability of land. In Andijan province, where population pressure on land is extremely high, new allocations fell well below the legally allowed limit and many were actually denied land. In Kashkadarya much larger allocations of unirrigated land were made to households, but lack of water limited what they could cultivate and many used the land to grow fodder crops.

other tasks among married sons. Corrective action by the researcher was clearly needed here to reconstitute the full domestic unit that made this young family viable. Indeed, families that do not cook and live together may none the less continue to cultivate common plots, share the produce and remain enmeshed in daily ties of sharing and exchange of products, labour and services structured along gender and seniority lines. This type of corrective action may be particularly difficult to accommodate in large scale surveys based on fixed sampling fractions and using teams of interviewers, assuming that local variations in budget control had been identified in the first place.

Conversely, common residence and a shared cooking pot may act to conceal the tacit separation of incomes and expenditures of co-resident families. Zuhra and Sodik are elderly pensioners cohabiting with a married son, his bride (*kelin*) and their unmarried children. They report cooking together. However, when asked about who keeps the household money and who asks for money from whom when necessary, Zuhra says; 'We keep and spend our own pension. They keep their own money'. Although they may share the produce of their land plots, they go their separate ways when it comes to cash expenditure. This tendency may have been exacerbated by the fact that pensions have become the sole source of cash income in many households where *kolkhoz* workers are paid intermittently and only in kind. Clearly, depending on circumstances, such sharing arrangements may be revised and modified. In one case, a widowed pensioner, Omina, decided to separate her cooking pot from her elder son, who already has four children, and to share her pension income only with her youngest married son who has no regular income and a disability. She justifies her initiative as follows: 'Why should I share my pension with all of them? The older children grow, the more they eat. To each his own, it's better that way'.

To complicate matters further, relational considerations may exercise a considerable influence on the reporting of even the most seemingly straight-forward items. The household survey in Andijan and Kashkadarya also included interviews with all cohabiting, adult women. This often meant that mother-in-law/daughter-in-law pairs had to answer the same questions (albeit separately). Concerning the ownership of household durables (such as televisions, sewing machines or furniture), the answers of co-habiting pairs tended to be identical, which was what one would normally expect. There was, however, a notable exception of a daughter-in-law who reported owning only a cupboard, the one she had brought with her trousseau, omitting to mention other household items that were plainly available. When I queried this apparent anomaly, I was informed that this *kelin* was having a par-ticularly bad relationship with her mother-in-law. This was evidently her way of signalling her disaffection with and alienation from her husband's family. In a rare twist of events, there was also one case of a bride reporting a car among household possessions, an item that was left out of her mother-in-law's account. This was a case where the older woman only had access to her pension money, whereas the bride claimed to be in control of general household finances.

These findings suggest that different levels of welfare and access to resources may apply to different categories of household members, depending on gender, seniority and the state of interpersonal relations between genders and generations. Although it has almost become a truism, especially in feminist literature, to point out that intra-household relations mediate individual access to resources (Agarwal, 1990; Bruce and Dwyer, 1988; Evans, 1989; Moore, 1992; Whitehead, 1981), these age-gender effects are not necessarily captured by household surveys unless they are specifically built into questionnaire designs. In the case of the household survey in Andijan and Kashkadarya, interviews with all co-resident adult women were extremely revealing with respect to intra-household discrepancies in access to income and leisure.

There were are at least three areas that pointed to significant disparities *within* households: budget control, and access to money and to leisure. Most women reported that the money in their household was kept either by their husband, or their father-in-law or mother-in-law. This meant that many women in waged employment handed over their earnings and had to approach the holder of the purse strings if they needed cash. Furthermore, as will be explained in greater detail in the sections dealing with employment and income, there are now more women than men who are either unemployed or are receiving their wages only in kind. These varying levels of discretion over money became quite apparent in the age composition of participants in all-women *gaps*, the rotating savings networks referred to above. Younger married women (*kelins*) do not generally participate in such occasions and if they do it is usually by consent of husband and mother-in-law. If a household is better-off, the *kelin* may be allowed to use the *gap* money on herself. Normally, she is expected to hand the money over, and does so. There may be conflicts in cases where the *kelin* who earns her own money and contributes to the *gap* through her own means feels resentful about having to hand over the proceeds to her husband or mother-in-law. In most instances, however, these hierarchies of domestic privilege are perceived as quite natural.

The distribution of domestic chores is also skewed in the direction of younger women who have a much longer working day. They are responsible for the more routine and onerous tasks of cleaning, fetching water, washing clothes, tending animals and the kitchen garden. Older women may oversee these activities and continue to cook, bake and keep an eye on children although they tend to delegate the more back-breaking tasks, such as kneading dough for bread, to their daughters-in-law or adolescent daughters. Adult men are usually exempt from domestic chores, although boys may be asked to fetch and carry, run errands and take care of animals. Age and gender therefore structure intra-household divisions of labour and access to leisure in powerful ways.

Patterns of intergenerational assistance and solidarity are shaped to a considerable extent by the patrilineal bias inherent in the local kinship system. Three of the most vulnerable households, bordering on destitution, consisted of elderly pensioners who only had married daughters and no sons. In one case, grandchildren had moved in to give the elderly couple a hand. In the other cases, although the daughters came in to help with household chores they did so on sufferance from their husbands. The elderly couples received no help at all with their household plots and had to lease them out. It is too early to speculate whether increasing dependence on offspring will give a further boost to already existing son-preference in Uzbekistan. At this point in time, there is some evidence to suggest that pensions, though much reduced in value, are still appreciated as a source of cash. Humphrey, for instance, cites a respondent in Siberia as saying 'It is better to have two live grandparents than to have two cows' (Humphrey, 1998: 465). However, I did not encounter any cases where a widowed woman was taken into a married daughter's household whereas widowed mothers of sons were routinely to be found in control of household finances, sometimes at a surprisingly advanced age. Some responses to a question concerning the number of co-resident families in a household suggested that both emotional and cultural considerations played a role in delineating boundaries. In some cases, widowed parents, with or without unmarried children, were considered to constitute a separate family, in other cases they were not. Divorced daughters who came back to live with their parents, with or without children, were considered as a separate family, pointing to the anomalous, and hopefully transitory, nature of their current status.[6] Neither the boundaries of constituent families within households, nor those between households are fixed entities. Rather, they may themselves become the object of negotiation and redefinition, depending on a range of material and emotional circumstances.

Domestic units are, therefore, best conceptualized as the site of multiple and interlocking sets of processes. These may activate different sub-sets of individuals who constitute appropriate units of analysis, depending on the nature of the research question posed. For instance, an understanding of family planning decisions may require a different unit of analysis than, say, the allocation of intra-household resources. Since the exploration of these boundaries is part and parcel of the research process, there is a sense in which units of analysis may sometimes emerge *a posteriori*. An adequate

---

6. Admittedly, this only happened in two cases since divorce is relatively rare in villages. There is, however, a patrilineal bias in setting the boundaries of families. A disabled, single older brother receiving benefit is considered as part of the same family in a way that a divorced daughter can never be. However, in the event of remarriage a divorced daughter's children are frequently taken in by their maternal grandparents since it is considered unseemly for a woman to bring children from a previous marriage into her new husband's household.

understanding of the different ways in which domestic units organize livelihoods and mutual assistance is particularly central to analyses of vulnerability, especially in a context where existing social safety nets are being eroded, and must be given the utmost priority. Gender analyses of poverty are more crucially dependent upon an accurate identification of the hierarchical allocational practices and power differentials enacted in domestic units.

The household survey in Andijan and Kashkadarya revealed that the links between co-residence, budget control and household divisions of labour (in both domestic and production tasks) are varied and complex as well as fluid. It also highlighted significant intra-household disparities in budget control, access to income and to leisure. Even the use of so-called 'filter questions' (in this particular case, trying to sort out households with a common vs. separate cooking pot at the outset) proved unequal to the task of identifying the boundaries of domestic units. Yet the general tendency in survey research is to assume that households correspond to officially registered units of residence and that these, in turn, constitute discrete budgeting units. A more flexible and exploratory approach clearly needs to be adopted, one that is more open to trial and error. The qualitative methodologies habitually employed at the pilot stage of surveys, whether these take the form of focus group discussions, participatory or observational techniques, may not be sufficient in themselves to secure adequate questionnaire design. However, an unexpected bonus of the survey method may reside in the heuristic value of the inconsistencies, gaps and apparent inaccuracies of the responses provided — what are normally dismissed as 'errors' rather than given detailed consideration. This is what the rest of this chapter will attempt to demonstrate, starting with the category of 'employment'.

EMPLOYMENT VS. LIVELIHOODS?

Although it is a commonplace that the concept of employment is itself an artifact of regulation (as most discussions on the informal economy keep reminding us), this is nowhere more apparent than in the republics of the former Soviet Union. In the case of our survey, a strikingly high proportion of respondents declared themselves 'unemployed', even as they gave detailed descriptions of their farming, animal husbandry or trading activities. This was not an attempt at dissimulation; they were, indeed, 'officially' unemployed.

In the Soviet Union (and currently in Uzbekistan) all employees are provided with a workbook (*trudovaya knizhka* in Russian, or *mihnat daftarchasi* in Uzbek) which is registered with their employer for the entire duration of their time with that enterprise. If a workbook is 'with the person himself/ herself' rather than with an employer this constitutes an interruption of service and reflects detrimentally on pension rights (with the exception of one and a half years allowed for maternity leave, or *dekret*). It is therefore important to keep one's workbook registered with an enterprise whether one is drawing a salary or not.

Alisher Ilkhamov (1998) notes the fact that farm restructuring in Uzbekistan consisted mainly of converting state farms, which were centrally funded, into collective farms which hold their own budgets. As a result, there was a 30 per cent increase in collective farms since 1991 and privatization took the rather cosmetic form of restructuring them as joint-stock companies now called *shirkat*. Since these enterprises are in permanent deficit, the pressure of having to pay salaries has resulted in either shedding some of their personnel or keeping them on the books without paying them wages. These new pressures created different categories of employees: those registered, and still receiving a salary (generally in managerial positions); those registered, without receiving a salary (some skilled workers who now work on their own account); those registered, but receiving irregular payment and only in kind (unskilled agricultural workers); and those who are struck off the books altogether and 'keep their own workbook'. These latter identify themselves as unemployed, regardless of what else they do and how much they earn. There are, in addition, different categories of non-employed. Housewives who are currently out of a job will report themselves as unemployed, whereas those who have never had a workbook will define themselves as housewives. Invalids receiving disability benefit, students with stipends, women on maternity leave, and pensioners constitute recognized categories of non-employed, distinctions that are seldom found in rural societies where such provision is non-existent.

It is also important to note that post-Soviet reforms have not been gender-neutral in their effects. Most commentators have pointed to the disproportionate rise in female unemployment in transitional economies (Buckley, 1997; Moghadam, 1993; Molyneux, 1994). In the labour surplus areas of Central Asia, the majority of those working outside social production were already identified as women before the break-up of the Union (Lubin, 1981). This existing tendency for female unemployment and underemployment has become further exacerbated, in both rural and urban areas, by the continuing loss of public sector jobs, although women constitute a major proportion of collective farm workers, especially in the seasonal operations of cotton-picking. One of the paradoxes of transition has been a simultaneous intensification of women's labour input into a range of subsistence and informal activities, more fully described in the next section, accompanied by a decline in their wage-earning opportunities and incomes.

Among the 'officially' employed, current patterns are also becoming increasingly complex, especially in urban areas. There are people who are registered with an enterprise for pension purposes but do not do the job they are registered for, nor do they draw a salary. There are also those who are registered in an enterprise, and do another job entirely. Not surprisingly, with the collapse of public sector employment and precipitous drops in wages, what used to be 'subsidiary' activities or 'unofficial' incomes now often become the mainstay of household budgets. However, for the purposes of surveys (an official activity par excellence) many will still report the place where their workbook is registered, and the 'official' salary that goes with it, regardless of what they actually do to make a living and how much they might actually earn.

This was quite apparent among registered *shirkat* workers in the survey (constituting the majority of rural workers) who reported a monthly wage that had by now become quite fictitious. This makes the calculation of household incomes quite problematic, as will be seen in the sections to follow. There is a sense in which this insistence on official wages has to do, at least partly, with a desire by respondents to depict their current situation as somehow 'anomalous', a situation that could not last indefinitely and might yet be put right. Especially now that no stigma attaches to informal activities, which are no longer considered illegal, this tenacity cannot be attributed to attempts at concealment. This could hardly be the case in the context of a survey where all other sources of income were gone into in considerable detail. I had to acknowledge the extent to which local understandings of what constitutes a 'proper' job and the benefits that go with it had been deeply conditioned by Soviet institutions. The sense of grievance experienced by those subjected to late payment of benefits, for instance, also conveyed a sense of outrage about a loss of normalcy. It is, of course, conceivable that a major overhaul of the welfare system and phasing out the work-books in favour of different arrangements may, in time, change people's apprehensions and expectations. It is also clear that this is an area where a great deal of resistance is likely to manifest itself.[7]

What is directly pertinent to the argument at hand, is that extreme vigilance is necessary when formulating questions on current employment status. The issue of whether salaries are actually received or not, at what intervals, the calculations of money equivalents of in-kind payments and the extent to which currently non-salaried jobs offer scope for non-official wages to be earned[8] must all be taken into account. This is difficult to achieve in view of

---

7. This became quite clear to me in discussions with Uzbek colleagues who expressed utter disbelief at the notion that pension rights could be tampered with or redefined. Verdery (1996) was right in pointing out that the social compact between state and citizen under socialism was based on the paternalistic promise of being provided for at the cost of restrictions of one's personal freedoms in market and political terms. The elimination of the former in the absence of an expansion of the latter, as is currently the case in all Central Asian republics, could occasion serious social disaffection and unrest.

8. Some categories of skilled workers are better placed in this respect. For instance, a carpenter-builder registered in a construction brigade but receiving no wages can ply his trade privately and work during the construction season. Tractor and combine drivers are likewise able to do jobs on their own account. Unskilled agricultural workers are least able to command unofficial wages and *shirkats* try to make sure they, at least, get paid in kind. Cotton harvesting wages are always paid in cash on a five-day basis since the supply of an adequate workforce during the peak season continues to be a problem.

an understandable reticence to report unofficial earnings. Informal activities, such as trading in markets, are reported with greater ease. These activities are, in fact, subject to regulation since it is necessary to register and pay the *bazarkom* (the officer in charge of allocating spaces and collecting charges) for one's stall or spot. On the other hand, it is common knowledge that although a *bazarkom*'s official wages may be quite low this is a sought after and profitable position offering plenty of opportunities for unofficial emoluments which provide a handsome supplement. This is a point I shall return to in greater detail when discussing the question of household incomes. First we must consider the crucial question of access to the main source of rural livelihood, namely land.

ACCESS TO LAND: MOVING THE GOAL-POSTS?

Among the republics of Central Asia, Uzbekistan is noted for pursuing a gradual strategy of partial changes in the area of agrarian reform (Ilkhamov, 1998; Spoor, 1995). Unlike neighbouring Kazakhstan and Kyrgyzstan, there has not been a disbanding of *kolkhozes* but rather the creation of what Ilkhamov has described as a three-tiered rural economy. This structure consists of collective farms, still occupying the major part of irrigated, arable land, a thin layer of private peasant farms, and a mass of collective farm employees who cultivate household smallholdings. Ilkhamov has cogently argued that the local élite has a stake in the maintenance of this type of agrarian economy since it ensures a minimum subsistence level for the peasantry whilst preserving the monopoly of the government and administrative élites over land and water resources and over cotton, the leading and most lucrative export commodity

However, despite the absence of *de jure* privatization, land is *de facto* increasingly becoming a commodity through the development of leasehold markets. Local administrations and collective farms face the contradictory pressures of having to simultaneously fulfil state procurement quotas for crops (cotton and wheat), continue to allocate private plots to households for their own use, and enter leasehold arrangements with farmers under the new rules of the Land Law. This is creating an unprecedented indeterminacy in the mechanisms of land allocation.

Villagers have access to different types of plots. The first type is the land plot on which their house is built and which may accommodate a small kitchen garden. This is held in perpetuity and is inheritable. The second type is the *tamorka* or private subsidiary plot to which all citizens have been entitled since Soviet times. After independence in 1991 the legal size of personal plots was increased substantially, from 0.1 ha to 0.25 ha of irrigated land and 0.5 ha of non-irrigated land. These are usually allocated from the land reserves of collective farms and, in densely populated areas, may be located some distance away from house plots.

On the collective farm itself, two types of land tenure arrangements may coexist; leasehold peasant farms, and sharecropping arrangements with farm management on annually negotiated terms. In principle, leasehold peasant farmers are free to market their own produce but, in practice, they also opt for a sharecropping arrangement with the collective farm on which they depend for inputs, transport and access to markets. Independent peasant (*dekhan*) farms are those with the status of separate juridical entities and the right to open their own bank accounts. They may hold leases of up to ten years. These are few in number and have been experiencing reverses rather than expanding. A TACIS report (1996) on the Samarkand district noted a decline in the number of independent peasant farms since 1995. The operations of peasant farms are, in fact, quite severely restricted since they have contracts with collective farms to grow particular crops under sharecropping arrangements. These frequently exceed the legal requirement of crops and quantities (50 per cent of wheat or cotton) they must deliver, but farmers have weak bargaining power in setting the terms of their contracts. Furthermore, the collective farm is often in arrears of payments, leaving independent farmers strapped for cash, unable to pay for essential inputs or acquiring them by selling produce privately and therefore falling short of their contracted production quotas. Some private farms were closed down with reference to Article 13 of the Land Law stating that if land is not used properly it should revert to the collective. There are, therefore, significant structural obstacles to the development of this type of tenure.

The household survey in Andijan and Kashkadarya reflected the land tenure situation described above quite accurately. Out of 100 surveyed households, only one was identified as an independent peasant farm. This conforms to the official data (1.5 peasant farms per 1000 population, approximating 150–170 households) reported by Ilkhamov (1998). The different categories of land tenure were also correctly identified. However, the precariousness of tenure from year to year was not adequately taken into account, leading to puzzling inconsistencies in the case of one particular village. Several households had mentioned rice as their most important marketable crop. However, the household plots reported and the crops grown on them did not include rice. Upon closer scrutiny, it became apparent that this rice was grown on subsidiary plots (*tamorka*) allocated during the past season. In the current agricultural season, the *shirkat* decided to take this land back to plant cotton. One can only surmise that there had been a shortfall in cotton production quotas. That meant the allocations of *tamorka* land would only be made on wheat land after the harvest, allowing households to grow vegetables only, which are both perishable and much lower in value than rice. This decision had created consternation since household budgets would be depleted by this serious loss of income.

Another crop which made an unaccountable appearance in one of the households was several tons of onions reported as sold but not as grown on

any of the plots to which the household claimed to have access. It appeared
that the head of the household had entered into a sharecropping
arrangement with the brigade chief (the overseer and manager of work
brigades) on the collective farm to plant onions after the wheat harvest in
return for a proportion of the produce. The degree of formality involved in
this and similar arrangements is not always entirely clear. A widow living
with her married sons also reported their household had harvested four tons
of carrots, one of which was given to the brigade chief 'for the village
kindergarten'. Whether this transaction took place in the context of a
formal sharecropping contract or not was, again, rather vague. What is
quite clear, however, is that since land allocation continues to depend on
collective farm managers this gives them considerable power. They have
discretion over the quantity, quality and distance from the homestead of the
plots leased out, over the terms of the lease and over whether a household is
allocated land or not. In one particular instance, one household was in
serious financial difficulty and had no land plots at all. It transpired that
they had not been allocated any after a falling out with the head of the
kolkhoz two years ago.

Aside from the vagaries of relationships with collective farm managers, a
more insidious underlying source of instability in current land tenure
arrangements, and therefore of growing vulnerability, resides in the inevitable tensions arising from simultaneously attempting to provide villagers
with a subsistence base (and even expanding it under the new Land Law) *and*
establishing land as a commodity through the expansion and diversification
of leasehold markets. Inevitably, the claims that rural households make to
the land which they are, in principle, legally entitled to cultivate may be
curtailed by the competing claims and priorities of farm managers. Given
that *kolkhoz* employees who no longer receive wages have become more
dependent than ever on subsistence farming (and the sale of their crops
whenever possible), there is a limit beyond which local administrators may
not squeeze them without creating serious distress and discontent. However,
there are already signs that this delicate balance may be tilting away from the
interests of smallholders.

It would appear that even the very partial process of commoditization
initiated by agrarian reform in Uzbekistan has set in motion changes that are
likely to result in new pressures on smallholder households. Better-off
households are able to enter into private hire arrangements with the tractor
and combine drivers of the *kolkhoz* who get paid either in cash or in kind. But
the shortage of cash and inability to pay for inputs has already meant that
the level of mechanization has dropped considerably for the great majority.
On the other hand, private ownership of tractors is rising and households
that can command both farming implements and some capital may look
further afield than their own village for land to lease. The notion that
outsiders who are not members of the collective may thus receive access to
land is bound to create great ambivalence and there is likely to be conflict

between communal norms and expectations and statutory rights under the new legislation.[9]

There are also signs that changes in land tenure and in the composition of rural livelihoods are shifting the balance of gendered divisions of labour within households and creating new burdens for women. The increasing reliance on personal subsidiary plots has meant an intensification of women's input into subsistence farming. In addition, women constitute the majority of workers who are officially registered in work brigades. There has been an increasing feminization of labour on collective farms since *perestroika*. Men tend to allocate their time to more lucrative contract farming activities, trade or even casual labour as *mardigar* (daily labourers hired for construction or farm work) where wages are higher than women's pay in agriculture. The wages women (and children) receive for the cotton harvest are considered too small and are sometimes referred to by men as 'cigarette money' although they often represent the only source of cash income since all other agricultural wages are paid in kind. Work on multiple plots (kitchen garden, additional subsidiary plots, *tamorka*, plots leased under contract and brigade work on the collective farm) represents a substantial intensification of women's labour input in the busy season in Andijan. In Kashkadarya, on the other hand, the combination of a herding and cereal-based domestic economy means that women who lose their employment on collective farms have no other work or income. The appearance of women *mardigar* in Andijan, seasonal workers hiring out their labour during the rice harvest, also suggests the emergence of an increasingly impoverished section of the village population. Male informants strenuously denied their existence, insisting that only men worked as casual workers. However, interviews with women suggested that some had started organizing all-female harvest teams with friends and were looking for seasonal employment. At the other end of the social scale, the wives of private *dekhan* farmers are also experiencing major changes in their work conditions. From being *kolkhoz* workers or public sector employees with attendant social benefits, they have become unpaid family labourers. At least one of the interviewees reported that cooking for all the hired help during the busy agricultural season created a heavy load which made the more leisurely pace of her former employment in the local administration seem enviable. Elson (1995) notes that market-oriented family farming systems in China and Vietnam have intensified gender gaps in health and education and led to an incipient 'market

---

9. In the course of an interview with a farm manager, I tried to highlight the problems of leasing village land to outsiders by asking whether I would be permitted to lease and cultivate a plot if I came forward with the requisite capital. I was assured that I would be welcome to do so and that I would even find willing partners to join me in this farming venture. In reality, leaving aside any existing legislation barring foreigners from such enterprise, this would constitute quite a scandal and be extremely negatively received whatever the formal rules might be.

patriarchy'. Ilkhamov (1998) partly concurs with this analysis in the case of Uzbekistan but puts his emphasis on the inadequate development of markets and the fact that the subsistence-based household economy is coming to dominate rural livelihoods. It is far too early to judge what the impact of family-based commercial farming might be in Uzbekistan, but it already seems evident that greater reliance on family labour for subsistence and market-oriented activities is affecting sexual divisions of labour.

It should be quite clear from the foregoing that this shifting landscape of access to land and wages means that livelihoods are now generated through a wider range of activities and take multiple forms. These have important implications for the calculation of household incomes.

HOUSEHOLD INCOMES: OFFICIAL, UNOFFICIAL AND INFORMAL

In his study of the Soviet informal economy, Grossman (1989) made a conceptual distinction between the informal *second economy* which was outside legal regulation and *informal incomes* that derive partly from the second economy and partly from illegal transfers such as bribes, embezzlement and misappropriation of public resources. He suggested that informal incomes constituted a sizeable portion of household budgets and that these tended to increase in both absolute and relative terms as one moved from north to south (particularly into Transcaucasia and Central Asia) and from major urban centres to smaller cities and the countryside. In an earlier ethnography of a Siberian collective farm, Humphrey (1983) showed that some unofficial or illegitimate roles were, in fact, essential to the smooth functioning of enterprises and that they could be deployed to perfectly legitimate ends such as securing inputs or marketing *kolkhoz* produce. Other research evidence (Mars and Altman, 1992) also highlighted that the second economy thrived in a symbiotic, if not parasitic, relationship to the formal sector and was, in some senses, an outgrowth of specific types of malfunction inherent in the command economy itself. The transition to the market and the crisis of the public sector have occasioned significant changes in the context and extent of informal activities and created new patterns of informalization which complicate the calculation of household incomes considerably. Indeed, as Humphrey (1998) notes in an update of her earlier work, the sphere of unofficial dealings which used to be kept in the background, both in view of its illegality and the fact that the official system of redistribution was still delivering, has now moved to centre stage as the arena where new survival strategies are enacted.

Rural households in Uzbekistan currently make ends meet through a combination of sources of livelihood. These are salaries and wages which may be paid in cash, in kind or through combinations of both, self-provisioning and sale or barter of produce from personal plots or animals, income from other trading or informal service activities, and benefits and entitlements (such as pensions, child, maternity and invalidity benefits) which are paid in cash. The financial crisis of collective enterprises and the fact that they are chronically in arrears with wages has resulted in a tacit 'informalization' of registered, official activities. Let us consider the case of a woman worker at the local poultry factory in a village of Andijan province. Her salary currently consists of eggs which she must take to market or sell to intermediaries who collect produce from households. This is received in payment for a registered, official job which, to take a monetary form, has to go through the medium of petty trading, an activity normally associated with the informal economy. Similar conditions apply to workers at the local towel factory, with a resulting periodic glut of towels on local markets whenever they receive their 'pay'.

The case of *kolkhoz* workers is equally complicated. Workers organized in brigades normally have responsibility for a specific acreage of land (commonly one hectare, hence the term *hektardji*) planted with cotton year round, for which they receive *only* in kind payment, except for the wages received for picking cotton. As stated above, the vast majority of workers in this category are women. Their payment usually consists of basic necessities such as flour, cooking oil and rice. A calculation I made on the basis of money equivalents of these goods showed that it translates into a monthly income well below the official minimum wage (Kandiyoti, 1998). However, membership of the collective farm also gives employees access to necessities which they would otherwise have to pay for such as the cotton stalks they use as fuel and animal fodder and the ability to graze animals on *kolkhoz* land. As a result, the calculation of money equivalents for in-kind payments becomes a less than precise exercise.

When payments in kind are not automatically translated into immediate contributions to the family budget, estimations of income become even more complicated. This point was graphically illustrated by the case of a villager who had grown melons and water melons on a plot of leased land and bartered them at the local commercial shop against one hundred cups and plates. These were meant not only for his own family but also for the trousseau of his daughter who was coming up to marriageable age. Acquiring crockery made the returns from his melons more inflation-proof than if he had received cash for them and will doubtless save him money in the longer run. This sequence of events also implies that his immediate need for cash was not so pressing and that he was sufficiently comfortable to cover himself against some future expenditure.

Finally, the calculation of unofficial wages presents even more intractable problems. By unofficial wage, I mean emoluments received privately by officially registered employees in the performance of their normal duties. Tractor and combine drivers on the *kolkhoz* do private work on the personal plots of villagers in exchange for a fixed cash payment per hectare, or a portion of the produce harvested in the case of combines. Although they pay for their own petrol, they use the machinery of the collective farm and do this work in lieu of wages. Workers in construction brigades may also work privately and offer their services for cash or wages in kind.[10] Likewise, a hospital nurse may give injections privately when called upon by villagers in need of treatment. There is nothing novel in these types of activities which would normally go under the label of 'moonlighting' or having a job on the side. The novelty resides in the fact that these incomes have superseded official incomes which none the less may continue to be reported in household surveys. Moreover, researchers may find that there is little consistency in reporting practices. One tractor driver in an Andijan village declared his private earnings, while another stuck to his fictitious monthly wage. Others were genuinely unable to put a figure on their earnings due to the fluctuating nature of the demand for their services.

There are other unofficial incomes of a far less innocent nature than the private sale of one's customary services. These are the bribes and extortions which those in commanding positions of administrative authority are able to exact from villagers. The example of *bazarkoms*, officials who allocate spaces in bazaars, was already cited as a position offering substantial scope for unofficial earnings. Ilkhamov (1998) also remarks that the scale of exactions by officials (such as traffic police) on roads between village and town is of such magnitude that it has become one of the major obstacles to the development of private farming. These types of incomes are, needless to say, not susceptible to detection except through the obvious discrepancies one sometimes encounters between declared incomes and ownership of consumer durables such as cars, videos and expensive furniture.

It would be quite accurate to say that there are significant differences between men's and women's relative abilities to command unofficial and informal wages, since the skilled/technical and administrative occupations are almost exclusively taken by men. There is a pattern of deepening feminization of unskilled agricultural labour (which is now paid only inter-mittently and in kind), while men tend to capture the more lucrative niches of market trading in the informal economy. This pattern is by no means new but builds upon existing cultural understandings of the marketplace as a male domain and the informal world of patronage and bribes as an exclusively masculine world. Certain categories of women, those who are older and freed of their domestic duties since they can rely on younger women for the upkeep of their households, may also be active in markets. However, they tend to occupy less advantageous positions in the retailing chain. Typically, women selling imported clothing items in markets (from China, India or Turkey) receive goods on commission from a wholesaler who has the capital to make bulk purchases. The wholesaler (usually male) passes on his wares to individual women for retailing at a minimum agreed price, with anything the

---

10. Some payments in kind are more appreciated than cash. Bottles of vodka, for instance, are inflation-proof, just like dollars.

women can make over that price retained as profit. This effectively protects the wholesaler from any losses which are passed on to the retailer who may end up making no or very small profits. Some of the women I spoke to insisted that the only way they could break this cycle was by acquiring capital of their own. Yet at this juncture the already existing wage and income gaps between the sexes, based on the concentration of women in lower paid, unskilled occupations, is turning into a 'cash gap' in the currently cash starved economy of rural Uzbekistan. Especially in Kashkadarya, a less developed province, some women reported 'not seeing money at all' in response to a question on who keeps the money in their household.

In addition to these complications, I was able to identify what we might call phenomenological discrepancies in what respondents themselves consider as 'income'. In one household, pensioners' benefits and proceeds from the household plot were the only sources of livelihood. When asked what the major source of income of their household was, they insisted they had no source of income whatsoever. This occurred on several subsequent occasions. Since these families were plainly living off something, their insistence that they had no income at all needed interpretation. It became apparent that benefits were not perceived as income since this was something they were entitled to. As for the produce from their own plot, it all went towards self-subsistence. They earned no wage and therefore had no income. It was not simply a matter of whether they received cash or not, since pensions are paid in cash. It was more a question of defining what types of returns qualified as income so far as the respondents were concerned. I entertained the possibility that this might be a problem of translation since the Uzbek term *daromad* equally translates as profit. However, I was surprised to come across another household reporting pensions as their major source of income. Commenting on this discrepancy, I was informed that they were sufficiently poor to report their pensions.[11] On the other hand, a sizeable proportion of registered workers receiving actual or theoretical wages did not report their wages as the major source of income of their households but mentioned their farming or animal husbandry activities instead.

There are thus numerous sources of inaccuracy and possible bias in the reporting of household incomes. Some of these difficulties have to do with the nature of the incomes in question, others with a reluctance to reveal certain types of earnings and yet others relate to ways in which the meaning of 'income' itself is interpreted by respondents. The issue of interpretation became even more crucial in relation to questions concerning household expenditure.

11. I am indebted to Nodira Azimova for heated and lengthy discussions on the meaning of some of these inconsistencies. She found it self-evident that better-off families would not consider benefits as income, whereas my own strictly monetary understanding dictated that all payments received must constitute income.

HOUSEHOLD EXPENDITURE: HERE YOU SEE IT, THERE YOU DON'T

Descriptions of the most important expenses incurred by households during the past twelve months took a variety of forms. In some cases, straightforward reporting of items, such as the repair or construction costs for a house, was followed by a specific sum of money spent. The purchase of consumer goods, such as a new battery for a car or a carpet, was likewise reported in monetary values. In other cases, outgoings were described as an outlay of animals, produce, cash or various combinations of these. The most common incidence of such combinations could be found in enumerations of the costs of a wedding feast, circumcision or funeral ceremony. In many households, these life cycle events were the most frequently cited source of major expenditure. A typical inventory of expenses might look as follows: two rams, one sack (50 kgs) of rice, one sack of flour, 20 litres of oil and 10 kgs of carrots. Deriving the money equivalents of these outlays was a relatively simple matter, frequently assisted by respondents' own mental calculations. Whether these constituted net expenses was another matter, given that the value of gifts received on such occasions may act to defray some of the costs. None the less, these were cases where all outgoings, whether they took the form of cash, livestock or produce were acknowledged as expenses.

I was alerted to the possibility that the concept of expenditure may itself be subject to differing interpretations by some findings from a village in the province of Kashkadarya. Here, one household identified the largest item of expenditure as the payment of 6000 sums for medical expenses for the treatment of the respondent's sick wife. In answer to a previous question, the same respondent had reported slaughtering two rams and one bull for various religious holidays and ceremonies (for *iftorlik*, the break of fast at Ramadan, for *kurbanlik*, the feast of sacrifice, and for a *sunnat toy*, the circumcision feast). Even the most superficial calculation suggested that the value of these animals far exceeded the amount reported as maximum expenditure, since a single ram would easily have fetched 6000 sums. Yet these animals were not mentioned as expenditure. When I probed into this discrepancy, I was informed that these animals did not count as expenditure *'because they were ours'*. Whereas they had to spend cash for medical costs, and therefore reported it as a major expenditure, they were able to meet their ceremonial needs from their own flock. Besides, whereas sickness constituted an unexpected misfortune, the slaughtered animals went towards meeting religiously sanctioned obligations. Clearly, this household was not thinking about the worth of its animals in terms of their market value or in money equivalents, highlighting the extent to which the concept of expenditure itself is relative to the degree of monetization of the economy as a whole.

Indeed, one of the characteristics of this particular village was the fact that few reported selling any of their produce on the market. This was a dry farming area with few marketable crops. Villagers grew wheat on their personal plots for their own consumption and some vegetables, if they could find water, but the principal form of wealth consisted in having animals, mainly sheep. Many necessities were obtained through barter and exchange. Only the poorest households reported that their women wove rugs (*kelims*) for sale on the market and when animals were sold as a means of raising cash for essentials this was a tell-tale sign of resource depletion. In addition, the actual cost of keeping animals was relatively minimal. The whole family, including children, participated in their care. Shepherding and taking animals to summer pastures could be achieved through informal arrangements with *kolkhoz* shepherds who added private flocks to those of the collective farm in exchange for an animal or two depending on the size of the flock. Similar arrangements could be transacted with kin and neighbours. This was also an area where most women reported having no access to cash at all and where *gaps*, the rotating savings associations reported in Andijan, were non-existent. As pointed out in my earlier discussion on incomes, women's discretion over money, and therefore expenditures, is drastically curtailed in a cash scarce economy where opportunities for earning wages are shrinking further.

This situation contrasts sharply with that of villages in Andijan province where the degree of monetization is much higher. In this area of irrigated farming many household smallholdings were producing crops for sale, particularly rice. The level of mechanization of production on even relatively small plots was considerable and the cost of production much higher.[12] Transactions to obtain inputs (such as access to fertilizers and machinery) were also monetized, whether payments were made in cash or in kind, since the money equivalents of in-kind payments were carefully calculated. One of the most striking findings here was that even what used to be a communal reciprocal helping arrangement, *hashar* (such as neighbours coming together to help build a house), now carries a hidden payment in the form of gifts considered to approximate the value of the services rendered. Unlike Kashkadarya many women were active participants in *gaps*, indicating a degree of discretion over money, although this generally applied to older women. The reporting of household expenditures in this region was more strictly monetized regardless of the type of outlays (whether they consisted of money, animals or other products).

These contrasts between findings in different regions are hardly surprising if we remember that the calculation of costs may always be a relative matter.

---

12. I was particularly struck by the fact that the number of women working as casual wage workers (*mardigar*) at the rice harvest was not particularly high, although the very existence of such women represents a departure from past patterns. If we compare this to Southeast Asia where harvesting and processing rice constitutes an important source of income for poor rural women we may better appreciate the differences. However, the increase of manual operations in households which can no longer afford to pay for machines, combined with rising unemployment on collective farms, may well push up the demand for and the supply of casual workers.

Even in the most industrialized countries of the North a householder keen on do-it-yourself who has just built himself a cabinet or a garden shed might report the cost of the materials purchased but treat his own labour as a 'free' resource (although it may be argued that the labour of this amateur has a less obvious market value than that of a good cow). The reason why this gains particular relevance in rural Uzbekistan at this point in time is that the ways in which costs and expenditures are reported are both diagnostic of the degree of monetization in any given locality and constitute an important baseline for monitoring the extent of penetration of a market economy. That is why rather than treating the concept of expenditure (or for that matter, income) as a self-evident, universal category (which implicitly presupposes a market economy) it may be more pertinent at this stage to achieve a better qualitative understanding of how these categories are mapped out and utilized in different locations.

CONCLUSION

Post-Soviet transitions have prompted a search for new policy tools and methods of data collection. The measurement of living standards and calculations of poverty lines have promoted the use of quantitative techniques and sample surveys as privileged tools for the collection of policy-relevant information. I have argued throughout this chapter that survey data is valuable only to the extent that it builds upon a solid bedrock of in-depth, qualitative information about the processes under investigation. In particular, in an environment where patterns of employment, redistribution and social provision are shifting rapidly the assessment of poverty requires a detailed understanding of new sources of vulnerability. The gendered practices and expectations leading to differential outcomes for men and women at different stages of their life cycles can only be fully apprehended through detailed and painstaking qualitative research. Using illustrations from a household survey carried out in four villages of the provinces of Andijan and Kashkadarya in Uzbekistan, I offered an analysis of the ambiguities surrounding five basic concepts; those of *household*, *employment*, *access to land*, *income* and *expenditure*. My findings suggest that not only are the processes and categories identified under these labels context-specific, but they are also likely to undergo further transformations as market reforms deepen.

This raises a host of methodological questions that are not amenable to easy, prescriptive answers within the scope of a brief chapter. None the less, some general observations can be made about crucial areas of indeterminacy that should receive particular attention in the design of household surveys. The first concerns the use of official records, such as *selsoviet* records, as sampling frames. These may or may not be adequate depending on the problem at hand. The illustrations provided in this chapter suggest that households identified on the basis of village records do not necessarily correspond to self-contained budgeting and consumption units. A more exploratory approach should inform the choice of units of analysis. This is particularly pertinent in view of the fact that the ways in which domestic units organize themselves (or fail to do so) to secure their livelihoods and deliver mutual assistance may represent the difference between destitution and relative security. Furthermore, the data at hand already indicates significant disparities along gender and age lines in access to employment, income and leisure. As resources shrink and services (such as education and health) become more costly we may expect already existing intra-household disparities to become exacerbated. The tools we use should be up to the challenge of capturing and monitoring such changes.

The second observation concerns the effects of 'transition'. These may be crystallizing around a growing disjuncture between 'official' occupations and wages and what people actually do to make a living. This disjuncture is reflected in the reporting of employment and incomes in ways that make an accurate evaluation of both work status and household finances quite problematic. At this point in time, there is a tendency in rural Uzbekistan to carry on reporting wages that have now become fictitious and 'registered' occupations (tied to the workbook system) that may no longer be related to a household's main source of livelihood. This may not simply be put down to a reluctance to report informal earnings but may also reflect a genuine internalization of Soviet definitions of what constitutes a 'proper' job — one that not only brings wages but a range of entitlements and benefits. As this system gets progressively eroded, the tendency for reported occupations to fall into line with major income-generating activities will undoubtedly increase. The same applies to wages. It will be crucial to monitor whether already existing gender gaps in wages become aggravated as women lose access to cash incomes, an incipient but clearly visible trend in rural Uzbekistan.

The particular combinations of cash and in-kind payments received at present and the 'informalization' of registered jobs described above all correspond to a particular phase of the transition process. This period of crisis of the public sector is accompanied in Uzbekistan, by an effort to keep as many workers as possible 'on the books', although youth and female unemployment are officially recognized as causes for particular concern. The government of Uzbekistan has made it an explicit policy goal to avoid the worst excesses of the market observed in other countries of the former Soviet Union (UNDP, 1998) and to 'cushion' the social costs of transition. However, even the piecemeal agrarian reforms adopted are creating contradictions which are becoming apparent in the area of access to land. The simultaneous attempt to provide smallholders with a subsistence base while developing and diversifying leasehold markets in land is creating new tensions. It is difficult to see how the existing situation may be sustained indefinitely. The fact that the rural population (a majority of just over 60 per cent in Uzbekistan) still retains a toehold in subsistence farming and smallholder production for the market and that movements of population are highly regulated (although much less so than under the Soviet system) has meant that urban poverty has been growing but is relatively contained. There has not been a significant influx of rural-to-urban migrants to cities. On the contrary, both the emigration of non-indigenous nationalities that are predominantly concentrated in urban centres, and the steep decline of urban wages has meant that, at least initially, there has been a slight decline in urban populations since independence. This situation may change drastically if rural livelihoods are threatened by further losses of jobs and access to land. This may deepen the feminization of agricultural work even further since there are indications that most seasonal migrants are men. The combination of the erosion of the welfare system and the squeezing out of smallholders may result in growing destitution unless vigorous programmes of rural industrialization and off-farm employment creation are established.

Finally, the calculation of household incomes and expenditures are currently complicated by the intricate mix of in-cash, in-kind, official, unofficial and informal payments. Furthermore, the reporting of incomes and expenditures may reflect different kinds of logic, depending on the degree of monetization of local economies. Whereas in one region (Andijan) all outgoings, regardless of the form they take (cash, produce or animals) are accounted for as expenses, in another region (Kashkadarya) variations were observed in whether households calculated their animal wealth in terms of market values. The deepening of a market economy may well bring about a homogenizing effect on the deployment of these categories. The use of sensitively designed, longitudinal surveys may not only serve to monitor these changes but may also make a substantial contribution to our currently limited understanding of transition from command to market economies in different regional and cultural contexts. We may yet break out of the poverty of methodology in assessments of poverty.

REFERENCES

Agarwal, B. (1990) 'Social Security and the Family: Coping with Seasonality and Calamity in Rural India', *Journal of Peasant Studies* 17(3): 341–412.
Bruce, J. and D. Dwyer (eds) (1988) *A Home Divided: Women and Income in the Third World.* Stanford, CA: Stanford University Press.
Buckley, M. (ed.) (1997) *Post-Soviet Women: From the Baltic to Central Asia.* Cambridge: Cambridge University Press.
Couduel, A., A. McAuley and J. Micklewright (1997) 'Transfers and Exchanges between Households in Uzbekistan', in J. Falkingham et al. (eds) *Household Welfare in Central Asia*, pp. 202–20. London: Macmillan.
Elson, D. (1995) 'Transition to the Market: Some Implications for Human Resource Development', in P. Cook and F. Nixson (eds) *The Move to the Market? Trade and Industry Policy Reform in Transitional Economies*, pp. 41–56. London: Macmillan.

Evans, A. (1989) 'Gender Issues in Rural Household Economics'. IDS Discussion Paper No. 254. Brighton: Institute of Development Studies.

Falkingham, J. and J. Micklewright (1997) 'Surveying Households in Central Asia: Problems and Progress', in J. Falkingham et al. (eds) *Household Welfare in Central Asia*, pp. 42–60. London: Macmillan.

Grossman, G. (1998) 'Informal Personal Incomes and Outlays in the Soviet Urban Population', in A. Portes et al. (eds) *The Informal Economy*, pp. 150–70. Baltimore, MD: The Johns Hopkins University Press.

Humphrey, C. (1983) *Karl Marx Collective: Economy, Society and Religion in a Siberian Collective Farm*. Cambridge: Cambridge University Press.

Humphrey, C. (1998) *Marx Went Away — But Karl Stayed Behind*. Ann Arbor, MI: The University of Michigan Press.

Ilkhamov, A. (1998) '*Shirkats, Dekhqon* Farmers and Others: Farm Restructuring in Uzbekistan', *Central Asian Survey* 17(4): 539–60.

Kandiyoti, D. (1998) 'Rural Livelihoods and Social Networks in Uzbekistan: Perspectives from Andijan', *Central Asian Survey* 17(4): 561–8.

Lubin, N. (1981) 'Women in Central Asia: Progress and Contradictions', *Soviet Studies* XXXIII(2): 182–203.

Mars, G. and Y. Altman (1992) 'A Case of a Factory in Uzbekistan: Its Second Economy Activity and Comparison with a Similar Case in Soviet Georgia', *Central Asian Survey* 11(2): 101–11.

Moghadam, V. M. (ed.) (1993) *Democratic Reform and the Position of Women in Transitional Economies*. Oxford: Clarendon Press.

Molyneux, M. (1994) 'Women's Rights and the International Context: Some Reflections on the Post-Communist States', *Millenium* 23(2): 287–313.

Moore, H. (1992) 'Households and Gender Relations: The Modelling of the Economy', in S. Ortiz and S. Lees (eds) *Understanding Economic Process*. New York: University Press of America.

Morris, L. (1984) 'Redundancy and Patterns of Household Finance', *Sociological Review* 33(3): 492–523.

Morris, L. (1987) 'Constraints on Gender: The Family Wage, Social Security and the Labour Market', *Work, Employment and Society* 1(1): 85–106.

Pahl, R. (1984) *Divisions of Labour*. Oxford: Blackwell.

Pahl, R. (1988) 'Some Remarks on Informal Work, Social Polarization and the Social Structure', *International Journal of Urban and Regional Research* 12(2): 247–67.

Spoor, M. (1995) 'Agrarian Transition in Former Soviet Central Asia: A Comparative Study of Uzbekistan and Kyrgyzstan', *The Journal of Peasant Studies* 23(1): 46–63.

TACIS/Government of Uzbekistan (1996) 'Pilot Integrated Development Programme, Bulungur District, Samarkand, Uzbekistan'. Final Report BS6-Land Tenure, Tashkent.

UNDP (1998) *Human Development Report — Uzbekistan*. Tashkent: UNDP.

Verdery, K. (1996) *What Was Socialism and What Comes Next*. Princeton, NJ: Princeton University Press.

Whitehead, A. (1981) 'I'm Hungry Mum: The Politics of Domestic Bargaining', in K. Young, C. Wolkowitz and R. McCullagh (eds) *Of Marriage and the Market*, pp. 88–111. London: CSE Books.

5

Gendering Poverty: A Review of Six World Bank African Poverty Assessments

Ann Whitehead and Matthew Lockwood

INTRODUCTION

Concern with poverty within the World Bank has ebbed and flowed over time. Its most recent appearance dates from the late 1980s, which saw the emergence of a 'New Poverty Agenda' and the 1990 *World Development Report* on poverty (Lipton and Maxwell, 1992). However, a key difference between the 1990s and, for instance, the MacNamara period is that awareness of issues to do with 'women in development' and 'gender and development' is far more pervasive. The literature on gender and poverty is now a mature, and very large one (see Baden and Millward, 1995 and Kabeer 1994, 1997 for recent reviews).

At one level, the relationship between gender disadvantage and poverty appears straightforward, and this approach has been readily taken up by development agencies such as the World Bank within a general set of arguments about the 'feminization' of poverty (Buvinic, 1983, 1997). However, on closer inspection, and at a deeper analytical level, the relationships between gender and poverty are far from straightforward, and there are concerns that objectives about unequal gender relations will become subordinated to an agenda about increasing welfare (Jackson, 1996).

This is the context within which this chapter examines gender in the World Bank's Poverty Assessments. Poverty Assessments (PAs) have emerged as the most important statements by the World Bank about poverty in particular countries. By 1996, almost fifty Assessments had been carried out, and for some countries there is more than one Assessment. The approach we have taken is to look at a relatively small number of Assessments (six from four countries) in some detail. Our chosen four countries are Ghana, Zambia,

This chapter is a shorter version of UNRISD DP 99 (Whitehead and Lockwood, 1999), which presents the evidence and arguments in greater detail. The not inconsiderable task of editing a lengthy chapter down to manageable proportions was undertaken by Bridget Byrne, to whom we are very grateful. We would like to thank Caroline Moser, Andy Norton, Alison Evans, Shahrashoub Razavi, Rosemary McGee, Jo Beall, Naila Kabeer and participants in workshops in Trivandrum and Oslo for helpful comments on earlier drafts of this chapter. We have also benefited from the comments of anonymous reviewers who read the chapter for *Development and Change*. The responsibility for the chapter's findings, including errors of fact or judgement, of course remains with us, the authors.

Tanzania and Uganda in sub-Saharan Africa.[1] Partly because both African populations and poverty are mainly in rural areas, and partly because our own experience has been in rural, as opposed to urban Africa, we have focused particularly on what the Assessments have to say about poverty and gender in rural areas. In our review, we have been helped by the fact that a number of high quality evaluations of the Poverty Assessments already exist which focus on complementary themes: a review of Assessments and public expenditure reviews in Africa by the Institute of Development Studies at Sussex (IDS, 1994); a comprehensive examination of twenty-five Assessments by a team at the Institute of Social Studies (ISS) in the Hague (Hanmer et al., 1997); an internal evaluation by the World Bank which focuses on the links between Assessments and other Bank processes (World Bank OED, 1996); and a review of the Participatory Poverty Assessments for the UK's Department for International Development by the Centre for Development Studies at Swansea (Booth et al., 1998).

The first section of the chapter outlines the ways in which gender concerns actually appear, or do not appear, in each of the six PAs we examined, and the institutional and organizational context in which they were produced. The rest of the chapter then seeks to explain exactly why gender appears in the forms it does, and at the points it does, in these documents. In this process, a number of points emerge not simply about the approach to gender within the World Bank, but also about the approach to poverty, to methodological issues, and to policy.

GENDER IN THE POVERTY ASSESSMENTS: AN OVERVIEW

How Does Gender Appear?

There is enormous variation in the extent to which women and/or gender issues are present in the six Poverty Assessments under scrutiny. Moreover, as the clumsy phrase 'women and/or gender' signals, the language adopted for the analysis and description of gender issues also varies widely. In some Poverty Assessments, the issues are addressed through talking about 'women'; other Poverty Assessments use the language of 'gender' and some of these have an elaborated set of concepts, including those of the gender division of labour, gender relations, gender discrimination and so on. By far the most common way in which women appear in the Assessments is in the guise of female-headed households. This is a frequently used way of disaggregating the quantitative nationally representative household surveys. Here, as elsewhere, gender is largely used to describe a relatively fixed status

---

1. These were chosen so as to give a geographic spread, but also to take advantage of the countries in which we have experience of first hand field research. The PA documents are World Bank 1992b, 1993a, 1994, 1995a, 1995b, 1996.

or category with little reference to its relational implications. Where there is an attempt to specify the link between gender and poverty, it mainly consists of identifying women's specific poverty characteristics. Most markedly, even where the main body of the PA has addressed the particular characteristics of poor women or gender issues in other ways, there is a substantial gap between these discussions and the extent to which gender is addressed in the final policy section of the main volume of each report. In these policy sections, gender sensitivity appears in highly fragmented references, largely to women and education and sometimes to the role of women in agriculture.

Readers will hardly be surprised at this lack of consistency. It mirrors the complexity — and confusions — of gender conceptualizations, analysis and language use in the development field as a whole. Academic attention to gender and development began with debates about language and appropriate concepts and recently public institutions and the donor community have come under increasing pressure to elaborate their languages of gender. There has been a commonly occurring shift away from women in development (WID) to gender and development (GAD) formulations within public policy, usually as a result of highly politicized debates about what the shift from women to gender means.[2] As Razavi and Miller (1995a) document, several important institutions have changed their gender language and we can see a trend towards a more uniform language in their public documents.

However, this has not happened at the World Bank. A recent review by Moser et al. (1998) contends that there is no agreement on what the term gender means in Bank policy documents. Arguably, this complexity and lack of coherence in gender language and gender approaches arises out of the relatively weak commitment to WID/gender issues within the Bank. Razavi and Miller (1995b) document the history of the relatively limited resources allocated to gender specialists in the Bank and their weak mandates and institutional position. There is a tendency to locate WID/gender concerns in the soft areas — such as human resources — in an organization giving strong analytical and policy priority to economics. In the period leading up to the Poverty Assessments, gender thinking in the Bank was relocated in a WID Division of the Population and Human Resources Department. Ravazi and Miller (1995b: 38) cite the Gender Team in the Africa region of the Bank arguing that the 1993 reorganization of the institution had led to a 'temporary slowdown of momentum in building up and sustaining staff gender capacity'. It is significant that poverty measurement was being expanded rapidly at a time when efforts to mainstream gender in the Bank had stalled.

By the late 1990s, this weak capacity had contributed to producing a diversity — in approaches to gender and development; in definitions of what

---

2. See, for example, the change from 'women in development' to 'gender and development' by the Development Assistance Committee (DAC) of the OECD. Whitehead (1998) discusses this shift. Goetz and Baden (1997) includes an interesting discussion of contentions around the use of the language of gender and/or women at Beijing.

gender analysis is; and in the potential components of a gender analysis — that Moser et al. document (1998). Their chapter argues the need for a common framework of gender analysis within the Bank. However, no attempt is made to associate the use of particular approaches or definitions of gender with other differences (for example, crudely between different schools of economic analysis, or between social development sections and others). As a result, it is unclear whether this diversity is accidental, whether it is associated with particular perspectives within different sections of the Bank and, crucially, whether it is the outcome of contestation.

Given this background, it is not unexpected that the six Poverty Assessments of our case study have such wide variations in their approach to gender. *Uganda II* and *Ghana I*[3] are two studies in which women and/or gender hardly figure at all in the documents. In *Ghana I*, for example, the only mention of gender issues is an occasional reference to female-headed households and a sudden appearance in an assertion that the agricultural labour force is becoming feminized. No evidence is offered for this generalization and it is not linked with any previous data discussion. It returns in the final section on policy, where the main mention of women is a recommendation for improvements in agricultural extension work with women farmers.

It is a very similar story in *Uganda II*. Household survey data are analysed in terms of differences in per capita expenditure between male-headed and female-headed households. Women are hardly mentioned anywhere else in the report. The policy section does not refer at any point to the gender of the beneficiaries and agents of economic growth, nor to the rural infrastructure and human capital programmes that it recommends.

Since both Uganda and Ghana have two successive Poverty Assessments, this allows us to examine whether there is evidence of a learning process. We might expect the gender sensitivity of PAs to have grown through the early 1990s. This seems to be borne out in the Ghana case. *Ghana I*, which is one of the earliest Poverty Assessments (1992), was followed by a 1995 assessment which is much more gender sensitive *(Ghana II)*. A general trend is belied, however, in the contrast between the two Uganda studies. *Uganda I*, undertaken in 1992, contains much more about gender than *Uganda II*, undertaken in 1995. What the *Uganda II* and *Ghana I* Poverty Assessments (with their scant attention to gender) seem to have in common is that they are the documents most dominated by a poverty strategy centred on macro economic growth. These Poverty Assessments are also largely content to use poverty lines, that is, income or consumption money-metric household definitions of poverty.

---

3. In our sample countries, both Uganda and Ghana have two successive Poverty Assessments, conducted in 1992 and 1995. In each case, the 1992 PAs are referred to as I and the 1995 PAs are denoted II. The 1992 Uganda PA was published in 1993 (World Bank, 1993a).

Tanzania and *Uganda I* are more eclectic in their approach. Each has an initial gender sensitivity in that a separate report on gender/women's issues was commissioned, with a summary appearing as a separate chapter in the final report. The content of these chapters is dominated by the kind of gender analysis that is prevalent in the country concerned, influenced by national literature and local feminist policy priorities. They have a much better developed language to describe gender issues. In *Uganda I*, there is a wholesale use of the language of gender. It appears for example in the idea of the gender division of labour, and in arguments about the need for gender-responsive actions and growth. The framework of gender analysis makes use of the idea of rights and obligations between men and women and the use of the law to establish women's rights to land, labour and other resources. The problem of women's time burdens, because of domestic responsibilities and their disadvantages in access to education, are also prominent, as are the effects on women of the high incidence of HIV and AIDS. The treatment of gender in a separate chapter does mean, however, that there is much less focus on women throughout the rest of the report, with the exception of female-headed households which are identified as one of the poverty categories. When it comes to the policy chapter, there is no mention of gendered agents, until a separate section makes a series of recommendations about women which arise directly out of the analyses in the gender chapter.

In the *Tanzanian* PA, the dominant gender language in the chapter on women concerns the 'status of women', with a stress on women's legal status and educational disadvantages, on advocacy and political mobilization. The *Tanzanian* PA is also one of three out of the six PAs that adopts new methodologies for the identification of poverty, with the commissioning of a Participatory Poverty Assessment (PPA). The women's chapter has a good discussion of the link, or lack of it, between poverty and female-headed households which draws on both household survey data and data from the Participatory Poverty Assessments. It also discusses intra-household gender equity, using as its sources already published qualitative case studies.

Despite all this, the main chapter on incomes, inequality and poverty barely mentions women, except in a suggestion that women choose under-employment. In the policy chapters, gender issues are reduced to two: female education and targeted social spending. There are other missed opportunities and inconsistencies, as for example when women (as an otherwise unqualified social category) are described as a 'vulnerable group'. The account of agri-culture and rural livelihoods is completely silent on the sex of farmers and the gender division of labour in agriculture. There is a rather good account of the causes of poverty in households with agricultural livelihoods that owes much to the findings of Participatory Poverty Assessment. Yet, while several of these findings have clear gender dimensions — such as the supply of inputs, savings, credit, access to livestock and labour — rural poverty is discussed in wholly gender blind ways.

The final pair of studies — *Zambia* and *Ghana II* — are documents in which gender is a palpable part of the Poverty Assessments, although neither has a separate chapter on women/gender. Rather, gender is integrated into the analysis with different degrees of success. In the *Zambian* case, the language of the gender analysis shifts around quite a lot. Gender is referred to as a 'social status'. 'Female-headed households' appear, as do 'women without support', but the 'gender division of labour' is a significant element of the arguments in the rural volume. Here the analysis centres on a model of the agricultural household which examines the effect of the gender division of labour on income from agriculture under a number of conditions. Female headship is listed as a cause of poverty in urban areas and female-headed households in general are included as a poverty category.

In *Ghana II*, the language of gender is largely descriptive, with frequent references to women, or women and girls. The report gives prominence to the role of women in agriculture and to some of the conditions which affect poor rural women, such as the time burden of water collection in the dry north. There is no data on gender and poverty in the account of the household quantitative data, except in a disaggregation by sex of household head, where there is also a discussion of some of the problems of defining female-household heads and of the importance of intra-household differences. There is an innovative discussion of gender biases in social spending.

Along with *Tanzania*, *Zambia* and *Ghana II* are the other two Poverty Assessments that have combined national level poverty line methodologies with specially undertaken Participatory Poverty Assessments. The influence of the findings from the participatory exercises is evident throughout the accounts and appears to be one vehicle for greater gender sensitivity. Additionally, in each of these Assessments, gender has been examined in one or more of the other studies commissioned to inform the findings. In the *Ghana II* case, this is apparent in the analysis of who benefits from social spending and in the *Zambia* case, in the agricultural modelling, which is the centrepiece of the rural analysis. Even in these two Poverty Assessments, the policy sections fail to match the visibility of gender in the rest of the reports. In the *Zambia* case, the implications have been reduced to the need for labour saving technology for 'female' tasks on smallholdings and a prioritizing of girls' education in human resource development policy. In *Ghana II*, the policy section contains very little reference to women. There is a final paragraph to the report listing the need for more research on gender and poverty as one of a series of priorities for future research.

The picture that emerges from this overview is one of inconsistencies, fragmentation and gaps, both between and within the six PAs being reviewed here. Where it is not ignored, gender is made visible in many different ways, with no attempt to systematize the gender analysis implied by these discussions. The inconsistencies between the Poverty Assessments suggest that the project teams had a good deal of autonomy about how they interpreted and prioritized gender issues. Indeed, the Poverty Assessments are very different from one another in a large number of respects. They do not appear to have a common work plan, yet, at the same time, the concluding policy sections, in which much less attention is given to gender or women, are much more uniform. All this raises questions about the organization of, and background to, the Poverty Assessments. What briefs were the project teams working to? How were the Assessments planned and carried out? What were the procedures for producing the final reports? What is the link between the Poverty Assessments and the Bank's move to prioritize poverty as its development goal since 1990?

How Were The Assessments Done?

The publication of the 1990 *World Development Report* (WDR) signalled a significant break from the past for the World Bank. It was the product of an evolving approach to poverty and policy within the Bank, influenced by thinking on growth and liberalization in Africa in the early 1980s, debates on the social costs of adjustment and the UNICEF critique. Since then, the approach to poverty and policy has continued to evolve under the influence of the *East Asian Miracle* report (World Bank, 1993b). In general, there has been a move away from the preoccupation with the perceived conflict between the market and the state. Poverty, and policy to reduce poverty, have moved to centre stage.

As a result of these shifts, by the late 1980s, the World Bank had begun to step up its country-specific analysis and measurement of poverty in order to fill the information gap. As noted in the WDR: 'The absence of reliable inter-temporal statistics on income distribution in most Sub-Saharan African countries makes any comprehensive account of trends in poverty there impossible' (World Bank, 1990: 42). In 1991, various directives and strategy chapters were combined and released as a new *Operational Directive on Poverty Reduction*, OD 4.15 (World Bank, 1991). This was accompanied by a *Poverty Reduction Handbook* (World Bank, 1992a) containing 'examples of good-practice analytical and operational work' (World Bank, 1991: 1). The Directive was intended to guide operational work for poverty reduction, including the collection of information on poverty.

The approach to policy in OD 4.15 is explicitly based on the 1990 WDR. The policy recipe consisted of: broad-based growth brought about by the removal of price distortions and the provision of credit and infrastructure (World Bank, 1990: 73), basic social services (ibid: 88–9), and safety nets (ibid: 101–2). There is a guide for content for the Assessments, based on this approach, clearly aimed at standardization across countries. However, the Directive does recognize that the scope of issues will vary across countries, as will data availability. The level of government commitment to poverty reduction is seen as a key variable for shaping individual Assessments. Further guidance on measurement, analysis and policy is spelled out in detail in the *Poverty Reduction Handbook* accompanying OD 4.15 (World Bank, 1992a).

In practice, almost all of the PAs we looked at did follow a common overall structure, roughly similar to the model laid out in OD 4.15 and in the Handbook.[4] Each starts with an attempt to lay out a poverty line, and provide an overall headcount indicator of poverty. Most then go on to provide associations of poverty with household characteristics, such as location, education and sex of head. The format does vary, with some including separate chapters on particular issues (for example, urban poverty in *Zambia*, and women in *Tanzania*). However, what is common across all of the examples is a concluding policy section. Not only is the policy section an inevitable feature of all the PAs; there are also core elements in that section which are common. Not surprisingly given the WDR 1990 background, these centre on achieving growth through macro-economic policies, public sector reform for the delivery of social services, especially education, and targeting of safety nets.

Bearing in mind the enormous variation in approaches to gender within our sample of six PAs, it is noteworthy that OD 4.15 gives no guidance on whether and how gender considerations should be included in the content of Poverty Assessment. The only mention of gender is the general statement which appears at the beginning of the document that: 'The burden of poverty falls disproportionately on women: so it is essential to increase their income-earning opportunities, their food security and their access to social services' (World Bank, 1991: 2). Gendered statements in the *Poverty Reduction Handbook* are confined to a breakdown of data by gender, a discussion of female education under public expenditure, women's land rights, and the targeting of agricultural extension services to women.

According to OD 4.15, overall responsibility for operational work on poverty, which includes the Poverty Assessments, was vested in Regional Vice Presidents. Country department directors were to ensure the quality of analytical work and consistency with Bank policies, while regional chief economists were responsible for determining the satisfactory completion of a PA and the position of the poverty line (World Bank, 1991: 3).

In practice, many Poverty Assessments ended up with only a loose articulation with the Bank itself. Many were funded directly by external donors, especially European ones. A team of national and expatriate consultants headed by a task manager from Bank staff typically carried them out. This relative autonomy meant that although PAs did contain certain overall elements dictated by OD 4.15 and the 1990 WDR, other aspects varied between countries, and even between two Assessments in one country (for details, see World Bank OED, 1996). The PAs are also products of country governments, with national consultants and government staff involved in their production. OD 4.15 makes it clear that PAs provide 'the

---

4.   The exception to this was *Uganda II*, which was in effect not a full poverty assessment, but
     a *Country Economic Memorandum* with a quantitative appendix on poverty.

basis for a collaborative approach to poverty reduction by country officials and the Bank ... [helping] to establish the agenda of issues for the policy dialogue' (World Bank, 1991: 4). As a result, there are different approaches to poverty lines, to poverty analysis, to background studies, and to themed chapters. Crucially, there are also important differences in methodologies for poverty measurement and analysis, especially in how far the team embraced information beyond quantitative surveys.

As noted, variation in the PAs disappears in the final sections dealing with policy. The key factor seems to be the peer review process, by which drafts of the Assessments circulated within the relevant parts of the Bank, and especially through the hands of the country director and regional chief economist. While relatively little attention was paid to the empirical details of poverty measurement and analysis, policy sections attracted heavy comments and, we suspect, rewriting.

The process by which PAs are produced gives some insight into where we should look to understand how gender issues are made visible, or rendered invisible, within the Assessments. The team approach goes some way to explaining variation in how gender appears in the documents, as described above. Since there is no common analysis of gender in the Bank (let alone amongst PA consultants), different teams tended to bring their own approaches, and task managers weighted the significance of gender differently. The 'terms of reference' for the Assessments encapsulated in OD 4.15 and the *Poverty Reduction Handbook* give minimal guidance. They contain virtually no gender analysis, and a limited range of fragmented pointers to where teams might single out women.

UNDERSTANDING GENDER IN THE POVERTY ASSESSMENTS

At one level then, we can see the variable treatment of gender in the PAs simply as the outcome of an absence of a clear analytical gender framework linked to the loose and over-directed manner in which the Assessments were carried out. However, these problems are themselves symptoms of a more subtle and pervasive malaise. Methodological choices have a powerful influence in shaping the ways in which gender appears or is made invisible in the evidence on poverty in the PAs. Moreover, rather different factors shape the ways in which gender is treated in the analysis of poverty, and discussion of policies to reduce poverty. In the absence of a clear analytical framework for understanding gender, the treatment of gender in the Assessments is effectively driven by, on the one hand, a set of epistemological and methodological choices about measuring poverty, and on the other, a set of prescriptions for reducing poverty which originate in the WDR 1990.

In the remainder of this study, two central questions are taken up. The first question focuses on the empirical evidence collated in the poverty profiles, and asks why gender appears as it does, or indeed, why it is rendered invisible in certain ways. Central to the question of how far and in what ways gender issues could be discussed in the PAs is the issue of how evidence is generated and presented. While all of the Assessments exploited data collected in surveys using households as units, some also used various other sources, including evidence collected through participatory techniques. These various approaches to data collection imply different possibilities for raising gender issues.

The second question asks why gender appears as it does (or again, does not) in the policy analysis of the Assessments. In most of the Assessments, there are significant gaps, as we move from the evidence on gender and poverty to the policy analysis. Unlike the country-specific poverty profiles, the policy sections of the PAs are heavily influenced by peer review, and hence by both the 1990 WDR model and by subsequent evolving ideas about poverty within the Bank. To understand how gender appears in the analytical and especially the policy sections of the PAs, it is therefore crucial to examine these ideas.

The Poverty Assessments display an instance of one of the most fundamental, yet at the same time difficult-to-grasp, aspects of gender and poverty. Gender considerations are not an add-on to poverty, or a way of finessing a basically sound analysis or policy. Rather, the ways in which we (or the World Bank) define, measure and analyse poverty will have profound consequences for the way in which we characterize gender relations and inequalities. Equally, a proper gender analysis makes possible a useful approach to poverty.

Measuring Poverty and Gender I: Household Surveys

The Poverty Assessments follow in a long line of attempts to define and measure poverty. The definition of poverty determines the approach to measurement and the types of evidence to be considered. Of the Assessments we examined, most start by asserting the multiple dimensions of poverty. This multi-dimensional approach has led some (four out of six) of the PAs to adopt specialist methodologies to get at the poor's own perceptions of poverty, or at least local understandings of what poverty is. None of the PAs translate the multi-dimensional nature of poverty into an interest in well-being, or quality of life indicators, and so ignore the whole debate about social indicators and their relation to poverty.

Table 1, which looks at the various ways in which poverty is measured in the PAs under review, makes it clear that there is no standard, agreed way of defining and measuring poverty across the Assessments. Money-metric poverty lines dominate the introductory sections on evidence on poverty but, at various points, additional or complementary evidence is also drawn upon, including health and nutritional outcome indicators. Ultimately, however, all give priority to an income and/or consumption definition, a money-metric

Table 1. Measures of Poverty in Six Poverty Assessments

	Money metric poverty line	Nutritional and health data	Education data	Participatory assessment
Uganda I	x	x	x	x
Uganda II	x	x	x	
Ghana I	x			
Ghana II*	x	x	x	x
Tanzania	x	x	x	x
Zambia	x	x	x	x

*Also contains a discussion of social spending by gender.

poverty line and a quantitative estimate of the percentage in poverty. There is also a great deal of variation as to how that poverty line is established. Of our six Assessments, half define poverty lines in absolute terms and half in relative terms. Absolute poverty lines are in two cases determined in relation to a 'minimum' food basket and in *Tanzania* simply as a level of expenditure. Relative poverty lines range from 0.33 to 0.5 of mean expenditure for lower poverty lines, and between 0.66 and 0.8 of mean expenditure for upper poverty lines. Finally, while most Assessments deflate household expenditure by average household size, *Uganda II* and *Zambia* use expenditure per adult equivalent. This variation makes cross-national comparisons impossible, although one of the rationales for using quantitative data is precisely that they are (in theory at least) comparable.[5]

Basing the definition and measurement of poverty on a single, money-metric dimension makes poverty into a simple characteristic. In a sense, this is a fundamental methodological choice, since it locks the PAs into reliance on expenditure data from surveys. As a result, poverty lines are a relatively weak guide to the *processes* of impoverishment. This point is strongly made in the ISS review which recommends dropping money-metric poverty lines in favour of a socio-economic analysis approach because of the way in which the former fails to produce an account of poverty processes and dynamics (Hanmer et al., 1997). There are gender implications here, since a gendered account of poverty must be based on an analysis of poverty processes and dynamics.

Money-metric poverty lines also lead to a heavy dependence on survey data collected on a household basis. None of the Poverty Assessments attempt a quantitative exploration of poverty *within* households. However, both *Zambia* (p. 3) and *Uganda I* (p. 33) show an awareness of the problems arising from the limitations of aggregated data, particularly in terms of masking inequities within households. These insights are not, however,

---

5. For example, for Uganda, a relative poverty line approach in 1992 is followed by an absolute food-basket based approach in 1995, making comparison across time very difficult (Appleton, 1996).

followed through in the analysis of the household survey data. In considering gender, all the PAs are confined to analysing their household survey data according to the differences in the sex of the household head. Lying behind the aggregated household approach is an implicit assumption of pooled income and consumption within the household, despite considerable evidence to the contrary, especially for West Africa. Such a household has a head and the characteristics of this head — age, sex and marital status — are invariably collected and form a ready basis for sorting the data. Thus, women can only be made visible as female heads of household. Consequently, some of the approach to gender in the Poverty Assessments is driven by data whose mode of collection embodies prior decisions about the level at which human agency and personhood can, or should be, appropriately conceptualized in policy analysis of this kind.

The contemporary analysis of gender began with the understanding that the family based household is never a terrain of equality. Well-being, power and often access to economic resources are all differentially distributed. Intra-household relations themselves have been shown to be a powerful determinant of individual access to utilities and capabilities. Twenty years of feminist argument and evidence about the need to analyse the household as a system of social relations (Evans, 1991; Folbre, 1996; Kabeer, 1994; Whitehead, 1981), plus the evidence of gender differentiated poverty outcomes, has led to several developments in the formal economic modelling of households (see Haddad, Hoddinott and Alderman, 1997). These important developments are not reflected in the methodologies adopted in the PAs we are considering. All lack any intra-household dimension to income.

Female-Headed Households

Despite the limitations, it is important to compare female and male-headed households, if only because of some claims that growing poverty in sub-Saharan Africa is associated with the growth of female-headed households, or that female-headed households are disproportionately poor.[6] When female-headed households are compared with male-headed within each PA, using the poverty measurement from the household surveys, there is no clear finding as to which is likely to be poorer. So, in *Tanzania* and *Ghana II*, female-headed households are reported as richer, while in *Uganda I and Zambia*, they are poorer. There was no comment on the level at which the sometimes very small differences have been shown to be significant, or indeed *if* they are. We were surprised that there had been no effort to compare female and male heads of households divided into urban and rural dwellers, or to

---

6. For discussions see, for example, Baden and Milward (1995); Buvinic (1993; 1997); Chant (1997a); Jackson (1996).

make regional comparisons given differences in labour markets, climatically linked types of agriculture and social organization. Such a comparison is positively crying out to be made in the *Ghana II* PA, in the light of the interesting finding in the Participatory Poverty Assessment that female headship in the south is not perceived to be associated with poverty, whereas in the North it is.

The evidence of the six PAs, as well as the extensive literature deconstructing the idea of female-headed households,[7] suggest that disaggregation by gender of 'household head' does not provide a very meaningful approach to gender and poverty. The category of female headship lumps together categories of household, generated by different processes at different life cycle stages and for different reasons, which are likely to have a variety of socio-economic circumstances and opportunities.[8] This makes any simple comparison between male-headed and female-headed households impossible to interpret.

A further point is that even where certain types of female-headed households are found to be poorer, this begs a further set of questions for which we need a processual, rather than snapshot approach to household formation. In discussions of the household characteristics of poor and poorest households, the household variables are always treated as if they were independent, but it is perfectly possible that the chain of causation runs the other way round. For example, lone widows may well be a significantly poor category of households in sub-Saharan Africa, but why do some widows end up living alone and others do not? Widowhood may be only a calamitous event for the poor because it is those widows who are poor whose children leave the household — perhaps on labour migration. When more economically secure women are widowed, they do not end up living alone. This suggests the need for policies that support the social management of household membership, which is such a priority concern for African people in very many areas (Bledsoe, 1995; Lockwood, 1997).

The decision then to prioritize money-metric poverty lines, based on households, as the unit of analysis as the measurement of poverty has profound consequences for any gender profiling of poverty. It is one of a number of methodological decisions which underlie the way in which gender is present, or absent, in the PAs. It undermines any perspective on the ways in

---

7. See Appleton (1996), Chant (1997a, 1997b); Lloyd and Gage-Brandon (1993).
8. Persistent definitional problems with SSA households (see Guyer, 1981; Guyer and Peters, 1987; Yanagisako, 1979) underlie some of these difficulties. Many household surveys (for example, the *Uganda Household Budget Survey*, the *Ghana Living Standards Survey*) contain relatively little discussion of how these difficulties have been resolved, but most of the country studies throw up examples of culturally specific household forms that do not tally with standardized definitions of household. A particular issue here is that we get very little sense of how polygamy is treated in relation to household definition and hence of what contribution polygamy makes to the category of female headship.

which intra-household inequalities might contribute to gendered poverty outcomes. Poverty lines may be politically useful for establishing entitlement in welfare states or as baselines for assessing changes in incomes. However, it is difficult to make a link between the measurement of poverty in this form and its causes, and therefore to any explanation and rationale for alleviation strategies. A major reason for this is the difficulty of establishing poverty processes using static measurements of this kind.

Measuring Gender and Poverty II: Gender and the Participatory Poverty Assessments

These kinds of limitations of conventional household level surveys of quantitative poverty indicators have been widely discussed. They undoubtedly influenced the Bank's decision to experiment in the Poverty Assessments with methodologies that incorporate a qualitative, or subjective, element through using participation as a key tool. The Participatory Development Group that was established within the Bank promoted the idea of commissioning Participatory Poverty Assessments (PPAs) to operational managers (Holland and Blackburn, 1998).

The growing popularity in participatory methodologies reflects an interest in both the values embodied in the use of participatory methodologies and in the use of specific methods, as both a planning aide and a form of research method. There are many different kinds of participatory methodology. A recent review (Guijt and Shah, 1997) list thirty-three separate approaches and sets of techniques, each with its attendant acronym and a substantial and multifaceted literature on their advantages and disadvantages over more traditional methods (for PRA, see Chambers, 1994).

The core idea in participatory methods is that of using a variety of techniques to elicit knowledge, characterizations and understandings which do not use the language, concepts and categories of the interviewer and researcher, who by definition does not share the economic and social reality of poor people. The open-endedness of participatory techniques, and especially their stress on local perceptions of poverty, allows for a fuller range of poverty concepts. In addition, participatory methodologies also incorporate a philosophy that valorizes the direct involvement of people in problem identification. They draw on a critique of literacy practices, which argues that these are more than a set of technical skills, but are also a key element in a nexus of power/knowledge relations. Participatory methodologies aim to deliver a bottom up approach and to report the voices of the poor.

One contentious area in participatory methodologies is their use of more traditional qualitative techniques as part of participatory methods. We were initially surprised to find interviews with key informants and unstructured interviews with farmers or urban traders being described as 'participatory', since we are accustomed to think of these as standard qualitative research methods. However, techniques such as conversational interviewing and semi-structured interviews are now normal practice in some kinds of participatory methodologies. Proponents argue that it is the participatory context in which these semi-structured interviews were carried out which is the important feature of the methodology (Norton: personal communication). Furthermore, the participatory element in using informal interviewing of individuals, as part of a PPA, does become difficult to pin down.

Contestation about what constitutes a participatory method and its relation to qualitative methods is not simply a turf war. It is an important link to the long-standing epistemological competition in the social sciences between quantitative and qualitative approaches to research. Within economics, the quantitative paradigm has a foundational status. The use of the new participatory methods within the Bank, whose research culture has been dominated by economics, represents a foothold for non-quantitative methods. However, this does beg the question of whether there should not be a greater role for the findings from more conventional research using qualitative methods in the Bank's discussions of poverty. Our six PAs make relatively little use of the existing published local level case studies that have used a variety of qualitative research techniques to produce data appropriate for the analysis of socio-economic processes.[9]

Four Participatory Poverty Assessments

Given the emphasis on flexibility and local ownership in participatory methods, we were particularly interested in how each of the Participatory Poverty Assessments had been done and how the findings were integrated into the PAs. Moreover, as men and women experience poverty rather differently, we would expect gender to be made more visible through PPA methodologies.

In our four examples, the *Uganda* study stands out. The PPA was conceived as providing an adjunct to existing data and was used in the war zones where the household level survey work, on which the rest of the poverty assessment depends, could not be carried out. This was a very early example of a PPA and the decision to use it as an 'adjunct' clearly had a lot to do with local circumstances. There is very little evidence that the results of the *Uganda* PPA in any way influenced the analysis in the PA, especially its policy discussion. Nevertheless, according to Robb (1998), the *Uganda* PA generated a widespread discussion in the Bank of the value of using qualitative methods.

---

9. Some recent PAs have examined this literature with many positive effects (see World Bank, 1995c).

The other three examples of PAs with PPAs, dated 1994, 1995 and 1996, all had the participatory element funded as a separate piece of research. The most comprehensive published PPA in our set is that from *Zambia* (1994). The account of the methods of the PPA in Volume 5 of the PA is detailed and it is immediately clear that the participatory data collection exercise included many forms of semi-structured interviewing of individuals and groups as a significant part of the research.

In contrast to the *Uganda* PA, it is much easier to see the influence of the PPA in the case of the *Zambia* assessment. However, moving backwards from the PPA volume (5), through volume 3 (on rural poverty), to the main report, volume 1, we witness a loss of many themes from the PPA. The specificities of rural poverty, which are well described in the PPA report itself, become dominated by analytical and policy agendas which are extraneous to the local situation.[10] It is in this process that the gender insights from the PPA become lost: first, because they are not used in the rural volume, which is dominated by other specially commissioned work, notably that on agricultural modelling; second, when these volume 3 findings make their way into volume 1, evidence there that the gender division of labour is not nearly as rigid as the model specified is ignored in favour of the findings of the model.

The design of the *Ghana* PPA and its findings are much less transparent. Very little of the design of the research and the findings appear in the PA itself. They are instead described in a separate discussion chapter (Norton et al., 1995) in the *Poverty and Social Policy Series*. The *Ghana II* case (1995) shows clear slippage or gaps between the PPA and the PA. In the PA itself, the findings from the qualitative interviews and the various participatory exercises appear as a separate chapter. This follows on immediately from the quantitative data description. Care is taken to discuss the linkages between the two kinds of findings; however, some of the key messages from the local conceptions of vulnerability and poverty of the PPA are not carried through elsewhere in the PA. Further slippage occurs when we come to the final chapter on the policy agenda. The prescription is a three-pronged set, namely broad-based growth (especially in agriculture); deepening of human capital through education and health; and the use of a targeted social fund. The appraisal of the health and education sectors made in the PPA are taken on board. However, the discussion of agriculture seems to derive little from the PPA findings. In the *Ghana II* case, there is no doubt that certain findings of the PPA are relatively well integrated into the PA and it does appear to influence the overall policy recommendations. Nevertheless, the internal evidence suggests that it is a very selective reading of the PPA findings. The

10. A fuller and more informed discussion on the influence of the Zambian PPA findings on the Poverty Assessment and other aspects of the policy process is to be found in Norton (1998a); Norton is one of the authors of the PPA.

gender findings of the PPA are among those that are subject to this selective reading.

Our final case is that of *Tanzania* (1996) which is both very individual and very interesting. Policy makers were consulted on what they wanted to know and this was incorporated in the terms of reference for the PPA. The research team's stress on credibility led them to design one part of their PPA as a semi-structured interview format, with a sample of households which was drawn in a statistically rigorous way as a sub-sample for the main survey. This methodology enables some of the PPA findings to claim statistical significance; others have a more strictly illustrative or qualitative role. There are several chapters of the PA where the findings of the PPA are apparently widely integrated into the analysis and discussion. The PPA results are not *only* used when they can be backed up by household economic survey evidence. A telling example of this occurs in the discussion of female-headed households. There is a stark difference in the findings from the main quantitative and PPA surveys about the poverty of female-headed households. According to the PPA data, 29 per cent of female-headed households are very poor, but the main survey data gives only 18 per cent. In the interesting discussion of this difference, it is suggested that people themselves perceive poverty as being about more than current income and resources, but also about long-term security. The discrepancy arises because more female heads lack long term security, since they are less likely to own capital assets than male heads and are also more isolated from supportive family networks. This discussion is judicious in its attempt to reconcile differences in the findings. This kind of serious comparison is rare and rarer still is a preference for the PPA evidence over that from a household survey.

Do the PPAs Improve Gender Analysis?

Our most important question, of course, is whether the PPAs improve the gender analysis in the Poverty Assessments. Participatory methodologies might potentially deliver a gendered profile of poverty because of their capacity to come closer to people's experience of poverty. However, despite the fact that those PAs with PPAs in our sample do show greater gender sensitivity, this does not seem to come from a direct delivery of gendered poverty analysis from the PPAs findings. Given the various claims made for participatory methodologies, this is both striking and disappointing. In the following analysis of several claims frequently made for participatory methodologies, we show that the potential for PPAs to improve gender analysis fails precisely because it is only a potential, not an intrinsic feature. In the absence of existing gender awareness, the PPA will add little that is new.

Booth et al. (1998) argue that one major benefit of the PPAs lies in the potential for *triangulation*. We are in complete agreement about the huge benefits of triangulation in an analysis of poverty, its incidence, character-istics and causes in sub-Saharan Africa, but there are few examples in our case studies that PPAs are being used in this way. The PAs appear to have a limited understanding of non-quantitative non-survey based methodologies, poor conceptualization of what PPAs can do, and very little idea about triangulation and how multi-stranded methods can be successfully com-bined. Indeed, as we have indicated, the PPAs sit very uneasily within the PAs. The PAs almost inevitably privilege the authority and use of quantit-ative data from household surveys over qualitative information, which effectively comes from the Participatory Poverty Assessments. The lack of methodological sophistication in resolving the tension between the different types of data represents yet another barrier between the potential for the PPAs contributing a gendered perspective on poverty and their actual failure to do so.

The claim that PPAs give a more dynamic picture of poverty is an important one (see Booth et al., 1998). It is made explicit in the *Ghana II* Assessment and is followed by a discussion of seasonal aspects of poverty and malnutrition, which introduces the idea of poverty as vulnerability. The qualitative PPA accounts certainly include the reporting of long-term changes in the environment which are having a critical effect on vulnerability. This is an important discussion. But it is 'dynamic' only in the simple sense that long-term trends are addressed; what is absent is an account of the economic and social dynamics related to environmental trends. In our three examples where there is a full PPA component, this has not produced a substantial account of poverty causes and poverty processes. Both methodo-logies — participatory and conventionally statistical — can be deployed to produce static pictures of poverty (cf. Baulch, 1996).

The Politics of Poverty

Booth et al. (1998) point out that participatory methodologies have come to be seen as 'a powerful tool' to establish how poor people perceive and understand poverty. Indeed one of the most frequently cited advantages of using participatory methodologies in the Bank's documents lies in their capacity to access the 'voices of the poor'. There is, however, unease as to what this means and how it should be done. In one or two cases, the results of the country's PPA are introduced with a composite picture of a poor person that is very close to being banal. This is not very different from the simple addition of human interest — to show poverty is a human tragedy, experi-enced by flesh and blood people, not by statistical units.

None the less, there are some cases where the perceptions of poor people have been used properly as evidence. Perhaps the most promising aspect of the PPAs is the detailed information they have provided on the reality of public service provision. Norton (1998b) identifies these policy areas as ones in which there has been a successful translation of findings into public policy. It is worth pointing out that the data collection in some PPAs was specifically geared to these aspects of public service provision. For example, in the Ghana PPA, the third round of data collection was specifically about this and this is reflected in the findings. It represents a priority of the data collectors and it is not clear how far it matches poor people's priorities.

There is scarcely any reporting on how the PPAs ensured that the voices of women were heard. One of the major literatures criticizing participatory methodologies has concerned their capacity to represent multiple and different voices (Guijt and Shah, 1997; Mosse, 1994). There has been a lot of concern that the voices of the farmers and the voices of the poor picked up through participatory methodologies may turn out to be the voices of men (and slightly wealthier men at that).[11] Without much more detail on the processes by which (and by whom) the PPAs were conducted, it is impossible to assess how widespread and systematic a gender-blind application of participatory method has prevented the PAs from including the voices of poor women.

Participatory methodologies were originally developed within the context of the design and implementation of projects, and were intended to change the ways in which decisions were made. Such issues of power are of course very different where they are directed towards national-level issues of measurement and policy. But within this new context, an important claim made for the PPAs was that, since they are locally owned in a way that conventional poverty measurement is not, they open up a national debate on poverty, making it visible and a legitimate issue for political discourse. Certainly, there is evidence that the Assessments are opening up lively and productive debates at national and international levels (Norton, personal communication). It is too early to judge whether, or how soon, this will lead to shifts in political priorities and policies.

The PPAs have involved larger numbers of people in the process of direct engagement with fellow citizens as a source of research evidence. Here, the key issue is the relatively neglected one of the politics of poverty research, which takes us back to the problem of voice. National debates may be generated, but existing political structures have important effects on the outcomes of these debates. These political issues have urgent relevance for the local politics of gender, as well as the local politics of poverty. The greater awareness of poverty created by the PPAs does not necessarily lead to a more gender aware national poverty debate or to capacity building for gendered poverty analysis. The national political discourses about poverty that are being promoted may remain aloof from the national debates about gender, depending on the existing character of the local and national politics of

---

11. See Cornwall (1997) for a full exploration of gender sensitivity in participatory methodologies.

gender. Changing the politics of poverty in Africa — whether in national arenas or in research culture — will not in itself change the politics of gender.

An Overall Assessment

The analysis in this section suggests that there are severe constraints militating against the potential capacity of the PPAs to produce gender-sensitive accounts of poverty. Participatory methodologies are neither intrinsically gender-sensitive nor gender-neutral (cf. Kabeer, 1997). It depends how they are conducted. There is a range of reasons why the PPAs do not deliver a set of gender messages that are then picked up and used in the PAs. Some gender differences did emerge in many of the PPAs, but so much of the PPA findings are left out of the final reports that this potential for gender analysis is completely lost.

At a more fundamental level, one factor explaining the gender weaknesses in the PPAs is the absence of gender analysis, of any depth, in the participatory methodologies that underlie them. Some feminist methodologies had very similar starting premises of participatory methodologies, especially in their analysis of the relationship between knowledge and power. The two schools also share sophisticated discussions of the link between research, empowerment and social differences.[12] Yet these feminist influences are often unexplored and unacknowledged by those advocating participatory methodologies.[13] In the last analysis then, it is not simply the marginalization of PPA findings within the PAs that reduces their gender impacts. Serious shortcomings in the theory and practice of participatory methodologies also play an important part.

We have addressed the participatory methodologies at some length because they are an important innovation in the PAs. Their use reflects widespread misgivings about the potential of money-metric poverty line measurements and definitions for dynamic poverty analysis. The use of the PPAs has been a learning experience, so that what they are meant to do in each PA is a bit of a moving target. Many of our criticisms of these PPA examples, which represent early attempts to incorporate the new methods, are being addressed in the plans for future PPAs. For us, two issues stand out. First, successful use of participatory methodologies has breached the monopoly over poverty measurement hitherto held by money-metric poverty methodologies. It opens up a space for more careful consideration of the use of alternatives to national household surveys. Our own view is that there is an important role here for integrating the findings of qualitative case studies

---

12. See Maguire (1984) and Mies (1983) for a positive assessment of the potential of participatory methodologies from a feminist perspective, and Mosse (1994) and Guijt and Shah (1997) who point out its limitations in practice. See also Cornwall (1997).
13. Robert Chambers's (1997) account of the theoretical influences on PRA is a case in point.

with national level findings, as well as instituting new studies using participatory methodologies. Secondly, there is an urgent need for future PPAs to be
much more gender-aware in how they are carried out and to be much more
fully-grounded in a gendered analysis of poverty.

Gender and Policy in the Poverty Assessments

There is a deeply embedded paradox in the Assessments. On the one hand,
there is considerable variation in the approaches to measurement, to the
identification of poverty causes and to the analysis of gender relations in the
PAs. On the other hand, there is a remarkable consistency of views expressed
on how to reduce poverty, with usually implicit, but occasionally explicit,
implications for the treatment of gender. These consistent views can be traced
to an orthodoxy in the World Bank regarding the nature of poverty and
policy on poverty reduction, which has its fullest expression in the 1990
WDR. The policy sections of the Assessments may therefore be read as
exercises in applying the framework of the 1990 WDR to particular countries, rather than being generated out of the study of poverty in those
countries itself. We suggested earlier that the resulting gaps between evidence
and analysis on the one hand, and policy on the other, reflect a process by
which policy sections of the Assessments came under much heavier peer
review. While differing empirical specifics of poverty are consistent with the
Bank's position on poverty reduction, different models for poverty reduction
are not.

The implications for gender, and particularly for the ways in which a
gender analysis informs, or fails to inform, policy in the Assessments, are
considerable. A major problem is the 'filtering out' of gender issues and
gendered perspectives. For example in the *Tanzania* PA, a lack of rural
infrastructure, education and safety nets are picked up on in the policy
section, whilst other issues, such as the detailed discussion of gender, are not
mentioned there. We noted above that this process starts as we move from the
PPAs to the main PAs, but it continues as we move from evidence, to analysis
and finally to policy.

The resulting 'gaps' in the treatment of poverty are analogous to those in
the treatment of gender. One of the most striking aspects of the six Poverty
Assessments is that the relationship between evidence about poverty and its
causes on the one hand, and policy recommendations on the other is highly
selective and highly partial. In the *Zambia* PA, the sophisticated programming model of household farming is used in the policy section, producing
recommendations which are belied by the relatively rich evidence and
analysis produced elsewhere in the report. Issues present in the evidence
appear with changed emphasis, or sometimes do not appear at all. For
example, issues highlighted in the PPA in the *Ghana II* report receive a much
lower emphasis in the policy section. Problems and solutions raised in the

analysis are overlooked in the policy section. Again, in the example of the *Tanzania* PA, the issue of remoteness is addressed by proposing more roads, rather than rethinking the liberalization of marketing that is suggested by the earlier analysis. In reports where country-level evidence is less extensive, there is a tendency to rely on international comparisons to make arguments and policy recommendations (for example, *Ghana I* or *Uganda II*). In the case of *Uganda I*, the policy section is explicitly based on the WDR 1990.

The 1990 WDR Model of Poverty

Other reviews of the Poverty Assessments also refer to the deep influence of the 1990 WDR. As we described above, the analysis and policy prescriptions in the PAs reflect not only this orthodoxy, but also an evolving approach to poverty and policy within the Bank over a longer period. We see the implications for gender emerging in three areas in the Assessments, matching the three-pronged 1990 WDR approach. These are the idea of market-led growth (particularly export-led agricultural growth), the role of education, and vulnerability.

In the early 1980s, the World Bank was embarking on structural adjustment as its core policy. The key World Bank document on Africa over the 1980s was known as the 'Berg Report' (World Bank, 1981). This put forward a view of African agriculture and an account of agricultural stagnation that is still clearly visible in the Poverty Assessments in the mid-1990s. The PAs also reflect the shift marked by the Bank's (1989) report, *Sub-Saharan Africa: From Crisis to Sustainable Growth*. A more nuanced agenda was introduced, emphasizing institutional reform, increased efficiency of service delivery and re-direction of expenditure towards primary rather than tertiary services. All the Assessments advocate liberalization of trade and domestic marketing. They state variously that farmers should not be overtaxed, need liberalized export markets and inputs such as roads, fertilizers and credit, as well as price incentives.

Until recently, the conceptual, largely micro-economic framework underlying the market-led growth approach was gender-blind. With the sole exception of the *Zambia* PA, there is no sustained thinking about gender in relation to the broad-based export-led growth model in our six PAs, except for brief assertions that agricultural extension services must target women. Even this last point usually enters under the policy sections on agriculture, not on broad-based growth.

The *Zambia* Assessment frames gender as a question of efficiency: rigidities in the gender division of labour are identified as potential barriers to the expansion of agricultural production. This approach very much reflects the main way in which micro-economists both inside and outside the World Bank (as opposed to social scientists), have taken up gender over the 1990s (see for example, Collier, 1994). Gender equity arguments have been recast as arguments about efficiency (Razavi and Miller, 1995b: 40–2, 47). This process has currently reached the stage that gender relations are now seen by some within the Bank as the *main* constraint to growth in sub-Saharan Africa (Blackden, 1998). The issues raised by feminist economists — of gender equity within households and the balancing of the productive and repro- ductive economies — are not reflected in the growth agenda.

Vulnerability

Social safety nets as they appear in the Assessments have picked up the UNICEF idea of vulnerability. UNICEF, in the publication *Adjustment with a Human Face* (Cornia et al., 1987) emphasized that adjustment involved costs to which some sections of the population were particularly vulnerable. This combined with the recognition that 'getting prices right' would not alone bring investment, stability and growth. In practice, the social dimen- sions of adjustment (SDA) programmes introduced in Africa rarely addressed the problems of the poor, especially the rural poor. They largely went to compensate public sector workers who lost incomes through cuts in public employment. The successors to SDA programmes — social funds — have also failed to act as proper safety nets (Tjonneland et al., 1998: 73).

There are sometimes considerable continuities between the UNICEF approach and the poverty groups that emerge in the PAs: compare, for example, the *Ghana I* PA with Cornia et al. (1987). However, when the social safety nets concept appears in the policy sections of the PAs, it does so in a different context from its original use. The concept of vulnerability in the Poverty Assessments is not used to mean vulnerability to economic change (including reform), but a more static sense of vulnerability to drought, other natural disasters, and a 'common sense' notion of social vulnerability. This approach is consistent with the Bank's continuing position that adjustment causes only 'transitional' poverty and that the majority of the poor have generally gained from adjustment (see Demery and Squire, 1996).

'Common sense' vulnerable groups often include orphans, the disabled, widows, female-headed households and rural producers in certain margin- alized regions. These are of course not categories that have been identified by the statistical analysis. They do, however, represent a kind of analysis of what poverty is (vulnerability), as well as referring to particular policy needs. Women are over-represented in these 'common-sense' vulnerable groups. This is explicitly or implicitly linked to a static gender-as-characteristic understanding of gender inequalities.

The Role of Education

Recognition of the limits of 'getting prices right', and the criticism levelled by UNICEF and others at school fees and health care charges, has resulted in a new orthodoxy within the Bank on the pivotal role of human capital. This orthodoxy has been strengthened by the Bank views on the role of education in enhancing growth rates in East Asia. Female education, in particular, began to be seen as a synergistic 'magic bullet' which would not only increase child welfare, but also reduce population growth and increase economic growth.[14]

It is widely stated in the Assessments that education is intimately related to agricultural productivity, and thus the escape from poverty. However, the evidence given is often weak, with apparent associations only loosely established and poorly analysed. One concern here is that a relationship between education and income is being read spuriously as causal, when both education and household income may be affected by underlying patterns of wealth organized through families. An alternative hypothesis — seeing educational outcomes as the result of patterns of wealth and poverty rather than the other way round — would be more consistent with the striking fact that, while there are strong statements about the desire for more and better schools in the PPAs, education is not mentioned as an important *cause* of poverty in any of those the PPAs reported.

The Bank orthodoxy concerning gender and education (see for example, Summers, 1994), if not about gender issues more broadly, is reflected within the Assessments, where female education appears in strikingly uniform ways. The analysis of female education in the Assessments is based exclusively on efficiency arguments: how female education is more efficient than male education in increasing child and household welfare, and development indicators more widely. It is not an analysis that says anything about the reproduction of structural gender inequalities, or anything substantive about how gender inequalities underlie educational outcomes. A gender gap in primary or junior secondary education is found in all cases (*Uganda II*: 64; *Uganda I*: 38–9; *Zambia*: 53; *Ghana I*: 19; *Tanzania*: Ch. 5; *Ghana II*: 33). The explanations of why these gender gaps exist are particularly problematic. They are either purely economistic, about expected future returns, or they are anodyne ('parental reluctance' and 'gender bias' are both cited by *Uganda I*, which seem so self-evident as to be virtually meaningless).

In conclusion, it is clear that there are gaps between the evidence on both gender and poverty issues in the Assessments, and their treatment in the policy sections, because the policy and analysis are much more heavily influenced by peer review and by the evolution of Bank thinking since the late 1980s. As a result, the discussions of growth and poverty in the Assessments we examined are almost entirely gender-blind, even in the case where the analysis of rural growth is more gendered (*Zambia*). This is a fairly striking invisibilization of the role of gender relations in rural African economies, considering that thirty years have already passed since Esther Boserup's

14. Summers (1994). For a critique see Green (1994) and Jackson (1992).

pioneering work in this area. The sole exception is the mention of targeting agricultural extension services to women, an approach that merely reinforces the sense that policy makers find it very difficult to engage with the gendered analysis of the economy.

Gendered policy appears to be more visible in the area of vulnerability and safety nets. However, it typically takes the form of 'common sense' statements about groups taken to be vulnerable as a whole, such as widows. Finally, the gender jewel in the policy crown is female education. This is the only high profile gendered policy prescription in most of the Assessments, and reflects the fact that this is the only gender issue on which Bank staff — from country-level right up to the President — can express clear consensus. It is also a prescription based on ideas about the developmental efficiency of female education, rather than gender equity.

GENDER AND POVERTY: PAYING ATTENTION TO PROCESS

At the beginning of this chapter, we suggested that the Poverty Assessments of the 1990s were conducted in a climate of development and aid which was much more alert to issues of gender equity as compared with the 1970s. Perhaps the most disappointing aspect of our review of these six case studies is how little influence the accumulating evidence — that men and women experience poverty differently — has had. The Assessments betray a lack of any substantial appreciation of the issues raised by the study of gender and poverty in Africa over the last two decades.

In our view, the quantitative evidence in the Assessments (on which so much importance is placed) is both under- and over-interpreted. In the 'poverty profiles', an opportunity to explore poverty dynamics through a series of comparative analyses is ignored in favour of a set of statistical associations which produce a static view of who the poor are. At the same time, the quantitative data are taken up selectively to illustrate *a priori* arguments about causes of poverty. The relationship between poverty and education discussed above is a good example.

The participatory poverty assessments (PPAs), which were done in four out of the six cases, have a greater potential to unpick this methodological lock, in that they can have the capacity to say something about perceptions of gender and poverty and of gender relations. Our review confirms the point made by a number of critical, but sympathetic, observers that PPAs are not intrinsically gender sensitive, and that considerable effort needs to be made to ensure that they are so.

There is, in our view, a further problem with the participatory methodologies as they are currently discussed, and their capacity to deliver a gendered analysis. The methodological tradition that has emerged within the participatory approach, as opposed to that underlying more conventional locality-specific case studies of poverty by sociologists or anthropologists, emphasizes the importance of how data is collected, but underplays the importance of interpreting or 'reading' data. This stage of participatory methodologies is relatively under-discussed but it is an important point where the voices of women, which may well be muted by local gender relations, become heard. 'Reading' PPA data also means becoming aware of, and open to, implicitly gendered statements about poverty coming from poor people.

Above, we suggested that there was a gendered gap between the main findings of the Assessments and their policy sections. While some of the gender findings of the PPAs did find their way into the reports, and the separately commissioned background chapters on gender were also represented in some PAs, this evidence and thematic discussion were usually lost when the policy section was reached. These gaps arise because the Poverty Assessments are, above all, policy documents. The status of the documents as World Bank chapters means that they are situated within a particular policy context or climate, which effectively imposes assumptions about what can or cannot be done, and what should or should not be done, in the realm of policy.

A major influence on the policy recommendations in the PAs is the underlying model of poverty causes developed within the Bank, and the associated approach to policy for poverty reduction policy. This strong Bank orthodoxy on poverty reduction strategy interferes with any detailed interpretations of the evidence and findings of the poverty assessments. It is the policy sections of the PAs that are the most influenced by the Bank's evolving but relatively universal model of poverty and poverty reduction. This model has built into it certain assumptions about gender.

The PAs apply a standard, pre-existing analysis, with its attached policy agenda, to each country. The model applied is largely based on the 1990 *World Development Report*, with some additional features that evolve out of the Bank's interpretation of East Asian experience. One of the important characteristics of the WDR 1990 analysis of poverty is that it is funda-mentally about the actions of individuals or individual households in markets. With the exception of the relationship between the market and the state, social and economic relations are absent from this analysis. We would therefore agree with the ISS evaluation that one of the main shortcomings of the PAs is the limited poverty analysis which they contain, and we would point to this lack of analysis of *relational processes of impoverishment or accumulation* as the critical limitation. This is similar to the point made by feminist economists, that gender-blind economics has failed to analyse how men and women are positioned differently in relation to the economy, and to each other.

A particularly clear example of this is in the discussions of agriculture. Many of the policy chapters of the PAs have long discussions of agriculture, which reflects the fact that huge numbers of poor people in sub-Saharan Africa gain their livelihoods in that sector. Increasing the productivity, output and returns to smallholder agriculture must be core objectives in any strategy of labour intensive and pro-poor growth. Yet, we found it hard to feel very confident about either the diagnosis of the processes which produce poverty amongst African agriculturalists, or the proposed remedies.

Absent from the analysis in the PAs are examinations of rural livelihoods, agrarian socio-economic processes, rural social relations and, despite the centrality of the gender division of labour to African agriculture, of course, gender relations. Only by including such examinations would the PAs produce the socio-economic categories of poor people that Hanmer et al. (1997) call for as a pre-requisite for an analysis of poverty. The accounts of rural processes found in sociological, anthropological, and in some cases historical, case studies hardly seem to have penetrated discussions of agricultural policy in the PAs. It is true that women sometimes make momentary appearances in the agricultural policy sections of the PAs. However, they usually do so in ways that are unrelated to the previous findings and analyses, but at the same time are highly similar to the few appearances of 'women' and 'gender' in the *Poverty Reduction Handbook.*

The only sustained discussions of women and agriculture centre on land rights, and occur in those PAs that have stressed the legal basis for gender bias. Gender equity demands attention to the land rights issue, and for some women discriminatory inheritance laws and poor land access are significant constraints. But in our view, it is only in a minority of cases that inadequate access to land, because of an inability to secure usufruct rights, is by itself a cause of poverty for the two-thirds of rural African women who are poor. The fact that land rights rarely emerged as a voiced concern of rural women in the PPAs lends some support to this view.

Access to land, as with other significant resources, is secured or lost through the dynamics of gender relations as they intersect with socio-economic processes, which are often, but not always, ones of impoverishment. Once again, the issue here is a contrast between the static analysis of categories and characteristics, and the dynamic analysis of social and economic relations. The link between gender and poverty lies at the level of process and relations. For this link to be established, poverty must be analysed as relation and process, as must gender.

REFERENCES

Appelton, S. (1996) 'Problems of Measuring Changes in Poverty over Time: The Case of Uganda 1989–92', *IDS Bulletin* 27(1): 43–55.
Baden, S. and K. Millward (1995) *Gender and Poverty*, Bridge Report for SIDA. Brighton: Institute of Development Studies.
Baulch, B. (1996) 'The New Poverty Agency: A Disputed Consensus', *IDS Bulletin* 27(1): 1–10.
Blackden, M. (1998) 'Gender, Growth and Poverty Reduction in Sub-Saharan Africa'. Washington, DC: The World Bank (mimeo).

Bledsoe, C. (1995) 'The Social Construction of Reproductive Outcomes: Social Marginalisation in sub-Saharan Africa', in T. Locoh and V. Hertrich (eds) *The Onset of Fertility Transition in Sub-Saharan Africa*, pp. 221–34. Liège: Ordina Editions.

Booth, D., P. Lanjouw, J. Hentschel and J. Holland (1998) *Participation and Combined Methods in African Poverty Assessment: Renewing the Agenda*. London: Department for International Development.

Buvinic, M. (1983) 'Women's Issues in Third World Development: A Policy Analysis', in M. Buvinic (ed.) *Women and Poverty in the Third World*, pp. 14–33. Baltimore, MD: Johns Hopkins University Press.

Buvinic, M. (1997) 'Women in Poverty: A New Global Underclass', *Foreign Policy* (Fall): 38–53.

Chambers, R. (1994) *Participatory Rural Appraisal: Challenges, Potentials and Paradigms*. Brighton, Institute of Development, University of Sussex.

Chambers, R. (1997) *Whose Reality Counts? Putting the Last First*. London: Intermediate Technology Publications.

Chant, S. (1997a) *Women Headed Households: Diversity and Dynamics in the Developing World*. London: Macmillan.

Chant, S. (1997b) 'Women Headed Households: Poorest of the Poor?', *IDS Bulletin* 28(3): 26–48.

Collier, P. (1994) 'Gender Aspects of Labor Allocation During Structural Adjustment: A Theoretical Framework and the Africa Experience', in S. Horton, R. Kanbur and D. Mazumdar (eds) *Labour Markets in an Era of Adjustment*. Washington, DC: The World Bank.

Cornia, G. A., R. Jolly and F. Stewart (eds) (1987) *Adjustment with a Human Face. Protecting the Vulnerable and Promoting Growth*. New York: Oxford University Press.

Cornwall, A. (1997) 'Gender Politics and the Politics of Difference', in I. Guijt and M. Shah (eds) *The Myth of Community: Gender and Participatory Development*, pp. 46–57. London: Intermediate Technology Publications.

Demery, L. and L. Squire (1996) 'Macroeconomic Adjustment and Poverty in Africa: An Emerging Picture', *World Bank Research Observer* 11(1): 39–59.

Evans, A. (1991) 'Gender Issues in Household Rural Economics', *IDS Bulletin* 22(1): 51–9.

Folbre, N. (1996) 'Hearts and Spades: Paradigms of Household Economics', *World Development* 14(2): 245–55.

Goetz, A. and S. Baden (1997) 'Who Needs (Sex) When You Can Have (Gender)? Conflicting Discourses on Gender at Beijing', *Feminst Review* (56): 3–25.

Green, C. (1994) 'Poverty, Population and Environment: Does "Synergism" work for Women?'. IDS Discussion Paper No. 343. Brighton: Institute of Development Studies.

Guijt, I. and M. Shah (1997) 'General Introduction: Waking up to Power, Process and Conflict', in I. Guijt and M. Shah (eds) *The Myth of Community: Gender and Participatory Development*, pp. 1–23. London: Intermediate Technology Publications.

Guyer, J. (1981) 'Household and Community in African Studies', *African Studies Review* 24(2-3): 87–137.

Guyer, J. and P. Peters (eds) (1987) 'Conceptualising the Household: Issues of Theory and Policy in Africa', *Development and Change* 18(2), special issue.

Haddad, L., J. Hoddinott and H. Alderman (eds) (1997) *Intrahousehold Resource Allocation in Developing Countries: Models, Methods and Policy*. Baltimore, MD and London: Johns Hopkins University Press for the International Food Policy Research Institute.

Hanmer, L., G. Pyatt, H. White (1997) *Poverty in sub-Saharan Africa: What Can we learn from the World Bank's Poverty Assessments?* The Hague: Institute of Social Studies Advisory Services.

Holland, J. and J. Blackburn (eds) (1998) *Whose Voice? Participatory Research and Policy Change*. London: Intermediate Technology Publications.

IDS (1994) *Poverty Assessment and Public Expenditure: A Study for the SPA Working Group on Poverty and Social Policy*. Brighton: Institute of Development Studies, Univiersity of Sussex.

Jackson, C. (1992) 'Questioning Synergism: Win-Win with Women in Population and Environmental Policies'. Norwich: University of East Anglia (mimeo).

Jackson, C. (1996) 'Rescuing Gender from the Poverty Trap', *World Development* 24(3): 489–504.

Kabeer, N. (1994) *Reversed Realities: Gender Hierarchies in Development Thought*. London: Verso.

Kabeer, N. (1997) 'Tactics and Trade-Offs: Revisiting the Links Between Gender and Poverty', *IDS Bulletin* 28(3): 1–13.

Lipton, M. and S. Maxwell (1992) *The New Poverty Agenda: An Overview*. Brighton: Instititute of Development Studies, Sussex University.

Lloyd, C. and A. Gage-Brandon (1993) 'Women's Role in Maintaining Households: Family Welfare and Sexual Inequality in Ghana', *Population Studies* 47: 115–31.

Lockwood, M. (1997) 'Reproduction and Poverty in Sub-Saharan Africa', *IDS Bulletin* 28(3): 91–100.

Maguire, P. (1984) *Women in Development: An Alternative Analysis*. Boston, MA: University of Massachusetts, Centre for International Education.

Mies, M. (1983) 'Towards a Methodology of Feminist Research', in G. Bowles and R. Duelli-Klien (eds) *Theories of Women's Studies*, pp. 173–91. London: Routledge.

Moser, C., A. Tornqvist and B. van Bronkhorst (1998) 'Mainstreaming Gender and Development in the World Bank: A Review of Progress to Date and Recommendations for Next Stages'. Washington, DC: The World Bank (mimeo).

Mosse, D. (1994) 'Authority, Gender and Knowledge: Theoretical Reflections on the Practice of Participatory Rural Appraisal', *Development and Change* 25(3): 497–526.

Norton, A., E. Bortei-Doku Aryeetey, D. Korboe and D. K. Tony Dogbe (1995) 'Poverty Assessment in Ghana Using Qualitative and Participatory Research Methods'. PSP Discussion Paper Series No. 83. Washington, DC: The World Bank.

Norton, A. (1998a) 'Some Reflections on the PPA Process and the Lessons Learned', in J. Holland and J. Blackburn (eds) *Whose Voice? Participatory Research and Policy Change*, pp. 143–8. London: Intermediate Technology Publications.

Norton, A. (1998b) 'Analysing Participatory Research for Policy Change', in J. Holland and J. Blackburn (eds) *Whose Voice? Participatory Research and Policy Change*, pp. 179–91. London: Intermediate Technology Publications.

Razavi, S. and C. Miller (1995a) 'From WID to GAD: Conceptual Shifts in the Women and Development Discourse'. Geneva: UNRISD.

Razavi, S. and C. Miller (1995b) 'Gender Mainstreaming; A Study of Efforts by the UNDP, the World Bank and the ILO to Institutionalize Gender Issues'. Geneva: UNRISD.

Robb, C. (1998) 'PPAs: A Review of the World Bank's Experience', in J. Holland and J. Blackburn (eds) *Whose Voice? Participatory Research and Policy Change*, pp. 131–42. London: Intermediate Technology Publications.

Summers, L. (1994) *Investing in All the People: Educating Women in Developing Countries*. Washington, DC: The World Bank.

Tjonneland, E., H. Harboe, A. J. Jerve and N. Kanji (1998) 'The World Bank and Poverty in Africa: A Critical Assessment of the Bank's Operational Strategies for Poverty Reduction'. Oslo: Norwegian Ministry of Foreign Affairs.

Whitehead, A. (1981) 'I'm Hungry Mum: The Politics of Domestic Budgeting', in K. Young et al. (eds) *Of Marriage and the Market*, pp. 88–111. London: CSE Books.

Whitehead, A. (1998) 'Women in Development (WID), Gender and Development (GAD): The New Politics of an Old Distinction'. University of Sussex Development Lectures. Brighton: University of Sussex.

Whitehead, A. and M. Lockwood (1999) 'Gender in the World Bank's Poverty Assessments: Six Case Studies from Sub-Saharan Africa'. Discussion Paper 99. Geneva: UNRISD.

World Bank (1981) *Accelerated Development in Sub-Saharan Africa: An Agenda for Action*. Washington, DC: The World Bank.

World Bank (1989) *Sub-Saharan Africa: From Crisis to Sustainable Growth*. Washington, DC: The World Bank.

World Bank (1990) *World Development Report for 1990*. Oxford: Oxford University Press.

World Bank (1991) *Operational Directive 4.15: Poverty Reduction*. Washington, DC: The World Bank.

World Bank (1992a) *Poverty Reduction Handbook*. Washington, DC: The World Bank.

World Bank (1992b) *Ghana I: 2000 and Beyond: Setting the Stage for Accelerated Growth and Poverty Reduction* (one vol. PA). West Africa Department. Washington DC: The World Bank.

World Bank (1993a) *Uganda: Growing out of Poverty* (PA). Washington, DC: The World Bank.

World Bank (1993b) *The East Asian Miracle: Economic Growth and Public Policy*. Oxford: Oxford University Press.

World Bank (1994) *Zambia: Poverty Assessment* (five vol. PA). Human Resources Division, Africa Regional Office. Washington, DC: The World Bank.

World Bank (1995a) *Ghana II: Poverty Past, Present and Future* (one vol. PA). Population and Human Resources Division, Africa Region. Washington, DC: The World Bank.

World Bank (1995b) *Uganda: The Challenge of Growth and Poverty Reduction*. CEM, Country Operations Division. Washington, DC: The World Bank.

World Bank (1995c) *Cameroon: Diversity, Growth and Poverty Reduction*. Population and Human Resources Division, Africa Region. Washington, DC: The World Bank.

World Bank (1996) *Tanzania: The Challenge of Reforms: Growth, Incomes and Welfare* (three vol. PA). Country Operations Division. Washington, DC: The World Bank.

World Bank Operations Evaluation Department (1996) *Poverty Assessment: A Progress Report*. Washington, DC: The World Bank.

Yanagisako, S. (1979) 'Family and Household: The Analysis of Domestic Groups', *Annual Review of Anthropology* 8: 161–205.

6

Rethinking Gendered Poverty and Work

Cecile Jackson and Richard Palmer-Jones

INTRODUCTION

Conventionally poverty has been assessed in terms of household income or calorie levels and poverty lines; more recently we have come to assess it at the individual level, in terms of the capabilities and functionings that individuals achieve (Sen, 1983). This has been in part a response to the critiques of gender analysts that showed the existence of unequal intra-household ill-being. The UNDP Human Development Reports build on the capabilities approach to represent disparities in well-being between men and women. However, in addition to comparing well-being outcomes it has been argued that we need to focus on the processes behind these outcomes, and that gender and poverty are distinct forms of disadvantage, which should not be collapsed into a 'feminization of poverty' notion of women as the poorest of the poor. Rather, poverty should be understood as a condition experienced and shaped by gendered actors (Jackson, 1996). By this we mean that gender identities, along with others, frame opportunities and constraints for access and control of material and discursive resources, and also offer a repertoire of responses to these opportunities and constraints. Here we apply this idea to an examination of the working lives of poor women and men who are largely dependent on manual labour for their livelihoods.

Work is central to current understandings of poverty, well-being and social exclusion, as well as to prescriptions for poverty reduction, as exemplified in the 'Washington Consensus'; but there has been relatively little attention to the character of work rather than simply as income-generating employment. This chapter suggests a framework, consistent with capability approaches, for analysing the character and embodied experience of work, especially its physical arduousness, through which we might reach a fuller understanding of how work and well-being are connected in gendered ways.

We conclude that high levels of work intensity have significant gendered effects on well-being, and are central to the embodied and gendered subjectivities of men and women and therefore relevant to intra-household 'bargaining' and the gender divisions of labour which emerge from it. We speculate that if women, as well as men, seek to sustain bodily well-being

A longer version of this chapter has been published as UNRISD Discussion Paper 96. We would like to thank the referees of *Development and Change* for their comments on this chapter.

through avoiding heavy work, to the extent that this is possible, then poverty reduction programmes need to consider carefully how a range of poverty reduction interventions may impact on their ability to do this.

In this chapter, we first develop a framework of connected concepts for thinking about embodiment and well-being, before critically assessing the measurement and modelling of work intensity; the chapter ends with some speculations on the possible implications for gender equitable poverty reduction interventions and research.

WORK INTENSITY, EMBODIMENT AND GENDER RELATIONS: A FRAMEWORK

Work intensity can mean many things. An everyday definition would emphasize that work that causes fatigue or stress is arduous, burdensome or intensive, and this is the sense in which we use the term. We do not use the term to refer to multi-tasking (Floro, 1995), nor should it be confused with labour productivity, since the focus is not on outputs but on the effort of work. Intensive work may also be more productive, but this association needs to be established rather than assumed.

In general there is very little direct consideration of work intensity in the social science corpus on development, which might seem strange given the centrality of labour in development theories, and studies of social change, over the decades. The ways in which development discourses in general, and poverty and gender debates in particular, have approached work are marked by particular western histories and preoccupations (Jackson, 1997), and one of the consequent absences is attention to labour as more than an abstract category, for example as physical experience. Historians of technical change have considered work intensity and fatigue (Rabinbach, 1990) but their focus is on western industrial contexts. Gender analysts of social change, after an early interest in sexual dimorphism as a determinant of sexual divisions of labour, quickly decided that male strength was a mystification, and that gender divisions of labour were more directly the consequence of the constraints of reproduction on women (Mukhopadhyay and Higgins, 1988). However, since interest has shifted away from singular and determining explanations for the subordination of women towards the structuration of social institutions involved in both production and reproduction (Giddens, 1984), and social theorists have developed approaches which integrate these fields (Moore, 1994), it is timely to reconsider how the physical character of work enters into gender relations and identities. This section considers a set of related concepts to guide such a journey. In brief it proposes that the bodily endowments of women and men, or what Moore (1994: 3) calls their 'lived anatomy', represent a neglected but important element of understanding the materially grounded subjectivities, that is, the self-conscious perceptions of persons, which shape agency. We know our worlds through our bodies: 'The material world that surrounds us is one in which we use our living bodies to give substance to the social distinctions and differences that underpin social relations, symbolic systems, forms of labour and quotidian intimacies' (Moore, 1994: 71). Gendered working bodies change and age over life courses in which women and men may experience, resist, or develop capabilities for physical work differently, experience (and contribute to) discourses of value in work differently, and express agency differently.[1] Our framework is developed from six inter-linked themes.

1. Beyond determinism and dualism: The neglect of the body in gender and development discourses is at least partly a result of anxiety about biological determinism which social theorists have, in different ways, moved beyond (Connell, 1987; Shilling, 1993). It is now possible to think about biology and bodies in ways which are not determinist, since biology is no longer conceived as fixed and unchanging, rather the human body is seen as an incomplete project whose material form is transformed, over the passage of a life, through the inscriptions of health and working experience, culture and the intentions and choices of actors.[2] Whilst twenty years ago 'body talk' invoked ideas of 'biology as destiny', it is now possible to see the body as central to the very antithesis of determinism, to agency.

The ways in which the body has re-emerged in social theory are diverse, but have been dominated by views of bodies as entirely socially constructed (Butler, 1990). More useful in our opinion are critical realist conceptions in which the body is both a discursive construct, and a broadly defined set of biological constraints and opportunities (Soper, 1995). The boundaries of the physical and the cultural are by no means clear, and are deeply contested, but we consider that there is a need to know about 'objective' well-being (Sen, 1987), and bodily outcomes, which we explore below. The juxtaposition of perceptions of well-being with actual physical outcomes offers a rich analytical field, with considerable existing research but little of it gendered. In the UK women experience illness more frequently than men, judged by attendance at GP surgeries, yet live longer than men (Whitehead, 1988);[3] also, women attempt suicide more frequently than men, but far more men than women die by suicide. Indicators of states of health and well-being are complex mixtures of physiological advantage and disadvantage in the face of disease and nutrition stresses, and socio-cultural (and personal) advantage and disadvantage in the ability of gendered subjects to achieve and sustain well-being.

The concept of embodied subjectivities offers a liberation from mind–body dualism (Moore, 1994). Our subjectivities — that is, our self-conscious

---

1. The terms women and men should not be taken to suggest an implicit essentialism, but merely as shorthand for the generally significant gender variations in social life, the content of which is, however, everywhere different.
2. Another factor is the focus in Western discourse on libidinous bodies, rather than labouring ones (Turner, 1996).
3. A similar phenomenon occurs in Kerala (Ramachandran, 1996).

perspectives as persons — are grounded in the lived experience of particular bodily existences, which, however, are constantly changing since bodies are never complete, and thus embodiment is a process rather than a state. The idea of embodied subjectivities retains the emphasis, in current understandings of poverty and well-being, on subjectivity (Chambers, 1983); that is, the experience and perceptions of women or poor people themselves, as subjects rather than as (only) the objects of development interventions. This is important not only for ethical and feminist reasons but because social action follows from subjectivities. However, we also insist on the importance of attending to the material condition of the body.

2. *Work and stress*: The burdensomeness of work, and its implications for well-being, is not only a function of its physical arduousness, discussed below; it is also related to the social relations and valuation of work, and personal experiences of the pleasures and pains of work. Among nutritionally challenged populations, however, we believe that the physical aspect is of great importance, and has not been well understood.[4] Further justifications for our emphasis on physical arduousness are, firstly, the continuing context of absolute poverty in populations heavily dependent on physically arduous activity in both agricultural and natural resource based livelihoods, and in urban areas where physically laborious livelihoods (for instance, rickshaw pullers in eastern India) prevail (Breman, 1996), and secondly, the danger of promoting high work intensity development interventions inappropriately. We assume in this chapter that heavy manual labour has disutility, which may be greater for small bodied, undernourished or unhealthy persons, and we ask whether the embodied states of women in south Asia might mean that the experienced burden of effort intensive work is greater for women. This is especially relevant if labour intensive development interventions are targeted on poor women. In any case an aversion to some forms of such labour would not be unexpected. Aversion to heavy manual labour is hardly unique to women — after all much of human 'development' has been about the evolution of technology to reduce drudgery and manual work and raise productivity — yet the 'controlled discomfort of work' (Scarry, 1985) is possibly experienced more acutely by subjects with female bodies, for example, if the work involves static loads, because women generally have less upper body strength, smaller stature and so on. Whatever the provenance of the gender differences in bodily endowment — and it appears that south

---

4. There has been extensive debate around the 'small but healthy' hypothesis (Seckler, 1982; Sukhatme and Margen, 1978/1982). It seems now generally accepted that while individuals and perhaps populations 'adapt' in being small, by changing their behaviour (Dasgupta, 1993; Payne and Lipton, 1994), and perhaps discriminating against certain categories of person (Giampietro and Pimemtel, 1992), there are significant functional and well-being 'costs' to these processes (Dasgupta, 1993, 1997; Osmani, 1992). This work only obliquely considers the gendered nature and health consequences of effort at low levels of nutrition in the ways explored here.

Asian cultures particularly amplify and embellish the limited sexual dimorphism of small children through differential care — the effects of different work patterns, and emergent gendered patterns of agency, may be to create considerable aversion in women towards heavy manual labour in agriculture. This is especially likely when the less negotiable reproductive labour of the conjugal contract already involves a burden of heavy work such as fuelwood and water collection.

3. *Time, effort and agency*: The interdisciplinary framework we propose here raises further questions for the gender analysis of labour. Whilst economic models give little consideration to the politics of what is considered to be work, what work is ideologically valued and devalued, how notions of skill are gendered, and what processes other than economic rationality influence divisions of labour, these are the strengths of gender analysis. Over the past twenty-five years gender analysts have: valued and rendered visible women's domestic labour; demonstrated the substantial contribution made to farm work and rural transport by women in a wide range of societies, not only those characterized as 'female farming systems' by Boserup; shown the caring labour, mainly done by women for children, the ill and elderly; indicated the community work contributed by women beyond household boundaries; and profoundly changed the ways work and value are conceptualized. Studies of gendered divisions of labour at household level have been concerned with how equitable these divisions are, and have tended to see the length of time of work as the important focus in establishing this (Dixon-Mueller, 1985; UNDP, 1995). The more limited research on the character and content of women's labour has been largely concerned with the extent to which child bearing constrains women's work, with 'decision making' power by women in social relations of work, with the ways in which women can or cannot command the labour of others, with levels of control over returns to work and incomes, with exclusions from technology, and with multi-tasking and juggling of livelihood components. Taken together, dominant approaches to work in gender analysis of development emphasize social relations of subordination and ideological constructs which devalue women's work, juxtaposing these with evidence of time use to demonstrate excessive work for women, double and triple burdens (Moser, 1993) and time-famine.

Two questions which seem to require further thought, however, are how these levels of over-work by poor rural women are reflected in well-being outcomes, and how (if one does not see patriarchy as all-determining) women as actors come to be victims of such an inequitable order? We suggest that there are shortcomings in the ways we have thought about gender and work with an over-reliance on time as a proxy for burden, effort and equity; this is partly the result of neglect of the lived experience of work of individual persons, which informs preferences and choices, and influences positions adopted in intra-household bargaining (implicit and explicit) over labour.

4. Body capital: We propose an analytical focus on the significance of the experience of work to illuminate both direct and indirect connections between work and well-being. By direct connections we mean how the burdensomeness of a task depends on the type of body one has (female/male, large/small, healthy/unhealthy, experienced/inexperienced), which we conceptualize as *body capital*. Body capital is the cumulative outcome of the bodily endowment at birth, the health history and social relations of work, and so on, of the person to date, and which affects how burdensome a particular task *feels* to a gendered subject. This raises the question of whether heavy work is likely to be objectively more burdensome to many women than men, and is discussed in the following section. By indirect connections we mean the ways in which these perceptions and experiences of burden enter into social relations of work, in both wage labour markets and intra-household negotiations over work, or time allocation more broadly. The concept of body capital is especially useful to poverty analysis because it attends to the endowment which poor people rely on more than any other — their bodies; that is, their physical endowments, their labour entitlements, their extended entitlements to the labour of others (or their products), their capabilities and functionings and their achievement of well-being. Notwithstanding objections to the commoditized implications of the term, it suggests a sense of active engagement of persons in the building up and the consumption of the body as a store of value, unlike the term bodily endowment which appears as a 'given'. Thus, lived experience is cumulated into the embodied subject. Also, body capital potentially converts to other forms of capital — in the pathways through which differently embodied persons experience differential returns to work (economic capital), differential cultural approval (symbolic capital), differential conjugal and community relations (social capital). If bodies are seen as valuable assets for the poor, and for women, we question whether development policies should encourage them to be extravagantly squandered in effort intensive activity.

5. Bargaining and effort: The indirect connections between work and well-being are transacted within households, as well as in labour markets, which we have insufficient space to pursue here, where bargaining metaphors (Sen, 1987) and models suggest implicit and explicit negotiations through which individuals in a domestic group arrive at allocations of work and rewards. Fundamental as bargaining discourses in general are to gender analysis of intrahousehold relations, there are some methodological problems around the slippage between population and household levels of analysis, without consideration of the implications of such an elision. One issue is that whilst population averages for gender differences may be distinct, there can also be considerable overlap between the ranges for men and women. Thus sexual dimorphism in a population may be clear, but what matters for intra-household bargaining is the *specific* dimorphism of particular spouses — that is, the relative differences in size, strength and bodily capabilities of men and women in a particular domestic group. Bargaining may be a useful way of imagining the strengths and weaknesses of a population-wide *gender categorical* 'bargaining', but this is not the same as describing the actual or implicit discourses between individual members of a domestic group. Thus, the social structures of constraint and opportunity may be valid as accounts of the circumstances faced by women as a social *category*, but inadequate for predicting *particular* bargained outcomes because of two important reasons: firstly, that women bear multiple identities and secondly that they are individually and socially situated to be able to resist and reformulate structures of constraint. Generalized fallback positions (outside marriage or within it[5]) of men and women are highly relevant to outcomes, but, given multiple identities and capacities for struggle, they cannot be complete accounts of weakness and strength in conjugal relations. Sen's elaboration of objective and perceived contributions and interests is a major step forward, but we suggest here that a focus on the embodiment of work is one way to understand the *linkages* between Sen's objective contribution response (work as an objective contribution), on the one hand, and his perceived contribution response (the perceptions of its value by household members) on the other. It seems likely that the differential recognition accorded different forms of work by household members, is not only a construct of gender ideology, but connected to either a personal bodily experience of what it means to do that particular work, or close observations of the bodily effects of that work on others — sweat and fatigue, injury, wastedness, vulnerability to disease. Where gender divisions of labour are relatively flexible, for example weeding in many African societies, then the former mode of appreciation may be significant, and where divisions of labour are relatively rigid then the latter is possibly more so. In both, discourses of value around assertions of the bodily demands of different kinds of work are likely to be significant in the *processes* by which women's work, men's work, and shared tasks not only create value but are understood to do so.

It is somewhat ironic to criticize economists for an absence of agency, since economics appears to be dominated by notions of free choice, but essentially this is a problem with bargaining models in which social institutions of patriarchy or wage differentials, for example, appear to float free from the structurating actions of women and men.[6]

6. *Agency and body projects*: In addition to the idea that personal experience of burden is part of the subjectivities informing 'bargaining' and possibly an incentive for avoidance of heavy labour, the concept of *body projects*

---

5. See respectively McElroy (1990) and Lundberg and Pollak (1996).
6. The term agency is used in a number of different ways in different discourses, but here we use it simply to indicate the indeterminate nature of human actions, and the capacity of men and women for willed and voluntary action which is not given by social structures (Giddens, 1984).

suggests that women (and men) may implicitly strategize a life course in which body capital is built up, maintained and carefully expended towards the achievement of social and personal goals (Jackson, 1997), as well-being states of various kinds. Thus reproductive intentions, both for desired family size and structures (Bledsoe, 1995), and working livelihoods, come together in the idea of an embodied subject husbanding their bodily resources, building up strength, avoiding its depletion, managing the hazards and demands of childbirth and reproduction, and of work, over a lifespan whose course is partly scripted by social and economic structures and ideologies, partly extemporized, and studded with unpredictable events and unexpected outcomes. It might be argued that it is mistaken to assume conscious strategizing behaviour in relation to body projects, but 'strategization' can be practical as well as discursive (Giddens, 1979), and based in praxis.

Body management and adjustment to body capability take place over a range of scales from the working day to the life course. Two examples are Catherine Panter-Brick's work in Nepal and Melissa Parker's (1992, 1993) in Sudan. In her Nepal study Catherine Panter-Brick (1997) argues that Nepali men and women pace themselves to sustain work throughout the day (a 'tortoise' strategy) rather than race to complete tasks (a 'hare' strategy), and that there are advantages to this. In addition to the physical advantages of taking frequent pauses in work, she points out that a measured tempo of work allows the participation of anaemic individuals, who would otherwise be unable to sustain such a fast pace of work, and that pregnant and lactating individuals can also participate fully. Under other relations — of wage labour of varying kinds, and seasonal timeliness constraints where tasks have to be completed urgently — hare strategies become necessary. In circumstances of a commodification of labour, and/or agricultural intensification (such as irrigation and double or cash cropping) which compresses the time available for tasks such as land preparation, the physical work capacity of women and men may become more central to the valorization of women's and men's work.

The Sudan study of the work patterns of women, some of whom were infected by bilharzia, doing agricultural labour in the Gezira, found an increased work pace but decreased work time among infected women (Parker, 1992, 1993). However, the activity time and intensity of domestic work were not affected by the infection; nor was the well-being of children, suggesting effective strategies and priorities in managing work intensity. The ways in which a woman faced with onerous and well-being threatening work may husband her body can include economic strategies (hire labour for the task), relational strategies (persuade a daughter-in-law, husband or child to do it), or technological or other ergonomic strategies to reduce drudgery. Relationships are resources that can be deployed in this way, and ideologies of work, like discourses of strength and masculinity, of endurance and femininity, may have real value to women in their body projects. Body projects are not governed by narrow self-interest, since one's own well-being depends on the well-being of others. The much commented upon altruism of women, and their concern for the well-being of others, such as children and spouses, may be not essential, or even socialized, goodness, but a reflection of the extent to which their personal material well-being indeed depends on the health of spouses, children, and so on. When Sen (1987) observes that women conceptualize their welfare in terms of family welfare, this may not be entirely the altruistic 'false consciousness' he suggests. Personal well-being is certainly relational, as gender analysts have long recognized — but the point bears repetition.

Broadly, the idea of body projects also suggests an intentionality in relation to health and well-being, of selves and others, rather than a passive experience of well-being as a condition[7] without, however, suggesting that social structures of disadvantage do not constrain the room for manoeuvre. Indeed it is likely to be interesting to discover what kinds of differences in control women and men have in achieving body projects and how far vulnerable individuals lose the ability to manage their own body futures. The advantages of an approach such as this, to understanding both gender divisions of labour, and gendered well-being, may be considerable.

This framework assumes that meanings are grounded in, but not determined by, culturally elaborated physical experiences. These experiences are more conventionally examined through the natural sciences and economics, and thus we now critically assess the sciences which address work intensity, to examine some of the questions implied by the above. The following are a non-exhaustive set of questions arising from our framework, which the following section goes on to address. What do we know about the impact of work intensity on physical well-being? What is the distribution of work intensity between women and men? Are there significant gender differences in embodiment, for example in physical work capacity, which affect potential for, and effects of, heavy labour? How do the bodily effects of high work intensity connect to the subjective feelings of stress and burdensomeness in work? Does it make sense to consider a focus on the body as an asset, as body capital, as a means of connecting work to well-being? Is a focus on body management in the short run and body projects in the longer term meaningful? Are there grounds for policy concern about effort intensive poverty reduction interventions?

MEASURING AND MODELLING WORK INTENSITY[8]

How do different levels of work intensity lead to different bodily states of health, and how are these states distributed between women and men? This

7. Economists have for long thought of well-being as related to whole life-cycle consumption (Friedman, 1957; Modigliani and Brumberg, 1955), and can readily conceive of borrowing productive potential from later in life, as noted above (Becker, 1985).
8. An earlier version of this chapter (Jackson and Palmer-Jones, 1998) goes into considerably greater detail on the issues discussed in this section.

question finds only partial answers in mainstream natural and social sciences. Nevertheless, these sciences, despite complexities and qualifications, do suggest that work intensity is an important factor for a gendered understanding of well-being and its determinants, and that the outcomes of many poverty oriented development interventions are likely to be sensitive to these considerations. In this section we discuss critically the science and economics of work intensity, mainly in the context of South Asia.

Nutrition Approaches Applied to Work Intensity

Nutrition science models well-being by comparing food intakes (or nutrient equivalents) with nutrient requirements. Energy intake is especially important since, in most circumstances, adequate energy intake for a healthy lifestyle entails adequate intake of other nutrients. Work intensity is not addressed specifically in this model, but, given the common understanding of work intensity as high energy expenditure, it would appear reasonable to assess work intensity from this model as the energy expenditure on work activity. What we learn from it (in relation to the working poor in south Asia) is that men tend to have somewhat higher levels of work intensity than women, which is partly but not fully compensated for in their greater calorie consumption, and that there tend therefore to be more adult men than women in groups with a vulnerable Body Mass Index (BMI). However, the nutrition approach does not answer our questions directly since it does not consider the *capacity* for heavy work, which is gender differentiated.

Conventional nutrition models (WHO/FAO/UNU, 1985) consider balance between energy consumption and expenditure as a requirement of bodily well-being, expressed in stable body weight among adults, and growth in height and weight in proportion to age for children. Calorie intake (energy consumption)[9] alone is an inadequate account of nutritional status since food needs are relative to an individual's sex, age, body size and activity level; furthermore, there is considerable variability even among individuals of the same height, weight, sex and activity level, but at the population level the conventional model appears quite robust for the purpose for which it was designed, namely, to predict food requirements for health.

Energy expenditure is calculated in the following way; energy is required to maintain the body (there is a Basal Metabolic Rate — BMR), and for

---

9. The nutritional effects of food intake depend on the nutrients contained in the food and made available through processing. We focus here only on the energy contents of foods and a person's energy balance, noting that other nutrients are also important, and indeed bear on work intensity. For example, anaemia related to low iron intake relative to need is very common amongst poor women and seriously affects work capability, independently of BMI.

activity. The activity component of energy expenditure is assessed from the energy expenditure on individual activities; for each activity, the energy expenditure of an individual on this activity is expressed as a multiple of the person's BMR, according to the 'energy intensity' of the activity. The energy intensity of an activity is its Physical Activity Ratio (PAR) in relation to BMR. Daily energy expenditure can then be calculated by multiplying the time spent on different activities during the day (24 hours) by their respective PARs. The average daily sum of time-weighted PARs is the Physical Activity Level (PAL) of that category of persons.

What this model tells us about work intensity and gender is that while women often work longer hours, men, through having a higher proportion of active body tissue and being bigger, have a greater BMR, have a slightly higher PAR per activity, and often undertake a higher proportion of high PAR activities (Gillespie and McNeill, 1992). Hence, in the labouring classes, men may have higher average PAL than women despite women's longer working hours.[10] Furthermore, when the calorie intakes of men and women were compared, it appears that in some circumstances the observed greater calorie intake of men might not even compensate for their greater average daily energy expenditure (Gillespie and McNeill, 1992).

Some supporting evidence for this conclusion comes from assessment of nutritional well-being of men and women. In the nutrition model Body Mass Index (BMI — weight, in kg, divided by height, in metres, squared) is widely used as an indicator of nutritional status because it adjusts for stature (Shetty and James, 1994). The few studies there are, from South Asia, do not support the view that among the working poor, women have poorer nutritional status than men (Gillespie and McNeill, 1992; Harriss, 1990; Kynch and McGuire, 1994).[11] Thus, in some cases it appears that men consume and expend more calories than women, but end up more nutritionally stressed because their

---

10. Panter-Brick (1997) brought together as many studies as she could find which compared men and women's PAL, using the factorial method. In most cases the samples were very small, in many too small to make reliable comparisons, but there were as many groups among whom PALs for women were as high or higher than men's as the reverse. Batliwala (1982), in a similar location to that of the Gillespie and McNeill study, found greater female energy expenditure. However, this study calculated the energy costs of women's activities by discounting the male energy costs by their relative BMRs (0.85), rather than 'standard' (although still questionable) tables of gender specific PARs.

11. However there is some controversy about the use of BMI to make gender comparisons. This is related to the greater percentage of fat in women's bodies at any BMI, which seems to account for their greater resistance to infection and ability to survive at low BMI (Henry, 1990). In emergencies severe malnutrition leads to oedema, but when body fat is mobilized in women it produces steroid hormones which prevent the escape of body fluid; men suffer from this to a much greater extent than women. It is thus difficult to compare the nutritional status of men and women because their bodies differ in form and function, but for both, well-being in terms of survival, production and reproduction demands adequate BMI. BMI is also a reasonably sensitive indicator of changes in energy stores, e.g. seasonally, in both men and women.

calorie intake allows them only to achieve stable body weight at lower nutritional status.

There are various other functional consequences of low BMI for women and men (Shetty and James, 1994). For women the effects on reproduction are varied — conception ceases at low BMI, and low BMI leads to low birth weight babies, but pregnancy is largely unaffected and low BMI has no effect on lactation (Shetty, 1997). The effects of low BMI on health is clear and connected to more days of illness (see Pryer, 1989, for poor urban males in Bangladesh). The effects of low BMI are gender differentiated in other ways too; women can survive at considerably lower BMIs than men, as studies of famine mortality show. There is also evidence that BMI is positively associated with wage earning (Strauss and Thomas, 1995).

Does this analysis of work intensity, understood as daily estimated energy expenditure in relation to energy intake and nutritional status, provide a satisfactory account of the concept? We do not believe that it does. This (factorial) nutrition model was developed to assess the nutritional requirements of populations in order to assess food requirements and sufficiency; it may tell us relatively little about *stress*, or the burden of work for the individual; it does not take into account physical work *capacity*, that is, the ability to work intensively, or other aspects of work activity such as musculoskeletal injury, or other health and safety issues. The physiological and ergonomic models of work address some of these issues.

Physiological and Ergonomic Models of Work Intensity

Briefly, these studies show that the physical work capacity of men is greater than that of women because of differences in muscle mass and stature, and thus one might conclude that this greater capacity for heavy work might compensate them for any nutritional disadvantage. However, there are few studies that tell us about the health effects for poor men and women of exerting this capacity — in circumstances where they have variable abilities to manage the pace of work. Bio-behavioural health studies show that the subjective experience of the burdensomeness of work requires an approach based on a broader concept of stress.

Physiological and ergonomic models are based on the argument that an individual's physical work capacity (PWC) is given by the maximum volume of oxygen (called VO_2max) that he/she can consume in performing activity (Astrand and Rohdahl, 1986; Dasgupta, 1993, 1997). This capacity depends mainly on a person's active tissue mass, which is much the same as his or her muscle mass, and represents the maximum rate at which aerobic work can be sustained. This maximum work rate can be sustained only briefly — a few minutes — and there is thought to be a negative exponential relationship between the 'endurance time' and the percentage of PWC. Thus, if work is done at less than PWC then it can be sustained for a longer period. Work physiologists suggest that a sustainable daily level of work is 35 per cent of PWC (Astrand and Rohdahl, 1986). This conclusion seems to have been based on standard western working practices, so it is not clear for how many hours per day (beyond the standard working day of eight hours) or how many consecutive days beyond the five–six days per week, this rate can be sustained without health impairment, or the need for holidays, and so on.

What is the significance of PWC or VO_2max for gender and work intensity? Men generally have greater stature, and higher PWC than women for the same stature and BMI, and therefore greater productivity potential, and there is growing economic evidence relating height and BMI to wage rates. This suggests that men have greater physical work capacity than women, which might mitigate relative disadvantage in nutritional status.[12] However, there is very little empirical evidence of work intensity in relation to PWC among the groups with which we are concerned (that is, profiles of daily activity expressed as percentage of PWC).

Furthermore, the experience of physical stress and burden may not be well related to physical work intensity measured in this way. Perhaps most significant is that observation of work commonly classified as heavy shows that it is managed by a combination of bursts of work at well above the sustainable 35 per cent level, interspersed with periods of rest (Kilbom, 1995; Mueller, 1953). The health correlates of different combinations of work and rest pauses, as compared to steady levels of activity, are not clear, but it is considered that frequent pauses relieve fatigue and enhance productivity more than the equivalent amount of time in a single longer rest (Hockley, 1983). Furthermore, some tasks require energy expenditures well above the maximum aerobic capacity (VO_2max) which in humans is relatively slight,[13] thus some tasks require short bursts of isometric strength or power whose level is not well tracked by heart rate or oxygen uptake.[14]

Also, there are other health dimensions to work not strictly related to energy-based understandings of work intensity, for example, musculo-skeletal injuries and fatigue. These well-known attributes of 'hard' work require an approach to work intensity based on a broader concept of *stress*

---

12. However, greater *potential* physical work capacity should not be assumed to result automatically in greater work intensity: as we saw above, women in some cultures appear to be engaged in activity which yield higher PALs than men.
13. For example, in a nutritionally challenged society such as that of the Nepalis studied by Strickland and Tuffrey (1997), PWC may be around 125 watts, whereas the peak anaerobic energy expenditure (based on scaling up PWC to maximum anaerobic capacity by the ratios found in Western populations) may be over 1000 watts (McArdle et al., 1996).
14. Maclachlan (1983), in his south Indian ethnography, devotes considerable attention to the importance of, and differential capacities of men and women to exert, isometric power of the type just discussed. Energy systems theorists hypothesize that power constraints are important limitations to productivity in human labour based economies (Giampietro and Pimentel, 1992).

which integrates the biological with the psycho-social aspects of work. High physical exertion is now known to have physiological consequences that operate through hormonal pathways which also link the experience of stress to negative psychological states.[15] Indeed, in the end we have to understand work intensity in terms of its health *outcomes*, which cannot be read off in a straightforward way from any of the measures of effort intensity *inputs* we have discussed so far. This is because the health consequences of effort expenditure are mediated by socially situated psychological states which determine the emotional evaluation of the activity.[16]

It might be argued that manual labour may be physically demanding but is not otherwise psychologically stressful and that therefore stress related ill-health is unlikely to be associated with manual labour; indeed, increased exercise is often prescribed as therapy for mental stress in the West. However, this would be a misconception because those dependent on manual labour typically have limited control over their livelihoods, live under stressed and insecure conditions, and therefore 'exercise' under negative emotional circumstances, which consequently stimulates health impairing physiological pathways. This brings us back to the argument that the embodied consequences of work intensity are closely connected not only to the 'energy intensity' of the work but to the social relations under which work takes place.

Another consequence of considering work intensity in these ways is that there is no simple way of dividing activities into work and leisure or rest; activities will have both positive and negative consequences. Thus an apparently non-productive activity like rest, should be considered not just a preferred leisure good, but a productive activity, which enhances 'work' productivity later. In this respect rest or leisure can be considered a form of *productive consumption* like food, education or some forms of health expenditure.[17]

---

15. Negative emotions in relation to work, possibly connected to the aversion to work which is physically painful or exhausting, can trigger what is known as the 'flight or fight response' in the body which has negative long-term health consequences (Lovallo, 1997).

16. Unfortunately examples for which there is some evidence are drawn from western situations where actors do not face the nutritional challenges of poverty and hunger. Thus, it is known that athletes are unduly liable to infection due to exercise related suppression of their immune systems. However, there is some reason to believe that physiological and immunological responses are triggered by the body's responses to hunger (Shetty, 1997) which are similar to those involved in the mobilization of bodily resources for intense physical activity, such as the training of athletes, and in physiological responses to emotional stresses.

17. Also, evidence from athletes shows that rest is necessary in response to severe and extended stresses that exceed the ability of the body to cope or adapt (Lovallo, 1997). It is not clear whether effort intensive livelihoods at low levels of nutrition can produce similar effects; nevertheless, behavioural models of health postulate clear linkages between stress and health, which presumably extend to the types of nutrition and effort induced stresses with which we are concerned.

The implications of this brief review for gender and poverty are that, in poor societies dependent on human labour, men are biologically somewhat better equipped for heavy dynamic and static force intensive work than women because of their physiology, stature, and absence of reproduction constraints, that both women and men are actually involved in effort intensive work, and the consequences of this for their well-being are likely to be significant. However, the science of work intensity takes us back to the need for interdisciplinary approaches that transcend mind–body dualism and consider the social and psychological contexts of work and well-being.

Economic Modelling of Work Intensity

So far we have focused on the 'costs' of work: what we have yet to consider is how women and men benefit indirectly, in markets and livelihood production, from work intensity. Economists and systems theorists such as those mentioned above, focus on the link between physical work intensity, or effort, and productivity, implying that greater effort intensity and physical work capacity result in greater command over commodities, and hence greater well-being. Among economists who have addressed these issues,[18] only Pitt et al. (1990), incorporate effort intensity directly into an analysis of the relationships between calorie consumption, health, work and income. Using a unitary household model, these authors incorporate the (presumed) energy intensity of work activities[19] in their account of intra-household allocations of consumption and effort.[20] In this model, the food consumption, health and work effort of individual household members are arguments in the household utility function (the first two increasing, the last decreasing, well-being). Individuals have their own specific endowments of 'healthiness', but belong to categories that have health and wage functions. Health of a class of individuals is produced by individual endowments, enhanced by consumption of food, and harmed by effort intensity. The wages of an individual of a given class reflect the health of the individual and the effort

---

18. Nutrition-productivity links have been of great interest to economists since Leibenstein (1957); see also Bliss and Stern (1978a and 1978b); Dasgupta (1993, 1997); Dasgupta and Ray (1990); Mirrlees (1975); Ray (1998); Stiglitz (1976). Two mechanisms have been invoked; one works 'automatically' such that people paid more to feed themselves better and are consequently more productive, while the other, efficiency-wage model (Weiss, 1990), operates through incentives. People paid in certain ways are more productive.
19. Pitt et al. (1990) only have categories of work activity which they classify into five intensity levels. They do not have either time or person and activity specific work intensity indicators.
20. See also Pitt (1997) on the problems of estimating such models; in particular there is the need for an exceptionally rich data set which must not suffer from omitted variables which might affect productivity.

intensity of their occupational class. Effort therefore has a direct negative effect on well-being, and indirect effects through the harm to health and increase in wages.

In Pitt et al.'s model, food consumption by an individual is a good in itself and also raises income through improving health and hence wages. Different classes of individual are assigned to different activities where the relations between health and wages are quite different; more effort intensive activities show higher returns to health and hence to consumption of food, and are more likely to be done by men, as in most South Asian circumstances. This is reflected in correlations between health, calorie consumption and wages for men but not for women, which may be reasonable for much of South Asia (but see Strauss and Thomas, 1995, who report a positive correlation between the BMI of women and their wages in Brazil), and this may go some way to rationalizing the greater consumption of food by men than women, and their greater stature. Hence, Pitt concludes that men indeed get 'calorie reinforcement' but not sufficient to compensate them for their extra calorie expenditure, and that people (males and females), with high health endowments (achieved 'healthiness'), are taxed to increase the welfare of others (Pitt, 1997: 36). This work does not explain why male efforts are rewarded in markets more than female, although it does provide an explanation for allocations of additional nutrient intakes where this affects 'the likelihood of being able to work in strenuous but high paying jobs' (Strauss and Thomas, 1995: 1917).[21]

In summary, economists see higher BMI and effort as well-being enhancing in that they attract higher wages for both men and women, but more so for men. Conversely, they see effort intensity as threatening to well-being, as characteristic of male work patterns and as justifying calorie compensation to men. Analyses such as these, of the gender distributions of health threats, are rather limited by the paucity of data on the effort intensity of some forms of women's work such as water and firewood collection, grain processing, and the characteristic simultaneous multi-tasking of women, which may be reflected in longer-run health outcomes, for example the life expectancy disadvantages of adult South Asian women compared to their Western or sub-Saharan African sisters. Finally, arduousness of work is, as we point out above, not confined to peaks of energy expenditure alone, and tasks such as weeding and transplanting suggest different kinds of burden. Nevertheless, economic models such as this do suggest grounds for caution in advocating labour-intensive policies, such as earthworks and construction employment which are effort-intensive, for certain people — notably, poor men already

---

21. However, as Pitt et al. note (1990: 1916): 'to the extent that the residuals incorporate ... omitted factors or specification error, then they may be correlated with a propensity to work in high return, more strenuous occupations' — which, as Pitt notes, would make the method of estimation invalid.

Figure 1. Model of Pitt et al., 1990

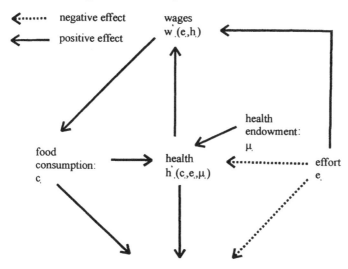

Utility or well-being is positively related to food consumption, and health status, and negatively related to effort for all household members:

$$U(c_{\cdot}, h_{\cdot}, e_{\cdot}), \; k=1, \dots m, \; i = 1, \dots n$$

Note: Pitt et al. first estimate a health production function, the residuals from which they use as health endowments. Then they estimate the intra-household calorie allocation equation using the individuals and gender disaggregated household average health endowments; they also estimate per capita household income and the probability of participation in work classified as exceptionally active. From these estimates they derive their conclusions.

reliant on wage labouring livelihoods, and poor women who also bear the bodily insults of childhood disadvantage.

IMPLICATIONS FOR POLICIES AND RESEARCH

By way of conclusion, we briefly comment here on some of the implications for research and policy that might follow from a deployment of the framework of concepts discussed above, and a renewed attention to embodied subjectivities, gendered well-being, ill-being and work.

Effort-intensive or Entitlement-intensive Growth?

The Washington Consensus on a 'New Poverty Agenda' envisaged routes out of poverty through labour intensive economic growth and targeted welfare and social security (Lipton and Maxwell, 1992). However, in this chapter we suggest that where labour intensive equates to *effort* intensive employment and social welfare it may not provide much of an escape from poverty. Appropriate technology for labour intensive growth which failed to distinguish between effort-intensive and entitlement or capability-intensive employment, would have very different implications for well-being outcomes compared to employment that yielded similar returns for lower levels of work intensity or greater returns for the same effort.[22]

The implications of a concern for effort intensity extend beyond employment policies, since labour is intricately bound up with other development policies. Evidence from African studies have pointed to the perverse effects of land reform in Zimbabwe on child nutrition (Kinsey, 1997) and many gender studies, since Hanger and Moris's work on Mwea (1973), have shown that when land is allocated to households as units under a male head, women can find their work loads increasing, in order to contribute to the labour needed for farming larger areas of land. 'Extensification' through land reform can have perverse effects on women within households; Angela Cheater (1981) demonstrated this in her work on small scale commercial farmers in Zimbabwe where polygyny, as a labour recruitment strategy, was part of a 'traditional idiom of accumulation' and came to be utilized to meet labour demands. Intensification through irrigation development has also generated resistance by women to increased demands made on women's farm labour (Carney, 1988; Jones, 1986). We would like to see the existing evidence for struggles over women's working bodies connected to a broader account of the trade-offs and dilemmas in managing one's own body *in relation to those of others*. The ideas of body capital and body projects suggest ways to look at changing divisions of labour as active constructions by women as well as men, and as patterned by prevailing social institutions, in which the logic of aversion to heavy labour, and the differential abilities of women and men to control and manage their body capital over a life course, may raise questions about effort-intensive development activities.

Targeting

Self-targeting through the labour test, i.e. offering employment to people at such low levels of reward that the non-poor would not compete for the jobs, for example in food for work programmes, has been envisaged to have a major role for both crisis and chronic poverty situations (Dreze and Sen, 1989). Since the labour test relies on the disutility of the work to screen out the less poor, it is by design disutility intensive; in many cases it is effort that

---

22.   The need to consider 'effort saving' in relation to the NPA has been noted elsewhere, but only in relation to the situation of poor women (Lipton and Maxwell, 1992: 11; see also Pitt, et al., 1990: 1155). In this chapter we put forward evidence which *prima facie* suggests that effort may be constraining for poor households in general and for individual men as well as women.

operates to deter all but the seriously poor in food for work or employment guarantee schemes.[23] Such programmes need to consider their well-being effects in the light of the possibility that they encourage those who are most vulnerable to expend their body capital for short term gain. Methods of implementation of effort intensive food for work programmes also need to consider the well-being implications of payment alternatives — piece rates are common, for example in paying per unit of soil dug, but will encourage greater bodily self-exploitation than daily rates in a manner similar to incentive oriented labour market institutions (Foster et al., 1994). Such self-targeting through the labour test may prove an energy trap for the poor and for women ill-equipped to bear the bodily costs of energy intensive work.

A further concern for policy implementation is the implication that targeting resources to vulnerable groups meets serious intra-household obstacles. It is possible that in human labour dependent livelihoods, where productivity is positively related to physical power, it may be advantageous to the domestic group for those with a greater capacity to exert muscular power to do so, but this may have negative health consequences for those individuals. Existing allocations oriented to favour 'productive' members may be quite resistant to attempts to alter them; thus feeding one member of a household through a programme may result in food that would have been allocated to that person being reallocated to others; similarly work patterns and gender divisions of labour within households may not be readily altered by involving women in extra-household employment, unless the returns to such employment are substantial. Against these arguments stand those that suggest that the impact of the *perceived* contributions of employed women to household income generates beneficial changes in intra-household gender relations. The questions for research are whether, where wages are very low, it is worthwhile in the longer term to transform body capital through adoption of hard labour into limited financial capital, but possibly significant symbolic capital? The answers will depend on prevailing local gender discourses and social settings, yet these are the processes and issues that require greater understanding.

Sustainability

Considerations of environmental sustainability in development policies also suggest increased human effort intensive technologies, or imply a less favourable ratio of human energy input to energy appropriated from the environment. Thus reduced use of fossil fuel based agro-chemicals and mechanical or

---

23. Other disutility causing factors can be the location or timing of work, its low status, or the poor quality of foods given out.

electrical power may increase the human contribution to energy costs of production and lower its productivity. A number of poverty reducing environment friendly interventions in Bangladesh, such as the treadle pump for irrigation of staple crops, and labour intensive infrastructure construction and maintenance, use technologies which are clearly effort intensive (Palmer-Jones and Jackson, 1997), and work with them needs to be paced.[24]

Lowering the burden of work as well as raising the capacity for work could help reduce poverty. This suggests increased focus on poverty reduction and egalitarian economic growth, including provision of water and sanitation and other public utilities or infrastructure that reduce human labour power constraints. It also implies that reduced experience of burden could be achieved even by poorly directed growth if there was some relief of nutritional constraints through adoption of productivity enhancing technologies. Thus, increase in agricultural productivity might go some way to enabling break out from 'agricultural involution', or a Malthusian trap, by kickstarting the type of virtuous growth of human labour based production, and investment of surplus into capital accumulation, including consumption raising human bodily capital, enabling further growth in net production and growth, that has been suggested for England during the 1730s (Fogel, 1994; Komlos, 1990). We might speculate that such a mechanism accounts in part for the medium term reductions in poverty that have been associated with Green Revolutions despite incomplete agrarian reforms and in the face of initial poor assessments (Lipton and Longhurst, 1989; Osmani, 1992; Singh, 1990). We can see in such arguments the possibility that exploitation of the environment in the short run may be a necessary evil in the transformations of poverty reduction.

Productive Consumption

If high work intensity, whether as peaks of energy expenditure or other forms of arduous labour, such as long periods spent at more moderate energy expenditure levels, can be damaging to well-being, as we argue here, then rest should be considered a form of productive consumption. The implications of this for research and development policy might be that we need to reconsider the crude use of time inputs alone as a measure of work burden, since an individual engaged in work producing fatigue needs time to recover, which should be factored into measures of work contribution. Similarly,

---

24. When work in relief projects is carefully observed we can note various effort sparing and work pacing practices; for example labourers in earthworks projects in Bangladesh and elsewhere carry loads for relatively short distances before exchanging them with another worker and walking back to pick up another load. This appears to be a form of work pacing, by dividing the work into bursts of relatively high intensity alternating with walking during which some recovery occurs (Palmer-Jones and Jackson, 1997).

multi-tasking may be an 'effort weighting' strategy where tasks can either be carried out simultaneously or interdigitated or sequenced within effort constraints. For development policy, one implication of treating rest as productive consumption would be to revise the idea that labour saving technologies such as domestic water service provision have to be justified by showing the 'productive' use of liberated time; it may be problematic, as Carr and Sandhu (1988) have argued, to require substitution of time formerly spent in water collection with more time farming. If rest time is seen as productive consumption then this recasts the issue of differential leisure not as utility versus production, but as forms of productivity.

Methodological Implications for Gender and Poverty Research

Understanding gendered disadvantage is deeply dependent on having a dynamic perspective over the life cycles of women and men. Age and gender interact in dramatic ways — in the northern Indian context, for example, depriving girls is associated with apparently better BMI for surviving adult women relative to adult men, who have been less deprived as boys (Kynch and McGuire, 1994). One implication is that successful attempts to reduce food and health care discrimination against the girl child in India might have to initiate labour saving technologies for adult women who, to the extent that these attempts are successful, may be expected to do more, harder work, and so face greater health challenges as adults. How widely and under what circumstances this pattern might occur is clearly an important topic for research. Does it occur in China, which also has an adverse males to females sex ratio, for example; and does it help to account for the reported greater work burden of women in sub-Saharan Africa?

We have also argued here against reductionist uses of bargaining models and the tendency to elide population and household levels in discussions of 'bargaining'. There remain thorny problems in economics over how to distinguish empirically between alternative models of households even when the income-pooling hypothesis is abandoned (Doss, 1996; Hoddinott et al., 1997). More challenging is the task of showing how an emphasis on agency can be incorporated into the bargaining approach. We have tried, in this chapter, to extend a relational gender analysis to men as well as women in order to understand the complex pattern of gendered disadvantage in poor rural societies. It seems important to avoid assuming universal, cross-cultural and ahistorical female disadvantage (Messer, 1997), and thereby both to ignore specific areas of male disadvantage, attention to which might also benefit women, and to miss the insights which follow from examining the spaces in which women are not disadvantaged. In addition to debates in terms of the assumptions of models, we argue for a proportionate attention to descriptions, the exploration of the mechanisms, and the importance of triangulating well-being outcomes with analytical accounts of processes. Real bodies matter; both processes and outcomes can be used as signs of relative disadvantage, but they need to be considered together and as a whole. For example, clear female disadvantages in processes such as education or employment, or domestic security, should not be considered independently of outcomes such as life expectancy. Life expectancy advantages of women do not cancel out these process disadvantages, but the life expectancy disadvantage of men suggests that in addition perhaps to 'natural' biological disadvantage there are also social processes that disadvantage men in health and longevity terms.[25]

Finally, on a practical note, comparative indicators of gender disadvantage such as those published by the UNDP might usefully include statistics on adult BMIs,[26] childhood stunting, and age specific mortality differentials in addition to time allocation and life expectancies, and further extension and refinement of PAR tables to offer fuller representation of the activities and situations of relevant (poor) populations, and in particular the wide range of domestic labour, would be a useful step towards allowing researchers to integrate effort analysis into studies of labour. Investigation of the various stresses experienced by poorer people in their labour dependent livelihoods and their health consequences would be perhaps most useful.

REFERENCES

Anand, S. and A. Sen (1995) 'Gender Inequality in Human Development: Theories and Measurement'. Human Development Report Office Occasional Paper 19. New York: UNDP.
Astrand, P. and K. Rohdahl (1986) *Textbook on Work Physiology*. London: McGraw Hill.
Batliwala, S. (1982) 'Rural Energy Scarcity and Nutrition: A New Perspective', *Economic and Political Weekly* 17(9): 329–33.
Becker, G. (1985) 'Human Capital and Effort', *Journal of Labour Economics* 3: S33–58.
Bledsoe, C. (1995) 'Numerators and Denominators in the Study of High Fertility Populations: Past and Potential Contributions from Cultural Anthropology', chapter given to the Seminar in Honour of John C. Caldwell, 'The Continuing Tradition', Australian National University, Canberra (August).
Bliss, C. J. and N. H. Stern (1978a) 'Productivity, Wages and Nutrition. Part 1: The Theory', *Journal of Development Economics* 5: 331–62.
Bliss, C. J. and N. H. Stern (1978b) 'Productivity, Wages and Nutrition. Part 2: Some Observations', *Journal of Development Economics* 5: 363–97.
Breman, J. (1996) *Footloose Labour*. Cambridge: Cambridge University Press.

---

25. This is not the place to elaborate this point except to point out firstly that there is increasing concern with the social construction of male health disadvantage, and secondly that there is some disagreement about the extent or even existence of biological female longevity advantage; for example, Anand and Sen (1995) and the UNDP (1995) support a five-year advantage, Murray and Lopez (1994) for the WHO support a two-year advantage. Ryan Johannson (1996) uses evidence of no gender difference among Seventh Day Adventists in the Netherlands to suggest no necessary female longevity advantage.
26. Re-emphasizing the importance of adult as well as child well-being (Reich, 1995).

Butler J. (1990) *Gender Trouble: Feminism and the Subversion of Identity*. London: Routledge.
Carney, J. A. (1988) 'Struggles over Crop Rights and Labour within Contract Farming Households in a Gambian Irrigated Rice Project', *Journal of Peasant Studies* 15(3): 334–49.
Carr, M. and R. Sandhu (1988) 'Women, Technology and Rural Productivity: An Analysis of the Impact of Time and Energy Saving Technologies on Women'. New York: UNIFEM (mimeo).
Chambers, R. (1983) *Rural Development: Putting the Last First*. London: Longman.
Cheater, A. (1981) 'Women and their Participation in Agricultural Production: The Case of Medium Scale Freehold in Zimbabwe', *Development and Change* 12(3): 340–77.
Connell, R. (1987) *Gender and Power*. Cambridge: Polity Press.
Dasgupta, P. (1993) *An Inquiry into Well-being and Destitution*. Oxford: Clarendon Press.
Dasgupta, P. (1997) 'Nutritional Status, the Capacity for Work, and Poverty Traps', *Journal of Econometrics* 77: 5–37.
Dasgupta, P. and D. Ray (1990) 'Adapting to Undernourishment: The Biological Evidence and its Implications', in J. Dreze and A. Sen (eds) *The Political Economy of Hunger: Volume 1: Entitlement and Well-being*, pp. 191–246. Oxford: Clarendon Press.
Dixon-Mueller, R. (1985) *Women's Work in Third World Agriculture*. Geneva: ILO.
Doss, C. R. (1996) 'Testing among Models of Intra Household Resource Allocation', *World Development*. 24(10): 1597–1610.
Drèze, J. and A. Sen (1989) *Hunger and Public Action*. Oxford: Clarendon Press.
Floro, M. S. (1995) 'Women's Well-being, Poverty and Work Intensity', *Feminist Economics* 1(3): 1–25.
Fogel, R. (1994) 'Economic Growth, Population Theory and Physiology: The Bearing of Long-Term Processes on the Making of Economic Theory', *American Economic Review* 84(3): 369–95.
Foster, A. D. and M. R. Rosenzweig (1994) 'A Test for Moral Hazard in the Labour Market: Contractual Arrangements, Effort and Health', *Review of Economics and Statistics* 76(2): 213–27.
Friedman, M. (1957) *A Theory of the Consumption Function*. Princeton, NJ: Princeton University Press.
Giampietro, M. and D. Pimentel (1992) 'Energy Efficiency and Nutrition in Societies based on Human Labour', *Ecology of Food and Nutrition* 28: 11–32.
Giddens, A. (1979) *Central Problems in Social Theory: Action, Structure, and Contradiction in Social Analysis*. London: Macmillan.
Giddens, A. (1984) *The Constitution of Society*. Cambridge: Polity Press.
Gillespie, S. and G. McNeill (1992) *Food, Health and Survival in India and Developing Countries*. New Delhi: Oxford University Press.
Hanger, J. and J. Moris (1973) 'Women and the Household Economy', in R. Chambers and J. Moris (eds) *Mwea: An Irrigated Rice Settlement in Kenya*, pp. 209–44. Munich: Weltforum Verlag.
Harriss, B. (1990) 'The Intra Family Distribution of Hunger in South Asia', in J. Dreze and A. Sen (eds) *The Political Economy of Hunger: Vol. 1*, pp. 351–424. Oxford: Clarendon Press.
Henry, J. (1990) 'Body Mass Index and the Limits of Human Survival', *European Journal of Clinical Nutrition* 44: 329–35.
Hockley, R. (ed.) (1983) *Stress and Fatigue in Human Performance*. Chichester: John Wiley and Sons.
Hoddinott, J., H. Alderman and L. Haddad (1997) 'Testing Competing Models of Intra-household Allocation', in L. Haddad, J. Hoddinott and H. Alderman (eds) *Intra-Household Resource Allocation: Models, Methods and Policy*, pp. 129–41. Baltimore, MD, and London: Johns Hopkins University Press for the International Food Policy Research Institute.
Jackson, C. (1996) 'Rescuing Gender from the Poverty Trap', *World Development* 24(3): 489–504.

Jackson, C. (1997) 'Working Bodies and Gender Divisions of Labour', paper given to workshop on Gender Differentials in Work Intensity, Sustainability and Development, School of Development Studies, University of East Anglia (3–4 July).

Jackson, C. and R. W. Palmer-Jones (1998) 'Work Intensity, Gender and Well-being'. Discussion Paper 96. Geneva: UNRISD.

Johannson, S. Ryan (1996) 'Excess Female Mortality: Constructing Survival during Development in Meiji Japan and Victorian England', in A. Digby and J. Stewart (eds) *Gender, Health and Welfare*, pp. 33–66. London: Routledge.

Jones, C. W. (1986) 'Intra-Household Bargaining in Response to the Introduction of New Crops: A Case Study from North Cameroon', in J. Moock (ed.) *Understanding Africa's Rural Households*, pp. 105–23. Boulder, CO: Westview Press.

Kilbom, A. (1995) 'Measurement and Assessment of Dynamic Work', in J. R. Wilson and E. N. Corlett (eds) *Evaluation of Human Work: A Practical Ergonomics Methodology*, pp. 640–61. London: Taylor and Francis.

Kinsey B. (1997) Email communication, 5 November, on Gender-cg network, reporting persistently lower levels of child nutrition amongst families which have benefited from land reform in Zimbabwe, as revealed in 15 year panel data.

Komlos, J. (1990) 'Nutrition, Population Growth, and the Industrial Revolution in England', *Social Science History* 14(1): 69–91.

Kynch, J. and M. McGuire (1994) 'Food and Human Growth in Palanpur'. STICERD Discussion Paper No. 57. London: London School of Economics and Political Science.

Liebenstein, H. (1957) 'The Theory of Underemployment in Backward Economies', *Journal of Political Economy* 65: 91–103.

Lipton, M. and R. Longhurst (1989) *New Seeds and Poor People*. London: Unwin Hyman.

Lipton, M. and S. Maxwell (1992) 'The New Poverty Agenda: An Overview', IDS Discussion Paper No. 306. Brighton: Institute of Development Studies.

Lovallo, W. R. (1997) *Stress and Health: Biological and Psychological Pathways*. London: Sage.

Lundberg, S. and R. Pollack (1996) 'Bargaining and Distribution in Marriage', *Journal of Economic Perspectives* 10: 139–58.

Maclachlan, M. (1983) *Why they did not Starve: Biocultural Adaptation in a South Indian Village*. Philadelphia, PA: Institute for the Study of Human Issues.

McArdle, W. D., F. I. Katch and V. L. Katch (1996) *Exercise Physiology: Energy, Nutrition, and Human Performance*. Baltimore, MD: Williams and Wilkins.

McElroy, M. B. (1990) 'The Empirical Content of Nash-bargained Household Behaviour', *Journal of Human Resources* 25(4): 559–83.

Messer, E. (1997) 'Intra-Household Allocation of Food and Health Care: Current Findings and Understandings — Introduction', *Social Science and Medicine* 44(11): 1675–84.

Mirrlees, J. (1975) 'A Pure Theory of Underdeveloped Economies', in L. Reynolds (ed.) *Agriculture in Development Theory*, pp. 84–106. New Haven, CT: Yale University Press.

Modigliani, F. and R. Brumberg (1955) 'Utility Analysis and the Consumption Function: An Interpretation of Cross Section Data', in K. Kurihara (ed.) *Post Keynsian Economics*, pp. 383–436. New Brunswick, NJ: Rutgers University Press.

Moore, H. (1994) *A Passion for Difference: Essays in Anthropology and Gender*. Cambridge: Polity Press.

Moser, C. (1993) *Gender Planning and Development Theory and Practice*. London: Routledge.

Mueller, E. A. (1953) 'The Physiological Basis of Rest Pauses in Heavy Work', *Quarterly Journal of Experimental Physiology* 38: 205–15.

Mukhopadhyay, C. and P. Higgins (1988) 'Anthropological Studies of Women's Status Revisited: 1977–87', *Annual Review of Anthropology* 17: 461–95.

Murray, C. J. L. and A. D. Lopez (eds) (1994) *Global Comparative Assessments in the Health Sector: Disease Burden, Expenditures and Intervention Packages*. Geneva: World Health Organization.

Osmani, S. (1992) 'On Some Controversies in the Measurement of Undernutrition', in S. Osmani (ed.) *Nutrition and Poverty*, pp. 121–64. Oxford: Oxford University Press.

Palmer-Jones, R. W. and C. Jackson (1997) 'Work Intensity, Gender and Sustainable Development', *Food Policy* 22(1): 39–62.

Panter-Brick, C. (1997) 'The Tortoise and the Hare: Physical Activity Levels, Effort and Endurance', paper presented at workshop on Gender Differentials in Work Intensity, Sustainability and Development, University of East Anglia (3–4 July).

Parker, M. (1992) 'Re-assessing Disability: The Impact of Schistosomial Infection on Daily Activities among Women in Gezira Province, Sudan', *Social Science and Medicine* 35(7): 877–90.

Parker, M. (1993) 'Bilharzia and the Boys: Questioning Common Assumptions', *Social Science and Medicine* 37(4): 481–92.

Payne, P. and M. Lipton (1994) 'How Third World Rural Households Adapt to Dietary Energy Stress: The Evidence and the Issues'. Food Policy Review 2. Washington: IFPRI.

Pitt, M. (1997) 'Specification and Estimation of the Demand for Goods within the Household', in L. Haddad, J. Hoddinott and H. Alderman (eds) *Intra-Household Resource Allocation: Models, Methods and Policy*, pp. 19–38. Baltimore, MD, and London: Johns Hopkins University Press for the International Food Policy Research Institute.

Pitt, M., M. R. Rosenzweig and M. N. Hassan (1990) 'Productivity, Health, and Inequality in the Intrahousehold Distribution of Food in Low Income Countries', *American Economic Review* 80(5): 1139–56.

Pryer, J. (1989) 'When Breadwinners Fall Ill: Preliminary Findings from a Case Study in Bangladesh', *IDS Bulletin* 20(2): 49–57.

Rabinbach, A. (1990) *The Human Motor: Energy, Fatigue and the Origins of Modernity.* Berkeley, CA: University of Berkeley Press.

Ramachandran, V. K. (1996) 'Kerala's Development Achievements', in J. Dreze and A. Sen (eds) *Indian Development: Selected Regional Perspectives*, pp. 205–356. Oxford and Delhi: Oxford University Press.

Ray, D. (1998) *Development Economics.* Princeton, NJ: Princton University Press.

Reich, M. R. (1995) 'The Politics of Agenda Setting in International Health: Child Health versus Adult Health in Developing Countries', *Journal of International Development* 7(3): 489–502.

Scarry, E. (1985) *The Body in Pain: The Making and Unmaking of the World.* Oxford: Oxford University Press.

Seckler, D. (1982) 'Small but Healthy: A Basic Hypothesis in the Theory, Measurement and Policy of Malnutrition', in P. V. Sukhatme (ed.) *Newer Concepts in Nutrition and their Implications for Policy*, pp. 127–37. Pune: Maharashtra Association for the Cultivation of Science.

Sen, A. (1983) 'Economics and the Family', *Asian Development Review* 1(2): 14–26.

Sen, A. (1987) *Gender and Cooperative Conflicts.* Helsinki: World Institute for Development Economics Research.

Shetty, P. S. (1997) 'The Gender Dimension in the Measurement and Interpretation of Nutritional Status and Energy Expenditure', paper presented at workshop on Gender Differentials in Work Intensity, Sustainability and Development, University of East Anglia (3–4 July).

Shetty, P. S. and W. P. T. James (1994) 'Body Mass Index: A Measure of Chronic Energy Deficiency in Adults'. Food and Nutrition Paper, 56. Rome: Food and Agriculture Organization.

Shilling, C. (1993) *The Body and Social Theory.* London: Sage.

Singh, I. (1990) *The Great Ascent: The Rural Poor in South Asia.* Baltimore, MD: Johns Hopkins University Press for the World Bank.

Soper, K. (1995) *What is Nature? Culture, Politics and the Non-human.* Oxford: Blackwell.

Stiglitz, J. E. (1976) 'The Efficiency Wage Hypothesis, Surplus Labour, and the Distribution of Income in LDCs', *Oxford Economic Papers* 28: 185–207.

Strauss, J. and D. Thomas (1995) 'Human Resources: Empirical Modelling of Household and Family Decisions', in J. Behreman and T. N. Srinivasan (eds) *Handbook of Development Economics, Volume 3A*, pp. 1886–2023. Amsterdam: North Holland.

Strickland, S. and V. Tuffrey (1997) *Nutrition, Adaptation and Social Inequality: A Study of Three Gurung Villages in the Nepal Himalayas*. London: Smith-Gordon.

Sukhatme, P. V. and S. Margen (1978/1982) 'Model of Protein Deficiency', *American Journal of Clinical Nutrition* 31: 355–65 (1978), reprinted in P. V. Sukhatme (ed.) *Newer Concepts in Nutrition and their Implications for Policy*. Pune: Maharashtra Association for the Cultivation of Science (1982).

Turner, B. (1996) *The Body and Society*. London: Sage.

UNDP (1995) *Human Development Report, 1995*. Oxford: Oxford University Press.

Weiss, A. (1990) *Efficiency Wages: Models of Unemployment, Layoffs and Wage Dispersion*. Oxford: Clarendon Press.

Whitehead, M. (1988) 'The Health Divide', in P. Townsend, N. Davidson and M. Whitehead (eds) *Inequalities in Health*, pp. 217–382. Harmondsworth: Pelican Books.

WHO/FAO/UNU (1985) 'Energy and Protein Requirements: Report of a Joint FAO/WHO/UNU Expert Consultation'. Geneva: World Health Organization.

7

Female Demographic Disadvantage in India 1981–1991: Sex Selective Abortions and Female Infanticide

S. Sudha and S. Irudaya Rajan

INTRODUCTION

Highlighted by sensational titles such as 'The Endangered Sex' (Miller, 1981) or 'More than 100 million women are missing' (Sen, 1992), studies have long pointed to the unfavourable life chances of females versus males in parts of East and South Asia. This female disadvantage is particularly concentrated in infancy and childhood years, and is rooted in long-standing social patterns of preference for male children. Practices regulating the numbers of female children in a family traditionally included the post-natal methods of female infanticide, abandonment or out-adoption of girls, under-reporting of female births, and selective neglect of daughters leading to higher death rates. Lately in China and South Korea, prenatal sex determination and selective abortion of female foetuses have been increasingly implicated (Asia-Pacific Population and Policy Report, 1995; Johansen and Nygren, 1991; Park and Cho, 1995; Yi et al., 1993). When fertility declines and preference for male children remains strong, parents still take steps to ensure the birth and survival of sons, and prenatal sex determination and selective abortion of females are apparently preferable to female infanticide or abandonment of baby girls. Prenatal sex selection techniques appear to substitute for post-natal methods in these regions, as shown by increasing masculinity of sex ratios at birth, coupled with more equitable sex ratios of infant and child mortality (Goodkind, 1996). That is, fewer girls are allowed to be born, but those who are born are more wanted and tend to survive.

These issues are also significant in South Asia, which shares with East Asia a long-standing tradition of son-preference. In India, the issue has mostly been examined in terms of the masculinity of the population sex ratios observed since the first census taken in 1871 under the British Raj (Irudaya Rajan et al., 1991; Kundu and Sahu, 1991; Raju and Premi, 1992; Srinivasan, 1997; Visaria, 1969). The persistent preference for sons and disfavour toward

This is a revised version of Working Paper No. 288 of the Centre for Development Studies, Thiruvananthapuram. It has been presented at the CDS-UNRISD Workshop on Gender, Poverty and Well-being, Centre for Development Studies, Thiruvananthapuram (24–7 November 1997), and at the T. N. Krishnan Memorial Seminar, Centre for Development Studies, Thiruvananthapuram (7–9 September 1997).

daughters, leading to the phenomenon of 'excess female child mortality'[1] and highly masculine juvenile sex ratios (counter to the global norm of female mortality advantage and moderately masculine sex ratios among children) have been discussed as key factors in this imbalance (Agnihotri, 1996; Kishor, 1993; Miller, 1981; Saith and Harriss-White, this volume).

An important dimension of inquiry, that of changes in the relative pattern of births and survival of male versus female children in India, has been comparatively neglected, mainly due to lack of data. Indian authorities do not routinely publish data on sex ratios among births reported in the Census or Sample Registration System enumeration years. A few regional studies suggest that cohort sex ratios at birth are anomalously masculine in some parts of the country, particularly in the North (Clark and Shreeniwas, 1995 for Gujarat; Mason et al., 1992 for Karnataka; Irudaya Rajan, 1996 and Visaria and Irudaya Rajan, 1996 for Kerala). Therefore, it is not clear whether parents in India, as in East Asia, are substituting prenatal for post-natal discrimination against girl children, or whether bias against females is lessening over time. One all-India study has examined changes in juvenile sex ratios (ages 0–4) between 1981 and 1991, alongside trends in mortality sex ratios and fertility rates, and concluded that during fertility decline in India, parents are not substituting prenatal for post-natal discrimination against girls, but are combining these two strategies. Male bias thus appears to be intensifying (Das Gupta and Bhat, 1997).

Our study explores this issue further, with more region-disaggregated and age-focused data. Using the 1981 and 1991 censuses of India, we present ratios among numbers of boys and girls aged 0 and 1 (taken together to minimize the effect of age misreporting). Next, using an unorthodox application of the technique of 'reverse survival' we estimate sex ratios at birth for these two census years. We also present sex ratios of child mortality probabilities (q5) from the censuses for these two time points. We examine variations by rural/urban residence and state/region, drawing attention to the specific sub-regions of India where changes have taken place over the decade. We summarize what has been reported about the incidence of prenatal sex selection and female infanticide in India, and place the evidence within the context of social and economic development in India, especially relating to the situation of women.

The rest of this chapter presents critical syntheses of prior research and reporting on gender-specific demographic trends in India. Arguments concerning the possible impact of social and economic development on gender stratification, and the consequent differences in the valuation and wantedness of male and female children, are summarized. Subsequently, the observed

---

1. 'Excess female child mortality' refers to the phenomenon of higher death rates of females among infants and children than males, in contrast to the 'normal' pattern of higher mortality among males.

and estimated birth and mortality ratios calculated from the censuses are presented. The concluding section discusses the implication of the arguments and findings.

GLOBAL PATTERNS IN SRBs

Sex ratios at birth (henceforward SRBs), refer to the ratio of male to female children born in a specific period, such as a year, or among all the children ever born to cohorts of women. In most human populations, more boys than girls are conceived, and despite greater male than female foetal wastage, more boys than girls are born. This leads to a fairly stable SRB observed among human populations in countries with good vital registration, of approximately 104 to 106 boys per 100 girls (Johansen and Nygren, 1991). Subsequently, mortality rates at every age are slightly greater for boys than for girls due to a combination of biological and behavioural factors. Thus, with increasing age, the population sex ratio balances out to a slight female dominance overall. Most societies irrespective of level of income or development exhibit this pattern.

In societies that have a marked preference for male children, however, a different pattern is seen. In South Asia, population sex ratios are persistently male dominant. In East Asia, period SRBs appear highly masculine especially in recent years. In South Korea and China respectively, both of which have good coverage of vital registration, SRBs as high as 112 and 113 males per 100 females have been observed among all births. First order births are within the normal range (approximately 104–6 in each society). Second and higher order births, however, soar up to 120 and more for China, and third and higher order births to 185 and more for South Korea (Asia-Pacific Population and Policy Report, 1995). Clearly, therefore, biological patterns of SRBs are in these regions being overwhelmed by behavioural factors rooted in parents' preference for at least one male child (Coale and Banister, 1994; Hull, 1990; Johansen and Nygren, 1991). These skewed SRBs combined with anomalously masculine sex specific survival rates have generated the problem of millions of 'missing' females in East and South Asia (Coale, 1991; Sen, 1992).

Several mechanisms are advanced to explain the phenomenon of excessively masculine SRBs. In China, mechanisms include non-reporting of female births (leading to omission of girl children in all subsequent official records, tantamount to denying their social existence), abandonment and/or out-adoption of girls, and female infanticide (Hull, 1990; Johansen and Nygren, 1991). All these mechanisms can be viewed as varying types of discrimination against female children. Lately, in China and South Korea where there is a combination of lowered fertility, continued strong son preference, and widespread access to medical facilities, the increased use of prenatal sex determination techniques leading to abortion of female foetuses is implicated in the phenomenally higher masculine birth order sex ratios observed there (Asia-Pacific Population and Policy Report, 1995; Park and Cho, 1995; Yi et al., 1993).

REGIONAL TRENDS IN JUVENILE SEX RATIOS IN INDIA

In India, most analyses focus on juvenile sex ratios rather than sex ratios at birth. This is firstly because of the concern that excess female child mortality, which arises from the selective neglect of girl children compared to boys, manifests itself in childhood years rather than around the time of birth (Das Gupta, 1987; Dyson, 1988). Secondly, data on period sex ratios at birth are difficult to obtain in India, as the Census of India does not publish this statistic. Such data are only occasionally published by the Sample Registration System (SRS) of certain states, and thus nation-wide or time-trend analyses are ruled out. Vital statistics registration is of varying quality and completeness in different parts of the country, as are hospital records. Thus all-India or time-trend investigations of period SRBs are difficult, although some intra-state analyses are emerging (Visaria and Irudaya Rajan, 1996, for Kerala).

Regional analyses of juvenile sex ratios in India on the whole indicate that more masculine juvenile sex ratios and higher female than male child mortality go hand in hand (Agnihotri, 1996; Clark and Shreeniwas, 1995; Das Gupta, 1987; Das Gupta and Bhat, 1997; Kishor 1993). That is, higher juvenile sex ratios at ages 0–4 are accompanied by higher female than male child mortality at ages 5–9. A well-known regional pattern is observed: the Northern and Northwestern parts of India, including the states of Punjab, Haryana, Rajasthan and Western UP, are areas most unfavourable to the life chances of female children. Other parts of the country, including the East, Central area and the South, exhibit more balanced rates.

A broad generalization has been made: the North/Northwestern regions of India fall within the so-called Northern cultural and demographic zone, distinguished by higher fertility, higher mortality, more masculine sex ratios, and lower status of women. This zone traditionally had a wheat-based agrarian economy (where women are less involved), and social systems marked by dowry, exogamous marriage[2] and the seclusion of women. In contrast, the South is broadly characterized by rice-based agrarian systems (with a greater role for women), endogamous marriage systems, marriage

---

2. Exogamy refers to the practice whereby the bride marries outside her natal kin, clan or lineage circles or village. It is argued that exogamous marriage makes women more vulnerable, by separating them far from their natal kin, and placing them in the position of outsiders in their marital families, until they 'prove themselves' by giving birth to sons and by bringing dowry and other gifts from their natal home. Conversely, endogamy refers to the practice of marrying within specific kin, clan or lineage circles or inside one's natal village, and is less detrimental to women.

payments that are more egalitarian between brides' and grooms' families, and less seclusion of women. Women's literacy and education levels are also much higher in the South than the North. The status of women is higher in the South, which also has lower fertility and mortality rates, and more 'normal' sex ratios (Dyson and Moore, 1983).

Other scholars rightly stress that the simplistic dichotomization of India into 'Northern' vs. 'Southern' zones is inadequate. The rice-cultivating Eastern region could never be fitted into either pattern. Within-region variations have been ignored in the dichotomization, such as the 'belt of female infanticide' in the Salem/Dharmapuri/Madurai districts of Tamil Nadu noted by Chunkath and Athreya (1997). Alternative spatial patterns ranging from five to nineteen clusters of India's districts have been proposed, taking into account ecological and economic sub-regions, areas with greater proportions of Scheduled Caste/Scheduled Tribe populations (who are characterized by more gender-egalitarian cultures), and other criteria. Even in these alternative groupings, however, juvenile sex ratios appear most masculine in the North/Northwestern region of India. A so-called 'Bermuda Triangle' for the female child exists in a zone of twenty-four districts including parts of Haryana, Western Uttar Pradesh, some of Rajasthan, and the ravine areas of Madhya Pradesh (Agnihotri, 1996).

FEMALE DEMOGRAPHIC DISADVANTAGE IN THE CONTEXT OF DEVELOPMENT

Globally, it should be pointed out that gender-imbalanced demographic measures are by no means simply associated with poverty or 'under-development', such that poorer nations have more female disadvantage. African, Latin American and Caribbean nations, all with varying development philosophies, levels of poverty and living standards, exhibit 'normal' sex ratios at birth and of mortality. Any gender inequalities these countries may have is apparently manifested in other domains. On the other hand, countries such as China, South Korea and India which have a socio-cultural pattern of preference for male children, irrespective of level of development and philosophy of economic organization, exhibit gender imbalances in demographic measures that persist over time.

In India, too, the relationship between social and economic development and female disadvantage is not clear-cut. On the broadest level of generalization, the process of development in India has been mostly to women's detriment. The 1974 Report of the Committee of the Status of Women in India (GOI, 1974) was the first to point out that despite the progressive promises and provisions of the Indian constitution, development since Independence had been accompanied by a deterioration in women's situation, indicated by worsening sex ratios, declining female work participation rates, and persistent shortfalls in literacy and female mortality.

Neither has the trend since that time been positive. The majority of Indian women are involved in the agricultural sector, and have been adversely affected by agrarian development. First, while land reforms focused on redistributing land to the landless, in practice ownership was invested in the *household* head, always seen as the senior male. Women's alienation from the most critical productive resource was thus progressively institutionalized. Women's use rights in land, where they exist, are exercised during the goodwill of the male kin who have effective control over the land (Agarwal, 1994).

Second, although the Green Revolution dramatically increased food production and allayed fears of population growth outstripping food supply in India, it adversely affected women's work participation. Evidence from Punjab, Haryana, UP, and Tamil Nadu shows that the Green Revolution narrowed the range of agrarian tasks, displaced women from traditional occupations, and placed them at the bottom of the new labour hierarchies. Women's occupations became increasingly impermanent and casualized due to technological changes coupled with traditional norms about the gender-based division of labour (Kapadia, 1992; Nayyar, 1989; Nigam, 1988; Sen, 1982). Although the initial impact of Green Revolution technology was to increase the demand for labour to fertilize, weed, and harvest the new High Yielding Varieties (HYVs), this trend was short-lived, and tended not to involve women. For example, farmers in Gujarat utilizing HYV technology preferred male to female labour since they felt that men were more efficient, more suited to the 'high-technology' innovations, could work for longer hours at a stretch, and could fulfil demands for group labour. Although women received lower wages than men for the same work, they had no training for even the simplest new tasks such as spraying, and were thus excluded (Hirway, 1979). In Bihar as in Gujarat, female work participation grew substantially less in irrigated districts, and the rise of mechanized dehusking and flour-making industries deprived women of significant work they had hitherto performed (Hirway, 1979; Sinha, 1988). Varghese (1991) states that rural Indian women's paid work participation is declining, and that women are highly concentrated (approximately 80 per cent of female workers) in the agricultural labour and unpaid family work sectors. The increased casualization of female labour is accompanied by consistently greater unemployment among women than men. He concludes that the 'female marginalization thesis' is supported in the Indian agrarian context.

Non-farm opportunities have not kept pace with the displacement of rural women. Though Deshpande (1992) shows that many urban women workers are absorbed into new occupations such as in export processing zones, and argues that despite low wages and poor working conditions they contribute up to one third of household income, pull their families above the poverty line, and thus gain a measure of respect and autonomy, Ramaswamy (1993) argues that the vast numbers of women (94 per cent of the total female work force) in the unorganized occupational sector indicates the failure of the Indian planning process with respect to women. The organized sector, depending on newly emerging technologies, offers little to the many women displaced from rural or sunset industries. There are opportunities only for those with education and skills. Though female literacy is rising, parents in much of India do not encourage their daughters to attend more than a few years of school, since higher education is seen as an unprofitable investment in girls who will marry and move to their husbands' households. Much of the impetus for girls' education comes from the increasing demand for literate brides on the part of young educated men. Women thus cannot compete for the new opportunities in significant numbers. Moreover, the masculine bias of the organized sector tends toward decreased security of even those women involved, as Indian trade unions usually downplay the needs of women workers, who have had to set up parallel organizations as a result. Ramaswamy (1993: 323) concludes that in India, 'developmental processes have only pushed women to states of survival'.

However, development has marginalized women in other less affluent nations too, which none the less continue to exhibit gender-balanced demographic measures. The fact that economic development devalues women is not sufficient on its own to make families discriminate against daughters. It is pointed out that both economic and cultural factors are jointly responsible for the variations in the status of women, and consequent sex differentials in the wantedness, birth, care and survival of male and female children (Kishor, 1993).

Socio-cultural trends in India also place women at an increased disadvantage. The traditional patrilineal, patrilocal, and exogamous marriage and kinship systems prevailing over much of the subcontinent have always placed women in a low-status, precarious position, until they earn their place in the patriline by bearing sons. Although the southern part of the subcontinent had more endogamous and egalitarian marriage systems, with matrilineal family forms in many Southwestern coastal communities, social change in these regions has tended to move towards normatively patrilineal systems. Significantly, scholars also note the spread of dowry[3] nationwide to communities and castes where it had never been the custom. Insufficient research attention has been paid to this phenomenon. The bulk of sociological or anthropological research in India on the topic of kinship is abstract and descriptive in nature, viewing women as objects of study and exchange, and not problematizing the underlying causal and consequential gender relations (Agarwal, 1994; Ramaswamy, 1993). Some scholars have begun to address this issue (for instance, Palriwala and Risseeuw, 1996), but there is

---

3. Dowry is the transfer of wealth, in the form of money, gold, consumer goods, or other assets, from the bride's parents to those of the groom. Although the custom is supposed to provide the bride with pre-mortem inheritance of her share of her family's property, in practice, she has little control over the dowry, and her in-laws dispose of it as they wish.

little scrutiny of the relationship between kinship organization, gender relations, and women's life and death chances.

Some attribute the spread of dowry to the process of 'Sanskritization', whereby lower castes achieve upward caste and class mobility by emulating the customs of the upper castes, including dowry and female seclusion. Others attribute the changes to the young age structure of the country: the greater ratio of young marriageable girls to potential mates in the higher age group increases the 'price' of grooms (Rao, 1993). The rise of consumerism is also implicated, drawing people into a growing web of expectations and demands. The continued importance of kin networks for economic resource mobilization, the spread of the dowry custom, the growing amounts of dowry changing hands, and the increasing importance of resource acquisition strategies for family status enhancement, have led to the concentration of wealth in families where the ratio of male children is greater, and female children are therefore increasingly seen as liabilities (Clark, 1987; Heyer, 1992).

The socio-economic bases of female mortality disadvantage have been examined with all-India level, and smaller-scale, localized analyses. All-India studies suggest that districts with higher indicators of conventional development, such as urbanization, industrial output, and agricultural productivity had significantly lower female vs. male survivorship, while girls in areas with a greater concentration of Scheduled Caste/Scheduled Tribe populations (with largely more gender-egalitarian norms than the Indian mainstream), endogamous marriage patterns, and greater female empowerment measured by women's labour force participation and education, fared better (Agnihotri, 1996; Kishor, 1993; Murthy et al., 1996). These studies identify a constellation of economic and cultural factors jointly affecting female mortality disadvantage, improving on earlier and simpler models of female agrarian labour force participation alone (Bardhan, 1974).

The findings of smaller-scale studies do not, however, lend themselves to such consistent generalizations. The role of women's education in ameliorating female child mortality disadvantage might seem self-evident, and the district-level studies cited above support the notion. However, smaller-scale studies in rural Punjab and Gujarat indicate that mothers with some education might actually be more efficient in discriminating against their daughters, particularly in asset-poor households. Schooling may make women more aware of health, hygiene and nutrition, but female education alone is not enough to transcend the nexus of conditions that leads families to consider daughters a liability. Education often domesticates women rather than liberates them (Clark and Shreeniwas, 1995; Das Gupta, 1987).

Regarding the role of economic assets, studies in rural Tamil Nadu suggest that female child mortality disadvantage is greater among the landed and upper-caste groups, where women are also more secluded and have lower rates of work participation (Harriss-White, 1998; Heyer, 1992). In one Green Revolution community of UP, and in a dairy co-operative region of rural

Gujarat, however, lower caste and landless groups are the ones where daughters appear in greater jeopardy (Clark and Shreeniwas, 1995; Wadley, 1993). While the specific castes involved depend on local conditions, the common factor is the family's effort to acquire land or other economic advantages through mobilizing kinship networks and manipulating the marriages of their sons and daughters. In a patrilineal kinship system where marriages are arranged on principles of dowry and hypergamy, and where women are objects of exchange along with other forms of wealth, excess female mortality is argued to be an inevitable outcome (Clark, 1987).

Contradictions notwithstanding, a pattern is discernible where increasing economic marginalization and social devaluation make daughters increasingly viewed as liabilities. Productive activities and resources are increasingly concentrated in the hands of men. Conventional socio-economic development accentuates rather than ameliorates this trend. Families therefore respond by discouraging the birth and survival of female children. Numerous studies document widespread gender inequality within households in the allocation of food and health care; women and girl children have last priority. This directly heightens female child mortality (reviews in Agarwal, 1994; Kishor, 1995; Miller, 1997). The role of selective neglect of daughters in excess female child mortality has been more extensively researched in the Indian context, and is not addressed in this chapter. We instead scrutinize the related practices of female infanticide and foeticide, which have been less examined in India for reasons obviously connected with the sensitivity of the issues. The main findings not surprisingly come from the documentation efforts of women's groups and NGOs active in these fields rather than from academic research.

FEMALE INFANTICIDE IN INDIA

Infanticide is an age-old post-natal practice among human populations to regulate the numbers of children and eliminate less wanted offspring. The practice of 'exposing' girls or weak or deformed babies was noted in ancient Roman and Greek society in the West (Scrimshaw, 1984). Little is known about female infanticide in India prior to the advent of British observers (Miller, 1987). However, since then, female infanticide has been widely recorded among upper caste (especially Rajput) groups in Northern and Northwestern India.

Historically, the main reasons for this practice in India included the system of hypergamy, whereby women must marry into a social sub-group above their own. Among the uppermost castes this was impossible. Since it was unthinkable that the rules of hypergamy could be transgressed, or that girls could remain unmarried, girls in these groups were killed and boys married females from sub-castes slightly lower than their own. Nineteenth century records show large groups of villages in Rajasthan and Gujarat, comprising several hundred upper-caste households, where no female child had been allowed to survive for many generations (Vishwanath, 1996). In that era female infanticide was also part of a set of household strategies among these same land-owning upper-caste groups, to acquire further holdings and improve and consolidate their socio-economic status. This was achieved through manipulating the marriage of sons and acquiring dowry from daughters-in-law; daughters, as dowry-takers, were clearly a liability in this scheme of things (Clark, 1983). Thus, the twentieth century socio-economic processes linked to female societal devaluation and demographic disadvantage discussed in the previous section, are foreshadowed in the nineteenth century.

Similar processes are suggested to explain the spread of female infanticide in modern India. Female infanticide has been recently noted among some castes in remote village clusters in South India, in Tamil Nadu state, a region where this practice was historically little known. Increasing landlessness and poverty, an escalating dowry custom, high gender differentials in wages, low education among women and few economic opportunities for them are suggested as reasons (Chunkath and Athreya, 1997; George et al., 1992). Newspaper reports describe the conditions of poverty and misery of the families who turn to female infanticide, and their suspicion of alternatives such as adoption offered by the Government and grassroots organizations in the region (Aravamudan, 1994). Government plans to tackle the problem range from a 'cradle baby' adoption system for unwanted girl children, to economic incentive packages for women who only have daughters and who agree to undergo sterilization. The coercive design of some of these schemes, and corruption and inefficiency in their management, have led to their falling short of their targets and having a very limited impact on the problem. In 1995, an estimated 3174 female infanticides occurred in Tamil Nadu state (George, 1997).

In rural North India, the historic practice of female infanticide apparently never died out. Jeffery et al. (1984) state that up to the 1900s female infanticide was practised among Rajput castes in Bijnor, UP state. Their study in the 1980s in villages around Bijnor town noted that part of a traditional birth attendant's duties continued to be disposal of unwanted (i.e. girl) children at birth. They also report that the practice is spreading across the social spectrum to caste groups among whom it had never been practised.

The same observation is made in rural Bihar state. In 1995, Adithi, an NGO working in rural Bihar and having an excellent rapport with its target population, conducted an in-depth investigation. It revealed that female infanticide, foeticide, and excess female child mortality due to selective neglect were widespread in the eight districts studied. Infanticide was carried out by *dais* (traditional birth attendants), who were coerced by the senior male kin of the woman giving birth, overriding the protests of the women in the family. Fear of reprisals, poverty, lack of alternative occupation, and socialization to obey the commands of those in authority led the *dais* to comply. Other medical practitioners such as compounders and doctors also carried out infanticide when approached by the family members of a newborn girl. There was no difficulty in committing infanticide, because the birth and death followed quickly upon each other, with no certificate recorded for either event. Unscrupulous medical practitioners also conducted abortion of female foetuses, especially after techniques like sonography became widespread. The traditional skill of *dais* in identifying the sex of a foetus in the seventh or eighth month of pregnancy is also used to avert the birth of a daughter. Estimating a count of 68,000 *dais* in seven contiguous and culturally similar districts of Bihar, and that each *dai* killed about two infants a month (according to the interviews), Adithi (1995) estimates that the number of female infanticides each year in these districts could total as many as 1,632,000.

The Adithi report noted that whereas previously only upper castes such as Rajputs and Brahmins practised female infanticide, the custom has now spread to all other groups in the rural spectrum, including Scheduled Tribes, Christians and Muslims. The main reasons are the spread of dowry with exorbitant demands, due to marginalization of women from traditional occupations and the concentration of income in the hands of men, with the consequence that women's seclusion and dependence on men increased, and men began to assert their right to emulate upper caste customs, including the practice of female infanticide. Emulation of upper caste social customs would enable the men to tap into upper caste economic networks to further upward class mobility. This spread of female infanticide across the Indian rural spectrum supports the arguments made above about the association of women's social devaluation and economic marginalization with female demographic disadvantage.[4] The underlying socio-economic processes, first analysed for the nineteenth century and intensifying in the twentieth century, can be seen as going hand-in-hand with the persistence of excess female child mortality and the spreading infanticide custom. The question of whether some families turn to female foeticide as an option thus arises.

PRENATAL SEX DETERMINATION AND SEX-SELECTIVE ABORTION IN INDIA

Unlike countries in East Asia, statistics on period sex ratios at birth, which would have enabled us to assess the birth patterns of boys versus girls and thereby make direct inferences regarding sex selective abortion, are not available for India. Statistics on abortion are also incomplete and largely unavailable. In order to examine the possibility of the spread of female

---

4. Violence against women is growing, within and outside the home. Bihar has extremely low female literacy: 23.1 per cent (Adithi, 1995).

foeticide in India, we thus turn to other kinds of evidence. In this section, we summarize reports from a variety of sources about the increasing availability and use of prenatal sex selection techniques. In the next section, we estimate sex ratios at birth from the available census data. We then discuss the picture that emerges from these complementary pieces of evidence.

Abortion was legalized in India in 1971, after a 1965 UN mission to India recommended this step to strengthen the population policy, and the report of the 1966 Shantilal Shah Committee also advocated it to reduce the numbers of illegal and unsafe abortions. Although the stated reasons for passing the Medical Termination of Pregnancy (MTP) Act were humanitarian (to 'help' victims of sexual assault), health-related (to provide an alternative to those whose contraceptive measures failed) and eugenic (to reduce the numbers of 'abnormal' children born), there was a strong population control motivation underlying the passage of the Act (Menon, 1996).

In 1975, amniocentesis techniques for detecting foetal abnormalities were developed in India, at the All India Institute of Medical Sciences, New Delhi. It was soon known that these tests could also detect the sex of the foetus, and doctors at the Institute noted that most of the 11,000 couples who volunteered for the test wanted to know the sex of the child and were less interested in the possibility of genetic abnormalities. Most women who already had two or more daughters and who learnt that their expected child was female, went on to have an abortion (Chhachhi and Sathyamala, 1983).

Between 1977 and 1985, in an effort to curb this misuse of the technique, three circulars were sent to Central and State government departments making the use of prenatal sex determination for the purpose of abortion a penal offense (Kulkarni, 1986). Women's groups, civil liberties groups and health movements also launched a campaign against prenatal sex determination and female foeticide (termed 'femicide'). In 1984, a broad-based coalition, the 'Forum Against Sex Determination and Sex Pre-selection' (FASDSP) was formed, with headquarters in Bombay, to monitor all aspects of the situation, and document the growing use of the technique, and the legal and policy steps taken against it. As a result of these efforts, the state government of Maharashtra passed the Maharashtra Regulation of the Use of Prenatal Diagnostic Techniques Act in 1988. The states of Punjab, Gujarat, and Haryana followed suit and the Central Government passed the Prenatal Diagnostic Technique (Regulation and Prevention of Misuse) Act in 1994. The Act states that determining and communicating the sex of a foetus is illegal; that genetic tests can be carried out only in registered facilities; and only offered to women who meet certain medical criteria, such as being over the age of 35, having a family history of genetic disorders, and so on.

However, these acts are full of loopholes. Most restrictions pertain to government facilities. Private laboratories and clinics are not banned from carrying out tests that can be used to reveal a foetus's sex: they must only be registered. While they are forbidden to communicate the foetus's sex, many evolve covert methods by which to do so. Second, the government can over-rule the decisions of the body set up to monitor facilities, which is empowered to suspend or cancel the licences of offending clinics or laboratories. The government can also exempt any facility from the Act. While in Maharashtra the monitoring committee included representatives of NGOs, the State Directorate of Medical Education and Research, and the Indian Council of Medical Research, the Central Government Act appointed only two State employees as regulators. Given the dubious record of the State as a monitor-ing body, the Act is thus considerably weakened. Further, an ordinary citizen cannot directly move the courts, but must approach the monitoring body, which can refuse to release any records if it is deemed in the public interest to keep them sealed. Moreover, these regulations cover ultrasonography facil-ities to a lesser extent, and this technique is also being widely used for sex determination. The possibility that newer technologies will be developed to determine a foetus's sex has not been allowed for (Arora, 1996; Menon, 1996; Sengupta, 1992). The result of such partial regulation is that sex determina-tion facilities have privatized, commercialized, and mushroomed. Doctors indicated that despite bans, they would continue to communicate the sex of the foetus to parents who wanted to know, verbally rather than in writing, and would hike the test fees to compensate for the legal risk. The Maharashtra bans did not have much impact as sex determination facilities continue to operate in that state (Kishwar, 1995). One study asserts that sex selection continues to be the major purpose of prenatal diagnosis in India (Wertz and Fletcher, 1993).

Systematic studies clearly indicate the increasing spread and acceptability of the techniques. A 1982 study in Ludhiana, an urban area in Punjab state, randomly sampled 126 individuals, of whom approximately half each were male and female and most of whom were educated and middle class. All the respondents had heard of the amniocentesis test; 66 per cent of them thought it was intended for sex determination; few knew that it was actually for detecting foetal abnormalities. While 73 per cent of the women and 59 per cent of the men believed that a girl should be aborted if the couple already had two or more daughters, only 25 per cent of the respondents felt that a boy should be aborted if the couple already had two or more sons. The reasons given indicated the nature of male-dominated society, dowry prob-lems, greater responsibilities in bringing up daughters, and social pressure to bear sons. Over 71 per cent of the respondents felt that amniocentesis as a sex determination test should not be banned (Singh and Jain, 1985).

These results were uncannily echoed over a decade later, in rural Maharashtra state, among six villages of Pune district, three with road and access to a health facility, and three others more remote and without these amenities. Results indicated that 49 out of the 67 women interviewed in-depth were aware of ultrasound and/or amniocentesis techniques and 45 per cent of those who knew approved of aborting female foetuses. Only four women were aware that such tests were actually for the detection of foetal abnormalities (Gupte et al., 1997). The spread of awareness of these techniques to rural areas is thus clearly documented.

The increase in number and reach of facilities offering sex determination and abortion is also clear. In the early 1980s, Jeffery et al. (1984) noted that in villages adjacent to Bijnor town in UP state, clinical services offering sex determination and abortion had already appeared. The first newspaper reports of private clinics offering sex selection techniques appeared in 1982–3, in cities such as Amritsar, Bombay, and Delhi. Within two to three years, the numbers of such clinics rose to several hundred in the larger cities, and several dozen in smaller towns in Maharashtra, UP, Punjab, and Gujarat states. A few clinics reportedly had begun to offer services from the late 1970s onward, but were brought to widespread public attention and formed the subject of a Parliamentary debate only in the early 1980s, after a senior and well-connected official's wife underwent an abortion of a foetus that was mistakenly diagnosed as female but turned out to be male (Ahluwalia, 1986). The ensuing media storm ironically only served to increase awareness of the techniques.

The use of these techniques thus became widespread not only in towns, but also among rural areas with access to a road or transport system to the nearest town. Newspaper reports describe mobile sex selection clinics, offering ultra-sound detection and immediate abortion if the foetus is female, in smaller towns of Haryana state in the mid-1980s. The clientele included farmers who had come from villages half-an-hour away by road (Vishwanathan, 1991). Remote districts that lacked basic amenities such as drinking water or electricity were reported to have sex determination clinics; where refrigeration and cold chain facilities for vaccinations were not available but amniotic fluid samples were sent in ice packs to towns for testing (FASDSP and Saheli Women's Resource Centre, nd, cited in Menon, 1996). Grassroots workers and concerned medical practitioners have observed an increase in female foeticide in all segments of society in rural Bihar state, especially after sonography techniques became common. Unscrupulous doctors identify the sex of the child, and provide abortion if it is female (Adithi, 1995).

Nor is the cost of the test (ranging over time from Rs 500 to over Rs 1000) a barrier. While we may expect that the largest consumers of such tests will be those with at least a modicum of disposable income, education, and aware-ness of medical technology, landless labourers and marginal farmers are also apparently willing to take out loans at high rates of interest to avail themselves of these tests (FASDSP and Saheli Women's Resource Centre, nd, cited in Menon, 1996). In 1981–2, the approximate average daily wage of a skilled male agricultural worker in Punjab was Rs 25, that of female and male field or other workers ranged from Rs 10 to Rs 13. In Haryana, the figures are Rs 18 for skilled workers, and Rs 7–15 for female and male field and other workers. By 1991–2, the figures were Rs 84 for skilled male workers in Punjab, Rs 77 in Haryana, and around Rs 40 in Bihar and Tamil Nadu. Field workers in these states earned Rs 30–40 in Punjab/Haryana, and Rs 20–5 in

Bihar and Tamil Nadu (Government of India, 1983; 1993). Thus, even taking the seasonality of wages, other expenses, and rural indebtedness into account, affording the price of a sex determination test would not be totally out of the question even for the poorer sections of rural society, especially in the relatively rich states of Punjab and Haryana. The logic underlying the motivation is illustrated by the now infamous slogan: 'Better Rs 500 today than Rs 500,000 tomorrow' that was widely used in the early 1980s to advertise sex determination clinics until protests from women's groups put a stop to it. The slogan may no longer be used, but the underlying logic — that an expenditure now (on the test) will save many multiples of the sum later (on dowry, if the foetus is a girl) — still holds.

Performing the tests has become an extremely profitable practice for doctors. A rough calculation may be made, that if the fee for a test is currently around Rs 1000, and a clinic performs ten to twelve such tests a day, based on a six-day work-week, a clinic can gross up to Rs 2.8 lakh (one lakh = one hundred thousand; currently approximately 42 rupees = 1 US $) per month. Some newspaper reports describe the tremendous wealth amassed by practitioners offering this facility, and how training doctors in the techniques has itself become a lucrative business. Nor is this trend toward exploitation confined to the 'modern' medical sector. In March 1991, health and consumer groups in Gujarat successfully lobbied the State Government to ban a best-selling herbal pharmaceutical product called 'Select' that, according to the manufacturer's claims, used an ancient Ayurvedic technique called 'Punsavana Prayog' to change the sex of a pregnant woman's foetus to male (VHAI, 1992).

Attitudes of medical practitioners reveal that they view sex determination tests as a 'humane' service they provide to couples not wanting any more daughters; as a regrettable but unavoidable result of the preference for sons in Indian society which they feel powerless to change; and as a necessary weapon in the 'population control' arsenal (Kulkarni, 1986). Many also argue that aborting a female is preferable to condemning an unwanted daughter to a lifetime of neglect and abuse. These attitudes are also echoed among large sections of the general public (Ravindra, 1995). Further, some eminent economists also endorse the argument that abortion of females is preferable to neglect, and assert that if the sex ratio of India further worsens as a result of these technologies, then the law of supply and demand will operate and raise the value of women; thus curbing these tests and techno- logies is unnecessary or even retrograde (Kumar, 1983a, 1983b).

Making even approximate computations of the numbers of such pro- cedures occurring in India is difficult. One retrospective estimate (Saheli Women's Resource Centre, cited in Arora, 1996) suggested that between 1978 and 1982 nearly 78,000 female foetuses were aborted after sex determination tests. Arora (1996) also cites a statistic purporting to come from the Registrar General of India, that based on hospital records alone, 3.6 lakh female foetuses were aborted in India between 1993 and 1994.

ESTIMATING SEX RATIOS AT BIRTH IN INDIA

To complement such reports, and to assess the geographical spread and the magnitude of impact of the increasing use of prenatal sex selection in India, we use data from the 1981 and 1991 censuses. We present sex ratios of children aged 0 and 1, i.e. under age 2. We then estimate sex ratios at birth by means of the 'reverse survival technique' (UN Manual X, 1983: Chapter VIII), using the counts of boys and girls aged under 2 and observed male and female q2 mortality probabilities in the 1981 and 1991 Census of India records, fitting to a South Model Coale and Demeny Life Table (Coale and Demeny, 1966). In essence, the technique is based on the notion that children aged x are the survivors of births that occurred x years ago. Therefore, it is possible to take the numbers of children observed at age x, and observed mortality probabilities for children in that population and, using a model life table suitable in shape and level of mortality for the population in question, 'resurrect' the numbers who have died. Here, we 'resurrect' the numbers of boys and girls under age 2 who died prior to the census enumeration, add them to the numbers of reported males and females aged under 2, and take the ratio of male to female children in the resulting total, to estimate a sex ratio at birth.

The authors warn that the reverse survival technique is sensitive to age misreporting, especially for children aged 0 or 1. Das Gupta and Li (in this volume) state that Indian census data show marked age-heaping, especially at young ages. Our estimates overcome this potential danger by basing calculations on children aged 0 and 1 taken together, i.e. those under age 2. (In calculations not presented here, we examine sex ratios among infants aged 0, and the results are very similar to those among infants aged < 2; none differed by more than 2 per cent.) Moreover, we use this technique to generate sex ratios among children ever born, not to present or evaluate estimates of actual fertility. Even if there is a nation-wide tendency to under-report the numbers of females (a contention doubted by Visaria, 1969), the comparison we present, that is the trend over time in sex ratios, should not be affected. In the absence of reliable statistics on abortions or on period sex ratios at birth, we argue that infancy sex ratios and estimated SRBs provide information that can illustrate and evaluate the impact of continuing son preference in India, under conditions of social change, economic development, declining fertility and mortality, and spread of new medical technologies.

It was pointed out some time ago that the distribution of prenatal sex determination facilities in India was greater in areas where females were more devalued, i.e. the North/North-west (Patel, 1988). During the decade covered in this study (1981–91), reports suggest that such techniques were more widely available in urban areas, although there is every indication that their awareness and use spread into the rural hinterlands too. Urban areas are characterized in developmental terms by higher female literacy, more non-agrarian employment opportunities, more paid employment opportunities for women, and better infrastructure, including availability of health services. Moreover, a more egalitarian ethos may accompany increasing education, income, and exposure to diverse groups and thoughts.

Thus, while scrutinizing the estimated SRBs, one might contrast urban/ rural SRBs over the decade, to investigate whether urban SRBs grow progressively more 'normal' with improved education and greater accuracy of reporting/recording births, and decreasing scope for female infanticide or abandonment of girls. On the other hand, if gender stratification in India is intensifying, attested by the increase of phenomena such as dowry and economic marginalization of women, many urban families would not necessarily have greater incentive to welcome daughters. They would also have more access to the means to avert their birth, i.e. prenatal sex determination and selective abortion, which may be seen as more acceptable and practicable alternatives to female infanticide, abandonment, or non-registration of girls' births. In fact, families with some amount of education and disposable income might have better access to these techniques and thus be more efficient in discriminating against their daughters. Particularly with fertility falling in many parts of the country, with urban areas in the forefront, Indian families may take steps to ensure that at least one son is born to them, as do Chinese or Korean families. Thus, if urban SRBs grow anomalously masculine over the decade, the most likely cause is the increasing use of prenatal sex selection techniques rather than under-reporting, infanticide, or abandonment of baby girls.

Appendix Table 1 presents the observed sex ratios among infants aged under 2, and the corresponding estimated SRBs for rural and urban areas of each state, for 1981 and 1991. Ratios are presented here as males per 100 females. There is, by and large, little difference between sex ratios at ages 0 and 1, and estimated sex ratios at birth. As may be expected, once mortality at infant ages is taken into account, most ratios lessen, but only very slightly. However, in some states, predominantly in rural areas, the ratios heighten slightly, such as in rural MP, North-eastern states (Mizoram, Nagaland, Arunachal Pradesh, Tripura), and the South (rural Kerala, Tamil Nadu and Karnataka, urban and rural Maharashtra and Orissa). In 1991, far fewer regions show this pattern: Himachal Pradesh, and urban parts of Sikkim, Goa, Dadra and Nagar Haveli, and Pondicherry. The census was not conducted in Assam in 1981, and in Jammu and Kashmir in 1991, thus the corresponding Table and Figure entries are blank.

Spatial and Temporal Trends in Estimated Sex Ratios at Birth

The spatial distribution of trends in estimated SRBs from the two censuses are presented in Figure 1, which identifies rural and urban areas of those states with 'abnormally' masculine SRBs (i.e. > 107). The actual sex ratio values on which Figure 1 is based are presented in Appendix Table 1.

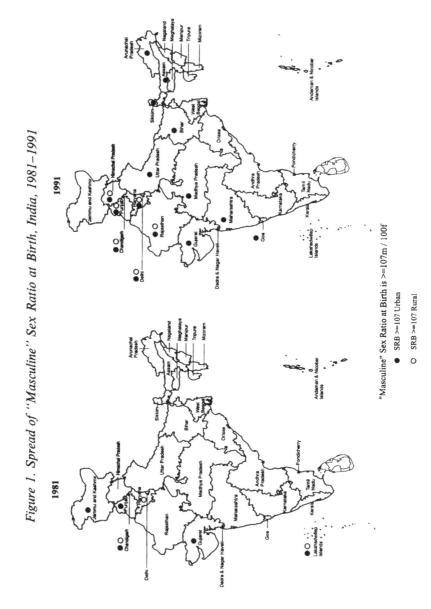

Figure 1. Spread of "Masculine" Sex Ratio at Birth, India, 1981–1991

Figure 1 shows that in 1981, most parts of the country exhibited SRBs that were not 'abnormally' masculine. The few masculine regions were mostly within the North/North-western zone such as urban Punjab, Jammu and Kashmir, and Chandigarh, also urban Gujarat in the West, and, surprisingly, the Lakshadweep Islands off India's South-west coast. Appendix Table 1 shows that the 'masculine' SRBs mostly have values at the lower end of the range (107–110). Thus, in 1981, we can conclude that SRBs in India were in general not very masculine. Appendix Table 1 bears this out by showing all-India values within the normal range.

In 1991, Figure 1 shows a greatly changed picture. We see masculine SRBs not only in the urban areas of the North/North-western zone (Himachal Pradesh, Punjab, Rajasthan, Haryana, Delhi, and Chandigarh), but in the corresponding rural areas, and a spread of anomalous masculinity outward from this zone to urban areas of Central and Western zone states, namely Gujarat, UP, MP, Bihar, Maharashtra, and Goa. Arunachal Pradesh, Assam and Sikkim in the North-east also have masculine SRBs. Appendix Table 1 shows a stark shift toward excess masculinity, with SRB values in the range of 107–118. The lowest abnormal values are 107 for urban Bihar, UP, and Goa, and the highest values reach 118 for urban Punjab and 116 for urban Haryana. Appendix Table 1 shows that the all-India urban area SRBs now reach 108, reflecting the increase in masculinity of urban SRBs of many states. The Southern states' SRBs appear normal in both decades. The Lakshadweep Union Territory (off the Kerala coast) that had masculine SRBs in 1981 is in the normal range in 1991.

For 1981, Appendix Table 1 shows some states (Andhra Pradesh and urban Tamil Nadu in the South; Manipur, urban Nagaland, Meghalaya and Arunachal Pradesh in the North-east; Madhya Pradesh, urban Orissa and rural Bihar in the Centre; Rajasthan and urban UP in the North/North-west; urban Dadra and Nagar Haveli) have SRBs that may be seen as 'feminine' (below 103). We speculate that this might be due to under-reporting of infants that might have been born alive but died shortly thereafter. They would not be enumerated, and would thus not show up in either the counts of infants, or the mortality statistics. Since neonate and infant boys have higher mortality than girls, boys may be over-represented in the uncounted children, leading to unusually feminine SRBs. In 1991, the phenomenon of excess femininity of SRBs has greatly lessened, now noted only in Dadra and Nagar Haveli, Nagaland, and rural Arunachal Pradesh, Manipur, Meghalaya, Andamans and Lakshadweep, and MP. This could be due to improved enumeration and tabulation, or lessening of male infant/child mortality due to the improvement in health facility coverage, or to the general country-wide trend toward the masculinization of SRBs.

We conclude that while SRB figures have grown anomalously masculine across several states, the numerical magnitude of the impact of sex selective abortion in India is not great as yet, at least according to these Census records. In East Asia, the impact of such practices amounts to about 5 per cent of female births (Asia Pacific Population and Policy Report, 1995). In India, the impact is less than this. Since the 1991 all-India rural SRB was within the normal range, if we examine the change in all-India urban SRB from 104 in 1981 to 108 in 1991, and consider that an SRB of 106 is the upper bound of 'normal', then only 2 per cent of female births are affected. This translates to a shortfall of some 74,600 female births (all-India urban), mostly in the North-west zone. Since official records of induced abortion in India are notoriously flawed and incomplete, Mishra et al. (1998) have estimated the likely number of abortions occurring in India using National Family Health Survey data (1992–3). They show that the possible numbers of induced abortions for all-India were over 207,000. However, the fact that the numerical magnitude of sex-selective abortion as judged from Census records is not very great, does not diminish the gravity of the issue, for two reasons. First, since Census records are only picking up the 'tip of the iceberg' of this phenomenon, the reality is probably greater than the figures show. Second, even Census records indicate that the phenomenon is increasing over time, which is itself a grave cause for concern.

SPATIAL AND TEMPORAL TRENDS IN FEMALE DISADVANTAGE IN CHILD MORTALITY PROBABILITY

We examined evidence that prenatal sex determination and selective abortion of female foetuses occurred on an increasing scale in India during the decade 1981–91, in specific urban areas. We also reviewed studies and reports that female infanticide is spreading across the rural Indian spectrum. We now turn to the examination of sex-specific child mortality probabilities, to examine whether girl children in India continue to face heightened mortality risks *vis-à-vis* boys. In Appendix Table 2, we present sex ratios of under-5 mortality probabilities for children (q5) for 1981 and 1991, for each state, for rural and urban areas. Mortality ratios that indicate female disadvantage (i.e. male to female q5 ratio < 100) are considered anomalous. Ratios that show male disadvantage are considered 'normal'. Figure 2, based on this table, maps the spatial and temporal distribution of female mortality disadvantage.

Figure 2 shows the spatial distribution of trends in mortality sex ratios across 1981–91, identifying rural and urban areas of those states with ratios showing female disadvantage. In 1981, all the Northern/North-western states (except Himachal Pradesh and urban Jammu and Kashmir) had excess female child mortality, in urban and rural areas. In 1991, all these areas continued to exhibit female mortality disadvantage, with the exception of Chandigarh, which along with urban Dadra and Nagar Haveli and Andaman Islands, were the only regions shifting to 'normal' female vs. male child mortality risks. Furthermore, in 1991, female mortality disadvantage appeared in areas that were 'normal' in 1981, namely rural

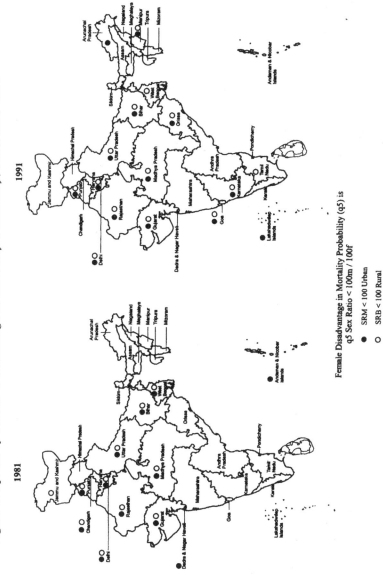

Figure 2. Spread of Female Disadvantage in Mortality Probability, India 1981–1991

and urban Orissa, Goa, and Karnataka, and rural Tamil Nadu (in keeping with reports of female infanticide in that state). Thus, the phenomenon of excess female child mortality not only persisted over the decade, but also actually spread across more of India.

Overall, levels of child mortality in India declined considerably from approximately 152 per 1000 (both sexes, all India) in 1981 (Government of India, 1988: 5), to 96 per 1000 in 1991 (both sexes, all India, in Irudaya Rajan and Mohanachandran, 1998, based on 1991 Census records). Appendix Table 2, however, shows that the sex ratio of mortality actually became more male-biased during 1981–91, indicating that mortality fell more for males than females, and that females still have higher mortality than males. Positive changes (i.e. lessening female mortality disadvantage 1981–91) are seen in only a few areas, such as Himachal Pradesh, the Union Territories of Delhi and Chandigarh, rural Punjab, urban Rajasthan, West Bengal, Mizoram, Dadra and Nagar Haveli and Andaman Islands. However, of these areas, only the small regions of Chandigarh, Mizoram, Dadra and Nagar Haveli and Andaman Islands show 'normal' male to female mortality risk ratios in 1991, the other regions still exhibit female disadvantage. Increasing female disadvantage appears in many North/North-western and Central states: rural Rajasthan, urban Haryana, all of UP, Bihar, MP, and Gujarat, which all had female mortality disadvantage in 1981. Orissa, which had 'normal' mortality sex ratios in 1981, shifts to female disadvantage in 1991. In South India, Karnataka, Goa, and rural Tamil Nadu also shift from 'normal' ratios to female disadvantage. Thus, substantial parts of India in 1991 exhibit persistent excess female child mortality, in keeping with research documenting persistent selective neglect of girls.

While the 1991 Census mortality figures for Kerala also indicate female disadvantage, infant and child mortality is generally so low in this state, that a small absolute difference between the sexes has translated into a large difference in the ratio in this case. Thus, in the case of Kerala, we do not suggest at this time that excess female child mortality has suddenly emerged in this state, since, unlike Tamil Nadu, no study has identified this phenomenon here. This logic also applies to some Union Territories and states in the North-east, that indicate extreme values of the mortality sex ratios. Values in 1981, such as 152 for urban Meghalaya or 128 for urban Sikkim, are an artifact of small sex differences in low reported levels of mortality.

To contextualize the scenario of birth and life chances of boys and girls in India, Appendix Table 3 shows fertility trends in different regions of India 1982–94. This decade witnessed a moderate fertility decline in the country as a whole (20 per cent), from a TFR of 4.5 in 1982 to 3.5 in 1994 (SRS Reports). However, we observe dramatic declines in the South, such that Kerala now has below replacement fertility and Tamil Nadu is at replacement level, and Karnataka and Andhra Pradesh are below the national average. The Eastern states register moderate declines, as do Gujarat and Punjab. The other Central and North/North-western states record more modest gains.

The demographic picture that emerges for the period 1981–91 is one of all-India declines in fertility and mortality, worsening sex ratios of child mortality in many major states, and increasing masculinity of SRBs in the North/North-west, and in urban areas of some Central states. Prior studies showed that higher birth order females were at the greatest risk of mortality in Northern and North-western India (Das Gupta, 1987; Kishor, 1995). It is therefore argued that with declining fertility, the proportion of births of higher order would decline, lowering excess female child mortality overall. Since the mortality ratios have not shown lessening female disadvantage in the face of declining fertility, this contention is clearly not upheld. Furthermore, SRBs in the North/North-west regions indicate increasing sex selection to ensure that the greater proportion of babies born are of the wanted (male) sex. Thus, excess female child mortality appears combined with prenatal sex selection in a specific zone of the country — the North/North-west — to create a 'double jeopardy' for Indian daughters there, with increasing female mortality disadvantage in other regions that have 'normal' SRB patterns.

CONCLUSION AND DISCUSSION

The first point we highlight is the great need for suitable data to be collected and released in a timely manner by the Government of India. The decennial census does collect information on the number and sex of births in the enumeration year. Statistics on period SRBs for all parts of India could be directly furnished, removing the need for indirect estimation to illuminate this important question. In our findings, it should be kept in mind that the SRBs have been estimated based on the reported numbers of infants aged under 2 years, and thus may be affected by any under-registration of female births or female infanticide, though we argue otherwise.

However, even with indirectly estimated measures, there is a clearly marked shift toward increasing masculinity of SRBs in North/North-west India, and urban areas of Central India. This suggests the rising use of prenatal sex determination and sex selective abortion there. The studies and reports we summarize, and the spatial distribution of the SRB figures we present, indicate plausibly that prenatal sex selection techniques are being increasingly used in these regions. The trend initially began (as might have been expected for a medical technological innovation) in urban areas and spread out over time to the rural surroundings, especially concentrated in those regions of the country that have a socio-cultural history of disfavour toward women. As we saw, in 1981, only urban areas of the North-western region had somewhat abnormal SRBs. By 1991, urban and rural parts of the North-west, and urban parts of Central regions, all had masculine SRBs, some with very high values. Since the increased masculinity is seen in urban areas, we cannot attribute the trend to increased under-reporting of girls, or rise in female infanticide, both of which are less likely to be successfully carried out in urban areas.

Some argue that increasing masculinity of SRBs could be caused by development, especially in the health sector, because improved health conditions provide better life chances to male foetuses that are by nature more frail and prone to die. The trend in many parts of India between 1981 and 1991 of SRBs moving from excess femininity to normal masculinity may be due to this factor. The intense masculinity in the North/North-west region is, however, a little difficult to attribute entirely to improved health. If improvements in health were mainly at the bottom of increasing masculinity of SRBs, then regions such as Kerala and urban areas elsewhere in the South would also have witnessed much more masculinity of SRBs than they have. We thus conclude that improved male survivorship is in itself an insufficient explanation for the temporal and spatial trend in sex ratios in India. Since, as discussed above, other alternative explanations such as female infanticide and under-registration of births are less likely in urban areas, the spread of prenatal sex selection is further implicated.

Evidence indicating women's increasing economic marginalization and greater socio-cultural devaluation underlines the contention that development in India has generally been to the detriment of women, and further research investigating how these trends are causally linked to female demographic disadvantage is needed. Families in India respond to developmental stresses by increasing discrimination against daughters, since this strategy fits with the matrix of choices deemed culturally acceptable, which are largely patriarchal in nature. Alternative strategies such as investing in girls' education, ensuring daughters' inheritance, and including females in the production process, are less considered. Resisting dowry pressures generated by a 'groom shortage' by marrying women to men their own age or younger, or leaving them unmarried, or finding a spouse of another caste or community, appear unthinkable. Despite gains in education, longevity, and income for some groups of women, large sections of Indian society apparently still consider daughters a liability, and may prefer to avert their birth. While infanticide in earlier eras had been confined to certain limited caste and geographical groups, neglect of daughters, female infanticide and foeticide now appear widespread in some parts of India, and have pervaded groups and classes where they were hitherto unknown (Adithi, 1995; Harriss-White, 1998; Jeffery et al., 1984). Selective neglect of daughters persists. In fact, the co-existence of female foeticide, infanticide, and selective neglect of girls renders the distinction between pre- and post-natal sex selection techniques invidious: the bias against girls is entrenched, and the choice of methods may depend on convenience rather than conscience. Some scholars have gone so far as to term the persistent and multi-layered bias against girls, as 'gender-cleansing' (Harriss-White, 1998).

However, while the aggregate statistics for 1981–91 indicate that pre- and post-natal sex selection methods co-exist in many regions, conclusions regarding additive rather than substitutive strategies should also consider whether some local differences are being obscured in the aggregate. A study of a rapidly urbanizing and changing rural area near New Delhi revealed that local parents of the Jat community had an ideal family composition of two sons and one daughter, and thus formed the clientele of the flourishing local sex determination clinics. However, the subsequent infant/child mortality rates among their children did not reveal female disadvantage any more (Khanna, 1995, 1997). This suggests that a pattern of substitution is indeed occurring. More such micro-level studies would better illuminate whether within any region, some families use certain strategies and others follow other methods, or whether the same groups are indeed following both strategies. Future research should prioritize examination of demographic behaviour, development trends and policies in India from a gender perspective, and focus on the nexus between macro-level cultural and economic structures and micro-level household organization and strategies.

The contention that selective neglect or infanticide affect mainly higher birth order girls and that therefore the gender imbalance in demographic rates and indicators should decline with decreasing fertility and mortality is clearly not upheld in this study. Consider that if the Jat families in the study just referred to could actualize their desired family size and sex composition, the community would show a TFR of 3.0 and an SRB of 200! In fact, the ideational shift to controlled fertility that includes acceptance of modern means of contraception has, in India, also meant a growing societal acceptance of medical technologies surrounding conception, prenatal sex selection, and abortion. Abortion selectively directed against female foetuses is acceptable to large sections of society in the name of 'population control', or couples' greater reproductive choice. The secular societal trend that increasingly devalues female lives remains largely unquestioned.

The argument that an adverse sex ratio will lead to a shortage in the supply of women, which will drive up their value since demand will remain high, is also unconvincing. The sex ratio in India has been noted to be adverse to females, and more or less steadily worsening, since the first recorded Census of 1871. The population sex ratio of India declined from 972 females per 1000 males in 1901 to 929 per 1000 in 1991. In this same period, the status of Indian women has been steadily eroded, despite gains made in some sectors by some groups of women. A 'shortage' of women does not lead to their increasing valuation, but to greater restrictions and control being placed over them. The increasing intensity of violence against women in all domains of life is testimony to this. Scholars predict increased social unrest in China once the shortage of females to males of the appropriate ages in the marriage market is felt, as a result of the skewed SRB patterns there (Tuljapurkar et al., 1995). The same might be said for India.

The trend toward greater use of prenatal sex selection despite legislative proscription, combined with persistent female disfavour in mortality ratios, combines to produce a scenario that is not likely to improve in the near future. These demographic phenomena are themselves only symptoms of the worsening situation of women in the Indian socio-economic developmental context. Policy measures addressing women's societal devaluation have either not been implemented, as in the Central Government scheme proposed in early 1997 of cash subsidies to girl children in all families identified as poor; or have had very limited impact, as illustrated in Tamil Nadu state's cash subsidy schemes or 'cradle baby' schemes (George, 1997). NGO strategies to tackle infanticide or female devaluation range from the very long-term (consciousness-raising), to the confrontational (reporting suspicious female infant deaths to the police), to the ineffective (attempting to dissuade parents from infanticide). Examples of plans that have successfully involved women and men in local development efforts are rare and recent, and their impact on demographic behaviour is as yet small.

Furthering the legislative drive against discriminatory practices, on 9 January 1996, the Indian Government announced a ban on the abortions of healthy female foetuses identified during permissible genetic tests. Under the new law, mothers, fathers, and doctors can all be punished with fines ranging from $300–$1500 and prison terms from three to five years, escalating for repeat offenses. Critics point out that women are rarely the primary decision-makers in the use of these technologies, and such legislation places a dual punishment on them. It is feared that women will be driven to seek terminations of unwanted pregnancies under illegal conditions, in a country where the majority of abortions are already reported to take place illegally. It remains to be seen how effective new legislative measures will be in reversing the trend of female foeticide, when past actions have not shown marked success. Our review of the literature suggests that any policy measures must not focus primarily on restricting technology used to women's detriment, but must also address the root causes of devaluation of Indian women, or they will not succeed in eradicating discriminatory practices but will drive them underground where they will continue to flourish.

ACKNOWLEDGEMENTS

This research was supported by a grant from the UNFPA Population and Sustainable Development Programme at the Centre for Development Studies, Thiruvananthapuram, as a 'Research in Support of Training' activity. We are grateful to the office of the Registrar General of India for providing the data and to the Centre for Development Studies for institutional support. We thank Dr P. Mohanachandran for technical advice, Dr R. Homan for programming help, and Ms A. Mini for research assistance. We are grateful to Tom Swasey and John Vogler of the Carolina Population Center for assistance in preparing maps. We thank Sarthi Acharya, Cecile Jackson, Helen Lambert, Alec Mercer, Uday Shankar Mishra, Richard Palmer-Jones, and Shahra Razavi for their helpful comments. The following NGOs generously shared their information with us: ADITHI, Patna; JAGORI, New Delhi; MATRIKA, New Delhi; M. S. Swaminathan Research Foundation. Chennai. S. Sudha thanks family and friends for child care, inspiration and moral support without which this chapter could not have been written.

APPENDIX

Table 1. Sex Ratios at Ages 0 + 1, and Estimated Sex Ratios at Birth: 1981–91

	1981				1991			
	Sex ratio (M/F)				Sex ratio (M/F)			
	Observed ratio 0 + 1		Estimated SRB		Observed ratio 0 + 1		Estimated SRB	
State/Region	Rural	Urban	Rural	Urban	Rural	Urban	Rural	Urban
INDIA	103	104	103	104	106	108	106	108
North/Northwest								
Himachal Pradesh	105	105	105	105	108	113	109	114
Jammu & Kashmir	105	110	105	110	—	—	—	—
Punjab	107	108	105	107	117	119	117	118
Rajasthan	103	103	101	102	108	111	107	110
Haryana	109	107	108	106	114	117	113	116
Delhi (UT)	105	104	105	106	111	111	110	110
Chandigarh (UT)	112	103	111	107	110	109	110	109
Uttar Pradesh	104	102	103	102	107	109	106	108
Central								
Bihar	102	104	101	103	107	108	105	107
Madhya Pradesh	101	102	102	101	103	108	102	107
Gujarat	105	108	104	107	107	112	106	111
Maharashtra	102	101	106	105	103	108	106	109
Orissa	101	103	102	104	104	104	103	103
Goa	104	105	104	105	103	106	103	107
East/Northeast								
West Bengal	102	104	103	103	104	105	103	104
Assam	—	—	—	—	105	108	104	107
Mizoram	103	100	104	100	102	104	103	104
Nagaland	101	103	102	103	99	103	99	102
Meghalaya	102	104	102	104	101	103	101	103
Arunachal Pradesh	100	105	102	105	101	109	101	109
Tripura	105	104	106	104	104	104	104	104
Manipur	101	101	101	100	103	105	102	105
Sikkim	105	99	104	98	105	123	105	124
South								
Kerala	102	107	103	106	106	106	105	106
Andhra Pradesh	101	102	102	102	103	104	103	103
Tamil Nadu	103	102	104	101	105	105	105	105
Karnataka	102	104	103	104	105	105	105	105
Union territories								
Andamans	102	94	104	95	100	104	100	103
Lakshadweep	109	110	109	108	102	106	102	106
Dadra Nagar Haveli	98	100	99	103	101	94	101	101
Pondicherry	102	102	103	103	103	105	103	106

Notes: Any value above 107 can be considered 'excessively' masculine. The census was not conducted in Assam in 1981, or in Jammu and Kashmir in 1991.
Source: Censuses of India 1981 (Government of India, 1988); and 1991 (Government of India, 1991).

Table 2. Sex Ratios of Child Mortality: 1981–91

	1981		1991	
	Sex ratio of child mortality q5 m/f		Sex ratio of child mortality q5 m/f	
State/Region	**Rural**	**Urban**	**Rural**	**Urban**
INDIA	93	98	89	95
North/Northwest				
Himachal Pradesh	104	107	108	110
Jammu & Kashmir	97	102	—	—
Punjab	87	92	92	92
Rajasthan	89	89	85	90
Haryana	81	89	81	82
Delhi (UT)	85	95	89	96
Chandigarh (UT)	88	99	107	110
Uttar Pradesh	83	86	79	82
Central				
Bihar	87	90	72	79
Madhya Pradesh	96	98	92	92
Maharashtra	101	106	100	104
Orissa	103	101	93	86
Gujarat	92	94	80	82
Goa	106	103	96	91
East/Northeast				
West Bengal	99	99	92	152
Assam	—	—	103	108
Mizoram	107	111	113	116
Nagaland	106	132	100	107
Meghalaya	105	126	104	105
Arunachal Pradesh	106	152	104	91
Tripura	105	108	102	104
Manipur	104	103	90	94
Sikkim	120	128	110	106
South				
Kerala*	113	101	94	88
Andhra Pradesh	105	107	103	108
Tamil Nadu	101	104	88	100
Karnataka	101	102	96	97
Union territories				
Andamans	107	92	112	102
Lakshadweep	121	105	136	91
Dadra Nagar Haveli	113	97	133	136
Pondicherry	103	104	107	103

*See explanation in the text. For all other cells, any value < 100 can be considered to indicate female disadvantage.
Sources: 1981: Government of India (1988); 1991: Irudaya Rajan and Mohanachandran (1998).

Table 3. Profile of Fertility Decline in Major States of India (1982–94)

State/Region	Total fertility rate (TFR)		
	1982	1994	% decline
INDIA	4.5	3.5	22.20
North/North-west			
Rajasthan	5.3	4.5	15.10
Uttar Pradesh	5.7	5.1	10.10
Haryana	4.9	3.7	24.50
Punjab	4.0	2.9	27.50
Central			
Bihar	5.6	4.6	17.90
Madhya Pradesh	5.3	4.2	20.80
Gujarat	4.2	3.1	26.20
Maharashtra	3.8	2.9	23.70
Orissa	4.3	3.3	23.30
East			
West Bengal	4.1	3.0	26.80
South			
Andhra Pradesh	3.9	2.7	30.80
Karnataka	3.6	2.8	22.20
Kerala	2.9	1.7	41.40
Tamil Nadu	3.3	2.1	36.40

Source: Government of India (1982, 1994).

REFERENCES

ADITHI (1995) *Female Infanticide in Bihar*. Report prepared by Viji Srinivasan, Vijay Parinita, Alice Shankar, Medha Mukul and Anita Kumari. Patna: ADITHI.

Agarwal, Bina (1994) *A Field of One's Own: Gender and Land Rights in South Asia*. Cambridge: Cambridge University Press.

Agnihotri, S. (1996) 'Juvenile Sex Ratios in India: A Disaggregated Analysis', *Economic and Political Weekly* 28 December: S3369–S3382.

Ahluwalia, Kishwar (1986) 'Amniocentesis, the Controversy Continues', *Times of India* 8 March.

Aravamudan, Gita (1994) 'Whose Baby is She Anyway?', *The Hindu* 16 October.

Arora, Dolly (1996) 'The Victimizing Discourse: Sex Determination Technologies and Policy', *Economic and Political Weekly* XXXI(7): 420–4.

Asia-Pacific Population and Policy Report (1995) 'Evidence Mounts for Sex-Selective Abortions in Asia', Report No. 34 (May–June). Honolulu, HI: East-West Center, Program on Population.

Bardhan, Pranab (1974) 'On Life and Death Questions', *Economic and Political Weekly* Special Issue (9 August): 1293–1304.

Chhachhi, A. and C. Sathyamala (1983) 'Sex Determination Tests: A Technology which will Eliminate Women', *Medico Friends Circle Bulletin* 95: 3–5.

Chunkath, Sheela Rani and V. B. Athreya (1997) 'Female Infanticide in Tamil Nadu: Some Evidence', *Economic and Political Weekly* XXXII(17): WS22–WS29.

Clark, Alice W. (1983) 'Limitations on Female Life Chances in Rural Central Gujarat', *The Indian Economic and Social History Review* 20: 1–25.

Clark, Alice W. (1987) 'Social Demography of Excess Female Mortality in India: New Directions', *Economic and Political Weekly* XXII(17) Review of Women's Studies: WS517–WS521.

Clark, Alice W. and Sudha Shreeniwas (1995) 'Questioning the Links between Maternal Education and Child Mortality: The Case of Gujarat', paper presented at the Population Association of America Annual Meeting, San Francisco (April).

Coale, Ansley (1991) 'Excess Female Mortality and the Balance of the Sexes in the Population: An Estimate of the Number of "Missing Females" ', *Population and Development Review* 17(3): 517–23.

Coale, Ansley and Paul Demeny (1966) *Model Life Tables and Stable Populations*. Princeton, NJ: Princeton University Press.

Coale, A.J. and J. Banister (1994) 'Five Decades of Missing Females in China', *Demography* August (3): 459–79.

Das Gupta, Monica (1987) 'Selective Discrimination against Female Children in Rural Punjab, North India', *Population and Development Review* 13: 77–100.

Das Gupta, Monica and P. N. Mari Bhat (1997) 'Fertility Decline and Increased Manifestation of Sex Bias in India', *Population Studies* 51: 307–15.

Deshpande, Sudha (1992) 'Structural Adjustment and Feminization', *Indian Journal of Labour Economics* 35(4).

Dyson, Tim (1988) 'Excess Female Mortality in India: Uncertain Evidence on a Narrowing Differential', in K. Srinivasan and S. Mukherjee (eds) *Dynamics of Population and Family Welfare*, pp. 350–81. Bombay: Himalaya Publishers.

Dyson, Tim and Mick Moore (1983) 'On Kinship Structure, Female Autonomy and Demographic Behaviour in India', *Population and Development Review* 9(1): 35–60.

FASDSP and Saheli Women's Resource Centre (nd) 'Information Sheet on Sex Determination and Sex Preselection Techniques', on file with Jagori (NGO) New Delhi.

George, Sabu R. (1997) 'Female Infanticide in Tamil Nadu, India: From Recognition back to Denial?', *Reproductive Health Matters* 10: 124–32.

George, Sabu, R. Abel and B. D. Miller (1992) 'Female Infanticide in Rural South India', *Economic and Political Weekly* XXVII(22): 1153–6.

Goodkind, Daniel (1996) 'On Substituting Sex Preference Strategies in East Asia: Does Prenatal Sex Selection Reduce Post-natal Determination', *Population and Development Review* 22(1): 111–26.

Government of India (1974) 'Towards Equality: Report of the Committee on the Status of Women'. New Delhi: Department of Social Welfare.

Government of India (1982) *Sample Registration System: Fertility and Mortality Indicators*. New Delhi: Office of the Registrar General of India, Ministry of Home Affairs.

Government of India (1983) *Agricultural Wages in India, 1980–81*. New Delhi: Ministry of Agriculture, Directorate of Economics and Statistics, Department of Agriculture and Co-operatives.

Government of India (1988) 'Census of India 1981. Child Mortality Estimates of India'. Occasional Paper No. 5, Demography Division. New Delhi: Office of the Registrar General of India, Ministry of Home Affairs.

Government of India (1991) 'Census Data C Series, Social and Cultural Tables'. New Delhi: Office of the Registrar General of India.

Government of India (1993) *Aricultural Wages in India, 1991–2*. New Delhi: Ministry of Agriculture, Directorate of Economics and Statistics, Department of Agriculture and Co-operatives.

Government of India (1994) *Sample Registration System: Fertility and Mortality Indicators*. New Delhi: Office of the Registrar General of India, Ministry of Home Affairs.

Gupte, Manisha, Sunita Bandewar and Hemlata Pisal (1997) 'Abortion needs of Women in India: A Case Study of Rural Maharashtra', *Reproductive Health Matters* 9: 77–86.

Harriss-White, Barbara (1998) 'Gender-cleansing: The Paradox of Development and Deteriorating Female Life Chances in Tamil Nadu', in R. Sundar Rajan and U. Butalia (eds) *Gender and Modernity in Post-Independence India*. New Delhi: Kali for Women.

Heyer, J. (1992) 'The Role of Dowries and Daughters' Marriages in the Accumulation and Distribution of Capital in a South Indian Community', *Journal of International Development* 4(4): 419–36.

Hirway, Indira (1979) 'Female Employment in Rural Gujarat: Some Issues', *Indian Journal of Labour Economics* 22(1).

Hull, Terence H. (1990) 'Recent Trends in Sex Ratios at Birth in China', *Population and Development Review* 16: 63–83.

Irudaya Rajan, S. (1996) 'Sex Ratios in Kerala: New Evidences', paper presented at the workshop on Target Free Population Policy, Health Watch Kerala, Trivandrum (27 September).

Irudaya Rajan, S. and P. Mohanachandran (1998) 'Infant and Child Mortality Estimates based on the 1991 Census of India: Part I', *Economic and Political Weekly* XXXIII(19).

Irudaya Rajan, S., U. S. Mishra and K. Navaneetham (1991) 'Decline in Sex Ratio: An Alternative Explanation', *Economic and Political Weekly* 21 December: 2963–4.

Jeffery, Roger, P. Jeffery and A. Lyon (1984) 'Female Infanticide and Amniocentesis', *Social Science and Medicine* 19(11): 1207–12.

Johansen, Sten and Ola Nygren (1991) 'The Missing Girls of China: A New Demographic Account', *Population and Development Review* 17: 35–51.

Kapadia, Karin (1992) 'Every Blade of Green: Landless Female Labourers, Production and Reproduction in South India', *Indian Journal of Labour Economics* 35(3): 266–76.

Khanna, Sunil K. (1995) 'Prenatal Sex Determination: A New Family-building Strategy', *Manushi* 86: 23–9.

Khanna, Sunil K. (1997) 'Traditions and Reproductive Technology in an Urbanizing North Indian Village', *Social Science and Medicine* 44(2): 171–80.

Kishor, Sunita (1993) 'May God give Sons to All: Gender and Child Mortality in India', *American Sociological Review* 58: 247–65.

Kishor, Sunita (1995) 'Gender Differentials in Child Mortality: A Review of the Evidence', in Monica Das Gupta, Lincoln Chen and T. N. Krishnan (eds) *Women's Health in India: Risk and Vulnerability*, pp. 19–54. Bombay: Oxford University Press.

Kishwar, Madhu (1995) 'When Daughters are Unwanted: Sex Determination Tests in India', *Manushi* 86: 15–22.

Kulkarni, Sanjeev (1986) 'Sex Determination Tests and Female Foeticide in the City of Bombay'. Report commissioned by the Secretary to the Government, Department of Health and Family Welfare, Government of Maharashtra.

Kumar, Dharma (1983a) 'Male Utopia or Nightmares?', *Economic and Political Weekly* 15 January: 61–4.

Kumar, Dharma (1983b) 'Amniocentesis Again', *Economic and Political Weekly* 11 September: 1075–7.

Kundu, Amitabh and Mahesh Sahu (1991) 'Variation in Sex Ratio: Development Implications', *Economic and Political Weekly* 12 October: 2341–42.

Mason, William, Alan Bittles, Marco Spinar, Sudha Shreeniwas and D. Natasha Singarayer (1992) 'Sex Ratios in India: Studies at National, State and District Levels', in L. M. Schell, M. T. Smith and A. Bilsborough (eds) *Urbanization and Ecology in the Third World*.

Menon, Nivedita (1996) 'The Impossibility of "Justice": Female Foeticide and Feminist Discourse on Abortion', in Patricia Uberoi (ed.) *Social Reform, Sexuality and the State*, pp. 369–92. New Delhi: Sage Publications.

Miller, Barbara (1981) *The Endangered Sex: Neglect of Female Children in Rural North India*. Ithaca, NY: Cornell University Press.

Miller, Barbara (1987) 'Female Infanticide', *Seminar* 331: 18–21.

Miller, Barbara (1997) 'Social Class, Gender, and Intrahousehold Food Allocations to Children in South Asia', *Social Science and Medicine* 44(11): 1685–95.

Mishra, U. S., Mala Ramanathan and S. Irudaya Rajan (1998) 'Induced Abortion Potential among Indian Women', *Social Biology* 45(3/4): 278–88.

Murthy, Mamta, Anne-Catherine Guio and Jean Drèze (1996) 'Mortality, Fertility and Gender Bias in India: A District-level Analysis', *Population and Development Review* 21(4): 745–82.

Nayyar, Rohini (1989) 'Rural Labour Markets and the Employment of Females in Punjab-Haryana', in A. V. Jose (ed.) *Limited Options: Women Workers in Rural India*, pp. 234–53. Geneva: ILO.

Nigam, Namita (1988) 'Employment Pattern and Educational Status of Female Workers in UP', *Indian Journal of Labour Economics* 31(4): 340–53.

Palriwala, Rajni and Carla Risseeuw (eds) (1996) *Shifting Circles of Support: Contextualizing Gender and Kinship in South Asia and Sub-Saharan Africa*. Walnut Creek, CA: AltaMira Press.

Park, Chai Bin and Nam-Hoon Cho (1995) 'Consequences of Son Preference in a Low-fertility Society: Imbalance of the Sex Ratio at Birth in Korea', *Population and Development Review* 21(1): 59–84.

Patel, V. (1988) 'Sex Determination and Sex Pre-selection Tests: Abuse of Advanced Technologies', in Rehana Ghadially (ed.) *Women in Indian Society*, pp. 178–85. New Delhi: Sage Publications.

Raju, Saraswati and Mahendra K. Premi (1992) 'Decline in Sex Ratio: Alternative Explanation Re-examined', *Economic and Political Weekly* 25 April: 911–12.

Ramaswamy, Uma (1993) 'Women and Development', in A. N. Sharma and S. Singh (eds) *Women and Work: Changing Scenarios in India*, pp. 323–37. New Delhi: B. K. Publishing Corporation.

Rao, Vijayendra. 1993. 'Dowry "Inflation" in Rural India: A Statistical Investigation', *Population Studies* 47(2): 283–93.

Ravindra, R. P. (1995) 'Myths about Sex Determination Tests', in Facts Against Myths: *Vikas Adhyayan Kendra Information Bulletin* II(3) June (Bombay).

Scrimshaw, Susan (1984) 'Infanticide in Human Populations: Societal and Individual Concerns', in Glenn Hausfater and Sarah B. Hrdy (eds) *Infanticide: Comparative and Evolutionary Approaches*. New York: Aldine Publishing Company Hawthorne.

Sen, Amartya (1992) 'More than 100 Million Women are Missing', *New York Review of Books* December: 61–6.

Sen, Gita (1982) 'Women Workers and the Green Revolution', in Lourdes Beneria (ed.) *Women and Development*, pp. 29–60. New York: Praeger Publications.

Sengupta, Amit (1992) 'Prenatal Diagnostic Techniques Bill: Loopholes Galore', *Women's Equality* (newsletter) April–June.

Singh, Gurmeet and Sunita Jain (1985) 'Opinions of Men and Women regarding Amniocentesis', *Journal of Family Welfare* XXXI(3): 13–19.

Sinha, R.P. (1988) 'Technological Change in Agriculture and Women Workers in Rural Bihar: A Case Study', *Indian Journal of Labour Economics* 31(4): 306–16.

Srinivasan, K. (1997) 'Sex Ratios in India: What they Hide and What they Reveal', in S. Irudaya Rajan (ed.) *India's Demographic Transition: A Reassessment*, pp. 89–94. New Delhi: MD Publications.

Tuljapurkar, Shripad, Li Nan and Marcus W. Feldman (1995) 'High Sex Ratios at Birth in China's Future', *Science* 267(5199): 874–6.

UN (1983) 'Manual X: Indirect Techniques for Demographic Estimation'. Population Studies, No. 81. New York: United Nations, Department of International Economic and Social Affairs.

Varghese, N. V. (1991) 'Women and Work: An Examination of the "Female Marginalization Thesis" in the Indian Context', *Indian Journal of Labour Economics* 34(3): 203–9.

VHAI (Voluntary Health Association of India) (1992) 'Banned: Select, a Drug to Alter the Sex of the Foetus', *Health Action Series* 4, December. New Delhi: VHAI.

Visaria, Pravin M. (1969) *The Sex Ratio of the Population of India*. Census of India 1961, Vol. 1, Monograph No. 10. New Delhi: Office of the Registrar-General of India.

Visaria, Pravin M. and S. Irudaya Rajan (1996) 'Fallacies about the Sex Ratio of the Population of Kerala', paper presented at the International Conference on Kerala's Development Experience: National and Global Dimension, Institute of Social Science, India International Centre, New Delhi (9–11 December).

Vishwanath, L. S. (1996) 'Female Infanticide and the Position of Women in India', in A. M. Shah, B. S. Baviskar and E. A. Ramaswamy (eds) *Social Structure and Change Vol. 2: Women in Indian Society*, pp. 179–202. New Delhi and Thousand Oaks, CA: Sage Publications.

Vishwanathan, Prema (1991) 'Haryana's Urban Convicts', *Times of India* 14 April.

Wadley, Susan (1993) 'Family Composition Strategies in Rural North India', *Social Science and Medicine* 37(11): 1367–76.

Wertz, D. C. and J. C. Fletcher (1993) 'Prenatal Diagnosis and Sex Selection in 19 Nations', *Social Science and Medicine* 37(11): 1359–66.

Yi, Zeng, et al. (1993) 'Causes and Implications of the Recent Increase in the Reported Sex Ratio at Birth in China', *Population and Development Review* 19(2): 283–302.

8

Gender Bias in China, South Korea and India 1920–1990: Effects of War, Famine and Fertility Decline

Monica Das Gupta and Li Shuzhuo

INTRODUCTION

The aim of this chapter is to examine how key events of the twentieth century have affected the extent of female disadvantage in child survival in China, South Korea and India, and how this in turn has shaped spousal availability, marriage payments and the treatment of women. These three countries represent South and East Asia, the parts of the world which show the highest levels of excess female child mortality. This is a longstanding pattern in all three countries, as evidenced by data from the nineteenth and early twentieth centuries (Kwon, 1977; Visaria, 1969; Xin, 1989). We explore how historical events have influenced the extent of excess female child mortality in the period 1920 to 1990, and look at some of the substantial social ramifications of changes in the level of gender-based discrimination.

In examining how the level of discrimination has been affected by events in the wider society which place households under severe stress, our focus is on three kinds of resource constraint. The first is the disruption and privation of *war*, which was experienced at the national level by China in the first half of this century and especially during the Second World War, and by South Korea during the Korean War of 1950–3. The second is *famine*, which was experienced on a large scale in China in 1959–61. The third is the substantial *fertility decline* which has taken place in all three countries in recent decades. Since these societies are characterized by strong son preference, this amounts to another form of resource constraint on the household because reducing the number of births means reducing the number of opportunities to have a son. Empirically, fertility decline in these countries has been accompanied by rising female disadvantage in survival even at low birth orders, and more masculine sex ratios of children (Das Gupta and Bhat, 1995).

There seems to be little evidence from South Asia or South Korea that the poor discriminate more against their daughters, the hypothesis being that sharper resource constraints force them to allocate resources to the more valued males.[1] However, resource constraints may affect discrimination in another way: people may increase the level of discrimination when they experience a tightening of circumstances relative to their *own* previous position, as when they are caught up in a war or famine. This is the hypothesis which we examine.

We also explore how the marriage market has been affected by the extent of discrimination, building on Caldwell et al.'s (1983) idea of the 'marriage squeeze'. The history of these three countries is quite different, and these differences are reflected in the extent of discrimination against girls. We explore how this has affected spousal availability in the three countries, and how the treatment of women is affected by whether they are in surplus or shortage.

We begin by discussing what drives this comparison of three countries which are so disparate in many ways. Despite their very different levels of economic and social development and political systems, they have fundamental similarities in the position of daughters in the family, and in the nature of marriage. We then examine the historical trends in female disadvantage and how they are related to major resource constraints. Finally, we look at trends in spousal availability and some of the social implications of these historical trends, including the implications for marriage payments, and the situation of poorer people and of women.

SIMILARITIES IN THE POSITION OF DAUGHTERS IN CHINA, SOUTH KOREA AND INDIA[2]

China and South Korea are culturally fairly homogeneous countries in which the majority of the population belongs to a culture of rigidly patrilineal and patrilocal kinship systems based on a clan system. India is more diverse. The dominant kinship system in North-west India is strikingly similar to that of China and South Korea. Other parts of Northern India have forms of patriarchy which are less rigidly organized. Southern India has elements of a more bilateral kinship system, and also exhibits far less son

---

1. Early censuses in India show that in regions with strong son preference, the higher castes had more imbalanced sex ratios than the lower castes (Das Gupta, 1987; Miller, 1981). Krishnaji (1987) and Murthi et al. (1995), using district-level data from India, found that, if anything, the rich discriminate more than the poor. Data from South Korea also suggests this (Das Gupta et al., 1997).
2. The discussion in this section draws on the voluminous literature on kinship and social organization in these three countries, as well as on our field interviews in the countries themselves. See, for example, Chang (1991), Chowdhury (1994), Chung (1977), Cohen (1976), Croll (1983), Das Gupta (1995b), Davis and Harrell (1993), Dyson and Moore (1983), Freedman (1965), Gates (1996), Goody (1990), Greenhalgh (1994), Hershman (1981), Hsu (1948), Hu (1948), Karve (1965), Kendall (1996), Kim (1988), Kolenda (1987), Lee and Campbell (1997), Lee and Wang (1997), Pasternak (1972), Pradhan (1966), Skinner (1997), Stockard (1989), Williamson (1976), Wolf (1968), Wolf and Huang (1980), and Yi (1975).

preference than the North. We therefore compare the three countries and then examine the case of North-west India, because that is the most directly comparable with China and South Korea in terms of kinship and the potential for gender bias.

In the following brief and broad brush sketch of how the position of daughters is affected by the system of kinship and marriage, we refer to a 'traditional' system. Traditions, of course, are far from immutable, and here we refer to the social arrangements prevalent in these countries through much of this century. These arrangements persist to a considerable extent today despite much social change. All three countries have experienced considerable socio-economic development, and South Korea in particular is highly developed and urbanized today. However, the kinship system in these societies are especially resilient,[3] and values relating to the family and marriage have been much slower to change.

In these rigidly patrilineal and patrilocal kinship systems, lineages are defined in terms of males alone. Lineages are strictly exogamous, so they import brides to produce the next generation of the lineage. Membership of a lineage and one's position in it is conferred by dint of being a particular man's offspring, and the identity of the mother is almost irrelevant to this. Women are thus merely biological reproducers for a lineage other than their lineage of birth, and men are the social reproducers, the ones who confer an identity to the newborn child. Rights to a woman are transferred to the husband's family at the time of marriage. It is understood that the woman's future productivity and services belong to the husband's family, whatever her parents' needs may be. Consequently, a daughter's birth is far less welcome than that of a son. The kinship system in these settings leads to strong son preference and accompanying discrimination against daughters.

A daughter's marginality to her family of birth also affects the way in which the question of her marriage is perceived. While her brothers are central members of the family and lineage, a daughter's appropriate place is in her father's home only until it is time for her to marry. As an adult she becomes extraneous to her family of birth, her appropriate position being a wife in another family. It is highly unusual for an adult woman to live with her parental family. In short, there is no socially acceptable role for a grown woman in her family of birth, except as a visitor. She must leave and make way for incoming daughters-in-law.

---

3. Other types of family system have shown more rapid change. Some of the most dramatic changes have taken place in matrilineal systems. These typically practice inheritance from mother's brother to sister's son, which means that men pass on their property to their nephews instead of their sons. This generates conflict of interest, especially when resources become scarcer, which encourages a shift to more patrilineal family systems. By contrast, patrilineal systems have much more congruence between the interests of lineage members, and are therefore more robust in the face of other social and economic changes.

The need to marry off one's daughter is also affected by the fact that premarital sex and especially premarital childbirth bring tremendous dishonour to a family. For many reasons, then, there is much pressure on parents to find a groom for their daughter and give her away in marriage. The norm was for marriages to be arranged: it was the father's duty to see to this, and after the father's death the duty fell to the brother. Parents of grown daughters are reminded of their obligation to marry off their daughters. It is culturally unacceptable to have daughters remaining single, as evidenced by the negligible proportions of women who never marry in these countries.

Marriages entail some costs for the groom's as well as the bride's family. Currently in India, the average net expenses of a daughter's marriage are far higher than a son's marriage, because large dowries are paid to the groom's family. In China and South Korea, the average net expenses of a son's marriage are several times higher than that of a daughter's marriage (Bae, 1997; Williamson, 1976; Xie, 1997). Yet even in the latter case, people resent even the relatively small payments they make for their daughters' marriages, because this is viewed as a net loss for the family. Relatively heavy expenses on a son's wedding are less resented because the money is still viewed as remaining within the family.

There are thus some critical points of similarity between these three countries in the nature of marriage, which distinguish them from most other cultures. For example, in large parts of rural Europe it was completely acceptable, and even the norm, for grown daughters to remain single for many years and look after their parents or work on someone else's farm (Arensberg and Kimball, 1968; Sieder and Mitterauer, 1983). Besides, marriage was a matter of the couple's own choosing, not the responsibility of the parents. In such societies, a shortage of available grooms would be more of a personal problem for a woman, not an intolerable situation for parents to avoid by whatever means possible. This is in sharp contrast with the pressure to find a groom for one's daughter in these East and South Asian societies.

DATA AND METHODOLOGY

Data

The data used in this chapter are from the national population censuses of China, South Korea and India. Where indicated, we have also used other sources. For China, these include the 1995 One Percent National Population Survey and the Annual Population Change Surveys for 1989 to 1993. For South Korea, they include the 1995 Korean Population and Housing Census and the Annual Vital Statistics from 1985 to 1992.

The accuracy of age reporting in the censuses is critical to our analysis. In the case of China and South Korea, the accuracy of age reporting is very high (Coale and Banister, 1994; Kwon, 1977), because almost everybody knows the animal symbol of their birth year, which helps pinpoint the year of birth. Error will thus be small and also not subject to age-heaping. This made our analysis for China and South Korea simple and robust.

By contrast, the quality of age-reporting in the Indian censuses is subject to serious age-heaping, making it impossible to use these data for many purposes. The data are officially smoothed, but the linear assumptions underlying smoothing break down for the youngest and oldest age groups.[4] Therefore we are unable to use these data to analyse sex ratios of annual birth cohorts, since this would require using the youngest age group. We are, however, able to use the smoothed data for the analysis of spousal availability, as the smoothing assumptions have greater validity for the relevant age-groups.[5]

Method of Calculating the Excess Sex Ratios

To calculate the proportions of girls missing in each birth cohort in China and South Korea, we use the methodology and the index developed by Coale and Banister (1994) in their study on 'missing' females in China. Thus we calculate the observed sex ratio of each single-year birth cohort and compute a five-year moving average of the ratio. We then estimate how excessively masculine this sex ratio is by comparing it to the expected ratio in the West model life tables (Coale and Demeny, 1966). This was calculated using the female life expectancy prevailing in the country at the time (see Table 4 in the Appendix), along with the conservative assumption that the normal sex ratio at birth is 1.06. These model sex ratios are based on life tables from a range of countries, and form a useful benchmark of the 'normal' sex ratio in the absence of discrimination. The censuses used for this analysis are those conducted between 1953 and 1990 in China, and between 1960 and 1990 in South Korea.

The estimated excess sex ratios for China and South Korea (Figure 1) reflect cumulative loss of females from birth until the time of the census, resulting from sex selective abortion, female infanticide and discrimination against girls and women which reverses their normal biological advantage in survival. To focus more on the discrimination in childhood, we use the most recent census data on each birth cohort. The method is described more fully

---

4. Personal communication from Mari Bhat, based on his extensive work on the Indian census data.
5. Normal smoothing methods do not eliminate systematic age errors which vary by sex. However, unless these systematic errors have changed substantially over time, the trend in spousal availability is more or less correctly reported by the smoothed sex ratios.

in the Appendix. The same method is also used for South Korea. For India, we were unable to apply this method because of problems of age-reporting, as mentioned above. Instead, we show the juvenile (aged 0–4) sex ratios of India from 1951 to 1991 to give some idea of missing girls in India.

Method of Estimating Spousal Availability

The index used in this chapter is the ratio of males to younger females for each five-year birth cohort at census time, using the observed average age gap at first marriage between men and women prevailing at the time in each country (Appendix Table 1). For each male birth cohort, we calculate the observed ratio for this cohort when they are aged 20–9.[6] The exception is the last calculation for each country, which uses males from age 5 in order to look at the future spousal availability.[7] For this last group, we use the current age gap at marriage.

To separate the effect of fertility decline from that of discrimination, we calculate the 'normal' ratios of males to younger females which should prevail in the absence of discrimination. For this, we estimate the expected number of females given the observed number of males of the same age and the 'normal' sex ratio from the corresponding life tables. The difference between the observed ratio and the normal ratio is the estimated effect of gender bias on spousal availability.[8]

There are several demographic models to investigate the marriage market. Park and Cho (1995) and Tuljapurkar et al. (1995) are primarily interested in the future marriage market, and therefore use the current age gap between spouses as the basis for their calculations. Bhat and Halli (1996) focus on the past marriage market, and hold the age gap between spouses constant in

6. In the case of China, the censuses were not carried out every ten years, so the age groups are wider in some cases. In such cases, there is a small difference in exposure to mortality, which will slightly affect our analysis insofar as there is a sex differential in this different exposure.

7. For the most recent estimates, we had to supplement the census data with data from annual statistics, in which we assumed the normal sex ratio at birth to be 1.06. This is because for China we do not know the inflators to match the 1995 1% census data with the 1990 census, and for South Korea the single-year age-distribution from the 1995 census data is not yet available. Thus for China we used the births from the 1989–93 annual population change surveys, and for South Korea we used the births from the 1985–92 vital statistics. For India no sex-specific data are available beyond the 1991 census, and so we could not extend the calculation beyond the 1980–4 birth cohort.

8. In the case of India, the data on spousal age gap and life expectancy before 1947 refer to pre-Partition India, including present-day Pakistan and Bangladesh, while those after 1947 refer to present-day India. However, the population base on which the calculations of spousal availability are made are taken from the post-Partition censuses. Thus our estimates of spousal availability, in Appendix Tables 2 and 3, reflect the situation in present-day India.

Figure 1. Excess Sex Ratios at Census Time by 5 year Birth Cohorts, 1920–1995, China and South Korea

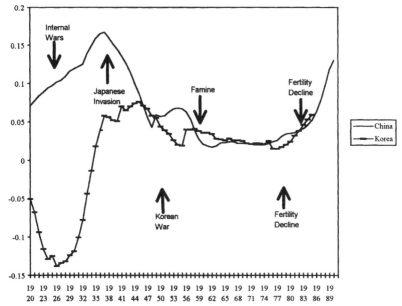

First year of 5 year period of birth

Note: The excess ratios peak amongst cohorts born just before a war or famine, because those who were young girls at the time of the crisis experienced the maximum excess mortality.
Sources: China, calculation based on data from 1953, 1964, 1982 and 1990 Population Censuses of China. See Department of Population Statistics, SSB (1985, 1988, 1993, 1997) S. Korea, calculation based on data from 1960, 1970, 1980 and 1990 Population Censuses of Korea. See Economic Planning Board (1960, 1970); National Bureau of Statistics and Economic Planning Board (1980, 1990).

order to estimate what would have been spousal availability had the age gap not changed. This approach takes into account the fact that the age gap between spouses is partly influenced by spousal availability. Of course, many other factors also influence the age gap between spouses, including socio-economic factors such as levels of female education, and changes in social norms. In the case of China, the age gap is also influenced by changes in marriage laws. Bhat and Halli's estimates are therefore designed to reflect the full extent of marriage squeeze which would have prevailed had the spousal age gap not changed, but are not designed to reflect actual spousal availability except at the time of the initial equilibrium. Our model has to allow for empirical changes in spousal age gap, as our primary motivation in this chapter is to estimate changes over time in actual spousal availability.

There are several aspects of the potentially complex dynamics of 'marriage markets' which we cannot take into account. For example, differences in the remarriage rates of widows and widowers influence spousal availability. Bhat and Halli (1996) are able to increase the complexity of the marriage market analysed by using the data from the Indian censuses on remarriage rates by sex. Unfortunately, the Chinese and South Korean data do not include information on remarriage rates, and therefore we have to ignore this potentially important factor. We also do not address the fact that people choose spouses on the basis of matching education, class and other characteristics. In addition, we do not consider the possibility that some people may choose not to marry: this is an important factor in some post-industrial societies, but not in these three countries during the period we are studying. Over 99 per cent of women aged 40–9 were classified as 'ever-married' in the 1990 censuses of China and South Korea. Our method provides an approximate estimate of spousal availability in the first marriage market (Appendix Table 1). That is, it gives rough estimates of the historical and present proportions of people never-married given their spousal age gap, and the future trend based on the current spousal age gap.

CRISES AND THE MANIFESTATION OF GENDER BIAS

In this analysis, it is only possible to examine the effect of major national-level crises. More localized events may have been very significant in themselves, but their impact is likely to be drowned in national-level sex ratios. Therefore our focus here is only on large-scale crises.

China

Of the three countries studied here, China has had the most eventful history during this century, at least from the point of view of households trying to make their way in life (Bianco, 1967; Chi, 1976). The briefest sketch of this history makes the vicissitudes of ordinary life apparent. The century began with the Qing dynasty in tenuous control of the country. In 1911 a revolution deposed the Qing dynasty and installed a nationalist government under Sun Yat Sen. The country was not united under one central government, and 'warlords' were battling hard for hegemony. Meanwhile, the Communist forces were gradually increasing in strength.

Through the first half of this century, the battles between the warlords, and between the nationalists and the Communists, created a situation of continuous uncertainty for people. One of the least manifestations of this was uncertainty about which set of authorities was in charge and had to be dealt with. This was interspersed with periods of chaos when people might face being forced to send family members to join the troops, having food supplies requisitioned, being pillaged by hungry troops, and occasionally having to flee in the face of advancing armies. All this is reflected in fairly high sex ratios of cohorts born during the 1920s and 1930s (Figure 1).

The most dramatic effect on sex ratios is evidenced when the Japanese invaded China during the Second World War. The Japanese had a presence in Manchuria from the early years of the century which they used to build up an agricultural as well as industrial base in this region rich in coal and iron and a thriving armaments industry (Chi, 1976; Cumings, 1981; McCormack, 1977). This was followed by a more formal occupation of Manchuria in 1931. In 1937, Japan launched a massive invasion of the main body of China. This caused havoc, as people fled in the face of the advancing army and also had to deal with the requisitions of their own armies. To add to the people's difficulties, they had two Chinese armies to contend with: the Nationalists and the Communists who, during the Japanese invasion, were at best in uneasy alliance, and at worst in open competition with each other.

As Japanese troops swept through the densely-populated eastern half of China in a blitzkrieg from 1937, the sex ratios shot up (Figure 1). Apparently the disruption was such that people felt they had to make some harsh choices about which family members to sustain. Stories about this period talk of female abandonment and infanticide (Tan, 1989). An interview with a woman in her sixties in Zhejiang province gives a firsthand account of such an experience: 'When I was six years old, my mother said that I should be sold. I begged my father not to do this, that I would eat very little if only they would let me stay at home'.[9] Increased discrimination against daughters during periods of crisis was also common in nineteenth century China. Using data from local gazeteers from several provinces of China, Xin (1989) describes how levels of female infanticide rose in times of famine, drought, war and other economic stress, with comments such as: 'After the war, the economy was in a slump. The land was deserted so drowning female babies was common'.[10]

The Japanese invasion would be expected to cause excess mortality of young men, but this is not visible here because they would have been born largely before 1920. During the 1950s, with the establishment of Communist rule, life became much calmer and more predictable for ordinary households. This peace contributed to a lowering of discrimination against daughters, helped by the Communist ideology of gender equality.

During the famine of 1959–61, the sex ratios went up again (Figure 1). Those who were young girls at the time of the famine experienced the maximum excess mortality, so the peak excess ratios are in the cohorts born in 1954–8, a few years before the famine. After the famine and through the 1970s, levels of discrimination remained fairly constant, with about 2 per cent of girls missing. In the early 1980s, the sex ratio began to rise once again. Since the mid-1980s, it has been rising at an accelerating rate, probably because the availability of sex-selective abortion makes it easier to

---

9. Interview conducted by Monica Das Gupta and Li Bohua in 1996.
10. The word 'common' is ours. The original translation was 'very popular'.

Figure 2. Juvenile (0–4 year) Sex Ratios in China, South Korea, India and Punjab, 1950s–90s

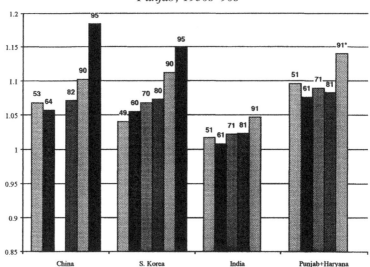

Notes: The census year is indicated above each bar. *The 1991 figure is the sex ratio of 0–6.
Sources: China, computed from 1953, 1964, 1982 and 1990 Population Censuses of China, and 1995 National One Percent Population Sample Survey of China (see notes to Figure 1). S. Korea, computed from 1949, 1960, 1970, 1980, 1990 and 1995 Population and Housing Censuses of Korea (see notes to Figure 1). India and Punjab, computed from 1951, 1961, 1971, 1981 and 1991 Popualtion Censuses of India. See Registrar General and Census Commissioner, Census of India, 1951–1991.

discriminate against daughters.[11] Sex ratios rose at a similar time in South Korea and India (Figures 1 and 2), and this is very likely to be for the same reason.

South Korea

Korea was annexed by Japan in 1910, and remained under Japanese colonial administration until the end of the Second World War. Thus there was no war on Korean territory during the Second World War (Han, 1970; Kim, 1981). From 1950, however, the country was racked by war, especially in the North. The Korean War caused havoc between June 1950 and March 1951 as the two sides pushed each other up and down the peninsula. After this, until the peace settlement in July 1953, there was continued fighting around the cease-fire line, and heavy bombing of North Korea which was held by

---

11. Zeng et al. (1993) report that the import of ultrasound machines into China rose sharply in the mid-1980s.

Communist forces. Actual fighting never reached the southern-most part of the Korean peninsula (Han, 1970; Hastings, 1987).

Interviews[12] with older people in South Korea reveal something of the havoc experienced when the northern troops pushed southwards at the beginning of the war:

> (old man in a village in Kyungsangpuk Province): When the North Korean troops came near our village, we fled into the hills with our families. Nevertheless, they managed to catch some of our men and forced them to work for their troops. When the South Korean troops recaptured our village, they asked 'Who worked for the North Koreans?' Anyone who admitted to it was shot. We feared both sides.

> (old woman in Taegu city): As the North Koreans advanced, we fled our village and headed to the deep South where we had some relatives. On the way there we were able to buy some food because we were fortunate to have some money, but I lost the child I was expecting ...

Equally revealing is the youth of those who died: the sex ratios indicate that substantial numbers of boys as young as fifteen years old were involved in the fighting. The Korean War caused so much mortality among young males that the sex ratios for the cohorts born between 1920–36 are excessively feminine.

The effect of the Korean War on girls is evident in the sex ratios. As in the case of the Chinese famine, the maximum brunt of excess mortality was borne not by those born during the famine but by girls who were young children at the time. These girls appear to have suffered discrimination, whether through neglect or abandonment. Note that the sex ratios reflect only the *excess* mortality of girls over and above the fact that children of both sexes undoubtedly suffered during the war.

Since the Korean War, there have been no major crises in South Korea which are likely to impact on sex ratios. This has been a period of peace and rapid economic and social development. During this period, the proportion of females missing in South Korea follows a path very similar to that of China, rising once again in the 1980s.

India

India has had perhaps the least eventful history during the period we consider here. Improvements in irrigation reduced the likelihood of harvest failure, and the construction of a railway network enabled the transport of grain to avert mortality from local harvest failures. As a result, there has been no major famine since 1920 with the exception of the Bengal Famine of 1943. From the point of view of our analysis, we would not expect to find an impact

---

12. Interviews conducted by Monica Das Gupta and Bae Hwa-Ok in 1996.

from this famine because it affected only one part of the country, and half of the affected region is no longer in India but in Bangladesh.

Neither has India experienced a war during this period. Indian soldiers participated in the Second World War in all the theatres where it was fought, but there was little fighting on Indian territory. Towards the end of the war the Japanese pushed briefly into the part of India bordering on Burma, but were quickly pushed back. As it happens, this part of India shows no son preference, so child sex ratios are unlikely to have been affected even if the war there had lasted longer. The Partition of India was obviously a very traumatic event for the country, as it was split into three sections on the basis of religion. Tens of thousands of people were killed, mostly in the months just before Partition and millions became homeless refugees, having fled from riots, arson and looting in their home areas.

For all this, Partition involved riots, not war. For a few months there were serious riots and some administrative disruption in Punjab and Delhi. Yet in the midst of riots and a large movement of population across the borders, the administration managed to set up camps for the refugees. Shortly after Independence, arrangements were made for some rough exchange of property between those leaving India and those leaving Pakistan. Although there was considerable disruption, the situation during Partition was not comparable to the breakdown (or absence) of State machinery during the Japanese invasion of China or during the Korean War.

Whatever impact Partition may have had on Indian sex ratios is reduced by two factors. One is that Southern India was very little affected by the riots. The second is that, as in the case of the Bengal Famine, only half the affected territory is still in India, reducing further the weight of the affected region in India as a whole. The region where we would expect the maximum impact of Partition is Punjab, because it has strong gender bias and experienced the greatest disruption during Partition. As discussed above, the poor quality of age-reporting in Indian censuses make it difficult to study this. However, the juvenile sex ratio for India in 1951 is higher than that for 1961. The difference is even sharper in the case of Punjab (Figure 2). This may reflect increased discrimination during Partition, but part of it may be due to ordinary fluctuations.

A number of points emerge from comparing the juvenile sex ratios of India with China and South Korea during recent decades when fertility has declined (Figure 2).[13] Firstly, the sex ratios for India are low compared with China and South Korea. This is because India is culturally heterogeneous and the South shows relatively balanced sex ratios. This regional pattern is remarkably resilient over time (Das Gupta and Bhat, 1995; Visaria, 1969). To illustrate excess female mortality in the region with the strongest gender bias,

---

13. Note that the Indian juvenile sex ratios may be underestimated because of age mis-reporting, with boys' ages being overstated (Mari Bhat, personal communication).

Figure 3. Total Fertility Rate of China, South Korea and India, 1960–1990

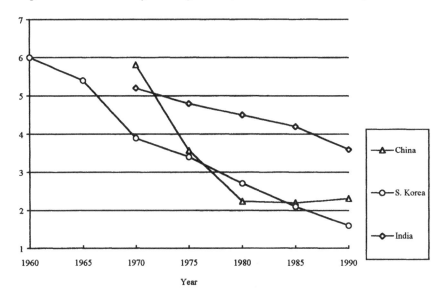

Sources: China: Yao Xinwu and Yin Hua (1944: 144). South Korea: Lee and Cho (1992). India: Registrar General of India, *Sample Registration System, 1970–1990*.

we show the juvenile sex ratio for the North-western States of Punjab and Haryana (Figure 2). These are higher even than those of China and South Korea. The second point which emerges from these data is that the main rise in sex ratios in all three countries is after 1980. This suggests that the impact of fertility decline on sex ratios is substantially raised by the spread of sex-selective technology during the 1980s.

SPOUSAL AVAILABILITY AND THE 'MARRIAGE SQUEEZE'

Improved child survival earlier in this century led to a growing population in all three countries, as in most of the rest of the developing world. Consequently, successive birth cohorts increased in size until fertility decline became well-established, after the 1960s (Figure 3). Given the fact that in these countries men marry women from younger cohorts than their own (Appendix Table 1), this means that the three phases of the 'demographic transition' are associated with different forms of marriage squeeze. In the pre-transition phase the size of successive cohorts was not growing rapidly and we expect discrimination to generate a surplus of men. With the child mortality decline that all three countries experienced earlier this century, there may be a surplus of *women* because birth cohorts are increasing in size.

The extent of this surplus depends on the extent of discrimination. More recently there has been fertility decline, which again makes for a surplus of men, both because younger cohorts will be smaller and because fertility decline can raise the level of discrimination. The period we examine, that is the birth cohorts of 1920–90, includes the period of mortality decline followed by fertility decline.

Our analysis is intended simply to illustrate changes in spousal availability and how it was affected by excess female mortality. Of course, excess female mortality is just one factor influencing spousal availability. Responses to the marriage squeeze are heavily influenced by cultural norms. For example, if it were more acceptable for women to remain unmarried or to marry men substantially younger than themselves, many of the effects we describe would be greatly mitigated. However, these options have limited cultural acceptability.

The age at marriage influences our illustration considerably. If men and women have the same mean age at marriage, the proportion of 'missing girls' would heavily influence the availability of spouses. However, when men and women differ in mean age at marriage, the rate of growth of the population and the average age gap between spouses become the main determinants of spousal availability (Caldwell et al., 1983). We discuss these dynamics in the context of each of the three countries, and then develop some hypotheses about how spousal availability may have affected marriage payments and the treatment of women.

China

In the absence of discrimination against girls, China should have had a shortage of marriageable men until 1970, since until then fertility levels were high and the size of successive cohorts was increasing. However, this shortage was largely removed by discrimination, and for most of the period before 1970 there was some surplus of men (Appendix Table 2). Even the dramatic rise in discrimination against girls during the Second World War resulted in only a moderate rise in the surplus of men, because its effect on spousal availability was heavily cushioned by population growth. The male surplus rose for the cohorts of men born between 1930–44, but only those born in 1935–9 experienced a substantial rise in the excess of men. This is despite the fact that an estimated 17 per cent of females were 'missing' from the birth cohort of 1937–41.

The famine of 1959–61 was accompanied by a slump in fertility, as famines usually are, followed by a brief post-famine recovery in fertility. These fertility fluctuations made for a shortage of spouses followed by a surplus of spouses. The net effect is of a somewhat balanced marriage market for men born in 1955–64.

Although the proportion of missing girls was highest at the time of the Japanese invasion, the problem of spousal availability is worse now because of fertility decline. From 1970–80 fertility declined rapidly in China, falling from 5.8 in 1970 to 3.6 in 1975 and 2.2 in 1980 (Figure 3). Since 1980, fertility levels have fluctuated and shown relatively little overall decline. The effect of the early period of rapid fertility decline was to sharply increase the shortage of marriageable women, as successive cohort size fell sharply. Men born in 1970–4 experienced a substantial rise in shortage of women. This was not offset by a surplus of available wives for subsequent cohorts of men, as these continued to register a smaller but steady surplus of men. This situation was aggravated even further for males born after 1985, when levels of discrimination against girls rose (Figure 1) as new technology made such discrimination easier. The cohort of males born in 1985–9 will suffer from the same shortage of spouses as those born around the time of the Japanese invasion. Their situation is worse than those born in 1935–9, however, because it is unlikely that the shortage will be reduced in the immediate future, building up an increasing shortage of women.

The effect on spousal availability of fertility decline and of discrimination are distinguished in Table 3. Men born in 1970–4 will experience greater shortage of available wives than any other cohort of men born during 1920–90. Most of this shortage is caused by fertility decline. For cohorts born after 1975, the effect of fertility decline is diminished, and for men born during 1985–9 most of the shortage of future wives is caused by discrimination against girls.

Men marrying in the late 1990s will experience the maximum shortage of spouses. This shortage will accumulate gradually and then receive another large boost in the second decade of the next century, when males born after 1985 enter marriageable ages. At least 12 per cent of these men will not be able to find wives. Given the continued rise in levels of discrimination against girls between 1990 and 1995 (Figure 2), the shortage of available wives will continue to rise in the foreseeable future, and higher proportions of men will not be able to find wives. Given the small age gap between spouses of around 1.7 years in China in 1990, even the unlikely event of a long-term rise in fertility will not do much to cushion the shortage of available wives. This shortage will continue to increase unless discrimination ends. Some of the problems associated with this are discussed briefly below.

South Korea

South Korea also has a history of discrimination against girls. However, because of rapid population growth and the four-year age gap at first marriage, there was actually some surplus of women available for marriage for males born between 1935–49. We do not analyse spousal availability for men born before that, since the heavy casualties associated with the Korean

War (Figure 1) affected both single men and those who were already married. The Korean War also caused some fertility fluctuations, with a drop in fertility during the war and a post-war recovery of fertility (Kwon, 1977: 141). The latter increased the surplus of women available for men born in 1950–4. However, this surplus was followed by the beginning of fertility decline, which caused a shortage of women, so the effect of some of the fluctuations in spousal availability for men born during the 1950s could be reduced by increasing the age range within which spouses are sought.

The fertility decline which began in 1960 changed this to a situation in which there was a shortage of women available for marriage. The increase in discrimination against girls since the mid-1980s has added to the effect of fertility decline (Table 3), such that there were nearly 25 per cent more males born in 1980–4 than females of the appropriate age. The average age gap between spouses was still three years in 1990, so shrinking cohort size still affects the availability of women.

As the fertility transition nears its end now, there will be less shortage of women resulting from reductions in the size of successive birth cohorts. Discrimination will now become the main factor creating a shortage of women. So far the trend has been for discrimination to rise (Figure 2), but without the added factor of fertility decline there will be a much smaller shortage of women. Fertility fluctuations will also affect this. For example, there has been a rise in the number of births during 1991–4 compared with 1984–90 (National Statistical Office, 1995: 20), probably because these are the births of the larger cohort born during the 'baby-boom' after the Korean War. Consequently, for males born in 1985–9 there is a surplus of only 7 per cent compared with females three years younger than themselves. This is of course substantial enough to cause a serious problem, but far less than the 25 per cent shortfall experienced by males born in 1980–4. Discrimination accounts for 6 per cent of the shortfall for males born in 1980–4, and all of the 7 per cent shortfall of females for males born in 1985–9.

The worst shortage of potential wives will thus be felt by those marrying in the early decades of the next century. This will be followed by a continuing shortage of women for the foreseeable future, caused mostly by discrimination against girls. There are already signs of the pressure of spousal availability, and some of this is resolved by importing women from elsewhere: for example, from amongst the ethnic Koreans in Northern China and from the Philippines.[14]

---

14. Based on field interviews in South Korea by Monica Das Gupta and Bae Hwa-Ok. The marriage of women from the Philippines was also reported in the *New York Times* in winter 1996–7.

India

India has had a surplus of women throughout the period we study, reversing only for the males born after 1980 (Table 2). The surplus has been substantial: for males born during 1920–59, there were approximately 9 per cent more women than men of marriageable age. Moreover, the female surplus has been steady, unmarked by even brief reversals in spousal availability which could ease the situation. Thus the pressure on women in the 'marriage market' has been intense throughout this period.

This consistent pattern of a surplus of women in India is generated by the fact that rapid population growth has created growing cohort sizes. With the steady mortality decline in the country since 1920, child survival increased, increasing the size of successive cohorts. The age gap between spouses has also been wider than in South Korea or China (Appendix Table 1), so the impact of growing cohort size on the availability of wives is larger. Another factor is the relative peace of the country's history since 1920, without any countrywide famine or war which might have raised discrimination against girls and reduced the surplus of women. Discrimination against girls is also lower on aggregate in India than in the other two countries, since only Northern India shows strong discrimination against girls. North-west India had a shortage of women at the turn of the century, but we cannot analyse spousal availability there in the same way because it is not a closed population: they could and did import women on a regular basis.

Fertility decline has taken place at a much slower pace in India than in South Korea or China (Figure 3), such that the size of successive cohorts has only recently begun to shrink. Combined with a larger age gap between spouses and less discrimination on aggregate than these countries, fertility decline did not quickly generate a surplus of men. Instead, it made for a balanced 'marriage market' (Appendix Table 2) for men born between 1965 and 1979. The next cohort (born 1980–4) will experience a surplus of men. Given the trend of continuing fertility decline, this surplus will increase, augmented by rising discrimination against girls (Figure 2).

SOCIAL IMPLICATIONS OF HISTORICAL TRENDS IN GENDER BIAS

Implications for Marriage Costs and Age Gap between Spouses

China and India provide an interesting contrast in their history of spousal availability during this century. Both countries experienced mortality decline and increasing size of successive cohorts until their recent fertility decline. However, there was a *surplus* of men to marriageable women throughout this period in China, while in India the opposite was the case. This is partly because China has higher levels of discrimination against girls than India has on aggregate. Moreover, levels of discrimination were raised in China by national-scale wars and famines, which India was spared during this period. Another factor is some differences in the cultural constraints on marriage choices: the average age gap between spouses was smaller in China than in India. These factors have several implications for marriage arrangements.

We calculate that there was a balance in spousal availability in India at the turn of the century, which changed from 1921 to a substantial surplus (around 9 per cent) of women. The sex ratio of males aged 17–26 to females 6–7[15] years younger than them was 1.02 (1881), 0.98 (1891), 0.90 (1901, following a decade of severe famines with excess male mortality), 0.97 (1911), 0.91 (1921), 0.92 (1931), and 0.92 (1951). This corroborates the view in several studies on India that there has been a surplus of women generated by improving child survival during this century, and that this has contributed to a shift from brideprice to dowry and dowry inflation. Caldwell et al. (1983) were the first to argue this, and other studies have concurred (Bhat and Halli, 1996; Billig, 1992; Rao, 1993). It is interesting to note that in field interviews people themselves attribute the rise in dowries to the surplus of women (Caldwell et al., 1983; Epstein, 1973).

We extend Caldwell et al.'s (1983) argument by hypothesizing that bride-price has continued to be practised in China because of a surplus of men through this century. Accounts suggest that there has also been inflation in brideprice, especially in poorer regions, because of the increasing difficulty of finding a wife (Zhu, 1992). In the case of India, the surplus of men that we can expect for birth cohorts after 1980 means that there is hope that dowry inflation will taper off. Using survey data from South-central India, Rao[16] has shown that there is indeed some sign of dowry inflation tapering off in recent years. However, the social arrangements surrounding marriage payments acquire some normative content, so marriage payments may not respond very quickly to this demographic shift. Another factor which may slow down this response is the consistent pattern of trying to marry girls into families of higher socio-economic status, since these transactions are smoothed by financial incentives.

Of course, some part of dowry inflation in India is due to efforts to be hypergamous: payments have to be higher the greater the gap in status between the households, and the more qualified the groom.[17] It is important, however, to clarify that the need for higher payments from the bride's family is analytically distinct from a rise in the *net* payments from her family. Marriage typically entails some costs for both the bride's and the groom's family. For example, with growing incomes and desire to find qualified grooms in China and South Korea, brides' families have been paying more

---

15. The average age gap between spouses used in these computations was 7 years for 1881–1921, and 6 years for 1931 and 1951.
16. Vijayendra Rao, personal communication. Unfortunately, no hard data are yet available on these trends in other parts of India.
17. Billig (1992), Caldwell (1983), Kapadia (1993), and Rao (1993).

for marriages (Kim, 1995; Xie, 1997), but the major share of marriage costs continue to be borne by the groom's family in line with earlier practices.

Studies in India have also drawn attention to the fact that the marriage squeeze puts pressure to reduce the age gap between spouses, in order to reduce the extent of the squeeze (Bhat and Halli, 1996; Caldwell, 1983; Rao, 1993). This argument can also be extended to China and South Korea, which have also experienced a marriage squeeze and a reduction in the average age gap between spouses (Appendix Table 1). However, increasing the age gap between spouses will not be an effective strategy for reducing the coming marriage squeeze in the next century, because with advanced fertility transition the size of successive cohorts will not increase steadily as during this century.

Does a Shortage of Available Wives Improve Women's Situation?

These three countries present an interesting comparison of how the 'marriage squeeze' affects the situation of women. The comparison is of interest because, as described above, the three countries show much commonality in kinship and marriage patterns, and in the position of young women within the family. This sharpens the comparison of outcomes when they show very different patterns of spousal availability. The contrast is especially sharp between China and India, because the first shows a long-term shortage of women while India shows a long-term surplus of them.

The situation of women in India has been negatively affected in several ways by the shortage of grooms. The fact of having to pay large dowries to marry off daughters puts enormous financial stress on families. In the parts of the country where the culture makes girls undesirable, this financial stress adds to the problem. In the South, where there was little gender bias in the past, there is evidence of some now. However, the persistence of cultural differences is notable: as compared with the South, Northern India has not only higher levels of discrimination against girls, but also a higher pace of increase in this discrimination as fertility has declined (Das Gupta and Bhat, 1995). This is despite the fact that the South has had more rapid fertility decline than the North and also experienced a shift from bridewealth to dowry and dowry inflation.[18]

Another negative consequence of this marriage squeeze for Indian women is that they are likely to be less valued because substitute wives are easily available. One aspect of this is the dowry-related violence which is widely reported, with husbands' families abusing women in order to extract more dowry from their parents. In extreme cases women are killed, for example by engineering an 'accident' in which the woman is reportedly burnt while

---

18. Caldwell (1983), Epstein (1973), Heyer (1992), Kapadia (1993) and Rao (1993).

cooking. The surplus of women increases the likelihood of being ill-treated in other ways too, by worsening the imbalance of power between men and women. It makes it easier for the man to be abusive and more compelling for the woman to accept abuse: if one woman does not seem desirable, she can be abused or cast off and another obtained if necessary.

We hypothesize that the marriage squeeze has led to a rise in dowry-related violence during this century. In the absence of time-trend data on dowry violence, this cannot be proved quantitatively, but there is considerable qualitative evidence on this. Field interviews stress that such violence was rare in the past,[19] and archival data indicate that brideprice was widespread (see also Kumari, 1989; Natarajan, 1995). This is logically consistent with the increasing surplus of available women. Perhaps the most compelling evidence that dowry violence has grown substantially during this century derives from the writings of social reformers around the turn of the century, who were deeply engaged in reforming the status of women. They discussed in detail various aspects of women's subordination and social practices which required reform. If dowry violence were prevalent at the time as it is today, it is difficult to believe that this would not have figured prominently in their writings.

China's experience is in sharp contrast to that of India. Through most of this century, there was some surplus of men. The surplus was very small amongst those marrying before 1950. We have little hard information on how women were treated at the time. However, literary sources (Buck, 1931; Lu, 1980, 1990) suggest that although women had very low status in the household, people were not resorting to desperate and violent means to obtain wives: they saved up for a wife and married when they could. People reportedly felt themselves lucky to obtain a wife, especially if they were not rich. The demand for wives was enough that a widow might be sold by the husband's family into marriage elsewhere. It also meant that during famine women could (and did) leave their husbands to live with another man elsewhere temporarily or permanently. Heightened discrimination during the Japanese invasion generated a substantial surplus of men born during the war years. However, these men would have married when there was strict Communist control at the community level, so there would be little question of resorting to desperate and violent means of obtaining wives.

In recent years the shortage of women in China has become more serious and sustained, and women are being subjected to violence because of the difficulty of obtaining wives. The fertility decline of the early 1970s generated a substantial shortage of women for men marrying in the 1990s. The shortage of women in China now is even larger than the surplus of women in India in earlier decades. Some people have resorted to buying brides who

---

19. Vijayendra Rao (personal communication), and field interviews by Das Gupta in Karnataka and Haryana.

have been kidnapped. There are many reports of women being kidnapped or lured by job offers and sold into marriage in distant provinces, and of the operation of criminal gangs in this kidnapping. The situation is serious enough for the Chinese government to pass an edict in 1992 to crack down on these criminals,[20] and for a women's magazine to publish advice on how to avoid being kidnapped or lured (Lu, 1994). Other means are also being used to secure wives, such as resurrecting the old custom of adopting and raising a little girl as a future bride for one's son, and families engaging their infants to each other (Zhu, 1992).

A kidnapped woman is largely powerless to recover her freedom if she does not like her situation. The husband's community overwhelmingly supports the man, feeling that since he paid for the woman his rights should be protected. Even the local police have in some cases taken this position, sometimes out of fear of retribution by local people. The community protects its men by refusing to divulge information on the location of kidnapped women, and even by co-operating to spirit them away during a police search (Zhang and Li, 1993).

Nor is it necessarily easy for a woman if she is rescued and returned home. The first problem is that she has been with a man. If she was already married, her erstwhile husband may not accept her. If she was single, she is likely to make a poor match, reducing her chances of a good life. Whether or not a kidnapped woman succeeds in escaping, her powerlessness subjects her to pressures which can even result in suicide. A case study of a suicide in China illustrates this point:

> A married woman in Shandong province was kidnapped and sold as a bride. Six months later, she succeeded in escaping and managed to return to her family. However, her husband said she had slept with another man, and everyone in the community knew that she had done so. On the second day after she finally got home, she killed herself.[21]

The second problem arises because her home village needs to balance its land resources. An adult woman's place is supposed to be with her husband, not her father. Consequently the village is under pressure to strike women off their fathers' records in order to be able to allocate land to incoming brides, as indicated by the following case:

> Fen-er was abducted and sold in marriage to a man in Shanxi province. After a couple of months she succeeded in tricking her husband to accompany her to her home area, where she reported him to the police as having bought her from her abductor. The police dissolved their marriage and sent her back to her parents. The following day the village head came to her father and said that since she had been married, her land had to be returned to the village at

---

20. *Min Zhu Yu Fa Zhi* May 1992: 41 (in Chinese).
21. Account of case study conducted by Michael Philips, and reported by him to a correspondent for the *Economist*. We are very grateful to Emily MacFarquhar for this information.

the end of the accounting year. Her mother argued that her marriage had been annulled, but a village meeting supported the head's position.[22]

Given the community-based allocation of land, the problem is one of the village, but in India the same problem applies to households, where daughters must move out to make room for the daughters-in-law.

In North-west India too, there has been a shortage of women in the past. As in the wealthier parts of China today, part of this was resolved by importing women from elsewhere (Hershman, 1981; *Report on the Census of Punjab, 1868*). However, this did not substantially increase women's control over their lives. They still became part of the husband's lineage property. A widow would be re-married within the lineage and would have little option but to accept whatever arrangements her husband's family made for her. A similar picture of being lineage property emerges from accounts of China, despite the shortage of women there.[23]

South Korea's pattern is similar to that which might have obtained in China if the level of discrimination in the latter had not been raised so much by decades of war till 1949. South Korea had some surplus of women for men born in 1935–59, though the surplus is very small compared to India. The costs of marriage seem to have been quite low. As one woman put it, exaggerating a little to make her point: 'All we took with us to our husband's home was our bodies'.[24] There was no shift towards the bride's family making larger net payments for marriage than the groom's family, which is consistent with the fact that spousal availability was not strongly imbalanced. In interviews, it was widely reported that it was common in the past for men to take a mistress if their wife did not have a son. This may have been made easier by having some surplus of women. The numbers of potential mistresses would also be increased by the ranks of abandoned wives, and by the fact that a woman could have more than one 'master' sequentially. In China, adoption (preferably within the lineage) was the usual solution to this problem, not concubinage, and this may well be related to the shortage of women there.

We have yet to see what will happen in South Korea with the large shortage of women they are about to experience. The country is now rich enough to be able to resolve some of this problem by importing wives from Manchuria and overseas. Being a relatively small country makes this easier to do: a country the size of China could never hope to emulate this example. Besides, it is now a highly urbanized country in which law enforcement is centralized. This is in contrast to the decentralized administration of largely

---

22. *Zhung Guo Fu Nu* August 1995 (in Chinese). The chapter mentions that since this particular case was publicized by some journalists, county-level officials took an interest in the case and saw to it that she could keep her land.
23. Zhang and Yin (1994), and Arthur Wolf (personal communication).
24. Interview conducted by Monica Das Gupta and Bae Hwa-Ok in 1996.

rural China, where there is vast potential for hiding women away in tightly-knit rural communities. Thus it is unlikely that the shortage of women in South Korea will lead to obtaining women by violent means.

Being in short supply does not seem to alter women's status and autonomy. These are determined by her position within the family and society, and can only be altered by efforts to alter the position of women in the family and society. China and North India are characterized by especially low autonomy of young women (Das Gupta, 1995b). However, it is likely that women are more subject to general abuse when it is easy to obtain another wife: this supply factor adds to the existing imbalance of power between husband and wife. This intuitively plausible statement is consistent with the widespread perception in India that dowry violence is rising, but there are no hard data on trends in such stress. The logic of our hypothesis, however, is consistent with the argument that a scarcity of women will raise their value but not their status in societies characterized by strong gender inequality in power (Guttentag and Secord, 1983; Pisani and Zaba, 1995). Their value may rise when they are in short supply because families may make more effort to ensure that they do not lose a wife, but this may not be accompanied by a rise in women's status as reflected in greater decision-making power within the household.

Who is Squeezed? Poverty and the Marriage Squeeze

It is largely the poor who suffer from the shortage of spouses. When there is a surplus of women, poor families are hardest pressed to find the wherewithal to marry off their daughters. Sometimes their daughters are forced to marry men who may be disabled or older widowers. When there is a shortage of women, it is poor men who are unable to find spouses. Wealthier men make more attractive partners, and manage to obtain wives one way or another. A saying in China refers to the marriage migration of women from poorer hill areas to richer plains areas:

'Women, like water, flow down the hill'.

In families with more than one son, the eldest son has a very high probability of being married, but if the family is under economic stress it is less likely to marry off younger sons. In fact, not letting some sons marry was one strategy for less affluent households to reduce subdivision of property and preserve resources for the following generation of the household (Das Gupta, 1995a).

That the burden of the shortage falls on the poor and on younger sons is evident from genealogical data collected in North-west India (Das Gupta, 1995a) and in North-east China (Lee and Campbell, 1997). It is also apparent in survey data collected in 1933 in Jiangsu, China (Li and Lavely, 1995). Across North India it was common for poorer men of the Rajput caste not to marry, since they practise strong discrimination against girls (Government of

India, 1931), and this helped households maintain a balance between their numbers and their resources. In China today the shortage of women has become unusually acute because of the combined pressure of declining cohort size and discrimination. It is especially difficult for men in poorer areas of China to find wives because even if they are able to put together a large sum for buying a bride, local women prefer to marry into a richer region. The desperation to find wives in China has already led to a situation in which some people resort to buying women from kidnappers.

CONCLUSIONS

China, South Korea and Northern India have commonalities in their kinship systems, which make for discrimination against female children. The extent to which this discrimination is manifested increased during periods of war, famine and fertility decline. Of the three countries, India has had the quietest history during the period under consideration, followed by South Korea, with one period of massive disruption during the Korean War, which led to a rise in discrimination. China has experienced the most crises: during the first half of this century, civil war and invasion in China led to an enormous amount of disruption, followed more recently by the famine of 1959–61. These events are reflected in sharp rises in the proportion of girls 'missing' in China.

As a result, there is a sharp contrast between China and India in the history of spousal availability. In China there has been a surplus of men in the marriage market throughout this period. The extent of discrimination offsets the expected tendency to have a surplus of women when men are marrying into younger cohorts which are larger than their own because of improvements in child survival. With its quieter history, India has conformed more to the expected pattern, shifting from a surplus of men to a surplus of women with the advent of steady mortality decline. These demographic shifts seem to have affected marriage payments in these countries.

Our findings are consistent with Caldwell et al.'s (1983) hypothesis that there has been a shift from brideprice to dowry in India because of a shift to a surplus of women. Alternative ways of resolving this imbalance, for example by having women remain unmarried or marry significantly younger men, were not culturally acceptable. We extend this argument to hypothesize that brideprice continues to be practised in China because of the continuing shortage of women.

There are a number of other social implications of demographic shifts during this century. It is likely that the reduction in the average age gap between spouses in all three countries during this period is at least partly a response to the marriage squeeze, as this reduces imbalances in spousal availability. Ceteris paribus, this should make for greater equality of power between spouses in these societies. There are also implications for the survival of different strata of the population: when there is a shortage of women, it is typically the poor who do not marry, as richer men make more attractive spouses. To some extent, this arises out of conscious household strategy: when times are hard for a household, younger sons may be required to remain single in order to conserve family resources.

In the societies we have examined here, which are characterized by strong son preference, fertility decline has made for a surplus of men not only because it leads to shrinking cohort sizes but also because it has led to increased discrimination against girls. China and South Korea will soon experience the maximum shortage of women in the marriage market, with substantial proportions of men unable to find a wife. In the case of India, the surplus of women will soon be replaced by a surplus of men. We hypothesize that as a consequence dowry inflation will taper off, along with dowry violence and some other aspects of ill-treatment of women. It is ironic that an increase of discrimination against girls may help reduce dowry pressures and thereby indirectly reduce the extent of violence against women.

One interesting question is whether the situation of women is improved when they are in short supply. Clearly being in substantial surplus is the worst scenario for women, in terms of the suffering of the great majority of women. Having to pay dowries makes parents less willing to have daughters, and husbands more prone to dowry-related harassment and violence. Moreover, the power imbalance between the sexes is worsened by the fact that it is easy for men to find another woman if necessary. When there was a small surplus of women in South Korea, women who were unable to fulfil obligations such as bearing sons were harassed by the possibility of their husbands taking concubines.

When women are in short supply, the daily lives of the majority of women are considerably improved because men are inclined to be more careful not to lose their wives. At the same time, a small proportion of women may be subject to new types of violence related to shortage of wives. For example in China, some women are kidnapped and sold into marriage to men desperate to obtain a wife. Even if these women succeed in escaping and returning home, there are serious obstacles to their re-integration in their earlier life whether in their husband's home or their parents' home. It seems that although the *treatment* of women improves when they are in shortage, their *autonomy* can only be increased by fundamental changes in their position in the family and society. Fortunately, such changes are taking place in these societies, albeit slowly.

ACKNOWLEDGEMENTS

Research was funded by the United Nations Population Fund. At the time of writing, Li Shuzhuo was a Bell Research Fellow at the Harvard University Center for Population and Development Studies; his fellowship was supported by the Ford Foundation, Beijing office, the MacArthur Foundation, the J. T. Tai and Co Foundation Inc., and the Richard Saltonstall

Population Innovation Fund. This research was presented at seminars at Harvard University, Brown University and the United Nations Population Division. The authors gratefully acknowledge comments from the seminar participants as well as from Nirmala Banerji, Judith Banister, Shelah Bloom, Mrinal Datta-Chaudhuri, Marcus Feldman, Supriya Guha, P. N. Mari Bhat, Emily MacFarquhar, Arup Maharatna, Jonathon Murdoch, Fabienne Peter and Arthur Wolf, which have been very helpful in revising this chapter.

APPENDIX ON METHODOLOGY

The Chinese censuses pose two potential problems for our analysis. The first relates to the ages of military personnel. These are not reported in the 1953 and 1964 censuses, and are listed in five-year age groups in the 1982 census and in single-year age groups in the 1990 census. This affects our analysis because most of the military personnel are male and so the estimated sex ratios are affected. Coale and Banister (1994) found a way of resolving this problem, and we have used the same approach, which we describe below. The second is the possible under-reporting of female births and very young girls in the 1982 and 1990 censuses. However, there is far less under-reporting of very young girls than of female births (Zeng et al., 1993). Since our analysis focuses on young surviving children, it may not be affected much by under-reporting.

Method of Estimating Proportions of Girls Missing

To illustrate how we used Coale and Banister's (1994) methodology to estimate the proportion of girls missing for each five-year birth cohort at census time, we show how we applied it to the data from China. First we calculated the sex ratios of each birth cohort, as they were recorded at each census (1953, 1964, 1982 and 1990). Then, following Coale and Banister's method, we adjusted for the omission of military personnel by using for cohorts aged 16–34 the highest ratio recorded in any census. The logic of this is that the sex ratios of these ages would be more accurately captured by the previous census, when these people would have been too young to join the army, or the following census, when they left the army. Differential mortality at these young ages is very low, and will have little effect on the analysis.

Thus, corresponding to each of the four censuses, we obtained sex ratio curves for each birth cohort (Figure 4). The female life expectancy used to fit the model life tables are shown in Table 4. The four curves are quite consistent because of the high quality of age-reporting. The only exceptions are the early birth cohorts, which show a difference in different censuses. This reflects the natural biological female advantage in survival, as these early birth cohorts are exposed to mortality over a long duration, so the later the census is taken, the more feminine the observed sex ratio.

In our final analysis, we used the most recent data on each birth cohort to obtain one combined observed sex ratio curve from the four censuses. Thus the 1953 census data are used for the period 1920–4 to 1948–52, the 1964 data for the period 1949–53 to 1959–63, and so on. This is easily done since the four curves are so consistent. This makes it possible to focus more on the impact of historical events on discrimination in childhood. It also minimizes the problem of model assumptions about the sex differentials in mortality over the life span.

We derived the curve of the model sex ratios in the same way, combining curves into one combined model sex ratio curve for the most recent cohorts for each five-year birth cohort at census time (Figure 4). The excess sex ratio for each five-year birth cohort at census time is derived by comparing the observed sex ratio to the model one, minus 1.0.

To estimate the excess sex ratios for the 1986–90 to 1990–4 birth cohorts in China, we used data from the 1995 One Percent National Population Survey. Since the model sex ratios are not very sensitive to small changes in life expectancy, and life expectancy was already very high in China by 1990, the model sex ratios for 1986–90 to 1990–4 birth cohorts are assumed to be the same for the 1980–4 to 1985–9 birth cohorts in the 1990 census.

Figure 4. Estimated and Model. Sex Ratios at Census Time by 5 year Birth Cohorts, 1920–1995, China

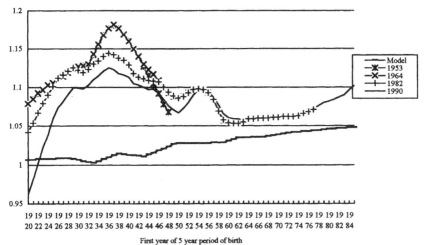

Sources: Estimated sex ratios: Calculation based on data from 1953, 1964, 1982 and 1990 Population Censuses of China, and 1995 National One Percent Sample Survey of China. See notes to Figure 1. Model sex ratios: Coale and Banister (1994).

Table 1. Singulate Mean Age at First Marriage in Population Censuses in China, South Korea and India, 1910s–90s

China				S. Korea				India			
Year	Male	Female	Gap	Year	Male	Female	Gap	Year	Male	Female	Gap
				1911	19.8	12.9	6.9				
				1925	21.1	16.6	4.5	1921	20.2	13.3	6.9
				1930	21.2	16.8	4.4	1931	19.0	12.9	6.1
				1935	21.4	17.1	4.3				
				1940	21.8	17.8	4.0				
1953			3.4*	1955	24.7	20.5	4.2	1951	20.6	15.2	5.4
				1960	25.4	21.5	3.9	1961	21.6	15.9	5.7
1964			3.1*	1966	26.7	22.9	3.8				
1970	23.1	20.4	2.7	1970	27.2	23.3	3.9	1971	22.4	17.2	5.2
1975	24.4	22.0	2.4	1975	27.4	23.6	3.8				
1980	25.0	22.9	2.1	1980	27.3	24.1	3.2	1981	23.3	18.3	5.0
1982	25.1	22.4	2.7								
1985	23.6	21.8	1.8	1985	27.8	24.8	3.0				
1990	23.8	22.1	1.7	1990	28.6	25.5	3.1	1991	24.2	20.0	4.2

Notes:
* Figures for 1953 and 1964 of China are respectively estimated from the age gap of currently married couples for cohorts born in 1925–9 and 1940–4 in the 1990 census of China. The numbers are somewhat underestimated due to the data tabulation feature.
Sources:
For China: estimates for 1953, 1964 and 1990 are based on the 1990 Population Census; for 1982 based on the 1982 Population Census, for 1970, 1975, 1980 and 1985 based on the 1988 National 2 Per Thousand Fertility and Contraceptive Survey.
For Korea: 1925–70 based on Kwon et al. (1975); 1975–90 based on National Statistics Office of Korea (1993).
For India: based on Bhat and Halli (1996).

Table 2. Observed Ratios of Males to Younger Females by Five-Year Male Birth Cohort, China, South Korea, India, 1920–89

Male birth cohorts	China	S. Korea	India
1920–4	1.01		0.87
1925–9	1.00		0.91
1930–4	1.07		0.93
1935–9	1.15	0.99	0.92
1940–4	1.05	0.92	0.89
1945–9	0.97	0.96	0.88
1950–4	1.03	0.79	0.91
1955–9	1.23	1.01	0.91
1960–4	0.89	1.05	0.94
1965–9	1.04	1.03	0.98
1970–4	1.17	1.16	0.97
1975–9	1.07	1.02	0.99
1980–4	1.03	1.25	1.06
1985–9	1.12[a]	1.07[b]	

Notes:
[a] Calculation based on data from the 1990 Population Census and Annual Population Change Surveys in China.
[b] Calculation based on Vital Statistics in South Korea.
Source: Computed from Population Censuses of China, S. Korea, and India.

Table 3. The Breakdown of the Ratios of Males to Younger Females by Five-Year Male Birth Cohort, China, South Korea, India, 1960–89

Male birth cohorts	China			S. Korea			India		
	Obser.	Normal	Dif.	Obser.	Normal	Dif.	Obser.	Normal	Dif.
1960–4	0.89	0.86	0.03	1.05	1.05	0.01	0.94	0.95	0.00
1965–9	1.04	1.02	0.02	1.03	1.01	0.02	0.98	0.93	0.05
1970–4	1.17	1.14	0.03	1.16	1.15	0.01	0.97	0.90	0.08
1975–9	1.07	1.04	0.03	1.02	1.00	0.02	0.99	0.94	0.05
1980–4	1.03	0.99	0.04	1.25	1.19	0.06	1.06	1.05	0.01
1985–9*	1.12	1.05	0.07	1.07	1.00	0.07			

Note:
* Figures for 1985–9 are based on data from the 1990 Population Census and Annual Population Change Surveys in China and Vital Statistics in South Korea.
Source:
Computed from Population Censuses of China, South Korea and India.

Table 4. Estimated Female Life Expectancy at Birth in China, South Korea
and India

Year	China	S. Korea	India
1900s	25.0	25.0*	25.0*
1910s	25.0	30.0*	25.0*
1920s	25.0	35.0	30.0
1930s	25.0	40.0	30.0
1940s	32.5	45.0	32.0
1950s	45.0	50.0	37.0
1960s	52.5	55.0	45.3
1970s	62.5	68.0	52.0
1980s	70.0	72.0	57.0

Note:
* Since the estimates are not available for South Korea and India before 1920, we assume these figures for these two decades.
Sources:
For China: Coale and Banister (1994).
For South Korea: Kwon (1977); National Statistics Office of Korea (1993).
For India: Bhat (1989); Registrar General of India (1985, 1995).

REFERENCES

Arensberg, Conrad and S. T. Kimball (1968) *Family and Community in Ireland*. (2nd edn) Cambridge, MA: Harvard University Press.

Bae Hwa-Ok (1997) 'Report on Field Interviews in Rural and Urban Korea, 1996', prepared for the workshop on Son Preference in China, South Korea and India, Harvard University, Cambridge, MA (February).

Bhat, P. N. Mari (1989) 'Mortality and Fertility in India 1881–1961: A Reassessment', in Tim Dyson (ed.) *India's Historical Demography*, pp. 73–118. London: Curzon Press.

Bhat, P. N. Mari and S. Halli Shiva (1996) 'Demographic Perspectives on Marriage Transactions in India'. New Delhi (mimeo).

Bianco, Lucien (1967) *Origins of the Chinese Revolution 1915–49*. Stanford, CA: Stanford University Press.

Billig, Michael (1992) 'The Marriage Squeeze and the Rise of Groomprice in India's Kerala State', *Journal of Comparative Family Studies* 23(2): 197–216.

Buck, Pearl S. (1931) *The Good Earth*. New York: The John Day Company.

Caldwell, John C., P. H. Reddy and Pat Caldwell (1983) 'The Causes of Marriage Change in South India', *Population Studies* 37(3): 343–61.

Chang, Hyun-Seob (1991) Unpublished PhD dissertation on the family in Korea, Cambridge University.

Chi, Hsi-Sheng (1976) *Warlord Politics in China 1916–28*. Stanford, CA: Stanford University Press.

Chowdhury, Prem (1994) *The Veiled Woman: Shifting Gender Equations in Rural Haryana 1880–1990*. Delhi: Oxford University Press.

Chung, Cha-whan (1977) *Change and Continuity in an Urbanizing Society: Family and Kinship in Urban Korea*. PhD thesis, University of Hawaii.

Coale, Ansley and Judith Banister (1994) 'Five Decades of Missing Females in China', *Demography* 31(3): 459–80.

Coale, Ansley and P. Demeny (1966) *Regional Model Life Tables and Stable Populations.* Princeton, NJ: Princeton University Press.

Cohen, Myron (1976) *House United, House Divided: The Chinese Family in Taiwan.* New York: Columbia University Press.

Croll, Elisabeth J. (1983) *Chinese Women since Mao.* London: Zed Books.

Cumings, Bruce (1981) *The Origins of the Korean War.* Princeton, NJ: Princeton University Press.

Das Gupta, Monica (1987) 'Selective Discrimination against Female Children in Rural Punjab, India', *Population and Development Review* 13(1): 77–100.

Das Gupta, Monica (1995a) 'Fertility Decline in Punjab, India: Parallels with Historical Europe', *Population Studies* 49(3): 481–500.

Das Gupta, Monica (1995b) 'Lifecourse Perspectives on Women's Autonomy and Health Outcomes', *American Anthropologist* 97(3): 481–91.

Das Gupta, Monica and P. N. Mari Bhat (1995) 'Fertility Decline and Increased Manifestation of Sex Bias in India', *Population Studies* 51(3): 307–15.

Das Gupta, Monica, Jiang Zhenghua, Xie Zhenming, Li Bohua, Nam-Hoon Cho, Woojin Chung and P. N. Mari Bhat (1997) 'Gender Bias in China, South Korea and India: Causes and Policy Implications', Report submitted to the United Nations Population Fund.

Davis, Deborah and Stevan Harrell (eds) (1993) *Chinese Families in the Post-Mao Era.* Berkeley, CA: University of California Press.

Department of Population Statistics, State Statistical Bureau, China (1985) *1982 Population Census of China.* Beijing: China Statistical Press.

Department of Population Statistics, State Statistical Bureau, China (1988) *China Population Yearbook 1988.* Beijing: China Statistical Press.

Department of Population Statistics, State Statistical Bureau, China (1993) *Tabulation of the 1990 Population Census of China.* Beijing: China Statistical Press.

Department of Population Statistics, State Statistical Bureau, China (1997) *Tabulation of the 1995 National One Percent Sample Survey.* Beijing: China Statistical Press.

Dyson, Tim and Mick Moore (1983) 'On Kinship Structure, Female Autonomy and Demographic Behavior in India', *Population and Development Review* 9(1): 35–60.

Economic Planning Board of Korea (1960) *Population and Housing Census, 1960.* Seoul: Economic Planning Board.

Economic Planning Board of Korea (1970) *Population and Housing Census, 1970.* Seoul: Economic Planning Board.

Epstein, T. Scarlett (1973) *South India: Yesterday, Today and Tomorrow.* London: Macmillan Press.

Freedman, Maurice (1965) *Lineage Organization in Southeastern China.* London: Athlone Press; New York: Humanities Press.

Gates, Hill (1996) *China's Motor: A Thousand Years of Petty Capitalism.* Ithaca, NY: Cornell University Press.

Goody, Jack (1990) *The Oriental, the Ancient and the Primitive: Systems of Marriage and the Family in the Pre-industrial Societies of Eurasia.* Cambridge: Cambridge University Press.

Government of India (1931) *Census of India, 1931.* New Delhi: Office of the Registrar-General of India.

Greenhalgh, Susan (1994) 'The Social Dynamics of Child Mortality in Village Shaanxi'. The Population Council Research Division Working Papers No. 66. New York: The Population Council.

Guttentag, Marcia and Paul F. Secord (1983) *Too Many Women? The Sex Ratio Question.* London: Sage Publicatons.

Han Woo-keun (1970) *The History of Korea.* Honolulu, HI: East-West Center.

Hastings, Max (1987) *The Korean War.* New York: Simon and Schuster.

Hershman, Paul (1981) *Punjabi Kinship and Marriage.* Delhi: Hindustan Publishing Corporation.

Heyer, Judith (1992) 'The Role of Dowries and Daughters' Marriages in the Accumulation and Distribution of Capital in a South Indian Community', *Journal of International Development* 4(4): 419–36.

Hsu, Francis (1948) *Under the Ancestors' Shadow*. New York: Columbia University Press.

Hu, Hsien-chin (1948) *The Common Descent Group in China and its Functions*. New York: Viking Fund.

Kapadia, Karin (1993) 'Marrying Money: Changing Preference and Practice in Tamil Marriage', *Contributions to Indian Sociology* 27(1): 25–51.

Karve, Irawati (1965) *Kinship Organization in India*. Bombay: Asia Publishing House.

Kendall, Laurel (1996) *Getting Married in Korea: Of Gender, Morality and Modernity*. Berkeley, CA: University of California Press.

Kim, Choong Soon (1988) *Faithful Endurance: An Ethnography of Korean Family Dispersal*. Tucson, AZ: University of Arizona Press.

Kim, Mo-Ran (1995) 'A Study of Marital Transaction in Korea', *Korean Journal of Sociology* 29(3): 533–58.

Kim, Son-ung (1981) 'Population Policies in Korea', in R. Repetto et al. (eds) *Economic Development, Population Policy, and Demographic Transition in the Republic of Korea*. Cambridge, MA: Council on East Asian Studies, Harvard University.

Kolenda, Pauline (1987) *Regional Differences in Family Structure in India*. Jaipur: Rawat Publications.

Krishnaji, N. (1987) 'Poverty and Sex Ratio: Some Data and Speculations', *Economic and Political Weekly* 6 June.

Kumari, Ranjana (1989) *Brides are not for Burning: Dowry Victims in India*. New Delhi: Radiant Publishers.

Kwon, Tai-Hwan (1977) *Demography of Korea: Population Change and its Components 1925–66*. Seoul: Seoul National University Press.

Kwon, Tai-Hwan et al. (1975) *The Population of Korea*. Seoul: The Seoul National University.

Lee, Hung-Tak, and Nam-Hoon Cho (1992) 'Consequences of Fertility Decline: Social, Economic and Cultural Implications in Korea', in Korean Institute for Health and Social Affairs, *Impact of Fertility Decline on Policies and Programme Strategies*, Seoul: Korea Institute for Health and Social Affairs.

Lee, James and Cameron Campbell (1997) *Fate and Fortune in Rural China: Social Organization and Population Behavior in Liaoning, 1774–1873*. Cambridge: Cambridge University Press.

Lee, James and Wang Feng (1997) 'Malthusian Mythology and Chinese Reality: The Population History of One Quarter of Humanity, 1700–2000'. Pasadena, CA: unpublished manuscript.

Li, Jiang-hong and William Lavely (1995) 'Rural Economy and Male Marriage in China: Jurong, Jiangsu 1993', *Journal of Family History* 20(3): 289–306.

Lu Xun (1980) *Selected Works*. Beijing: Foreign Language Press.

Lu Xun (1990) *Diary of a Madman and Other Stories*. Honolulu, HI: University of Hawaii Press.

Lu Zhenglai (1994) 'Some Hints for Rural Women Working Outside', *Zhong Guo Fu Nu* August 1992 (in Chinese).

McCormack, Gavan (1977) *Chang Tso-lin in Northeast China, 1911–28: China, Japan and the Manchurian Idea*. Stanford, CA: Stanford University Press.

Miller, Barbara (1981) *The Endangered Sex: Neglect of Female Children in Rural North India*. Ithaca, NY: Cornell University Press.

Murthi, Mamta, A. Guio and J. Drèze (1995) 'Mortality, Fertility and Gender Bias in India, A District-level Analysis', *Population and Development Review* 21(4): 745–82.

Natarajan, Mangai (1995) 'Victimization of Women: A Theoretical Perspective on Dowry Deaths in India', *International Review of Victimization* 3(4): 297–308.

National Bureau of Statistics and Economic Planning Board of Korea (1980) *Population and Housing Census, 1980*. Seoul: National Bureau of Statistics.

National Bureau of Statistics and Economic Planning Board of Korea (1990) *Population and Housing Census, 1990*. Seoul: National Bureau of Statistics.

National Statistical Office of Korea (1993) *Social Indicators in Korea*. Seoul: National Statistical Office.

National Statistical Office of Korea (1995) *Annual Report on the Vital Statistics 1994*. Seoul: National Statistical Office.

Park, Chai-Bin and Nam-Hoon Cho (1995) 'Consequences of Son Preferences in a Low-fertility Society: Imbalance of the Sex Ratio at Birth in Korea', *Population and Development Review* 21(1): 59–84.

Pasternak, Burton (1972) *Kinship and Community in Two Chinese Villages*. Stanford, CA: Stanford University Press.

Pisani, Elizabeth and Basia Zaba (1995) 'Son Preference, Sex Selection and the Marriage Market', London (mimeo).

Pradhan, Mahesh C. (1966) *The Political System of the Jats of Northern India*. Bombay: Oxford University Press.

Rao, Vijayendra (1993) 'Dowry Inflation in Rural India: A Statistical Investigation', *Population Studies* 47(2): 283–93.

Registrar General of India (1985) 'Estimates of Vital Rates for the Decade 1971–81 and Analysis of the 1981 Census Data', Paper 1 of 1985. New Delhi: Office of the Registrar-General of India.

Registrar General of India (1995) 'SRS-based Abridged Life Tables 1988–92'. Occasional Paper 4 of 1995. New Delhi: Office of the Registrar-General of India.

Registrar General of India (various issues) *Sample Registration System, 1970–90*. New Delhi: Office of the Registrar-General of India.

Registrar General and Census Commissioner (various issues) *Census of India, 1951, 1961, 1971, 1981, 1991*. New Delhi: Office of the Registrar-General of India.

Report on the Census of Punjab, 1868. Lahore (1870).

Sieder, Reinhard and Michael Mitterauer (1983) 'The Reconstruction of the Family Life Course: Theoretical Problems and Empirical Results', in R. Wall et al. (eds) *Family Forms in Historic Europe*. Cambridge: Cambridge University Press.

Skinner, G William (1997) 'Family Systems and Demographic Processes', in D. I. Kertzer and T. Fricke (eds) *Anthropological Demography: Toward a New Synthesis*, pp. 53–114. Chicago, IL: University of Chicago Press.

Stockard, Janice E. (1989) *Daughters of the Canton Delta: Marriage Patterns and Economic Strategies in South China 1860–1930*. Stanford, CA: Stanford University Press.

Tan, Amy (1989) *The Joy Luck Club*. New York: Putnam's.

Tuljapurkar, Shripad, Li Nan and Marcus W. Feldman (1995) 'High Sex Ratios in China's Future', *Science* 267: 874–6.

Visaria, Pravin (1969) *The Sex Ratio of the Population of India*. Census of India 1961, Vol. 1, Monograph No. 10. New Delhi: Office of the Registrar-General of India.

Williamson, Nancy E. (1976) *Sons or Daughters?* Beverly Hills, CA: Sage Publications.

Wolf, Arthur and Chieh-shan Huang (1980) *Marriage and Adoption in China, 1845–1945*. Stanford, CA: Stanford University Press.

Wolf, Margery (1968) *The House of Lim: A Study of a Chinese Farm Family*. Englewood Cliffs, NJ: Prentice Hall.

Xie Zhenming (1997) 'Demand of Childbearing of Chinese Farmer and its Changes in Zhejiang Province, China', paper presented at the workshop on Son Preference in China, South Korea and India, Harvard University, Cambridge MA (February).

Xin Long (1989) 'The High Sex Ratio in the Modern Population of China', in *Wei Ding Gao* 8: 53–9 (in Chinese).

Yao Xinwu and Yin Hua (1994) *Basic Data of China's Population*. Beijing: China Population Press.

Yi, Kwang-Gyu (1975) *Kinship System in Korea*. New Haven, CT: Human Relations Area Files.

Zeng Yi, Tu Ping, Gu Baochang, Xu Yi, Li Bohua and Li Yongping (1993) 'Causes and Implications of the Recent Increase in the Reported Sex Ratio at Birth in China', *Population and Development Review* 19(2): 283–302.

Zhang Fu and Yin Min (1994) 'Black Hand under the Sunshine', *Min Zhu Yu Fa Zhi* November (in Chinese).

Zhang Hua and Li Xiaojin (1993) 'Rescue Action in Taihang Mountain', *Min Zhu Yu Fa Zhi* December (in Chinese).

Zhu Min Mei (1992) 'Unbalanced Sex Ratio in Rural Area is Worry for People', *Zhong Guo Fu Nu* August (in Chinese).

9

Export-Oriented Employment, Poverty and Gender: Contested Accounts

Shahra Razavi

INTRODUCTION

Alice Amsden (1994) recently remarked that not long ago the issue of labour standards in economic development was fairly straightforward. Employers and right-of-centre social scientists and economists tended to be against them; trade unions and their left-of-centre allies tended to be for them. In the final decades of the twentieth century, she suggests, the issue has become more 'murky'. Conservative views have stayed the same, but a geographical division has emerged between the South and 'neo-institutionalist' or 'internationalist' labour advocates in the North (ibid: 185).

This chapter probes the murkiness surrounding labour standards and international trade by exploring it from a gender perspective, which adds further qualifications to the debate. It will do so by looking at what neo-classical, institutionalist and feminist advocates have to say about the implications of female employment for poverty and well-being.[1] While the neo-classical approach advocates reliance on market forces (trade liberalization) to expand female employment, reduce wage discrimination by gender, and thereby alleviate female poverty, institutionalists remain deeply sceptical as to whether market forces can deliver such desirable outcomes without regulations at both the national and global levels. They identify the power relations between labour and capital as the pivot around which the terms and conditions of work will have to be negotiated and codified. It is also increasingly recognized that the social arrangements for negotiating and bargaining the conditions of work will have to incorporate the voices of hitherto excluded social groups, in particular women workers.

---

1. It should be noted at the outset that this categorization, like most others, has weaknesses. 'Institutionalism' constitutes a broad range of approaches, and overlaps extensively with the work of many feminist authors. In this chapter, following the distinction made by Meagher and Yunusa (1996), institutionalism is used to refer to the perspective that is very often associated with the ILO, which draws attention to the negative effects of deregulation and informalization, and emphasizes the need for enlightened state intervention to facilitate a positive response. The more structural-historical approaches to labour market institutions which see the state itself implicated in the informalization process (e.g. Breman, 1996) are therefore not included under this label.

As is well-known, the neo-classical approach tends to downplay the political economy of 'real markets', that is, the diverse ways in which markets are 'substantiated' through the interaction of real social groups (Hewitt de Alcantara, 1993: 3). These insights into the concrete operation of markets have contributed to the feminist analysis of liberalization, particularly in the context of industrial relocation and labour market deregulation.

However, institutionalist authors, in their preoccupation with labour market structures and hierarchies and capital/labour conflicts, have tended to overlook other sites of struggle (domestic, familial) mediating women's labour market engagement which are intimately interwoven with their experiences of work, their perceptions of its value, and the everyday politics of production. Women face the labour market as gendered subjects and the fact that their entry, withdrawal and experiences of labour market engagement, although far from homogeneous, are distinct from men's in some ways, raises important policy questions. It is argued here that neither the neo-classical advocates nor the institutionalists have dealt with the distinctiveness of women's labour market engagement in a satisfactory manner. It is also arguable that institutionalist understandings of how power operates in the labour market have not adequately explained why seemingly similar forms of industrial production play out very differently in diverse contexts. Such diversity has been grappled with much more effectively through comparative feminist research which takes workers' gendered subjectivities seriously, and which sees labour regimes as *negotiated* orders rather than as institutional reflections of capitalism's historical tendencies (Hart, 1996; Lee, 1995).

To give the chapter a point of convergence, it will be looking at women's incorporation into the export-oriented manufacturing sector. This is admittedly a narrow focus, but a pertinent one, given the kinds of issues to be explored. First, the argument, made most vehemently by neo-classical proponents, that trade liberalization can facilitate labour-intensive, pro-poor growth capable of 'including' hitherto 'excluded' social groups such as women, is one that is very often made with the female-intensive export-oriented manufacturing sector in mind. It is also a view that is widely shared across the political spectrum — some feminists included — and deserves critical reflection in the context of current debates on gender and poverty. Second, the export-oriented manufacturing sector also figures prominently in institutionalist arguments about the need for global monitoring of labour conditions, and the incorporation of a 'social clause' in the agreements on the liberalization of international trade. Within this general discourse, women workers in particular have been portrayed as a vulnerable segment of the work-force, recruited by international capital in ways that undermine existing labour standards. Finally, within the gender and development literature itself, there has been a long-running debate about the implications of labour market inclusion for women. In the context of export-oriented industrial strategies, where women have been highly visible, interpretations of women's encounter with capital have been very divided, often reflecting deep methodological and epistemological differences.

Inevitably these complexities and ambiguities are rarely reflected in the debates on international trade and labour standards given the way in which the whole issue of women's entry into export-oriented manufacturing has become — and probably, has always been — polarized. It seems important, however, to assess these issues in a more dispassionate manner. The larger and more important question that is hinted at but not pursued here is whether 'social clause' type proposals can constitute the basis for transnational feminist politics in the same way that reproductive rights issues have coalesced women's groups across national boundaries. This chapter does not pretend to offer any answers or solutions to this debate. It has a far more modest intention, namely to summarize some of the relevant literature around it, and to draw attention to some of the thorny and unresolved questions.

EXPORT-ORIENTED EMPLOYMENT, POVERTY AND GENDER: NEO-CLASSICAL ARGUMENTS AND THEIR CRITICS

The 'New Poverty Agenda'[2] has identified *labour-intensive* growth as one of the most effective means of getting people in labour-abundant countries out of situations of poverty and destitution. The reasoning behind this assertion is the oft-cited premise that labour is 'the poor's most abundant asset'. It also finds support in theories of trade which suggest that the comparative advantage of poor countries lies in their relatively abundant labour supplies.

A recent neo-classical statement on how the interlinkages between labour and poverty work, together with relevant policy prescriptions, appear in the 1995 World Development Report, *Workers in an Integrating World* (World Bank, 1995). In order to expand employment opportunities that make intensive use of labour, the further opening of national economies to international market forces — import and export trade, foreign direct investment and capital flows — is stressed. In addition, governments and interest groups are urged to refrain from introducing 'distortions' in domestic labour markets. Women in particular, it is argued, have been frequent victims of well-meaning labour market regulation, and thus stand to gain from labour market deregulation. The policy conclusion is therefore reached that workers' interests are better served if public policy creates the conditions for market-driven growth capable of generating productive employment, rather than attempting to intervene directly in the labour market.

Before we turn to labour market issues, and the way gender is explicitly tackled in that context, some general observations need to be made about the key policy prescriptions considered to be essential for creating broad-based,

---

2. The 'New Poverty Agenda' (Lipton and Maxwell, 1992) refers to the poverty-oriented policy agenda most clearly articulated by the World Bank in the *World Development Report 1990* on poverty.

labour-intensive growth, namely policies facilitating trade and financial liberalization.[3] At this level of analysis, gender issues tend to enter the discussion only marginally, and it is arguable that women as a distinct set of social actors are of secondary importance, or maybe even irrelevant, to some aspects of these debates, such as whether there should be greater regulation of global financial markets or not, or what the degree and timing of state intervention in the industrial sector should be. Implicit assumptions are nevertheless made about the relevance and the implications of the proposed policies for women, which deserve some attention.

Interpreting the East Asian 'Miracle'

A prominent theme in the neo-classical literature is that industrial protection favours inefficient capital-intensive operations, while an open trade regime, referred to as 'neutral' (World Bank, 1990: 61), favours the emergence of industrial establishments that use resources, including labour, more efficiently. It is argued that the global market frees workers from the constraints imposed by domestic demand, given the fact that global markets are not only larger than any single domestic market, 'but also generally more stable' and capable of accommodating newcomers (World Bank, 1995: 55). The 'high-performing' East Asian economies are very often cited as evidence for the hypothesis that liberalized trade can lead to wage employment growth as well as real wage increases and massive poverty reduction (World Bank, 1991; 1993).

The important questions which have been raised about both the limits of growth through export trade, and the neo-classical interpretation of the history of events in East Asia, are by now quite well-known and will not be repeated here (see Castells et al., 1990; Jomo et al., 1997; South Centre, 1996). This critique has no doubt been very useful in questioning the neo-liberal interpretation of events in East Asia, highlighting the mix of policies that were very often used, as well as the diversity of experiences across the region.[4]

---

3. The debates about financial liberalization are beyond the scope of this chapter. I take it that the Asian financial crisis of 1997–8, more than the 1980s crisis in Latin America, has questioned the wisdom of financial liberalization. Many observers, including some mainstream economists, argue that the presumed benefits of liberalized trade will crucially depend on the state of the world economy and thus see an urgent need for regulation of short-term capital flows to prevent the systemic shocks and instabilities generated by unregulated capital flows.

4. It should be noted that the much-cited World Bank publication, *The East Asian Miracle: Economic Growth and Public Policy*, acknowledges the role of industrial policy in Japan and the first-tier newly industrializing countries (NICs), but maintains that the results of industrial policy have been ambiguous, and that it is the second-tier NICs, which have not pursued explicit industrial policies, that 'may show the way for the next generation of developing economies to follow export-push strategies' (World Bank, 1993: 25).

But very often missing from these debates are the critical voices of some observers, including feminist scholars, who have expressed concern about 'the other side of growth with equity' (Greenhalgh, 1985).

Ironically, some of the most disparaging assessments of women's entry into export-oriented manufacturing were made in the context of the first-tier NICs like Hong Kong and Taiwan. While there is no doubt that incomes and wages, including women's wages, rose spectacularly over a short time, the gender gap in wages, as well as the degree of occupational segregation, in Taiwan, South Korea and Hong Kong remains large by international standards and shows little sign of diminishing over time (Joekes, 1995). These quantitative indicators, however, only tell a small part of the story.

In-depth anthropological studies carried out in the 1970s and 1980s suggested that in the East Asian societies with sizeable ethnic Chinese populations, such as Hong Kong, Taiwan and Singapore, family and kinship systems marked by strong gender and age hierarchies and emphasis on intergenerational obligations were producing a perverse 'dutiful daughters' syndrome, whereby parents took their daughters out of school early and pushed them into the labour market, while they channelled their daughters' earnings into the education of their sons (Greenhalgh, 1985; Kung, 1983; Salaff, 1990). Despite earning money, opting out of familial residential arrangements was constrained by the expectation that women remain at home until married, by the obligation to 'repay' parents and also by public housing policies by which housing was either given only to families, according to need criteria (Hong Kong), or was organized through tightly supervised dormitories (Taiwan) (Salaff, 1990). Indicative of the extent to which the East Asian family system had dampened the transformatory potential of factory work was the observation that one of the few ways in which these young women gain satisfaction is by repaying their 'debt' (of birth and upbringing) to their families (Lim, 1990).

More recent studies have begun to question the model of the patriarchal Chinese family and its associated notion of filial piety invoked in some of these earlier studies. In Shenzhen (southern China), for example, young migrant factory women take much of the initiative to enter factories, often with individualistic objectives in mind (Lee, 1995). Such evidence is useful in contesting static notions of Asian patriarchy and rigid models of the Chinese family. It also highlights the need for context-specific analyses of women's work, and the problems in applying models developed in one setting to seemingly similar cultural and kinship systems observed elsewhere. None the less, the analytical contributions of the above-mentioned anthropological studies remain significant — namely that the meanings and implications of labour market entry cannot be divorced from the context-specific kinship and familial relations that pattern the connections between work and well-being.

244   *S. Razavi*

Trade Liberalization and Feminization: Some Ambiguities

A related argument frequently made by neo-classical advocates is that import-substitution industrialization (ISI) provided jobs for a male 'labour aristocracy', whereas the types of industry that expand in response to foreign market opportunities in an open trading regime rely heavily on the use of a female work-force. It is further argued that in the long-run trade will raise aggregate incomes and wages in developing countries, and reduce the gender gap in wages. The assumption behind this assertion seems to be that in a trade-expansionary context the demand for female labour increases faster than for male labour, so that female wages also rise faster than male wages, and eventually converge (Joekes, 1995).

As was noted above, the import substitution/export promotion dichotomy is somewhat misleading. Most of the successful industrializing economies of East Asia practised both policies, systematically and simultaneously. Even in Southeast Asia, where it is claimed there has been no explicit industrial policy, the Thai government has probably come close to the Japanese and South Korean strategy of linking effective protection to export promotion (Jomo et al., 1997). Similarly many Latin American countries also began early to explore ways of generating foreign exchange in pockets of non-traditional export production without changing their generally protectionist policy stance. It is therefore important, from a policy point of view, not to see these two options as mutually exclusive.

This important qualification notwithstanding, there is some empirical evidence which suggests that export promotion and trade liberalization policies, *where successful*, lead to the feminization of the labour force.[5] The relationship between export-oriented industrialization and feminization is particularly strong for economies specializing in commodities that require low skill content and labour-intensive methods of production. The crucial point, however, is that the phenomenon of female-led and export-led growth has been geographically patchy as well as being highly volatile (Pearson, 1998). Even in Asia and Latin America — the epicentre of this genre of manufacturing — export-oriented and female-intensive firms have gained a foothold only in some countries, while complex political and economic factors have precluded their emergence in most parts of sub-Saharan Africa and the Middle East.

Moreover, where the workforce is feminized, it would be wrong to see this as an irreversible and sustainable process. The emergence of new low cost competitors in the Asia-Pacific region and the erosion of Hong Kong's own cost advantage caused growth in manufacturing industries to slacken and eventually decline in the late 1980s, matched by a wave of outward

---

5. See Cagatay and Ozler (1995); Joekes (1995); Joekes and Weston (1994); and Standing (1989).

investment to countries with lower wage costs (such as southern China). The implications for manufacturing employment, and especially for the women who have made up the majority of the rank-and-file workers, it is argued, have been serious and more complex than the 'frictionless' picture painted by the government and by many economists (Chiu and Lee, 1997). Micro-level studies provide an account of the 'fading of the Hong Kong dream' which has 'pushed working class women down the class ladder and backward to domesticity as their gender destiny' (ibid: 759).

There is also some evidence to suggest that technological and skill upgrading of export products, especially multi-skilling of flexible labour engaged in high-performance production, can lead to a process of de-feminization of manufacturing labour, since women seem to be dis-advantaged in the processes of production which are capital-intensive and which rely on skilled labour.[6] The fall in the share of women in the manufacturing labour force of Mexico's export border zone (*maquiladora*) between 1982 and 1985 was attributed to product diversification, elimination of low-skill operators' jobs held by women, the need for higher levels of training as well as trends towards certification, and experiments with new work schedules (Beneria, 1995; Pearson, 1991a).

In addition to the patchiness and volatility of women's participation in the manufacturing labour force, questions have also been raised about the causes, implications and meanings of labour market inclusion for the women concerned. In some contexts, such as in Mexico during the 1980s, the income distributive aspects of structural adjustment policies have been associated with falling wages (especially urban wages) and rising urban poverty. It has been argued that these income distributive effects have in turn 'pushed' women into both formal and informal sector employment, representing a distress sale of labour, with women's wages barely making up some of the shortfall from declining male wages and social sector cut-backs. Commenting on this situation, Gonzalez de la Rocha (1998: 25) argues that 'where men are losing their capacity to perform their socially assigned role as providers and women are emerging as the new "bread-winners", receiving very low wages, it is difficult to talk about a development model "for the girls" '.

Moreover, what lies behind the *demand* for female labour, seems to be its docility and 'cheapness' — notions which have been deconstructed by several writers to show that they are not simply a question of absolute wage relativities, but also include working conditions, employers' contribution to the social wage, and the manual dexterity and patience of the work force to perform highly repetitive and tedious tasks with little formal training, as well as non-militancy and acquiescence given the lack of more attractive employ-ment options (Pearson, 1998).

---

6. See Elson (1996) for evidence of such reversals in some developed countries (e.g. elec-tronics plants in the Republic of Ireland and Scotland, and textile manufacturing in the United Kingdom).

Trade Liberalization and Feminization: Wages and Wage Gaps by Gender

Even though most writers agree that discriminatory forces underpin women's emergence as the preferred labour force in a significant part of the labour-intensive manufacturing sector, there is not a clear consensus as to whether the discriminatory forces which characterize women's employment here need to be assessed in relative (national) or absolute (universal) terms, and what space, if any, should be given to the accounts and views of women workers themselves. Here the debate touches on a number of thorny methodological issues.

Both Lim (1990) and Joekes (1995), for example, take a relativist position and criticize some strands of the feminist literature for assessing the terms of women's employment in export-oriented manufacturing from an absolutist perspective. The evidence they and others cite with regard to women's earnings in factory jobs indicates that compared to alternative low-skilled female occupations — such as farm labour, domestic work, small-scale local industry and service sector activities — these factory jobs are certainly better paid.

However, an assessment of this question, Joekes (1995) adds, would also have to include some comparison of wage rates in export-oriented manufacturing with wages in the rest of the manufacturing sector, the evidence for which is not available. Taking the EPZs and TNCs (for which there is more evidence) as a proxy for export-oriented manufacturing, Joekes is able to sketch a picture that is very mixed both across countries and over time: in many cases EPZs pay higher wages than in the surrounding national economy, but in others (India and Mauritius) the wages they pay are definitely lower (Joekes, 1995: 27). Assessing the linkages between export-oriented manufacturing and gender discrimination in wages is even more problematic. The availability, reliability and interpretability of the data on pay relativities by gender pose major problems, especially if a comparison between export and non-export sectors is attempted. In some cases the gender gap in wages appears to be smaller in export-oriented industries, while in other cases the opposite seems to hold.

There are two problems, in particular, that make the interpretation of the data difficult. First, the very high share of women in certain export-oriented industries renders direct comparisons of pay relativities (or wage discrimination) between export and non-export sectors problematic, and sometimes meaningless. If with industrial diversification women become increasingly confined to a narrow range of occupations, a dual (male/female) wage structure may gradually emerge. It is imperative, therefore, that the issue of gender discrimination be raised in a broader sense (including some comparison of conditions of work, health risks, opportunities for training and skill acquisition). Second, even if the level of wage discrimination is lower in the export-oriented sectors, the result will look less benign if it signifies that men who work in feminized industries fare badly compared to other male workers. In other words, in these export-oriented feminized sectors the entire wage structure may be dragged down. This seems to be the case in Bangladesh, for example, where wage levels in the garments industries are generally lower than those in the rest of the manufacturing sector due to the absence of collective bargaining arrangements and social mechanisms for the enforcement of the national minimum wage (Bhattacharya and Rahman, 1998).

One piece of research, frequently cited in the neo-classical literature, is by Tzannatos (1995). It asserts a positive correlation between trade liberalization and reduced gender wage gap, based on wage data for Côte d'Ivoire, Brazil, Colombia, Philippines, Thailand and Indonesia. Leaving aside issues of statistical coverage and reliability, it is difficult to attribute the apparent closing of the gap in wages in these six countries to trade liberalization *per se*; the analysis, for example, does not take into account the rise in women's educational attainment relative to men's over the same period (Joekes, 1995). Evidence presented by Joekes (ibid: 30–1) for a number of other countries reveals no systematic divergence or convergence over time.

The other major problem with some of the evidence on wage convergence (including the study by Tzannatos) is that it does not make a distinction between convergence of male and female wages through a process of 'harmonizing up' and 'harmonizing down' (Elson, forthcoming). In other words, is the gender gap in wages narrowing because women's wages are catching up with men's, or is it rather because men's wages are being levelled down? In some contexts, such as in Singapore during the late 1970s, successful export-oriented industrialization did create a tight labour market for both men and women, and women's wages in particular did rise somewhat faster than men's. But as Pasuk Phongpaichit (1988) rightly argues, Singapore's population is small and hence its experience somewhat different from that of many Asian countries which rely on migrant labour from a much wider rural hinterland. In Bangladesh, for example, the availability of a generally elastic supply of unskilled female labour has meant that wage increases in the garments manufacturing sector have been more or less the same as wage increases across a wide range of other sectors, despite a substantial rise in garments manufacturing profit margins and real value added over the same period (Bhattacharya and Rahman, 1998).[7]

Do wages and wage relativities sufficiently capture the different nature of livelihoods and capabilities in the two contexts? A simple indication of the limitations of such comparisons is the non-trivial qualification that where factory jobs are far away from workers' homes a significant proportion of their wages is eaten up by transportation costs (see, for example, Hart, 1995 on South Africa; Dunn, 1996 on Dominican Republic and Jamaica) — a cost that is not relevant for women working in family-based farms and

---

7. Even the small rise in wages in the garments industry, the authors note, may have been eroded by the demand for longer working hours.

enterprises. More importantly, women workers now encounter new and serious issues around safety of transport which require novel solutions, and which are indicative of the qualitative changes in their life circumstances.

The difficulties of making meaningful comparisons between export-oriented manufacturing and the rest of the manufacturing sector also become apparent when we turn to those conditions of work which impact on workers' health and well-being. Here there is some agreement across the political spectrum that physical working conditions — in terms of levels of heat, dust, noise and hygiene — are probably much better in the export-oriented factories than in the informal sector (Edgren, 1982; Joekes, 1995; Lim, 1990). But this favourable assessment needs to be tempered with other compelling evidence which shows the deleterious health hazards — both physical and mental — of working in some of these industries. This is very often due to the use of carcinogenic substances, the long working hours, and also the nature of the work which is repetitive, monotonous and fast, leaving the young workers prematurely 'burnt out' or 'used up' in the labour process (Edgren, 1982; Heyzer and Kean, 1988; Lee, 1995).[8]

The debate on the de-skilling or up-grading effects of modern technology continues, but one of the trends that seems to be supported by the available evidence is that of skill polarization (Standing, 1989). The educational qualifications of the female work-force in the export-oriented manufacturing sector vary widely from country to country, over time and across industries.[9] It is generally agreed, however, that women workers occupy the lower rungs in both garments and electronics manufacturing even though, in terms of education, they may not be disadvantaged compared to their male counter-parts.[10] Women are very often recruited as unskilled workers (usually as apprentices to begin with), given very little training and face limited promotion prospects. As a result they very often practice 'job hopping' from one firm to another as a way of improving their grade and earnings (Bourqia, 1996; Edgren, 1982; Kibria, 1998).

---

8. In the case of new technology clerical work (e.g. data entry), while there is an extensive literature on health hazards for developed countries, documenting muscular-skeletal disorders, eyesight injuries, stress and fatigue, skin complaints and reproductive hazards, very little research has been undertaken to monitor the health implications of working with new technology in developing countries (Pearson, 1991b).

9. The following statement is quite indicative, 'I have seen similar tasks in multinational electronics factories being performed by primary school dropouts in Singapore, where labour is scarce, and by high school graduates and even part-time college students in the Philippines, where unemployment rates are high' (Lim, 1990: 107). Within the same country, the education level tends to be higher in the electronic industries compared to the clothing/garments industries.

10. Detailed analyses of Moroccan employment and wage data, for example, suggest that there is strong selectivity in participation by educational level. The female urban labour force in Morocco is on average better educated than the male, despite a significant gender gap in education even in urban areas (Belghazi, 1996).

Doing low-skill, repetitive and monotonous work under tightly controlled conditions can generate feelings of alienation and monotony, as well as having deleterious affects on the workers' health and well-being, as was already noted. It also raises important questions about their fate in the process of industrial diversification and technological up-grading. Elson (1996) makes a useful point in this connection. She argues that organizations of and for women workers should be concerned with 'enhancing the skills and education of those workers, so that if workers lose their jobs, they have acquired something of permanence — more self-confidence, more organisational and advocacy skills, more knowledge of how their society works' (ibid: 50). The comments of one Malaysian woman worker (from an electronics factory) who was retrenched during the 1985 recession captures the problem succinctly:

> After eleven years of working, I realize that I have learnt nothing that is of any use to me. The government has told me to find another job, not to be choosy. How can I be choosy? I have nothing anyone wants. (cited in Lochead, 1988: 288).

To sum up, even though gender issues are not extensively explored in the discussion of trade liberalization and macro-policy prescriptions, the overall thrust of the argument seems to be that trade liberalization will deliver considerable benefits to women — both in terms of the sheer quantity of employment it can offer them and also in terms of employment conditions (reducing gender wage discrimination). A contextualized analysis of feminization, I have argued, provides a more qualified picture, mapping both the *uneven* 'gendered landscape of the new international division of labour'[11] across time and place, as well as the *contradictory* implications of 'inclusion' for those specific groups of women who have been incorporated into these new forms of work — a theme that will be pursued further in our discussion of institutionalist approaches.

Labour Market Interventions

The neo-classical conviction regarding the unmitigated benefits of trade liberalization is further underpinned by their views on labour market policies. It is argued that in heavily regulated labour markets women have frequently lost out as a result of 'paternalistic' labour standards. They thus stand to gain from a less interventionist labour market policy.

As is well-known, neo-classical advocates generally view labour standards as impediments to labour market clearing. 'Excessive labour standards' increase labour costs, cause unemployment and allocative inefficiency, jeopardize growth and drive a wedge between protected and unprotected

---

11. This phrase is borrowed from Pearson (1998).

workers, benefiting protected workers at the expense of the unprotected. Women workers, in particular, are very often seen as the victims of regulation. Regulations that are paternalistic — such as those which prevent women from working in 'dangerous' occupations or at night — tend to reduce the demand for women workers (World Bank, 1995: 44). Given this trade-off between labour standards and employment, in order to maintain their jobs workers are advised to forego standards and act with maximum flexibility.

To what extent do these allegations stand up to empirical scrutiny, and do they justify the policy conclusions that are drawn? While it is true that some forms of *protective* legislation can be inimical to women workers' interests, as the long-running feminist debate on the subject has recognized, the above statements provide a somewhat selective representation of the nature and the process of labour market regulation for women. Some of the earliest ILO conventions, such as the Night Work (Women) Convention, 1919 (No. 4) reflected the approach that is criticized by the World Bank report. But in response to pressure from the feminist equal rights lobbyists (both inside and outside the organization) since the 1930s, these conventions have been revised to ensure that protective legislation did not diminish women's employment opportunities. In the post-war years, standard-setting activities in the area of equal rights continued. National legislation in some countries may not have changed in line with this new approach, but it seems unreasonable to restrict the policy options in this area to either paternalistic regulations or no regulations at all. There is another policy option, along the lines of equal rights followed by the ILO, which in *some* contexts women's organizations and trade unions *may* be able to pursue.

The neo-classical proponents also argue that maternity leave and other special benefits for women typically require employers to bear the cost, effectively increasing the cost of hiring women workers, and thereby depressing their wages or discouraging their employment. The World Bank report admits that one way of providing women workers with special benefits without reducing their wages or hurting their employment is for these special benefits to be financed through general taxation and not be wholly borne by individual employers. However, due to the practical impediments — 'administrative difficulties and the risk of abuse' — the final verdict of the report is that women in low income countries will be better off without such benefits (World Bank, 1995: 74).[12]

Again, it has been recognized for some time now that legislation that grants generous maternity benefits to women can work against the interests of the very women it seeks to protect, especially when such benefits are financed mainly by the employer (Bullock, 1994; Hensman, 1988). Precisely

---

12. Administrative difficulties and risks of abuse do not seem to dampen the current enthusiasm for targeted welfare schemes and social safety nets.

for this reason the relevant ILO convention sets out the principle that maternity pay or benefits must be provided through a social security scheme or government funds, so that employers are not individually liable. It needs to be acknowledged that social security schemes may be underdeveloped or overstretched in many countries, so that the employer ends up paying for maternity provisions. It also needs to be recognized that access to public funds is a political, rather than a legal or technical, affair. In *some* contexts women's organizations and trade unions may be able to explore alternative policy options, such as new forms of shared cost or social insurance systems, rather than abandoning maternity provisions altogether. In Burkino Faso, for example, the unions on the tripartite governing body of the social security department have secured an agreement that working mothers will be covered by social security during their three months' leave, to redress employers' reluctance to hire young women (Cissé, cited in Bullock, 1994). Provisions such as these are unlikely to be applied in a uniform manner, given the weak bargaining power of many women workers, the rigid opposition by employers against regulatory measures, and the social identity of decision-makers and bureaucrats at all levels of the public administration down to the labour inspectors. But they provide at least a resource that some women's organizations may be able to use to facilitate women's labour market engagement on fairer terms.

In order to highlight the undesirable outcomes of labour market regulation, the charge of labour market dualism is emphasized at great length in the neo-classical literature. The efforts to regulate labour markets and provide citizens with social and economic rights have been feeble in many, if not most, Southern countries. The provision of permanent, full-time jobs with pension rights and other benefits was never extended beyond a small portion of the working population — mainly urban and mainly male. However, the extent to which such dualisms actually exist in the 1990s is questionable given the extensive casualization of employment practices which has taken place across both public and private sectors in many Southern countries.[13] So the labour market problem that the neo-classical literature identifies as the most central may be less serious today than it was fifteen years ago. Moreover, this has happened by dismantling workers' rights (male workers in particular) and 'levelling down' the labour process to the conditions that have been hitherto associated with the informal sector.

However, to demonstrate the redundancy of labour market regulations and the self-optimizing potential of markets, an idealized picture of the informal sector is painted. According to the World Bank report, 'ties of solidarity', 'social customs' and 'tradition' ensure a fair and tolerable

---

13. See Amsden and van der Hoeven (1996) on the rates of real decline in manufacturing wages in the 1980s; likewise they argue that it is no longer warranted to consider the formal manufacturing work-force as a labour aristocracy.

livelihood for workers in the informal sector which includes 'an element of insurance and risk sharing'; it is common for 'employers to provide loans to workers who face unexpected expenses, or to support older workers or those unable to work for health reasons' (World Bank, 1995: 87).

These arguments bear little relation to the everyday life in the unorganized sector as it is reflected in well-researched anthropological writings on the subject. Such notions of 'fairness' are rarely part of the labour market conditions in the unorganized sector. 'If they were ever practised so widely and generously', Breman (1996: 13) observes, 'they are certainly now out of date'. The informal economy is heavily screened with gender, class, caste and ethnicity, and the members of bottom castes and classes, and women, find it difficult to get access to informal sector jobs which are better-paid, higher-skilled and more regular because they lack the relevant skills, capital, access to state resources and connections. In some instances powerful agents construct and maintain the boundaries between different segments of the labour market, or occupational niches, using a wide range of exclusionary tactics (Breman, 1996; Meagher and Yunusa, 1996).

At the same time, it needs to be recognized that to be 'excluded' from the more permanent and secure labour market niches may also carry some advantages, giving the worker greater independence, autonomy and space for resistance. Hart's (1991) research on agrarian change in the Muda region of Malaysia, for example, documents that women casual labourers who are excluded from political patronage relations and whose material circum-stances are increasingly precarious, are nevertheless more capable than male workers of asserting their identities and interests as workers. She attributes women's greater militancy in this context to their exclusion from patronage relations, while poor men are caught up in relations of deference and dependence. Some workers may even exclude themselves from permanent contracts that carry deeper meanings of deference, and may choose casual employment which is freer. Breman (1996: 238) shows the landless Halpati women and men of south Gujarat grasping every opportunity to escape permanent employment with a landowner belonging to the dominant Anavil Brahmin caste.

> They choose the more risky but freer life of a day worker ... Away from the village and from agriculture they earn a few extra rupees, mostly countered by greater effort besides the longer journey and work times. Their motivation for migrating is the anonymity which accompanies them in the outside world ... they are certainly treated there as commodities, but at least they are not immediately identified and stigmatized.

This does not deny the exploitative nature of the casual labour contracts that these lower caste men and women enter into, nor does it confirm the idealized picture of the informal sector depicted above. But it does highlight the complex motivations that underpin workers' choices (albeit constrained choices) and the *trade-offs* they sometimes have to make between economic security, on the one hand, and independence and dignity, on the other. The theme of trade-offs is a recurring one in this chapter. As we will see later, young women entering the export-oriented manufacturing sector make other kinds of painful trade-offs: between intense supervision in the factories, on the one hand, and relative freedom (from parental supervision) and autonomy in their personal lives, on the other.

In rejecting labour market dualism as harmful, neo-classical advocates throw out the baby with the bathwater, wilfully ignoring another policy option, that is, the gradual extension of security and protection to the huge work-force adrift in the rural and urban informal sector economy (Breman, 1996). This may be particularly important from the point of view of many women, given the greater flexibility and independence that homeworking types of arrangement may give them in carrying out their reproductive responsibilities, and maintaining their social networks. The neo-classical approach advocates relying on market forces to bring about improvements in labour conditions. They argue that such improvements follow from growth or come about as a result of increased demand for labour standards by consumers or by growth in productivity. In the long run, outward orientation and the resulting high growth rates translate into increasing wages and better working conditions. The argument thus comes full circle: to increase employment and wages, and reduce poverty and gender inequality, economies need to become outwardly-oriented and governments and unions need to refrain from interfering in the labour market — as in the East Asian 'miracle' economies.

THE INSTITUTIONALIST PERSPECTIVE ON LABOUR MARKETS, LABOUR STANDARDS AND GENDER

Quite a different understanding of markets underpins the institutionalist perspective, which is itself far from monolithic. At the risk of simplifying what is a very diverse literature, some of its key features will be outlined here.

Rooted in a political economy approach, institutionalists highlight the unequal market power of employers and workers, and the subordination of labour to capital in the process of production. They advocate a variety of social compacts or corporatist arrangements to manage socio-economic conflicts, and to facilitate bargaining and compromise over key issues that affect the performance of the macro-economy, the livelihoods of workers, and the process of industrial accumulation.[14] To reduce labour-related insecurity and unemployment, the proponents of this approach advocate

---

14. While there is a wide variety of corporatist models, spanning both developed and developing countries, the most well-known are the corporatist regimes of Western Europe. They evolved in a context of what has been called a 'historic class compromise' for balancing the conflicting interests of capital, labour and the state. See Bangura (1997) for a useful summary of the literature and references.

macro-economic frameworks that are expansionary and employment-creating, coupled with an institutional structure that focuses on the promotion of labour process security. Keynesian economic theory provides the intellectual underpinning of the institutionalist project.

Trade Unionism and Gender Bias

As far as gender equality is concerned, the institutionalist record is somewhat mixed (Cagatay, 1996). On the one hand, the gender biases which were historically embedded in some labour standards were at times the direct outcome of trade union strategies which systematically excluded women's voices. As feminist scholars have argued, in industrialized countries, various forms of protective legislation, restrictions on child labour, and the demands of unions concerning the 'family wage' in the nineteenth century helped create the gender-based division of labour between women's unpaid domestic labour and largely men's paid labour activities (Hartmann, 1979). On the other hand, there is also evidence from different contexts for the post-war period suggesting that in industries or firms that are unionized the gender gap in wages tends to be narrower compared to non-unionized sectors (Standing, 1992). Cross-country studies for industrialized economies also suggest that in countries with more centralized wage bargaining systems, the gender earnings gap is lower compared to those with more decentralized bargaining systems (Howes and Singh, 1995).

More recently, changes in patterns of production in some of these countries, which have involved greater labour flexibility through outwork and homework, and the disastrous decline in union membership drawn from large workplaces, have further catalysed union responsiveness to women members (Tate, 1994). At the same time the issue of homework has also been re-examined. In some cases, such as in Australia and Canada, women trade unionists have been able to work from within mainstream trade union organizations — in the clothing sector, for example — to reach home-workers and even to organize them in response to structural changes in that sector (ibid).

At the analytical level, the reality of women's extensive entry into the labour force, the erosion of the male breadwinner/female homemaker model and the questioning of women's wages as 'pin money' have been assimilated, although unevenly, into a wide range of institutionalist writings (for example, Gore, 1994; Howes and Singh, 1995). However, some critics would argue, as both Fraser (1997) and Jackson (1998) have done, that the emphasis on labour-based exclusions as the source of social exclusion and poverty, which is central to both European social policy thinking and institutionalist approaches to the labour market, has a problematic gender sub-text. It assumes autonomy and 'breadwinning' as unproblematized requirements of a universal 'worker' whereas 'livelihoods for women need to

be seen as including a legitimate reliance on men (and the state) for compensation for reproductive labour' (Jackson, 1998: 26). These authors
highlight the stigma that has become attached to 'adult dependency' in post-
industrial contexts (the disappearance of 'good' dependency, as Fraser calls
it) and the dilemmas this raises for many women. This critique raises many
discomforting questions, not only for institutionalists, but also for neo-
classical advocates who, as we have seen, see labour market inclusion *along
male norms* as an unproblematic and desirable livelihood strategy for women.

As is well-known, in many Southern countries the activities of trade unions
have eluded the demands and interests of large groups of women and men
who remain confined to the more informal work sites. Homeworkers, who
very often include a significant proportion of women, have very often been
seen by trade unions as cheap labour ('outlaws' or 'scab labour') under-
cutting those in organized workplaces. Commenting on the poor record of
Southern trade unions in organizing women workers in particular, Mitter
(1994) notes that the culture and procedures of the trade union movement, a
champion mainly of workers in the organized sector, have understandably
over time assumed a male bias. Traditional trade union ways of organizing,
for example, are out of tune with the lives of working women.

However, there may also be deeper reasons for trade union disinclination
to show solidarity with unorganized workers. Commenting on the casual
labour market in the city of Surat in south Gujarat, Breman (1996) notes that
in addition to employer resistance and government disinclination —
plausible, but defensive, explanations that unions very often give for their
own inaction *vis-à-vis* casual workers — the attitude of established trade
unions towards casual and unprotected workers also constitutes an important obstacle. He describes their approach as a 'combination of indifference
rising almost to enmity' underpinned by the 'fear that pressure from below
would lead to gradual erosion of the rights gained during a long struggle'
(ibid: 247). Both trade union leaders and the rank-and-file, he argues, are
convinced that the mass of workers at the bottom is too numerous to be
accommodated within the formal sector system. Whether the casualization of
work in the formal sector will facilitate trade union solidarity with workers in
the unorganized sector, including many women workers, along the lines that
has been happening in some industrialized countries (Tate, 1994), remains to
be seen.

However, even in organized workplaces mainstream trade unions have not
sufficiently addressed the needs of working women. It is rarely recognized
that women workers may have different priorities from male workers: some
form of childcare support, for example, may be much more important for
them than having a minimum wage. In an insightful study of women's
employment and organizational strategies in an electronics factory in India,
the authors show how the demands and priorities voiced by women workers
related to specific problems they had experienced *as women* (Chhachhi and
Pittin, 1996). Women workers had initiated and organized to demand

transport and uniforms, which had been granted by management. Transport was seen as essential to avoid sexual harassment on public transport buses, especially in the late evenings when they worked overnight; the company bus also allayed the fears of parents, especially of unmarried women. The demand for uniforms was linked to the problems arising from the fact that women in this factory came from different socio-economic backgrounds and many could not afford the higher standards set by the better-off. Male workers, however, interpreted this differently:

> Girls do not know how to raise demands. They fall into the trap laid by management. They ask for general facilities while the real issue is wages ... now the girls have a bus, uniforms so they are just happy with that. They don't ask for wages (cited in Chhachhi and Pittin, 1996: 115–6).

The fact that women engage with the formal labour market more inter- mittently than men, while they shift to other forms of work that are more compatible with their reproductive responsibilities during certain periods of their life, also means that better ways of valorizing their alternative work experiences and skills may have to be found. As Jean Gardiner (1998) has recently argued, there are also important arguments for conceptualizing household activity as investment in human capital; like any other form of training and skill acquisition, through the experience of motherhood women acquire certain capabilities which contribute to successful performance in the workplace. But this form of human capital is rarely explicitly recognized or valued in the workplace. These are presumably the kinds of issues that gender-aware labour organizations would have to take up and prioritize.

International Trade and Labour Standards: The 'Social Clause'

According to the institutionalists, the causal link between standards and outcomes runs contrary to the neo-classical arguments (Cagatay, 1996). In their view standards encourage the adoption of new technologies that enhance productivity.[15] Transposing this understanding of labour standards to the global scene, institutionalists have more recently argued that without social regulation, competitive pressures in global markets would lead to a downward harmonization of labour standards, locking the global economy in a vicious low wage/low productivity cycle (Lee, 1996). Various proposals have therefore been put forward by international trade unions, policy think-tanks and academics, in the form of 'social charters', 'social clauses' or

---

15. One variant, or off-shoot, of this general approach is the post-Fordist view of industrial-ization with 'flexibility' which emphasizes a high-wage, high-skill and high-tech path of industrial growth based on Japanese industrial models, applied to other contexts (Kaplinsky, 1994 on South Africa).

'workers' rights clauses' which attempt to tie labour standards to trade liberalization.

Some of the most controversial proposals have involved relatively broad interpretations of labour standards which include wage increases commensurate with productivity increases and the pegging of Southern production and environmental practices to Northern levels. These proposals have been fiercely contested in the context of the ILO annual conferences and WTO ministerial meetings, as well as in the international media and academic literature. Other proposals have adopted a more flexible approach. They emphasize absolute, or core, standards such as the abolition of slavery and child labour, the outlawing of discrimination and the freedom of association on the grounds that these are basic human rights which do not cut into Southern countries' labour cost advantages (Brett, 1994).[16] Although the debate has moved in the direction of core labour standards or workers' rights, rather than a 'world minimum wage diktat', North/South tensions do not appear to have subsided. Southern governments have continued to resist any form of trade–labour standards linkage, because of its 'essentially protectionist motivation' (Brazilian Ambassador to the UN) and because it goes against the spirit of the ILO which is based on 'voluntarism, tripartism and free choice of social partners' (Indian Labour Secretary, cited in Raghavan, 1994).

It would seem problematic to collapse the interests of different Southern social groups with those of their governments. International labour organizations and others (Brett, 1994) argue that international pressure via trade sanctions on governments which defy basic labour rights can strengthen the bargaining position of national trade unions *vis-à-vis* their employers and governments and halt the spiral of declining labour standards.[17] In an age when global market forces wreak havoc with people's livelihoods, there is a need for different social groups to find support outside their own national borders in order to reinforce their capacity to cope within them. Whether the international labour movement can facilitate transnational alliances by trying to *link* labour standards to trade issues is, however, a moot point in view of the deep tensions and power asymmetries between North and South that continue to mark the on-going trade negotiations.

A number of factors have shaped these North/South divisions. One is the changing dynamics of employment in both North and South: the deterioration of labour standards and real wages, coupled with de-industrialization and mass unemployment in the North, and the growth of manufacturing employment in selected countries and regions of the South. Many of those in

---

16. Child labour is one of the issues that is seen as an absolute or core standard by some, and a relative standard by others.
17. It is of course not very clear whether Southern trade unions carry the same voice in these international labour organizations as their Northern counterparts which tend to be stronger, better-resourced and better organized.

the Northern labour movements see these two trends as complementary. Other observers point to the contractionary macro-policies which have been pursued since the 1970s in the OECD countries as a far more significant, and insidious, factor behind the current Northern predicament (Amsden, 1994; Howes and Singh, 1995).

While there is disagreement on these issues, what is clear is that unlike in the 1950s and 1960s, in many respects the North today is as concerned about competition from parts of the South as the other way around (South Centre, 1996). Such perceptions have important implications for the South, especially in the post-Cold War era. At the same time, the new trade agenda being pushed by the industrialized countries has been described by some Southern observers as no more than an attempt to win what was given up in the Uruguay Round negotiations, and facilitate a TNC-led integration of developing countries reminiscent of the liberal order of the nineteenth century (Raghavan, cited in Khor, 1996). Given this political context, the Northern arguments for tougher Southern labour standards as a means of protecting workers' rights in the South, have not been very persuasive. They have been described as 'ad hoc protectionism' (South Centre, 1996: 73), 'self-serving' and ineffective in inducing growth in Southern economies (Amsden, 1994).[18] Southern observers, otherwise sympathetic to labour market interventions and labour standards, have been placed in the awkward position of having to resist the demands for higher labour standards being launched at the international level (Kabeer, 1998; Raghavan cited in Khor, 1996).

The main weakness in the argument has been the lack of critical reflection on the institutional arenas through which progressive social forces hope to implement these social clauses. It is very often suggested that the implementation of the social clause should be a joint operation between the WTO and the ILO, given the competence of the latter in setting standards and supervising their application, and the might of the former in enforcing trade sanctions. However, given the marginalization of Southern governments and non-governmental groups from the WTO (Khor, 1997), there are serious grounds for being sceptical and concerned about its ability to act in the interest of Southern workers. There is also the non-trivial question about whether tougher labour standards can be monitored at the national level — an issue that needs to be seriously engaged with.

One group of Southern workers who tend to be spoken about in these discussions are women workers. According to the International

18. Amsden (1994) in fact argues that in the case of small 'profit-led' economies like Singapore and Puerto Rico experiments with a high-wage policy have been disastrous, causing both unemployment and economic stagnation; in borderline economies such as in Mexico, tying wages to productivity is also likely to be counter-productive; in large wage-led economies like China and India (where a sizeable domestic market exists) Northern arguments are likely to have greater relevance, but still will probably be ineffective.

Confederation of Free Trade Unions (ICFTU), they constitute an 'under-class of international capital', exploited and forced to work in TNCs under appalling conditions. Similar images of the 'submissive, exploited oriental girl' are very often portrayed in the Western press. Such stereotypes may be politically expedient, but how far does the institutionalist analysis clarify the changing dynamics of the international division of labour and its implications for women workers and how women workers themselves may view their position in this new order? We take up these two questions in turn.

'Global Feminization'?

In the context of supply-side macro-economic policies of the 1980s, Standing (1989) argued that the global feminization and flexibility of the work-force are interlinked phenomena which have been closely related to an erosion of labour regulations. This interpretation, however, has been questioned by several feminist writers.

In many instances the growth of women's share of industrial employment reflects the faster growth of labour-intensive sectors in which women have always been employed, such as textiles, clothing and footwear, and the decline of jobs/sectors previously dominated by men, rather than the substitution of 'cheaper' women for men (Elson, 1996; Joekes, 1995). In some cases substitution of this type does happen as a cost-cutting strategy, as Humphrey (1987) documented for factory work in São Paulo, Brazil, but it cannot be generalized.

The second and more fundamental problem, analysed by Elson (1996), is that the global feminization thesis confounds two distinct processes which, she argues, are not intrinsically interlinked: flexibility of production made possible by technological changes, and the erosion of workers' rights made possible by the unfettered mobility of capital and political decisions by states and employers to eschew responsibility for workers' well-being. Elson also makes the critical observation, from a gender perspective, that male 'norms' of full-time employment may not necessarily be the desirable norm to which all workers do and should aspire.

In fact more women have tended to take on casual, part-time, and homework compared to men across a wide range of economies, because of the flexibility it offers them. It is arguable that the vast majority of women who have domestic responsibilities have an immediate interest in a more flexible job structure that can offer them greater choice about hours and patterns of work and getting skills recognized and used (Elson, 1996). The key issue, as Elson goes on to argue, is not so much the disintegration of previous norms of 'regular' employment, which were in any case always more applicable to men than to women. Rather, the critical question is about how workers can secure decent livelihoods to support themselves and their dependants. What forms of organizing and what visions of social policy are needed to make this happen? And more importantly what role, if any, can a 'social clause' type of proposal play in this context?

The burning issue of course is whether in the present global economic context developing countries face a trade-off between higher wages/better employment conditions, on the one hand, and the quantity of employment, on the other. It is arguable that these low-end, poorly paid jobs, may be providing a pool of relatively accessible first-entry jobs which can help integrate young women migrants from rural areas. How far will a high-wage, high-technology path of industrial accumulation be able to retain the mass of rural, predominantly female, migrants who have been absorbed into export-oriented manufacturing? Some observers fear that the 'high-tech' road to industrialization — with high wages, skilled work-force, good working conditions — even if it could be constructed, would probably only include better-off men (Hart, 1995). This is particularly problematic given the fact that one of the peculiarities of late twentieth century capitalism is the dispersal of labour-intensive industry into predominantly rural and populated regions of the South.

Industrialization in successful Asian economies in the second half of the twentieth century, Hart (1996) argues, despite all the diversity within and across them, was preceded by a redistribution of resources that provided a social security net. Land reform, state-subsidized housing and transport and other forms of social security, lowered the money wage while maintaining the social wage. In the case of many developing countries today these *broadly-based* redistributive measures may be more effective than lower wages or higher technology for coping with intensified global competition. The useful point emerging from Hart's contribution is that it encourages ways of thinking about broad-based social security systems — maybe land reform in the present South African context, but state-sponsored housing and trans-port elsewhere — that can ensure a higher standard of living for the workers without jeopardizing their jobs.

Labour Market Structures and Multi-Layered Subjectivities

How do these young women themselves assess their work in the export-oriented factories? What weight should these 'subjective' assessments carry, and more controversially, how should they be read? One of the contentious issues dividing feminists who are writing on this subject concerns the inter-pretation of women workers' voices. According to Gita Sen (this volume) the fact that young women sometimes voice a preference for this type of work over going back to the confines of rural patriarchal households only emphasizes how harsh the conditions of rural poverty and rural patriarchal dominance are for these women, rather than being a positive indicator of the conditions of work in the factories. Providing a somewhat different reading of women's voices, Kabeer (1995) has argued that work in export industries (in Dhaka) has helped households meet basic survival needs, improved their security, and begun a process by which women are being transformed from representing economic burdens on their families into economic assets.

One of the analytical insights that emerged from the 1980s gender and development literature, and which can be seen as an area of cross-fertilization (or overlap) between feminism and critical institutionalism, was the gender critique of markets, captured in Whitehead's (1979) distinction between gender relations that are 'intrinsically gendered' (conjugal relations) and those that become the 'bearers of gender'. The labour contract was seen as a poignant illustration of the latter, and was elaborated by Elson and Pearson (1981) in their path-breaking work on women's incorporation into export-oriented manufacturing in world market factories.

In many ways this early analysis was nuanced and insightful enough to stand the test of time. Rather than providing a deterministic framework, the authors distinguished 'three tendencies' in the relation between factory work and the subordination of women which suggested that factory work could either *intensify* the existing forms of gender subordination, *decompose* them, or *recompose* new forms of gender subordination (ibid: 31). However, as Pearson (1998) herself has recently argued, their analysis left uncontested the idea that women workers' interactions with capital and patriarchy were somehow structurally determined rather than open to negotiation and reconstitution by women workers themselves. Structuralist accounts, critics argued, rendered women workers 'faceless and voiceless' (Wolf, 1992: 9) and attributed much more personality and animation to capital than to the women it exploits (Ong, 1988: 84). At a more general level, the oversight highlighted some of the difficulties of integrating an actor-orientation in structuralist analyses.

Some of the feminist research that was recording women's own under-standings of their work, and their experiences of engagement with factory management, provided diverse answers to some of the key questions that Elson and Pearson (1981) had raised. The Javanese factory daughters who figured prominently in Wolf's (1992) account of industrialization in rural Java did not seem to submit their needs to the betterment of the family economy in the way that Taiwanese daughters did. Wolf in fact argued that factory work in Java was giving young women the tools with which to 'hack and whittle away at parental and patriarchal controls over their lives, at least for a certain period, with longer-term implications such as deciding when and whom to marry' (Wolf, 1992: 254). A similar conclusion was emerging from some of the situated analyses of garments factory workers in Dhaka, Bangladesh (Kabeer, 1995).

The phenomenon of factory women was in many ways remarkable for a country where women's entry into the public domain in search of employment had been generally associated with dire economic need. Factory work, it was argued, had not altered some of the striking features of gender subordination in this context, such as women's dependence on male *protection* (even though it may have reduced their dependence on male *provision*). Nevertheless the ability to earn a wage (whether their wages disappeared into a common pool, were retained under their own management or handed over to or appropriated by household heads or other senior members), had made a difference in how women were perceived and treated, as well as their feelings of self-worth. The increased sense of power became even more visible in moments of crisis when the expanded possibilities offered by the strengthening of women's 'fall-back position' allowed them to walk out of, or not enter into, relationships which undermined their agency in unacceptable ways (Kabeer, 1995: 35).

While Kabeer (1995) did not explore the gendered patterns of shop-floor politics, Wolf (1992) argued that the increased field of manoeuvring that factory work had offered the Javanese daughters at home was matched by different patriarchal controls in the factory setting that kept these factory women 'relatively acquiescent, poorly paid and vastly unprotected in industrial jobs that are often dangerous' (ibid: 254). Moreover, the increased voice and agency in the familial sphere did not seem to carry over into the factory, despite the attempts of some women to 'rock the boat'; the managers and the work discipline seemed to be much less flexible and much more overwhelming than were parents in their rules and discipline.

Ching Kwan Lee's (1995) comparative analysis of two gendered regimes of production in Shenzhen (southern China) and Hong Kong, however, showed how two factories owned by the same enterprise, managed by the same team of managers, producing the same products, and using the same technical labour processes, developed distinct patterns of shop-floor politics. These gendered regimes were in turn explained in terms of local and communal institutions like localistic networks, kin, and families which underpinned the social organization of the labour markets. The comparative analysis also highlights the negotiated (rather than imposed) aspects of a factory regime where the workers themselves actively engage in the construction of cultural notions of workers' gender. In the Shenzhen factory, where the labour regime was strongly hierarchical and 'despotic', Lee (1995: 385) tries to explain why young women subscribed to the notion of 'maiden workers' and came to terms with localistic, despotic control:

> Many of these young women had fled home to evade arranged marriages. Many also had personal goals like gaining experience, saving for dowries, or financing their educations. Because they intended to marry at some point, factory employment was preferred to other service jobs because of the popular association between factory work and endurance for hardship and disciplined labor, traits deemed desirable for future wives. Thus, entering the factory meant preserving the appropriate femininity of maidens while earning a cash income and enjoying the freedom to explore romantic relationships.

The export-oriented production processes had in some ways reproduced gender hierarchies, providing employment that was in many ways exploitative under working conditions that were far from ideal — Lee's account of labour control in the Shenzhen plant, in particular, provides a vivid illustration of this point. But these 'despotic' labour regimes were at the same time social constructions that were both contested, and invested with different meanings and purposes by different parties. In the Hong Kong plant, Lee shows how the women workers used familial discourses as a pretext for circumventing certain managerial demands; women cited gender-based inconvenience and their mothering burdens at home to reject management demands for assignments which required cross-border commuting and overnight stays.

These fine-grained feminist accounts which provide a contextual analysis of labour force formation (workers' histories, familial and kinship relations and localistic networks) and take workers' subjectivities seriously, can also provide better insight into issues relating to collective action — why traditional trade union strategies have proven so problematic in some contexts. In South Africa, for example, where Taiwanese industrialists have invested in garment factories employing women, Hart (1995) argues that the fact that trade unions have experienced extreme difficulties in organizing clothing workers to press for higher wages and better working conditions reflects not only the adamant opposition of the foreign industrialists, but also broader processes of labour force formation and the desperate search by huge numbers of dispossessed people for a modicum of economic and social security.

CONCLUDING REMARKS

This chapter has tried to sketch some of the ambiguities and qualifications that a gender perspective would bring to the current debates on the interlinkages between employment, labour standards and poverty/well-being.

The overall thrust of the neo-classical argument has been that trade liberalization will deliver considerable benefits to women — both in terms of the sheer quantity of employment it can offer them, and also in terms of employment conditions (reducing wage discrimination by gender). The empirical literature suggests that the ability to create successful export-oriented manufacturing has been geographically uneven; nor has it been sustainable in all contexts. The argument that export-oriented industries provide higher wages to women, and exhibit lower levels of wage discrimination raises further questions. Setting aside issues around statistical coverage and reliability of the wage data, there are thorny issues around data interpretation. While the wage levels in export-oriented industries are higher than those offered for agricultural labour or domestic work, the basis for such comparisons may be shaky. Moreover, the kinds of issues that women workers may confront under the two labour regimes may be qualitatively different (including health risks generated through the labour process, issues around safety, skill acquisition, and so on). There are similar questions about the interpretation of the wage discrimination data: do the lower levels of wage discrimination in the export-oriented industries signify that men's wages are lower there? How significant is the wage discrimination data, when the export-oriented sectors are predominantly female? The thrust of the argument in this chapter has been that a meaningful assessment of what these jobs have meant for women would have to include some indication of the qualitative changes generated in their lives, in terms of life-long earning prospects, bodily well-being, changing social relationships (parents, siblings, husbands, co-workers), and issues around dignity, autonomy and self-worth.

Institutionalist analyses have been useful for understanding how labour markets can become 'bearers of gender', that is, how gender-based hierarchies are substantiated through labour market institutions. Institutionalist accounts, however, have not been sufficiently attentive to women workers' understanding of their work, its implications for their personal lives, and 'every day' forms of resistance on the shop-floor. The more situated feminist accounts, which have complemented structural analyses of labour market institutions with the perceptions and accounts of women workers themselves, have shown how the response to the wage contract is contextually specific and gendered. As Nancy Fraser (1997) puts it, the moral is that the wage contract requires looking beyond the boss/worker dyad. At the very least one must see the trade-off between subordination in paid employment against the potential for relative freedom from subordination outside it.

The free mobility of capital, the downward spiral of labour conditions, and political decisions by states and employers to eschew responsibility for workers' well-being are clearly important concerns for large numbers of men and women. Political responses and the search for coalescing strategies will most probably be shaped at the juncture of three sets of issues: (a) despite being problematic, there is a need to maintain these jobs, and the chances are that very few women would like to see their jobs disappear; (b) the high wage/ high tech road may be an option available to only a few countries and may be open to a limited number of men (and even fewer women); (c) the agenda for social and gender-equitable development needs to be widened to include the conditions for social reproduction that can effectively subsidize the social wage — this is an area that needs to be explored creatively from a gender perspective. The political processes to drive this agenda include national and international acts of solidarity, but in either context the extent to which the interests of women workers can be genuinely represented will depend critically on their politicized presence in those movements. The message that may be drawn from women's experiences with trade unions at the national level is that the 'obvious workers' priorities' may be implicit male priorities; the claim to represent 'global workers' priorities' may have to be subjected to similar qualifications.

ACKNOWLEDGEMENTS

The author would like to thank Yusuf Bangura, Solon Barraclough, Nilüfer Cagatay, Naila Kabeer, Carol Miller and Ruth Pearson for their useful comments on earlier drafts of this chapter. Nilüfer Cagatay deserves a special mention for her inspiring work on gender and labour standards and her support and feed-back on various drafts of this chapter. Responsibility for the content of the chapter, however, lies with the author.

REFERENCES

Amsden, A. (1994) 'Macro-sweating Policies and Labour Standards', in W. Sengenberger and D. Campbell (eds) *International Labour Standards and Economic Interdependence*, pp. 185–93. Geneva: International Institute for Labour Studies.

Amsden, A. and R. van der Hoeven (1996) 'Manufacturing Output, Employment and Real Wages in the 1980s: Labour's Loss until the Century's End', *The Journal of Development Studies* 32(4): 506–30.

Bangura, Y. (1997) 'Policy Dialogue and Gendered Development: Institutional and Ideological Constraints'. Discussion Paper No. 87. Geneva: UNRISD.

Belghazi, S. (1996) 'Determinants et Discrimination des Salaires Feminins dans le Secteur du Textile Habillement'. Geneva: UNRISD (mimeo).

Beneria, L. (1995) 'Toward a Greater Integration of Gender in Economics', *World Development* 23(11): 1839–50.

Bhattacharya, D. and M. Rahman (1998) 'Female Employment under Export-Propelled Industrialization: Prospect for Internalizing Global Opportunities in Bangladesh's Apparels Sector'. Geneva: UNRISD (mimeo).

Bourqia, R. (1996) 'Désavantage Social et Discrimination Salariale: Les Femmes et l'Emploi dans l'Industrie Textile'. Geneva: UNRISD (mimeo).

Breman, J. (1996) *Footloose Labour: Working in India's Informal Economy*. Cambridge: Cambridge University Press.

Brett, B. (1994) *International Labour in the 21st Century: The ILO — Monument to the Past or Beacon for the Future?* London: Epic Books.

Bullock, S. (1994) *Women and Work*. London and New Jersey: Zed Books.

Cagatay, N. (1996) 'Gender and International Labor Standards in the World Economy'. Salt Lake City: University of Utah (mimeo).

Cagatay, N. and S. Ozler (1995) 'Feminization of the Labor Force: The Effects of Long-term Development and Structural Adjustment', *World Development* 23(11): 1883–94.

Castells, M., L. Goh and R. Y.-W. Kwoh (1990) *The Shek Kip Mei Syndrome: Economic Development and Public Housing in Hong Kong and Singapore*. London: Pion.

Chhachhi, A. and R. Pittin (1996) 'Multiple Identities, Multiple Strategies', in A. Chhachhi and R. Pittin (eds) *Confronting State, Capital and Patriarchy: Women Organizing in the Process of Industrialization*, pp. 93–130. Basingstoke: Macmillan, in association with the Institute of Social Studies.

Chiu, S. W. K. and C. K. Lee (1997) 'After the Hong Kong Miracle: Women Workers under Industrial Restructuring', *Asian Survey* 37(8): 752–70.

Dunn, L. L. (1996) 'Women Organising for Change in Caribbean Free Zones', in A. Chhachhi and R. Pittin (eds) *Confronting State, Capital and Patriarchy: Women Organizing in the Process of Industrialization*, pp. 205–43. Basingstoke: Macmillan, in association with the Institute of Social Studies.

Edgren, G. (1982) *Spearheads of Industrialisation or Sweatshops in the Sun?: A Critical Appraisal of Labour Conditions in Asian Export Processing Zones*. Bangkok: ILO-ARTEP.

266   *S. Razavi*

Elson, D. (forthcoming) *Labor Markets as Gendered Institutions: Equality, Efficiency and Empowerment Issues*.

Elson, D. (1996) 'Appraising Recent Developments in the World Market for Nimble Fingers', in A. Chhachhi and R. Pittin (eds) *Confronting State, Capital and Patriarchy: Women Organizing in the Process of Industrialization*, pp. 35–55. Basingstoke: Macmillan, in association with the Institute of Social Studies.

Elson, D. and R. Pearson (1981) 'The Subordination of Women and the Internationalisation of Factory Production', in K. Young, C. Wolkowitz and R. McCullagh (eds) *Of Marriage and the Market: Women's Subordination Internationally and its Lessons*, pp. 18–40. London and New York: Routledge.

Fraser, N. (1997) *Justice Interruptus: Critical Reflections on the 'Postsocialist' Condition*. New York and London: Routledge.

Gardiner, J. (1998) 'Beyond Human Capital: Households in the Macroeconomy', *New Political Economy* 3(2): 209–21.

Gonzalez de la Rocha, M. (1998) 'The Erosion of a Survival Model: Urban Household Responses to Persistent Poverty'. Geneva: UNRISD (mimeo).

Gore, C. (1994) 'Social Exclusion and Africa South of the Sahara: A Review of the Literature'. Discussion Paper No. 62. Geneva: International Institute for Labour Studies.

Greenhalgh, S. (1985) 'Sexual Stratification: The Other Side of "Growth with Equity" in East Asia', *Population and Development Review* 11(2): 265–314.

Hart, G. (1991) 'Engendering Everyday Resistance: Gender, Patronage and Production Politics in Rural Malaysia', *Journal of Peasant Studies* 19(1): 93–121.

Hart, G. (1995) ' "Clothes for next to nothing": Rethinking Global Competition', *South African Labour Bulletin* 9(6): 41–7.

Hart, G. (1996) 'The Agrarian Question and Industrial Dispersal in South Africa: Agro-industrial Linkages through Asian Lenses', *Journal of Peasant Studies* 23(2/3): 245–77.

Hartmann, H. (1979) 'The Unhappy Marriage of Marxism and Feminism: Towards a More Progressive Union', *Capital and Class* 8: 1–33.

Hensman, R. (1988) *Trade Unions and the Gender Division of Labour: A Case Study in India*. Brighton, Sussex: Institute of Development Studies.

Hewitt de Alcantara (1993) *Real Markets: Social and Political Issues of Food Policy Reform*. London: Frank Cass.

Heyzer, N. and Tan Boon Kean (1988) 'Work, Skills and Consciousness of Women Workers in Asia', in N. Heyzer (ed.) *Daughters in Industry: Work Skills and Consciousness of Women Workers in Asia*, pp. 3–30. Kuala Lumpur: Asian and Pacific Development Centre.

Howes, C. and A. Singh (1995) 'Long-term Trends in the World Economy: The Gender Dimension', *World Development* 23(11): 1895–911.

Humphrey, J. (1987) *Gender and Work in the Third World: Sexual Division in Brazilian Industry*. London: Tavistock Publications.

Jackson, C. (1998) 'Social Exclusion and Gender: Swimming Against the Mainstream?'. Norwich: University of East Anglia (mimeo).

Joekes, S. (1995) 'Trade-Related Employment for Women in Industry and Services in Developing Countries'. Occasional Paper No. 5. Geneva: UNRISD.

Joekes, S. and A. Weston (1994) *Women and the New Trade Agenda*. New York: UNIFEM.

Jomo, K. S. with C.-Y. Chung, B. C. Folk, I. ul-Haque, P. Phongpaichit, B. Simatupang and M. Tateishi (1997) *Southeast Asia's Misunderstood Miracle*. Boulder, CO: Westview Press.

Kabeer, N. (1995) 'Necessary, Sufficient or Irrelevant? Women, Wages and Intra-Household Power Relations in Urban Bangladesh'. IDS Working Paper No. 25. Brighton, Sussex: Institute of Development Studies.

Kabeer, N. (1998) ' "For a Handful of Rice": Third World Women and the Double Edged Ethics of International Trade'. Brighton, Sussex: Institute of Development Studies (mimeo).

Kaplinsky, R. (1994) ' "Economic Restructuring in South Africa: The Debate Continues": A Response', *Journal of Southern African Studies* 20(4): 533–7.

Kibria, N. (1998) 'Becoming a Garments Worker: The Mobilization of Women into the Garments Factories of Bangladesh'. Occasional Paper No. 9. Geneva: UNRISD.

Khor, M. (1996) 'Reflection, not Adventurism needed at Singapore', *Third World Economics* 16–31 August (143): 4–6.

Khor, M. (1997) 'The World Trade Organization and the South: Fighting against the Tide', *Development* 40(4): 73–7.

Kung, L. (1983) *Factory Work in Taiwan*. Ann Arbor, MI: UMI Research Press.

Lee, C. K. (1995) 'Engendering the Worlds of Labour: Women Workers, Labour Markets, and Production Politics in the South China Economic Miracle', *American Sociological Review* 60: 378–97.

Lee, E. (1996) 'The Political Economy of International Labour Standards', paper prepared for the UNRISD conference on Globalization and Citizenship, UNRISD, Geneva (9–11 December).

Lim, L. (1990) 'Women's Work in Export Factories: The Politics of a Cause', in I. Tinker (ed.) *Persistent Inequalities: Women and World Development*, pp. 101–19. New York: Oxford University Press.

Lipton, M. and S. Maxwell (1992) 'The New Poverty Agenda: An Overview'. Discussion Paper No. 306. Brighton, Sussex: Institute of Development Studies.

Lochead, J. (1988) 'Retrenchment in a Malaysian Free Trade Zone', in N. Heyzer (ed.) *Daughters in Industry: Work Skills and Consciousness of Women Workers in Asia*, pp. 3–30. Kuala Lumpur: Asian and Pacific Development Centre.

Meagher, K. and M.-B. Yunusa (1996) 'Passing the Buck: Structural Adjustment and the Nigerian Urban Informal Sector'. Discussion Paper No. 75. Geneva: UNRISD.

Mitter, S. (1994) 'A Comparative Survey', in M. Hosmer Martens and S. Mitter (eds) *Women in Trade Unions: Organizing the Unorganized*, pp. 3–14. Geneva: ILO.

Ong, A. (1988) 'Colonialism and Modernity: Feminist Re-presentations of Women in non-Western societies', *Inscriptions* 3(4): 79–93.

Pearson, R. (1991a) 'Male Bias and Women's Work in Mexico's Border Industries', in D. Elson (ed.) *Male Bias in the Development Process*, Manchester: Manchester University Press.

Pearson, R. (1991b) 'New Technology and the Internationalization of Office Work: Prospects and Conditions for Women's Employment in LDCs'. Gender Analysis in Development Sub-Series No. 5. Norwich: University of East Anglia.

Pearson, R. (1998) 'Nimble Fingers Revisited: Reflections on Women and Third World Industrialisation in the Late Twentieth Century', in C. Jackson and R. Pearson (eds) *Feminist Visions of Development: Research, Analysis and Policy*, pp. 171–88. London: Routledge.

Phongpaichit, P. (1988) 'Two Roads to the Factory: Industrialization Strategies and Women's Employment in South East Asia', in B. Agarwal (ed.) *Structures of Patriarchy: The State, the Community and the Household*, pp. 151–63. London: Zed Press.

Raghavan, C. (1994) 'North-South Polarization in ILO Trade-Labour Link', *Third World Economics* 102: 1–15.

Salaff, J. (1990) 'Women, the Family, and the State: Hong Kong, Taiwan, Singapore — Newly Industrialised Countries in Asia', in S. Stichter and J. Parpart (eds) *Women, Employment and the Family in the International Division of Labour*, pp. 98–136. Philadelphia, PA: Temple University Press.

South Centre (1996) *Liberalization and Globalization: Drawing Conclusions for Development*. Geneva: South Centre.

Standing, G. (1989) 'Global Feminization through Flexible Labor', *World Development* 17(7): 1077–95.

Standing, G. (1992) 'Do Unions Impede or Accelerate Structural Adjustment? Industrial versus Company Unions in an Industrialising Labour Market', *Cambridge Journal of Economics* 16: 327–54.

Tate, J. (1994) 'Organizing Homeworkers in the Informal Sector: Australia and Canada', in M. Hosmer Martens and S. Mitter (eds) *Women in Trade Unions: Organizing the Unorganized*, pp. 67–82. Geneva: ILO.

Tzannatos, Z. (1995) 'Growth, Adjustment and the Labour Market: Effects on Women Workers', paper presented at the Fourth Conference of the International Association for Feminist Economics, Tours, France (5–7 July).

Whitehead, A. (1979) 'Some Preliminary Notes on the Subordination of Women', *IDS Bulletin* 10(3): 10–13.

Wolf, D. L. (1992) *Factory Daughters: Gender, Household Dynamics and Rural Industrialization in Java*. Berkeley, CA: University of California Press.

World Bank (1990) *World Development Report 1990: Poverty*. New York: Oxford University Press.

World Bank (1991) *World Development Report 1991: The Development Challenge*. New York: Oxford University Press.

World Bank (1993) *The East Asian Miracle*. New York: Oxford University Press.

World Bank (1995) *World Development Report 1995: Workers in an Integrating World*. New York: Oxford University Press.

10

Engendering Poverty Alleviation:
Challenges and Opportunities

Gita Sen

Poverty eradication has re-emerged as an important item on the agenda of global development. As the contributions to this volume show, in recent years understandings of poverty and what constitutes well-being have been significantly broadened. At the same time, what the volume also demonstrates is that the richness of concepts sits uncomfortably with the poverty of methods and data: the unresolved methodological problems that plague the measurement and analysis of poverty, especially from a gender perspective, and the lack of timely and reliable data. These are important considerations not only from an 'academic' point of view, but also as far as the arena of public action is concerned, an arena which is becoming increasingly 'knowledge-based'.

In this short chapter, however, I want to move away from the methodological questions posed by the other contributors, and point to another irony that is evident in the area of poverty research and action: namely, the diversity of concepts versus the uniformity of strategies for poverty eradication. Changes in the political and ideological climate during the last two decades pose major challenges to how anti-poverty strategies are conceptualized and implemented. This note does not attempt to address these issues in a comprehensive manner, but only highlights certain aspects of the context and the challenges, as well as pointing to the potential for new directions.

The Context

In the 1970s, strategies for poverty eradication were part of a larger belief in the importance of 'growth with redistribution' and of meeting basic minimum needs through focused government policies. The 1980s, an era of fiscal belt-tightening in both South and North, saw a shift in the approach of major multilateral and bilateral development agencies, away from redistribution and basic needs and towards structural adjustment and market-oriented economic reforms. Poverty, as such, was relatively low on the priority list during the 1980s. By the 1990s, a 'new poverty agenda' had surfaced (its first major appearance being in the World Bank's *World Development Report 1990*) as a counterpart of the so-called 'Washington consensus' on structural reforms.

This new agenda stresses the importance of market-led growth itself as *the* most important method to address poverty. The role of the state, and of focused anti-poverty strategies, is viewed as secondary in this approach. The state's role is limited to policies in selected social sectors such as health and education, and to programmes focusing on safety-net provision for the particularly vulnerable who cannot take part in regular labour markets. In other sectors, it is argued that the state need do little to address poverty directly, beyond supporting the competitive functioning of markets and removing distortions to efficient resource allocation. Overall, government's role is viewed as at most a market-supporting one, not a proactive one.

In downgrading the role of the state, the new poverty agenda has shifted the terrain of debate away from such issues as the conditions under which land reforms (or asset redistribution more generally) and basic needs provisioning are effective in reducing poverty. Instead, the focus now is on the types of economic growth that may be most conducive to poverty removal, and how state policies can promote such patterns of growth. In most countries of the South, proponents of the new poverty agenda hold that earlier policies favouring capital-intensive industrialization and import-substitution have been misguided. Structural adjustment reforms have argued strongly against such policies, supporting instead policies favouring agriculture and labour-intensive export sectors as most in line with these countries' factor endowments and comparative advantage.

The growth history over the last two decades of some countries in Southeast Asia, as well as others such as Mauritius and Chile, are often held up as proof for these theses. However, the empirical testing of these two hypotheses — first, the effectiveness of a market-driven approach to poverty reduction, and second, the success of labour-intensive growth in reducing poverty — is far from satisfactory. The UNDP's Human Development Report Office has argued both theoretically and empirically against the former through various issues of the *Human Development Report* (in particular *Human Development Report 1997*). Focused government policies directed at reducing poverty through various mechanisms including employment guarantee schemes, food-for-work programmes, consumption subsidies, credit programmes, and empowerment programmes, together with strong social sector programmes that will strengthen human 'capabilities' have resulted in poverty reduction even where growth rates have been moderate or low. While the question of the sustainability of poverty reduction is certainly a legitimate one, there have been few attempts to compare the relative social costs of poverty reduction through direct state support versus reliance on the growth process.

The extent to which the empirical evidence of Southeast Asia supports the thesis of labour-intensive growth being poverty reducing is also open to question. It is certainly true that countries in this region have experienced rapid growth as well as significant reductions in measured poverty rates during the last two decades, and prior to the current financial crisis. Female employment in labour-intensive exports has also been an important factor, as is well known. But possible causal links between the three have not been probed adequately. During the same period, there has been considerable direct involvement by the state in each of these countries, in ways that may well have contributed to poverty reduction. Examples are the Basic Minimum Needs programme in Thailand, redistributive and affirmative action policies in favour of the *bhumiputras* (Malay sons of the soil) in Malaysia, and anti-poverty programmes in Indonesia during the economic crisis of the early 1980s. How much of the observed reduction in poverty and improvement in living standards is due to labour-intensive growth per se and how much to such programmes is not clear. In reality, it is probable that both have played a role but their relative importance is not obvious.

The potential of labour-intensive growth to reduce poverty, female poverty in particular, is diminished by the fact that much of this use of female labour has been at relatively low wages and under poor working conditions in the informal sector and in export-processing zones. Piece-work payments, extremely long working hours, sweatshop conditions, considerable occupational health risks, and high job insecurity are the hallmarks of the jobs done by the young women workers employed in the various industries in this sector. A number of countries have gone back on ILO conventions guaranteeing different rights to workers in order to attract foreign investment into export-processing zones. The fact that young women, when interviewed, sometimes prefer this type of work to going back to the confines of rural patriarchal households is not necessarily a positive indicator of the working conditions in their jobs. It only emphasizes how harsh the conditions of rural poverty and rural patriarchal dominance are for young women in particular. An important and hitherto poorly explored research question is the linkage between female labour-intensive employment and actual poverty reduction, where poverty is viewed in both income and asset terms and also in terms of human capabilities. Some of these issues are addressed in the contributions to this volume (Razavi, Kabeer).

The work of the Human Development Report office and of organizations such as UNRISD have broadened the concept of poverty beyond a narrow income definition to include other dimensions of human deprivation that are critical to quality of life. This broadening of concepts is clearly reflected in some of the contributions to this volume — the use of sex ratios as indicators of relative female deprivation (Sudha and Irudaya Rajan, Das Gupta and Li); and the general emphasis on a wide range of social indicators (Saith and Harriss-White, Kabeer). This broadening of concepts has gone hand in hand with a broader approach in terms of methods of poverty reduction, to include such aspects as empowerment and political participation that may be as central to the question of sustainability as the issue of financial costs of a poverty programme (Kabeer). These methods go beyond the traditional focus on raising incomes, to involving people, communities and civil society organizations more centrally. In a sense they may be seen as using a widened view of 'assets' to include not only tangible resources but also such vital intangibles as power and knowledge. From the perspective of gender, these broader concepts and methods are valuable in that they allow a better treatment of multidimensional aspects of gender than a focus purely on household income levels.

Another recent trend that has been more positive, especially during the 1990s, is the greater visibility of gender concerns through the series of UN global conferences. Any realistic assessment of these conferences (UNCED in 1992, Human Rights in 1993, ICPD in 1994, the Social Summit in 1995, the Women's Conference in 1995, and Habitat II in 1996) has, however, to recognize a dichotomy in the extent of actual commitment to implementation by countries, once the dust of a particular conference has settled. There has been greater willingness to seriously consider finances and methods for implementation with regard to conferences that are not seen as directly threatening the larger global economic system. But conferences such as UNCED and the Social Summit have made less headway in terms of implementation. Notwithstanding this stalemate, these conferences have provided fora for organized women's groups and visibility to gender at the global level. It is well recognized that women's groups were among the best and most effectively organized at a number of conferences, an impetus that has strengthened networking and joint action thereafter.

Overall, an assessment of the context within which anti-poverty strategies are currently placed thus reveals both positive and negative changes. While the concept of poverty itself and the approaches considered effective in addressing it have been widened in scope, actual implementation has become more constrained by the ideological shift towards a belief in the efficacy of the market, and by the erasure of asset-redistribution strategies such as land reform from the policy agenda of major development institutions. As Whitehead and Lockwood show in this volume, despite the diversity in the approaches to poverty measurement and analysis across different Poverty Assessments carried out by the World Bank, there is remarkable uniformity of views expressed on how to reduce poverty; policy agendas very often reflect the policy prescriptions drawn from the *1990 World Development Report,* rather than using country-specific evidence to construct an analysis from which to generate policy.

The Challenges

There are both conceptual and institutional challenges to engendering poverty reduction strategies and programmes. Gender systems, structures and biases, and forms of oppression and subordination, work at multiple levels, and are both powerful and resistant to change. Anti-poverty strategies and programmes often attempt to sidestep gender systems. Sometimes this can be successful, particularly if the programme shows that it benefits both the powerful within a community or in the household as well as the women themselves. At other times, where a programme inherently challenges gender power relations, gender may have to be addressed head-on if the programme is to be effective.

It is well known that existing gender systems are oppressive to women in two distinct but related ways:

- unequal division of and access to different kinds of resources, unequal division of labour within and outside the home, and the associated ideologies and behavioural norms;
- non-recognition of the 'care economy' which shapes the resources, labour and ideologies that go into the reproduction of human beings in both daily and generational terms.

Unequal gender systems can impinge on the formulation, implementation and impact of anti-poverty strategies or policies through either or both of the above. For example, a strategy to provide credit or training to poor households may increase gender disparities if these resources are provided only to men, or may increase women's work burdens unintentionally. Anti-poverty strategies that focus ostensibly on women may be ineffective if they do not take the labour and resource needs of the 'care economy' sufficiently into account. Or they may place unconscionable burdens on the already stretched time and health of poor women.

In some sense these two key aspects of gender systems provide the touchstones for assessing how effective development institutions are in engendering their anti-poverty strategies. But the challenges that institutions face operate at different levels — global, national, and local — depending on the level at which the institution itself functions, and the strategies it espouses.

The Global Level

Over the last decade and a half, the growing dominance of neoliberal development ideas has been mirrored in the increased importance of the Bretton Woods institutions relative to the rest of the United Nations system in terms of both multilateral development resources, and the ability to shape the development agenda. The ability of the UN system to provide alternative development thinking through agencies such as UNCTAD or the Centre on Transnational Corporations has been significantly reduced. As a result of this, development strategies, and certainly those attempting to engender anti-poverty programmes, are increasingly shaped by the neoliberal agenda of the Bretton Woods institutions, particularly the World Bank. The recent round of internal restructuring within the World Bank is designed to make its operations more efficient, among other things, by becoming more sensitive and responsive to local communities. How well this will work in practice, to alter the incentive structure that determines the behaviour of the Bank's task and operations managers in favour of greater gender-sensitivity, still remains to be seen.

It is also not clear how the new approach at the project level will mesh with the macro-level of macroeconomic stabilization and adjustment policies which has not seen significant change. This is a serious challenge. In a way, the more community-responsive project approach favoured by the World Bank's current president, James Wolfensohn, carries further the 'participatory' approach that has become generally accepted in the development literature on poverty, rural development, and social sectors such as education. The contributions to this volume (Whitehead and Lockwood, in particular) highlight some of the ways in which 'participatory' poverty assessments, despite their greater potential to say something about perceptions of gender and poverty and of gender relations, may miss women's voices — or misread them. Their chapter also provides useful methodological suggestions for realizing the potential that these methods have in accessing women's voices.

A second challenge, however, is the actual meaning that terms such as 'participation' and 'empowerment' take when translated into programmes and projects. Kabeer's contribution to this volume explains the history of 'empowerment' as the concept has entered the policy domain; an important aspect in this difficult process of translation has been the quantification imperative. Many community-based organizations have begun to ask what it takes to ensure genuine participation by women and communities in the planning, implementation and evaluation of programmes, so as to remove the fuzziness that has plagued the way in which development institutions have tended to address the issue of 'participation'.

A third challenge at the global level is the as yet weak capacity of civil society organizations to hold global institutions accountable. Over the past three decades, a plethora of non-governmental organizations have come into existence, providing development services and support to communities, or challenging governments and the for-profit sector when their actions are perceived to pose threats to the livelihoods or survival of the poor. The large majority of such organizations function at the local level. There are few that function at the national level, and only a handful at the global level. Despite limited numbers, their impact has been significant in terms of making powerful global institutions take notice, as for example, in the work of the Narmada Bachao Andolan (the people's movement against hydroelectric projects on the River Narmada) or the new SAPRI (Structural Adjustment Programme Review Initiative), a tripartite initiative of NGOs, the World Bank, and participating governments. But their capacity to intervene at the global level, while useful when it comes to drawing attention to potential threats, is still quite weak with regard to ongoing engagement in monitoring or modifying the work of global institutions. Women's organizations at this level are few in number and need considerable capacity building before they can become truly effective.

National Level

Among those concerned with mainstreaming gender in development, the weakness of gender's institutional home within governments has long been a subject of debate. Whether in the form of women's bureaux, departments, or ministries, this home has typically been near the low end of governmental hierarchies, thus making it difficult to put effective national-level policies or strategies in place. But a worse problem is that the last two decades have seen a considerable erosion in state capacity to govern in any form at all. Many factors have played a role, not least among them the fiscal pressure on states and the severe cutbacks in expenditures that have been experienced in a number of countries. Drawing an analogy from the home, the problem is not just that women have been confined to the dark and smoke-filled kitchen, but that the house itself is crumbling. A major challenge is how to get governments that are under fiscal constraints and expenditure cuts to take 'new' issues such as gender seriously.

A second challenge to anti-poverty strategies at the national level is the rapid growth of the so-called informal sector and the growing phenomenon of the working poor among whom women are present in large numbers. Here the challenge is how to organize workers who may work long hours but still do not earn enough to ensure the security of family incomes or livelihoods. In the face of national policies that have been shaped by governments vying with each other to provide favourable conditions to investment in export processing zones, the pressures on those who try to organize such workers (quite apart from the inherent difficulties in organizing informal sector workers) can be quite severe. Traditional labour organizations have to learn from the SEWAs of the world if they are to make any headway in this area (see Razavi, this volume, on how important gender concerns have often been missed by traditional, male-dominated trade unions).

Local Level

Three critical challenges are present at the local level. The first is the need to move beyond the assumption that gender power relations at the local level are embedded in conjugal, intra-household relations alone. The structures of power that women confront at the local level operate not only within the home, but also in the terrain of communities, local markets and local government officials. Empowering women as part of a process of engendering anti-poverty strategies means strengthening their capacity to address and confront all these loci of power, and their interrelations.

A second major challenge is access to information. Historically, one of the most important sources of women's lack of power has been lack of information. If anti-poverty strategies are to enhance women's capabilities, then access to information is critical. Formal education and literacy, while important, are not the only needs. For instance, if women are to ensure that the local labour contractor in a government-funded public works programme does not cheat them, they need to be able to access information on wage rates and contracts. If village communities are to ensure that development funds earmarked for particular projects are actually spent on those projects, they need to be able to get that information. Formal literacy may be necessary but is not sufficient for this. Governments have to be challenged to make information available to their citizens if programme efficiency is to improve and corruption is to be eliminated.

Finally, as much as at the global level, the strengthening of capacity among women and women's organizations at the local level is crucial if strategies to engender anti-poverty programmes are to be truly effective on the ground.

Notes on Contributors

Naila Kabeer is a fellow of the Institute of Development Studies (IDS), University of Sussex, Falmer, Brighton BN1 9RE, UK. She is a socio-economist with research interests in gender, poverty, population and household economics. She has authored *Reversed Realities: Gender Hierarchies in Development Thought* (Verso, 1994), and *The Power to Choose: Structure, Agency and Bangladeshi Women Workers in London and Dhaka* (forthcoming).

Ruhi Saith recently acquired her doctorate in Medicine at Oxford University, and is currently a research officer in Queen Elizabeth House, Oxford University (21 St Giles, Oxford OX1 3LA, UK). Her recent work includes a journal article related to infertility in *Human Reproduction Update*, a paper on new methods for the analysis of household characteristics for the targeting of anti-poverty policies, and an UNRISD discussion paper on the gender sensitivity of development indicators.

Barbara Harriss-White is Professor of Development Studies at Queen Elizabeth House, Oxford University. She started research into social welfare while at the London School of Hygiene and Tropical Medicine where she worked as a research fellow in food policy in the Department of Human Nutrition from 1981 to 1987. Her latest book on this subject (with S. Subramanian) is *Illfare In India: Essays on the Social Sector in Honour of S. Guhan* (Sage, New Delhi, 1999).

Deniz Kandiyoti is Senior Lecturer in the Department of Development Studies at the School of Oriental and African Studies, University of London (Thornhaugh Street, London WC1H 0XG, UK). She is the author of *Women in Rural Production Systems* (UNESCO, 1985), the editor of *Women, Islam and the State* (Macmillan, 1991) and *Gendering the Middle East* (I. B. Tauris, 1996). She is currently working on post-Soviet transitions in Central Asia, with special reference to agrarian reform in Uzbekistan.

Ann Whitehead teaches social anthropology and gender and development at the University of Sussex, where she also contributes to graduate programmes. She has carried out research in Ghana and Uganda. She can be reached at the School of Social Sciences, University of Sussex, Falmer, Brighton, BN1 9QN or at awhitehead@juniper.u-net.com

Matthew Lockwood is Head of International Policy at Christian Aid (PO Box 100, London SE1 7RT, UK). He is writing in a personal capacity. He recently published *Fertility and Household Labour in Tanzania* (Oxford University Press).

Cecile Jackson and **Richard Palmer-Jones** are at the School of Development Studies, University of East Anglia, Norwich, NR4 7TJ, UK. Cecile focuses on gender analysis of environmental change, conceptualizing gender and poverty, and the social theory of the body; she recently co-edited *Feminist Visions of Development* published by Routledge. Richard's current research includes relations among water markets, agricultural growth and poverty in Bangladesh, the spatial analysis of sex ratios in India, and the implications of effort intensive livelihoods at low levels of nutrition for the intra-household allocations of well-being.

S. Sudha is a post-doctoral fellow at the Carolina Population Centre, University of North Carolina, Chapel Hill, NC 27516-3997, USA (e-mail sudha@email.unc.edu); when this chapter was written, she was an associate fellow, Centre for Development Studies, Thiruvananthapuram, Kerala, India. A sociologist and demographer; her research interests include investigating well-being outcomes over the life-course, focusing on the impact of social structures such as gender, ethnicity and the state. Her recent publications include a study of the impact of ethnicity, state policy and family factors on children's education in Malaysia, and the role of ethnicity in health care preferences of elderly persons in the southern United States.

S. Irudaya Rajan is an associate fellow at the Centre for Development Studies, Thiruvananthapuram, Kerala, India (e-mail: sirajan@giasmd01.vsnl.net.in). He has conducted research on historical and social demography, population and development, family planning, ageing, and studies on Kerala. He is the co-author of a recent book, *India's Elderly: Burden or Challenge?* (Sage, New Delhi) and is a member of the team which has just completed the Kerala Migration Survey.

Monica Das Gupta is a member of the Development Research Group, The World Bank, 1818 H Street NW, Washington, DC 20433, USA. Her research interests include population, development and social organization.

Li Shuzhuo is based at the Population Research Institute, Xi'an Jiaotong University, Xi'an, Shaanxi Province, 710049, China, where he focuses on population and development issues in China.

Shahra Razavi is project leader at the United Nations Research Institute for Social Development (UNRISD), Palais des Nations, CH-1211 Geneva 10, Switzerland. She is currently managing the Institute's multi-country research project on Gender, Poverty and Well-being. Her recent publications have been on the gender dimensions of institutional change.

Gita Sen is a Professor at the Indian Institute of Management, Bannerghatta Road, Bangalore 560 076, India, and an adjunct faculty member at the Center for Population and Development Studies, Harvard University. Her recent work includes research and policy advocacy on the gender implications of globalization and economic liberalization, the gender dimensions of population policies, and the linkages between population and the environment.

INDEX

Printed and bound by CPI Group (UK) Ltd, Croydon, CR0 4YY

09/06/2025

14686120-0005